Distributed Decision Making

WILEY SERIES

NEW TECHNOLOGIES AND WORK

Series Editor: **Bernhard Wilpert** *Technische Universität Berlin*

NEW TECHNOLOGY AND HUMAN ERROR

Edited by Jens Rasmussen, Keith Duncan and Jacques Leplat

THE MEANING OF WORK AND TECHNOLOGICAL OPTIONS

Edited by Véronique de Keyser, Thoralf Qvale, Bernhard Wilpert and S. Antonio Ruiz Quintanilla

DEVELOPING SKILLS WITH INFORMATION TECHNOLOGY

Edited by Lisanne Bainbridge and S. Antonio Ruiz Quintanilla

NEW TECHNOLOGY AND MANUFACTURING MANAGEMENT
Strategic Choices for Flexible Production Systems

Edited by Malcolm Warner, Werner Wobbe and Peter Brödner

DISTRIBUTED DECISION MAKING
Cognitive Models for Cooperative Work

Edited by Jens Rasmussen, Berndt Brehmer and Jacques Leplat

Please return to room 240

Distributed Decision Making

Cognitive Models for Cooperative Work

Edited
by
Jens Rasmussen, Berndt Brehmer and **Jacques Leplat**

JOHN WILEY & SONS
Chichester · New York · Brisbane · Toronto · Singapore

Other Wiley Editorial Offices

John Wiley & Sons, Inc., 605 Third Avenue,
New York, NY 10158-0012, USA

Jacaranda Wiley Ltd, G.P.O. Box 859, Brisbane,
Queensland 4001, Australia

John Wiley & Sons (Canada) Ltd, 22 Worcester Road,
Rexdale, Ontario M9W 1L1, Canada

John Wiley & Sons (SEA) Pte Ltd, 37 Jalan Pemimpin 05-04,
Block B, Union Industrial Building, Singapore 2057

Library of Congress Cataloging-in-Publication Data:

Distributed decision making : cognitive models for cooperative work /
edited by Jens Rasmussen, Berndt Brehmer, and Jacques Leplat.
p. cm. — (New technologies and work)
Based on a workshop sponsored by the Werner Reimers Foundation,
Bad Homberg, and Maison des sciences de l'homme, Paris.
Includes bibliographical references and index.
ISBN 0-471-92828-3
1. Decision-making—Congresses. 2. Decision support systems—
Congresses. I. Rasmussen, Jens, 1926- . II. Brehmer, Berndt.
III. Leplat, Jacques. IV. Werner-Reimers-Stiftung. V. Maison des
sciences de l'homme (Paris, France) VI. Series.
HD30.23.D57 1990
658. 4'03—dc20 90-12462
CIP

British Library Cataloguing in Publication Data:

Distributed decision making.
1. Organizations. Decision making
I. Rasmussen, Jens *1926-* II. Brehmer, Berndt III.
Leplat, Jacques
658.403

ISBN 0-471-92828-3

Typeset by APS Ltd, Salisbury, Wiltshire
Printed in Great Britain by Biddles Ltd, Guildford, Surrey

Contents

Section 5: Experimental Studies in Simulated Task Environments

Section 6: Simulation of Decision Processes

Section 7: Methodological Conclusion

Advisory Board

List of Contributors

Robert Allard
Uppsala Universitet
Dept of Psychology
Box 1854
S-751 48 Uppsala
Sweden

Professor Berndt Brehmer
Uppsala Universitet
Dept of Psychology
Box 1854
S-751 48 Uppsala
Sweden

Professor Dietrich Dörner
Max Planck-Project Gruppe
Kognitive Anthropologie
Frauenstrasse 6
D-1000 Berlin 45
FRG

Dr Pierre Falzon
INRIA
Bt 09
Domaine de Voluceau Rocquencourt
BP 105
F78153 Le Chesnay Cedex
France

Catherine Kasbi
Electricité de France
Direction Etudes et Recherches
'Human Factors Group'
Bat J2
1 Avenue General de Gaulle
F92 Clamart
France

Professor Dr Véronique de Keyser
Université de Liège-au-Sart-Tilman
Institut de Psychologie
Bat B32
B-4000 Liège 1
Belgium

Professor Paul Koopman
Vrije Universiteit, Amsterdam
Faculty of Psychology and Pedagogics
Dept of Work and
Organizational Psychology
De Boelelaan 1081
NL-1081 HV Amsterdam
The Netherlands

Professor Zvi Lanir
Tel Aviv University
Faculty of Social Sciences
Department of Political Science
Ramat-Aviv,
69978 Tel-Aviv
Israel

Professor Jacques Leplat
Ecole Pratique des Hautes Études
Laboratoire de Psychologie
du Travail
41 rue Gay-Lussac
F-75005 Paris
France

Professor Morten Lind
Danmarks Tekniske Hojskole
Servolaboratoriet
2800 Lyngby
Denmark

Professor Maurice de Montmollin
3 Avenue de Stalingrad
F91120 Palaiseau
France

Dr J. Pool
National Hospital Institute
PO Box 9697
NL-3506 GR Utrecht
The Netherlands

Professor Friedrich Rapp
Universität Dortmund
Abteilung 14
Postfach 50 05 00
D 4600 Dortmund 50
FRG

Professor Jens Rasmussen
Risø National Laboratory
PO Box 49
DK-4000 Roskilde
Denmark

Professor James Reason
University of Manchester
Dept of Psychology
Manchester M13 8PL
UK

Dr Janine Rogalski
CNRS-Université de Paris 8
URA 1297—Psychologie Cognitive
2 rue de la liberté
F-93526 Saint Denis Cedex 2
Paris
France

Dr Renan Samurçay
CNRS-Université de Paris 8
URA 218—Psychologie Cognitive
2 rue de la liberté
F-93526 Saint Denis Cedex 2
Paris
France

Dr Kjeld Schmidt
Cognitive Systems Group
Risø National Laboratory
PO Box 49
DK-4000 Roskilde
Denmark

Professor Agnès Van Daele
Université de Liège-au-Sart-Tilman
Institut de Psychologie
Bat B32
B-4000 Liège 1
Belgium

Series Preface

This volume is part of a publication series emerging from an international interdisciplinary study group on 'New Technologies and Work (NeTWork)'. NeTWork is sponsored jointly by the Werner Reimers Foundation (Bad Homburg, Federal Republic of Germany) and the Maison des Sciences de l'Homme (Paris). The NeTWork study group[1] has set itself the task of scrutinizing the most important problem domains posed by the introduction and spread of new technologies in work settings. This problem focus requires interdisciplinary cooperation. The usual mode of operating is to identify an important problem area within the NeTWork scope, to attempt to prestructure it, and then to invite original contributions from European researchers or research teams actively involved in relevant analytic or developmental work. A specific workshop serves to cross-fertilize the different approaches and to help to integrate more fully the individual contributions. Four volumes of NeTWork activities have so far appeared in the Wiley Series 'New Technologies and Work'.[2]

Bernhard Wilpert

---

[1]Members (1988) are: Prof. Dr L. Bainbridge, UK; Dr A. Borseix, France; Prof. Dr P. Drenth, Netherlands; Prof. Dr K. Duncan, UK; Dr J. Evans, UK; Prof. Dr V. de Keyser, Belgium; Prof. Dr U. Kleinbeck, FRG; Prof. Dr J. Leplat, France; Prof. Dr M. de Montmollin, France; Prof. Dr O. Pastré, France; Prof. Dr F. Rapp, FRG; Prof. Dr J. Rasmussen, Denmark; Prof. Dr J.-D. Reynaud, France; Prof. Dr R. Roe, Netherlands; Dr S. A. Ruiz Quintanilla, FRG; Prof. Dr T. Qvale, Norway; Prof. Dr B. Wilpert, FRG.

[2]J. Rasmussen, K. Duncan and J. Leplat (eds): *New Technology and Human Error*, 1986

V. de Keyser, T. Qvale, B. Wilpert and S. A. Ruiz Quintanilla (eds): *The Meaning of Work and Technological Options*, 1988

L. Bainbridge and S. A. Ruiz Quintanilla (eds): *Developing Skills with Information Technology*, 1989.

M. Warner, W. Wobbe and P. Brodner (eds): *New Technology and Manufacturing Management*.

Preface

The aim of the book is to explore the basis for design of decision support systems in different kinds of complex, collective modern work environments. Frequently, decision making has been analyzed and modelled in terms of isolated 'decisions' made by one person. In reality, however, decision making is a continuous, interpersonal process aiming at dynamic control of the state of affairs in a work domain and several decision makers typically will cooperate in this control.

Furthermore, decision making in social groups usually has been studied from the economic, management or sociological point of view, mainly having theoretic or normative perspectives. What is urgently needed for analysis of the implications of modern information technology is a cognitive approach to models of distributed decision making in actual, complex work settings. It is the aim of this book to identify the state of the art of modelling such distributed decision making, to identify the problems posed by modern high-tech systems and to formulate promising research avenues.

The book is based on a workshop sponsored by the Werner Reimers Foundation, Bad Homburg, and Maison de Sciences de l'Homme, Paris.

Section 1

Introduction: an Overview of the Field

The selection of participants in the workshop and, consequently, the topics and points of views presented in this book are intended to promote a particular view of decision making as being a control function in a dynamic environment, and to discuss the research required for modelling decision making, in particular distributed decision making in complex work domains.

It appears to be very timely to present a thorough discussion of this topic now, because of the rapid development toward integrated workstations and information networks. Work normally takes place in a collective context, a fact which has so far not attracted much attention from a cognitive point of view. Previous decision-making research typically is irrelevant to decision making in cooperative work, on the one hand, because this research never seems to involve any task to be performed by the group (except making a decision) and, on the other, because it never involved the dynamic contexts of the kind we find in modern work.

To set the stage for the discussion in the following chapters, Chapter 1 is a brief review of the recent literature dealing explicitly with distributed decision making.

1. Distributed Decision Making: Some Notes on the Literature[1]

Berndt Brehmer
Uppsala University, Sweden

A system is characterized by distributed decision making to the extent that it lacks a centralized control agent, or decision maker. The need for distributed decision making or control arises because of the complexity of the problems facing the decision makers. As the complexity increases, it becomes impossible to embody the required control structure in a single decision unit, especially when this unit is a human with limited processing capacity.

Distributed decision making differs from *group decision making*, where the problem is to achieve consensus among a number of persons, all of whom are capable of understanding the problem as a whole. For problems requiring distributed decision making, this is not the case. Instead, each decision maker has a model of a limited part of the problem. However, there is some relation between the field of distributed decision making and that of *group problem solving*, which often requires the pooling of cognitive resources. The problems studied in group problem-solving research are usually such that each of the group members is able to understand the whole structure of the problems. The difficulty is that, initially, each subject does not have all the information needed to solve the problem. Thus, research on group decision making and group problem solving is of little help for understanding distributed decision making, where the problem is too complex for any one person in the organization to understand it in its entirety. Here, the problem is to coordinate the efforts of agents that have limited models of the problem as a whole, and that these agents may never achieve a global understanding of the problem.

There are at least three reasons for the current interest in distributed decision making. The first is the complex character of modern work. Traditionally, the solution to the problem of complexity has been to partition the task into a number of subtasks. The best example of such partitioning is perhaps found in the Taylorized organization of production. However, in modern forms of

Distributed Decision Making: Cognitive Models for Cooperative Work
Edited by J. Rasmussen, B. Brehmer and J. Leplat

production such partitioning is no longer a viable alternative. What can be divided into well-defined subtasks is now usually automated, and the task of workers in modern forms of production have become those of planning, supervision, and detection and diagnosis of system failures. In short, modern automated and flexible manufacturing systems make work more cognitive: work is a question of problem solving and decision making, rather than actual manufacturing. Moreover, it is not possible *a priori* to divide the task into convenient subtasks, as, in many cases, we do not know what the tasks will be. If there is to be any subdividing, it will have to be done by the workers themselves. Thus, whereas distribution of activity in Taylorized forms of production was a consequence of the fact that a single person could only *make* so many things, modern forms of production require distribution, because one person cannot *form a model* of the complexity needed to control the plant. Therefore, not only the manufacturing but also the decision making must be distributed among workers.

Distribution of tasks leads to a need for coordination. In traditional systems this function was handled by foremen at the lowest level and production departments at a higher one. Foremen and production departments could fulfill these roles in part because they had a virtual monopoly on information, i.e. only the foreman would know what happened during one shift and only the production department knew what was produced by all shifts. Because information was centralized in this way, special staff were needed for the long-range decision making and planning functions.

Modern information technology has largely abolished the need for this kind of function. An information system in a modern process plant can now supply operators with all the information needed for production planning, for example, and for the coordination of work within the shift. This makes it difficult to justify the old forms of hierarchical organizations, and creates possibilities for distributing decision making at lower levels in the companies.

At the same time, demands for autonomy in the workplace lead to a call for a greater share in decision making on the shopfloor. Modern information systems make this possible, as required by the complexity of tasks in modern production.

A third source of interest in distributed decision making is to be found in the changed conditions on the modern battlefield. Military systems have always been characterized by distributed decision making. Commands from above in the military hierarchy tend to have the form of goals for the lower level, rather than specific orders, and the commander at the lower level is generally left to work out how to achieve these goals with his resources. Coordination of units at a given level is obtained by the level above by judicious selection of goals for the commanders at the level below.

Two developments changed this form of command and control. The first was the greatly increased pace of battle. Modern forms of communication and transportation make it possible to deploy troops much faster than when current command systems were developed, and these systems are now often too slow. Second, a precondition for the hierarchical command and control system is that communications can be maintained, a precondition that is now even less certain. This has led to an interest in distributed decision making in the absence of communication or under conditions of limited communication.

Research on distributed decision making can take two forms. The first involves the study of various systems characterized by distributed decision making to find how they perform for different kinds of tasks. For example, one method could compare different forms of organization and communication. The other could involve designing various forms of architectures for distributed decision making and testing their effectiveness.

Given the developments described above, we would expect to find a considerable amount of research on both problems. In fact, research on distributed decision making tends to be limited to the second problem. Moreover, this research is concerned mainly with artificial intelligence (AI) systems rather than with human ones. Moreover, it is related more to distributed problem solving than to distributed decision making. However, the difference between problem solving and decision making in complex environments, where a decision can usually only be reached after considerable analysis and model building, is, perhaps, not important in the present context.

Even though they are not concerned with human systems as such, analyses of distributed decision making from an AI perspective provide useful tools for analyzing problems of distributed decision making. AI systems also may provide possible base lines and simulation models that could aid the study of human distributed systems. Moreover, attempts to build artificial systems reveal what kinds of capabilities must be assumed to make distributed systems work. Thus, the analysis of artificial systems should give important information about when and how distributed systems could function.

CONCEPTS

Decker (1987) provides a very useful review of distributed problem-solving techniques. He describes a taxonomy of problems for distributed AI systems that is also useful for the problem of distributed decision making in human systems in that it yields a number of useful concepts. The taxonomy has four dimensions:

(1) The level of decomposition (granularity);
(2) The distribution of expertise;
(3) The methods for achieving distributed control;
(4) The process of communication.

The level of decomposition can be very fine (statement level) to coarse (problem level). Distributed AI is to be found at the coarse problem level, as would, presumably, most distributed decision-making systems involving humans. As for the distribution of expertise, distributed AI systems would usually involve units with a range of expertise rather than highly specialized people. Such a range of expertise would presumably also characterize most human distributed systems. Thus, in the analysis of distributed decision making we would be concerned with systems decomposed in terms of problems, and involving people with expertise such that a problem could be solved by more than one person.

In discussing decomposition we must not forget that decomposition often cannot be performed *a priori* since we may not always know what problems will be faced by the system. Instead, we must assume that the partitioning of a problem, in so far as it is the result of a decision, must be carried out by the decision makers themselves. To understand partitioning into subtasks is one of the many problems for research in distributed decision making.

As for control, distributed systems could vary along three dimensions: cooperation, organization and dynamics. Cooperation may vary from full cooperation to antagonism. Most distributed decision systems would, of course, be cooperative to some degree. This means that the decision makers would be willing to change their goals to suit the needs of other decision makers and the system as a whole. But goal adaptation would require communication, and a cooperative system of decision makers would presumably have to pay a high price in communication, especially when the subproblems are not independent, to achieve adaptation of the goal. In computer systems communication usually requires more time than does computation, so a cooperative computer system would presumably be inefficient compared to a non-cooperative system for the same kinds of problems. This is presumably also true for a human system, and for such a system, the goal-adaptation process may be even more difficult, and may require even more communication than a computer system.

However, there may be no alternative, especially when it is not known *a priori* which problems the system will have to tackle. If they are not known, it will not be possible to specify which tasks each person should perform and which information he or she will have to communicate (Lesser and Corkhill, 1981). In the face of uncertainty, coordination is presumably only possible by means of communication.

Davis and Smith (1983), as well as many others, point to the need for keeping down communication costs, and propose that this should be done by having not only a communication protocol but a problem-solving protocol as well. As a solution, they propose a *contract net*, where agents in an AI distributed system negotiate about which should do what. When an agent encounters a problem that it cannot solve, either because the problem is too large or because the agent lacks the expertise, it seeks help from others. When the problem is too large, the agent partitions it, and requests bids from other agents in the system to perform the parts. When the agent lacks expertise, the whole problem is offered to others. Other agents not currently engaged in processing problems of their own and which find that they have the expertise needed may then make bids to solve the problems offered. The original agent then selects one or more from the bids offered, and assumes control for the solution of the task.

This kind of architecture makes it possible for the system to reconfigure itself as problems arise. It seems to be useful both as an approximate description of many human distributed systems and as a normative model for such systems.

However, the goal to keep down the amount of communication is not likely to be shared by human agents. If implemented in a human system, the contract net would presumably lead to much more communication than would be found in AI. Moreover, a human system may not be composed of benevolent agents of the kind assumed in the AI system of Davis and Smith, so the negotiation process may be considerably more difficult than envisaged in AI applications. However, the communication costs of this structure may be lower than in many others.

Under certain conditions, cooperation can be achieved without communication by one agent reasoning about other agents and what they may do. This has been called *tacit bargaining* (Schelling, 1970). Presumably, this would require that these other agents in the system would be highly predictable in their response to the problem at hand. It would also require that each agent would have at least as much information about the problem as the other agents in the system, whose behaviour they have to predict. In military circumstances, such predictability is created by doctrine. In civilian organizations, similar results could presumably be obtained by standard operating procedures and 'company spirit'. However, as noted by Hamill and Stewart (1986), there are limits to what can be achieved by doctrine. First, each agent may have different situational information and may thus apply the doctrine in a different way. Second, there is the problem of the weakest link. By promoting action compatible with all units it sacrifices localized effectiveness to achieve uniformity of control. This may lead to independent actions at the lowest level of effectiveness and a loss of all synergistic effects to be achieved by cooperation. In actual systems, when the decision makers know each other, some of the risk of this worst outcome may be less, but it never becomes negligible.

Organization

Distributed systems need some form of organization to guide the communication of goals and results. Such organizations may range from very loose (teams or committees) to very strict hierarchical ones. In the former there is no hierarchical organization at all, and the problem is solved when one of the members proposes a solution. In the latter, lower-level agents are required to react to the commands of their superiors and provide no input of their own. Thus, as pointed out by Decker (1987), the former are data driven while the latter are goal driven. In between we find the more typical hierarchical organizations. Here, each level is responsible for processing at its own level, interpreting data from the level below, passing these interpretations upwards in the hierarchy and receiving its goals from the level above, interpreting these in the light of its information and transforming the goal received to a goal for the level below. This is a typical form of military organization (see Brehmer, 1988).

Kornfeld and Hewitt (1981) have proposed an organization where different agents have different functions, rather than positions in an organization. They call their proposal the *Scientific Community Metaphor*. This involves parallel systems with general problem-solving goals: *proposers* that propose different solutions, *proponents* that collect and present evidence in favour of each proposal, *sceptics* that collect evidence against the proposals and *sponsors* or *evaluators* that evaluate the results and direct the system so that the effort is concentrated on those proposals that seem most valuable. This structure is not necessarily incompatible with that proposed by Davis and Smith. One could easily imagine a system characterized by both negotiation and specialized functions. This serves to remind us that in analyzing organizations for distributed decision making it is important to analyze not only the organizational structure but also the various functions involved.

Many other forms of organization are possible, of course, and the literature on organizations provides a rich source. As noted by Decker, however, this literature is inconclusive with respect to which form is best. This is hardly surprising, for such a question can hardly have a general answer. Which form of organization is best must depend upon which task the organization is to perform. However, research on organizations tends to ignore the question of the relation between the task and the organizational form, and therefore little is known about how organizations and tasks should be matched. To investigate this problem is one of the many urgent tasks for research on distributed decision making.

Control structures

Even a distributed system will need some form of control structure. One possibility is to give the system its organizational form when it is set up, and then let all problems that occur be handled through communication. Another is to create one structure when the system is designed then let this structure change during problem solving to take advantage of new opportunities. Decker (1987) calls this a *dynamically opportunistic organization*. This seems to be the form that most human organizations actually take. That is, when an organization has been in existence for some time an informal organization will emerge that relies upon the capabilities of the people in the organization rather than upon those assumed in the organization chart. This suggests that there are considerable possibilities for self-organization, and that this will be used to get the job done.

The procedure of offering tasks and bidding for them described by Davis and Smith's metaphor of contract nets may well explain how such informal organizations arise.

However, the negotiation metaphor explains mainly the selection of tasks arising within the organization. It ignores the organizational environment, and a system may need to select among problems arising in its environment. That is, the system needs a *focusing* agent that controls the focus of attention of the system. Kornfeld and Hewitt's sponsors fill this role for tasks generated within an organization.

An organization that cannot foresee all the problems that it will encounter, nor all the resources that it will command, must rely upon self-organization to solve its tasks. How the capability for self-organization is to be built into an organization is something of a mystery, if not an outright contradiction.

Communication

Communication is the cement of the organization, and the greater the need for coordination and cooperation, the greater the necessity for communication. However, as noted above, communication requires resources, and it is desirable to keep communication at a minimum. Decker (1987) discusses this problem under three headings: the paradigm by which communication takes place, the semantic content of the information and the protocols adopted to effectively use the limited bandwidth available. We have already commented above upon the last of these.

As for the paradigm for communication, Decker (1987) distinguished between communication via a shared global memory and message passing. The model most often discussed for the former kind of communication is the blackboard model (Hayes-Roth, 1985). Here, the global memory functions as a blackboard (hence the name) upon which messages and partial results are written and where one turns to find information. Such an architecture ensures that every agent in the system will have access to the same information. However, the blackboard may easily become a bottleneck, and may make the system vulnerable if there is a failure of the global memory. A solution is to introduce a series of blackboards, perhaps in some hierarchical organization where different agents have access to different blackboards. However, this becomes identical to message passing, where messages are passed between agents. The new forms of electronic communication may make the construction of blackboards from messages quite easy, since all messages will have to pass through the same system. As shown in a series of studies by Chapanis and his associates (e.g. Weeks *et al.*, 1974), problem solving using written messages of the kind required by electronic mail is less efficient than face-to-face communication, even when the problem solvers have the requisite typing skills.

THE PROBLEM OF CONSISTENT PLANS

We have defined the problem of distributed decision making as that of achieving coordination among agents with limited models of the problem as a whole. In many (perhaps most) situations we will have to assume that these models will not be mutually consistent, and that they may therefore lead to inconsistent plans of action. This problem has recently been discussed by Durfee *et al.* (1989) in a paper on the *Cooperative Distributed Problem Solving* (CDPS) approach. This assumes limited communication among nodes, and as a consequence, it stresses the relative autonomy and adaptability of the problem-solving nodes to a greater extent than other AI approaches to the problem. Specifically, it is assumed that each node possesses sufficient problem-solving knowledge that its particular expertise, which results from its unique perspective on the problem, can be communicated and applied without the assistance of other nodes in the network. That is, each node can formulate a solution to the problem as a whole that is at least partially adequate to the problem as a whole. This seems like a very desirable property for a human network, where some overall understanding will be required, not only to help the individual worker to find some meaning in his or her work but also to show the need for cooperation.

The problem faced by a CDPS network is that each node must make decisions about problem solving and communication based on a local view that is likely to be incomplete and possibly inconsistent with that of other nodes. To resolve these problems there are a number of alternatives: negotiation, functionally accurate cooperation, multi-agent planning, organizational structuring and sophisticated local control. We have discussed negotiation and organizational structuring above, so here we will concentrate on the other three approaches.

In the *multi-agent planning approach* the nodes form a multi-agent plan that specifies all their future actions and interactions. This form of planning is typically used to avoid conflicts over resources (Durfee *et al.*, 1989, p. 76), and is obviously difficult to achieve in a distributed network. To succeed, each node needs models of the other nodes, as well as a protocol for resolving conflicts. The extent to which the nodes will converge on a common plan is dependent on the extent to which the nodes have accurate information about themselves and about the other nodes. When the nodes have incorrect information or incorrect views of the information available to other nodes, convergence on an optimal plan cannot be guaranteed (Rosenschein and Genesereth, 1987). Since inaccurate information is likely to be the rule rather than the exception, the best we could hope for would therefore be acceptable coordination.

An interesting alternative in the multi-agent field is the partial global planning approach of Durfee and Lesser (1988). Here, nodes build local plans, and share those with the other nodes to identify potentials for improving coordination. However, no overall plan has to be formed before the nodes act; action is on the basis of the local plans. This makes it possible to interleave action and planning, and is particularly important in dynamic domains, where no node may have complete information. The partial global planning approach is thus a step towards solving the main problem of the multi-agent approach. This is that it will probably never achieve the plan needed for action in a dynamic environment, since the new information coming in will require constant reformulation of the plan and prevent the system from taking any action.

The main concept in the *functionally accurate cooperation approach* is to tolerate inconsistency and to let the network function, despite inconsistencies (Durfee *et al.*, 1989). However, if the system tolerates inconsistencies, it also needs to be able to resolve them. To do so, the system should make it possible for nodes to exchange partial solutions, so that one or more of the nodes will have enough information to resolve the inconsistencies. Such partial solutions also constitute predictive information that nodes can use to predict the characteristics of the final solution to the problem (Durfee *et al.*, 1989). This speeds up the process of finding this solution.

A node also needs to be able to tolerate inconsistencies in its control information. Especially in complex networks in dynamic environments, the costs of recomputing the network control for each minor change may be prohibitively high, and it may therefore be cost effective to leave some inconsistencies in the control information, provided that the network can recover from errors (Durfee *et al.*, 1989).

The cost involved in this approach is that it makes local problem solving more complex, in that it requires that the whole plan be eventually developed in one or more single nodes. Thus, this approach is probably not adequate to the highly complex problems that require distributed decision making.

The *sophisticated local control approach* acknowledges the fact that a node in a CDPS network must have more sophisticated problem-solving abilities than one working alone. Thus, it must not only be able to reason about the problem at hand, it must also be able to reason about other nodes, and about its own problem-solving activities and how they fit into the activity of the network as a whole. It is not sufficient for effective problem solving merely to give a communication interface to a number of individually effective problem solvers, as anyone who has tried to organize a research team must know.

Sophisticated local control networks therefore concentrate on building nodes that can 'understand' the implications of their own actions and communication on the goals and plans of other nodes, and to choose their actions and communication accordingly. Thus, such networks will involve nodes that can decide for themselves when and how to communicate, rather than having a fixed communication protocol imposed upon them.

This requires the nodes to have a communication policy which guides their information exchange. It must be based on considerations of *coherence*, i.e. it must consider how well the nodes work as a team. Durfee *et al.* (1988) list three important characteristics of communication that affects the coherence of a network: *relevance* (the extent to which a given item of information is consistent with the overall solution being derived by the network), *timeliness* (the extent to which a message will affect the current activity of the network), and *completeness* (the extent to which a message covers the complete solution). If a message is irrelevant, it may divert the receiving node from a basically correct path. Thus relevant messages lead to more coherence. However, even though a message may be relevant, it may arrive at the wrong time, and have no effect. Therefore, timeliness is important to achieve coherence. Finally, completeness is important in that it leads more quickly to convergence.

Durfee *et al.* (1989) evaluated different communication policies experimentally in a dynamic game, and found that the effectiveness of communication policies depends on characteristics of the problem situation (for example, the extent to which the subproblems of the different nodes overlap, and how much data each node has). When the nodes were aware of which of their partial solutions were locally complete, giving them information about the potential impact of sharing their preliminary partial solutions with other nodes allowed them to communicate less but better.

SUMMARY AND CONCLUSIONS

The aim of this chapter has been to examine what current research on distributed AI can teach us on distributed decision making by humans. It is therefore necessarily rather superficial in its treatment of the AI research reviewed in that it has been concerned more with what kinds of problems AI researchers have found in attempting to model human cooperation than upon how they have tried to solve these problems. A number of important points have nevertheless emerged.

First, as should be obvious from what has been said above, we do not know very much about distributed decision making. We do not know how efficient different forms of organization will be for different kinds of tasks, nor do we know how to design efficient distributed systems.

However, some lessons can be learned from the literature reviewed. One is the *importance of communication*: if we want distributed decision making, we need to provide opportunities for communication. Since communication is costly in terms of resources, this may well appear to lead to a system that is inefficient. On the other hand, there may be no alternative. If the system is complex, some form of distributed control is necessary, and if all problems that the system will face cannot be foreseen, communication is needed for the system to reconfigure itself. It is necessary not to introduce organizations that make such reconfiguration impossible. How this is to be done remains an unsolved problem.

Another lesson is that the decision makers in distributed networks need to be able to reason about their own decision-making activities in relation to those of other decision makers in a network. Thus, effective distributed decision making may require a higher level of conscious processing than ordinary individual decision making. The need for communication will, in itself, be an important factor in developing this more reflective kind of decision making. However, reflectiveness is also a prerequisite for effective communication. We should therefore not expect distributed networks to function effectively until after the mutual processes of improving communication and reflectiveness have had a chance to develop. This means that we will need to give the network time to settle before we evaluate and change it. It also suggests that it will not always be easy to introduce new members in teams whose work is characterized by distributed decision making.

The challenge for research on distributed decision making is now to give more substance to these hypotheses, i.e. to find concrete guidelines on how communication should be organized and how reflectiveness can be developed to make distributed networks function effectively.

NOTE

[1]This study is part of the project 'Computer Supported Human Work', supported by a grant from the MDA.

Address for Correspondence:

Professor Berndt Brehmer, Uppsala Universitet, Dept of Psychology, Box 1854, S-751 48 Uppsala, Sweden.

REFERENCES

Brehmer, B. (1988) Organization for decision making in complex systems. In L. P. Goodstein, H. B. Andersen and S. E. Olesen (eds), *Tasks, Errors and Mental Models.* London: Taylor & Francis.

Davis, R., and Smith, R. G. (1983) Negotiation as a metaphor for distributed problem solving. *Artificial Intelligence*, **20**, 63–109.

Decker, K. S. (1987) Distributed problem-solving techniques: A survey. *IEEE Transactions on Systems, Man, and Cybernetics*, **SMC-17**, 729–40.

Durfee, E. H., and Lesser, V. R. (1988) Using partial global plans to coordinate distributed problem solvers. In A. H. Bond and L. Gasser (eds), *Readings in Distributed Artificial Intelligence.* San Mateo, California: Morgan Kaufman, pp. 268–84.

Durfee, E. H., Lesser, V. R., and Corkhill, D. D. (1989) Trends in cooperative distributed problem solving. *IEEE Transactions on Knowledge and Data Engineering*, **1**, 63–83.

Hamill, B. W., and Stewart, R. L. (1986) Modeling the acquisition and representation of knowledge for distributed tactical decision making. *Johns Hopkins APL Technical Digest*, **7**, 31–8.

Hayes-Roth, B. (1985) A blackboard architecture for control. *Artificial Intelligence*, **26**, 251–321.

Kornfeld, W. A., and Hewitt, C. E. (1981) The scientific community metaphor. *IEEE Transactions on Systems, Man, and Cybernetics*, **SMC-11**, 24–33.

Lesser, V. R., and Corkhill, D. D. (1981) Functionally accurate, cooperative distributed systems. *IEEE Transactions on Systems, Man, and Cybernetics*, **SMC-11**, 81–96.

Rosenschein, J. S., and Genesereth, M. R. (1987) Communication and cooperation among logic-based agents. *Proceedings of the 6th Phoenix Conference on Computing and Communication*, Scottsdale, Arizona, pp. 594–600.

Schelling, T. C. (1970) *The Strategy of Conflict.* Cambridge, MA: Harvard University Press.

Weeks, G. G., Kelley, M. J., and Chapanis, A. (1974). Studies in interactive communication. V. Cooperative problem solving by skilled and unskilled typists in a teletypewriter mode. *Journal of Applied Psychology*, **59**, 665–74.

Section 2

Approaches to Modelling the Organization of Cooperative Work and Decision Making

Modelling the organization of cooperative work and decision making can be approached from different points of view, i.e. 'top-down' from representation of the structure of social interaction and 'bottom-up' from the structure derived from an analysis of the control requirement presented by the work content. This section is focused on the various concepts and taxonomies emerging from the research in differing professions in order to identify their relationships and their prospects for development of predictive models.

The significance of the section is the demonstration that models developed within social and engineering sciences and work psychology are becoming increasingly compatible, which has been facilitated by recent developments within cognitive sciences that bridge the traditional gap between the technical studies of work performance and the behaviour-oriented, social science studies.

Part 2.1

Taxonomy of Organizational Models

In this part, Koopman and Pool set the scene for the discussion of modelling approaches by mentioning the limited usefulness of the classical decision-making models. Such models normally consider only one decision maker, and this decision maker has only one goal, which can be stated in quantitative terms. Finally, there is only a limited number of solutions which are known to the decision maker who can therefore 'calculate' the best alternative. Typically, these models consider decision making as a logical process, i.e. they are normative. Koopman and Pool then review alternative approaches which are less normative and take into account organizational decision making. One characteristic feature of these approaches appears to be that they are concerned with factorial analysis of observation of organizational behavior and management structures without explicitly discussing the technical, functional content of the work which is to be controlled by 'decision making.' They do not take into account the fact, mentioned by Thompson (1967), that 'the technical parts of the system provide a major orientation for the social structure. There are both instrumental and economic reasons but the instrumental question is prior to that of efficiency.' The basic reason for the traditional point of view can be partly that decision making and organization have normally been studied within a separate academic paradigm, e.g. economics or social science, without the necessary cross-disciplinary intuition supplied by professional knowledge of the real-life work domain, and partly it can be caused by the past lack of conceptual, cognitive frameworks which could serve to link content of work domains with higher-level management and decision making.

Another point of view is that social structure can be recognized in the design of technology. Even if technology in general will tend to structure the kind of organization which will evolve, this organization will, in turn, be reflected in the design of particular systems.

2. Organizational Decision Making: Models, Contingencies and Strategies

Paul Koopman
Vrije Universiteit, Amsterdam

and

Jeroen Pool
National Hospital Institute, Utrecht

In many of the contributions to this book decision making is regarded as a logical process. Training and technical improvements are applied in endeavours to optimize the process. In this chapter attention is directed to the fact that many decisions in organizations have both logical and political aspects. Decision making is not a neutral event; it generally takes place in a force field in which different preferences and different definitions of social reality play a role. When this is the case, successful decision making will typically bring together the logical and political aspects to a solution. Sometimes, too, the nature of the topic forms a threat to the decision makers or endangers their reputation. This can also upset the rationality of the decision-making process.

Much research done on the course of organizational decisions and the behaviour of the decision makers is summarized in this chapter. It will become evident that the classical rational model has but limited validity. Borrowing Morgan's (1986) use of metaphors and models, we have attempted to sketch the broad palette of organizational decision making. For instance, attention is directed to the limited cognitive capacities of decision makers, the ambiguity in decision-making situations, the role of information and power, the participation issue, etc.

Subsequently, several situational factors which are important in decision making are discussed. We might think of the newness and complexity of the topic, the type of organization, the nature of the environment and characteristics of the decision makers themselves. As we shall see, the validity of the various decision-making models is related to these situational factors. The power relations in the organization are especially important here.

Distributed Decision Making: Cognitive Models for Cooperative Work
Edited by J. Rasmussen, B. Brehmer and J. Leplat

In designing and executing complex decision-making processes the responsible managers are confronted with a number of dilemmas. Examples are: what degree of openness is desired, is it to be a top-down or bottom-up approach, how much should be delegated, how strongly planned and formalized should the process be, how to deal with conflicts, etc. Systematically answering these questions leads to two basic decision-making strategies which are presented at the conclusion of this chapter. The question of what situational factors favour which strategy will also be discussed there.

DECISION-MAKING MODELS

The classical or rational model

The classical or rational model is normative in nature: it prescribes the ideal way of acting in decision-making situations and offers a basis for quantitative disciplines such as econometrics and statistics. The model assumes that the decision maker strives for a decision with a maximum yield. It also makes the rather simplistic assumption that the decision maker is aware of all alternatives and their possible consequences, at least the short-term ones.

The model's usefulness is thus largely limited to situations with the following characteristics:

(1) There is only one decision maker.
(2) The decision maker has only one goal.
(3) The goal can be described in quantitative terms.
(4) There is a limited number of solutions and they are known to the decision maker.
(5) The best alternative can be 'calculated'.

Other variants of the rational model allow for several decision makers and more than one goal. However, the basic assumptions are always known goals,

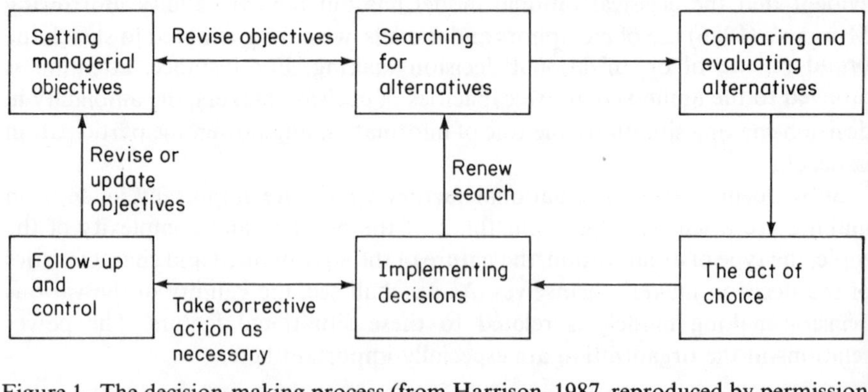

Figure 1. The decision-making process (from Harrison, 1987, reproduced by permission of Houghton Mifflin)

unlimited availability of information, the lack of cognitive limitations as well as limitations in time and costs, quantifiable alternatives. Decision making is regarded as a logical process in which decision makers try to maximize their objectives in an orderly series of steps (see Figure 1). In doing so, they continually assess what actions or alternatives, with what chances of success, will contribute to which fairly short-term goals.

Several models have been developed as alternatives to the normative rational model, and are based more on the actual behaviour of decision makers in organizations. Research has shown that, in practice, decision makers behave entirely differently than recommended by the rational model. In addition, the assumptions made by the rational model with respect to the situation have seldom been found to be realistic. We will now review several of these.

The information model

An initial adaptation of the rational model to the practice of decision making concerns the information-processing capacity of decision makers. Simon (1947, 1957) and March and Simon (1958) focused attention on several frequent restrictions with which decision makers are faced. For instance, because of their limited cognitive capacities, decision makers use only part of the relevant information. Time and money considerations also play a role in determining if there will be a search for more information and how long it will last. The search process generally stops when a 'satisficing solution' has been found: alternatives are not studied exhaustively.

Other researchers, mostly involved in laboratory research of decision-making behaviour, have pointed out more specific limitations of human decision making (Tversky and Kahneman, 1974). Oversimplification processes primarily occur in more complex, ambiguous decision-making situations. Schwenk (1984) investigated several of these mechanisms, most of which are seen in strategic decision making. Basically, decision makers become fixated upon one solution at an early stage and give insufficient consideration to other alternatives. The catastrophic results this can have are well explained by Janis (1982). His 'group-think' concept, or the phenomenon that many highly unrealistic assessments of reality can exist in a small group of relatively isolated decision-makers, serves as an explanation of catastrophes such as the Watergate affair and the Bay of Pigs crisis.

If we look, with Simon (1957), at information seeking in decision-making situations we see the following picture. The search for solutions mostly starts close to home. First, solutions are explored with which the organization successfully tackled its problems in the past. By following existing procedures and current policy, people try to avoid uncertainty. Only when old recipes and rules of thumb fail to work do they start to look for new possibilities.

Other characteristics of Simon's model are that the goals are fairly broad, that there are limited and subjective chance estimates, that not all alternatives are known and that the process is often poorly structured and shortsighted. The 'administrative man' makes do with the alternative that offers him just enough satisfaction with respect to his aspirational level, while avoiding as many unnecessary investments in time as possible.

Nutt (1984) studied the manner in which solutions to complex problem situations were generated. In his analysis of 73 decision-making processes he distinguished five different phases (formulation, concept development, detailing, evaluation and implementation) and three main activities (search, synthesizing and analyzing). The combination of phases and activities led to a typology of five different ways in which 'solutions' were found, and these were termed as follows:

(1) *Historical process (41%)*: In this case solutions or ideas of others (e.g. other organizations) are imitated, even if there is no immediate problem. The problem follows the solution. A subcategory is the 'pet idea', hobby horses of decision makers for which an occasion to put them into practice is sought.
(2) *Off-the-shelf (30%)*: This approach uses the tender method. Competition arises among various solutions offered from outside, and these offers are then evaluated.
(3) *Appraisal (7%)*: This is an attempt to find 'objective data' to back up a chosen solution. However, Nutt's remark that this resembles the scientific method is not entirely correct.
(4) *Search (7%)*: Possible solutions are sought to a newly discovered problem. There are no firm ideas about this. The search is passive and takes place through familiar contacts. If a solution is found, it is immediately adopted.
(5) *Nova process (15%)*: Solutions are designed either by outsiders (advisors) or by the decision makers themselves.

If we compare this classification with the work of other researchers, then its correspondence to the work of Mintzberg *et al.* (1976) is immediately apparent. Their division of the development phase into search-and-screen and design activities is clearly recognizable in Nutt's classification.

In Nutt's typology, solutions do not always follow problems, but sometimes precede them. In some cases it is not so much the solution which must be sought but the problem! O'Reilly (1983) discussed the role of information in decision making and also recognized these possibilities. Preferences or desired solutions are often present before the search for information starts. Information is then used to support, sell or defend these preferences. Naturally, we can no longer speak of an objective or rational choice in such a case.

The organization model

The limitations inherent in individual decision making as described above can be reduced by creating the proper sort of organization. Limited personal information processing and analysis of the environment are compensated by establishing various organizational units and creating a division of labour (March and Simon, 1958).

There are, however, also a number of limitations within the organization. For instance, organizational goals are seldom entirely clear. There are often several changing goals which must be achieved to a certain level of acceptance. Decision makers often have insufficient control of relevant situational factors here. This makes feasibility an important criterion.

The result is that decision making often takes place step by step. This is called 'incrementalism' and 'muddling through' (Lindblom, 1959). Gradually, decision makers develop a definition of the situation which is workable for them. It is a simplified model of reality, embracing both goals and solutions. Often the goals are not clear from the start, but are defined or elaborated along the way.

An example of this is how a government staff works. The precise goals of the minister for whom the staff must prepare policy are often not explicitly known. Civil servants at various levels use many different methods of anticipating a possibly desired policy. Often they must rely on isolated remarks by the minister or replies to questions in Parliament. From such signals they try to infer what proposals might be acceptable to the higher echelon. In this way, policy gradually takes shape by means of interaction between top and staff. Van der Krogt and Vroom (1988) therefore called this the dialogue model.

Lindblom's attempt to adjust the rational (or, as he called it, the 'root' or 'synoptic') model so that it more clearly described what actually took place in organizational practice has evoked many reactions. An often mentioned point of criticism was the inherent conservatism which appeared from it (Etzioni, 1967). The step-by-step method of working makes the introduction of fundamental changes a laborious process. Quinn (1980), however, showed that a step-by-step sequence is the only 'logical' possibility in complex and ambiguous situations from the point of view of feasibility.

Another point which requires attention when decision making is seen as an organizational activity is that an organization is not a unity. Organizations are composed of departments, divisions or other units, and are not 'unitary' structures (Allison, 1971). The task division in organizations leads to a limited view of problems and solutions. Production workers readily see problems as caused by inefficient production methods, sales people by improper marketing techniques, and so on. At the same time, they try to seek the solution in the area of production or sales and thus to safeguard the involvement and influence of the department (Hickson *et al.*, 1971).

Cyert and March (1963) also discussed decision making in the light of the organizational context, and presented four characteristics. The first is that conflicts which arise from the diversity of interests and preferences of the coalition partners are usually not really resolved. They are reduced to acceptable proportions by means of a variety of procedures ('quasi-resolution of conflict'). To ensure a certain coherence among the various subsolutions, the organization strives for satisficing rather than maximal results, and devotes its attention to the successive achievement of contrasting goals, where time acts as a buffer (Cyert and March, 1963). A second characteristic of organizational decision making is the avoidance of uncertainty, for example, by bringing the environment under control as much as possible through agreements and contracts (Thompson, 1967; Pfeffer and Salancik, 1978). Third, organizations only seek solutions to specific problems. Once a problem is solved, the search stops. The search process takes place according to three rules: first look in the neighbourhood of the problem, then in the neighbourhood of known alternatives, and then try to pass off problems as much as possible to weak sectors of the organization. The fourth and final characteristic is that organizations learn from their experiences. This implies that search procedures (the rules according to which attention is divided) and the goals of the organization are adapted in the course of time to the changed circumstances.

The bureaucratic model

The organization can be seen as the context within which decision-making processes take place. This means that such processes are subject to the structural division of authority and tasks that prevails in the organization. 'For decision making, an organization *is* the rules of the game,' as Hickson *et al.* (1986) stated. There are large differences in the number of decision-making procedures in different types of organizations. Governmental organizations are frequently characterized by detailed rules and delineation of authority, while business and industry often have fewer such rules. The delegation of authority—traditionally, more or less hierarchical—is not fixed, but can itself be the subject of decision making (Child, 1972; Bobbitt and Ford, 1980).

Most decisions take place within the network of accepted rules and agreements. This is primarily true of operational and tactical decisions, which are often made at middle and lower levels (Nutt, 1976). Sometimes, however, a decision is so new and exceptional that the existing structure is not adequate. Wilson *et al.* (1986) named four factors that make routine decisions impossible:

(1) Unusual facts;
(2) Conflicts between players;
(3) New topics;
(4) An unusual source from which the problem arises.

These factors mean that the usual rules and procedures are no longer applicable. The bounds are broken, so new negotiations must be held about the rules of the game. The more powerful players, those who control important resources or skills, are naturally in the strongest position.

Rather than use the existing organizational structure, agreements can be made about the procedure to be followed for each individual decision-making process. Mintzberg *et al.* (1976) called the use of such 'decision controls' *meta-decision making.* Under this heading come agreements about who does what when, what criteria will be applied and what the planning will be (Van Aken and Matzinger, 1983). This is actually the determination of the structure of the decision-making process (Kickert, 1979) or—as Van der Krogt and Vroom (1988) put it—decisions about the way in which decisions will be made. The latter authors viewed these as the most important or strategic decisions, because they establish the limits of the rest of the decision-making process. In this way, the top of an organization can exert significant influence on the final result without necessarily making direct decisions. However, firm agreements about the procedure to be followed can also work out unfavourably. For instance, the formalized procedures of governmental bodies often elicit counteractions: lower echelons learn to apply the rules to their advantage (Morgan, 1986). This decreases flexibility and increases administrative immobilization (Allison, 1971; Koopman *et al.*, 1986).

In addition to organizational structure and meta-decision making, legislation is a third constraint. For example, the Dutch Works Council Act states that the Works Council has the right to advise management or to endorse decisions in a number of areas. The Large Companies (Structure) Act (1971) and the Civil Code also set down certain competencies and obligations for the board of directors and board of management (De Jongh, 1987). Finally, trade union organization can insist on being involved in a number of decisions (such as reorganizations, mass dismissals, mergers) on the basis of collective labour agreements or the Socio-Economic Advisory Council's merger code. Several international studies (IDE, 1981; Heller *er al.*, 1988) showed that formal regulations largely determine the division of influence in decisions.

Legal regulations, the organizational structures which are based on them, and decisions about decision making form the framework in which decision-making processes should take place.

The garbage can model

In the 'garbage can model' organizations are seen as 'organized anarchies', characterized by unclear or inconsistent goals, a technology which is obscure and little understood by members and a highly variable member participation. Cohen *et al.* (1972) based their description of this model primarily on experiences with decision-making processes at universities. The university is considered the prototype of the garbage can model. According to these authors, organizations can be viewed as collections of (1) problems, (2) solutions, (3) participants and (4) choice opportunities (i.e. situations in which participants are expected to link a problem to a solution, and thus make a decision).

These four elements are more or less randomly mixed together in the 'garbage can'. Combinations arise almost unpredictably. There is no *a priori* chronology. Solutions can precede problems, or problems and solutions can wait for a suitable opportunity for a decision. Clearly, the traditionally assumed order 'identification and definition of the problem, search for solutions, consideration of alternatives and selection' (see Figure 1) is reversed. 'Although it may be convenient to imagine that choice opportunities lead first to the generation of decision alternatives, then to an examination of their consequences, then to an evaluation of those consequences in terms of objectives, and finally to a decision, this type of model is often a poor description of what actually happens' (Cohen *et al.*, 1972, p. 2).

Concepts such as the 'garbage can model' and 'anarchy' can be misleading. The authors certainly do not imply that no systematic decision making can be discovered in such organizations. On the contrary, the central message of these authors is that the seeming anarchy has a structure and an organization which form a reasonable, although not optimal, answer to the great environmental uncertainty in which the participants find themselves.

In order for decision making to progress it is essential that the organization manages to attract sufficient attention from the participants to solve the problems in question. However, participants generally have more on their minds. Thus it is not unusual that decision making takes place without explicit attention to the problem, or even by simply postponing the problem. The authors, however, see it as the task of management to coordinate and steer the required attention in a direction desired by the organization.

The political or arena model

Where the garbage can model emphasizes the variable participation of the members and the lack of clarity of the system, the arena model assumes that the various players have divergent and sometimes contrasting goals. Conflict and the way in which it is handled are thus the focal points of the arena model. The organization is seen as a band of changing coalitions, and decision making is primarily a political process in which negotiations play a central role (Bacharach and Lawler, 1986; Pettigrew, 1973). The primary criterion is not the 'right' decision but a decision acceptable to all.

The division of tasks among organization members mentioned under the organization model has one inevitable side effect: differences in the division of power. In their 'strategic contingencies theory of intra-organizational power', Hickson *et al.* (1971) described how the division of power in organizations lies in the control of critical dependencies. The power of departments is dependent on the extent to which (1) they can reduce environmental uncertainty for the organization, (2) they can be replaced, and (3) the activities are central (that is, how large a part of the organization will come to a standstill if a department discontinues its work).

The strategic contingencies theory is an extension of the earlier work of Emerson (1962). Pfeffer and Salancik (1978) also expanded the theory for external relations (relations of the organization with the environment). Their 'resource-dependence' model is based primarily on two ingredients: the importance of a resource and its scarcity. Resources can be anything: money, expertise, information, production facilities, etc.

Another view of power is that there are demonstrable power sources. In their classical article, French and Raven (1959) distinguished five sources of power: reward, force, legitimacy (accepted or legitimate power differences, as in stratified organizations), reference (the power that comes from identification with popular persons, charisma) and expertise. Another important power source is control of the available information (Pettigrew, 1973; O'Reilly, 1983). The person who determines how, on the basis of what information or which alternatives, a decision will be made often has more influence on the final result than those who actually decide.

In order to play the game successfully, a person must not only have access to sufficient power sources but also the will and the capacity to use them (Mintzberg, 1983). Use of language and legitimation of the exercise of power are essential elements of the power game (Pfeffer, 1981; Clegg, 1987). Many studies have shown that the 'logical rationality' (factual argumentation) of decision-making processes is often made inferior to the 'political rationality' (internal power relations).

An important question that has been studied is: 'What requirements must the political constellation—that is, the system of power relations within the organization—meet in order to be able to implement strategic changes?' A recent study by Pettigrew (1986) indicated that this is possible only in large organizations under extreme pressure from the environment. Excellent managers generally turn out to be very skilful at utilizing the situation!

The participation model

As the above models have shown, the participation of various groups in the decision-making process is an important factor. Here, however, we want to devote our attention specifically to the participation of lower organization members in decision making. The Netherlands has several forms of participation, set down either by law or by custom.

In the first place, there is the Works Council, which is compulsory for companies and organizations employing over 35 persons. Government organizations (local or national) have similar bodies. Second, many companies have forms of consultation at the departmental level. In the 1970s they were generally called work consultation, while nowadays newer forms such as quality circles are popular. Third, in the past decade, the trade unions encouraged union work in the company as a form of participation, because the unions did not want to commit themselves to company policy through the Works Council (Poole, 1986). This form of participation never really took hold in the Netherlands.

Participation can be considered to have positive effects for several reasons. First, on idealistic grounds, it is assumed that workers have a *right* to participate. Democratizing the organization, it is said, will lead to a breakdown of the exclusive rights of management in favour of the workers. This line of reasoning was frequently heard during the democratization movement of the late 1960s and early 1970s. In addition, because it utilizes the capacities and expertise of employees, participation was expected to lead to *higher-quality decisions*. This is the basis of more modern forms of consultation, although the priority here lies in improving the quality of the production or service. It should be distinguished from the approach that sees the increasing satisfaction and involvement of employees as the result of participation. This is hoped to lead to a greater *acceptance* of decisions. By taking into account, factually or procedurally, the opinion of those involved, a certain commitment to the decision is created, thus raising the level of acceptance.

Broadly speaking, the many and extensive studies have yielded little consistent support for the expected positive effects of participation (Locke and Schweiger, 1979; Wagner and Gooding, 1987). Solutions to the lack of consistent findings were sought in more complicated contingency models, in which the effectiveness of participation was considered dependent on certain situational factors such as the amount of conflict, pressure from the environment and the phase in which participation takes place (Koopman, 1980; Heller *et al.*, 1988). Although this clarified some findings, participation is generally useful only if it makes a functional contribution (in terms of utilizing expertise or promoting acceptance) to the decision making. The original expectations turned out to be too high after all, not in the least in the context of automation (Koopman and Algera 1987; Child, 1988).

The results of research on the use of the Works Councils in decision making are not markedly positive either. Usually the Works Councils exert only a marginal influence, especially on more strategic decisions (Koopman, 1980; Andriessen *et al.*, 1984). Replication of this research ten years later yielded only slightly better results. Changes in the Dutch Works Councils Act (1979) and other political, economic, technological and socio-cultural changes led to a somewhat higher influence of the councils. The increase in influence took place mainly in the area of strategic decisions, such as reorganizations, mass dismissals and large investment decisions. On this basis, it was concluded that the Works Council had reached a certain maturity (Pool *et al.*, 1988). Despite its generally modest position, a number of positive effects of Works Council involvement can be named (IDE, 1981: Looise and De Lange, 1987):

(1) Better acceptance of decisions;
(2) Greater openness and a more careful approach to policy formulation and execution, better decisions;
(3) Better promotion of employees interests.

One way to explain the contrast between marginal infuence and positive effects is the preventive effect of the Works Council. Although there is little noticeable direct influence on decisions during the meetings between management and the council, the position of the Works Council is taken into consideration prior to the meeting.

The dynamic phases model

Several of the models described above share a characteristic in that they subtract something of the *behavioural* rationality which is assumed or advocated in the classical model. They note that the rationality of this behaviour (striving for maximal achievement of goals) is compromised by limited cognitive capacities, insufficient time and resources, lack of insight in the functioning of the organization and, finally, by conflicting interests of participants.

Emphasis in the dynamic phases model lies on the *process* rationality. These two categories are not mutually exclusive; however, the point of view is different. Assuming that, in strategic decisions, logical and political problems should be brought together, the question of how this does or should take place arises.

There are several phase models of decision making in the literature. A typical example is the model of Brim *et al.* (1962), in which the following steps take place: (1) identification of the problem, (2) seeking information, (3) generation of possible solutions, (4) evaluation of alternatives, (5) selection and (6) implementation of the decision. Such a model was shown in Figure 1. Other authors use a somewhat rougher classification, because a sharp distinction between steps 2 and 3 and between 4 and 5 is seldom found in practice (see e.g. Witte, 1972). Based on a study of 25 strategic decisions, Mintzberg *et al.* (1976) observed that three central phases were always found: 'identification', 'development' and 'selection' (see Figure 2).

Several supporting processes run parallel to these three central decision-making phases: decision-making control processes, communication processes and political processes. In addition, the picture is further complicated by the effect of several 'dynamic factors'. Interruptions, delays and feedback loops are important in complex decision-making processes. Strategic management is not a matter of steady progress from one activity to the next but a dynamic process with acceleration and delays, 'comprehension cycles', in which those involved gradually get more grasp of a complicated question, and 'failure cycles', in which they must return to previous phases, when, for example, no acceptable

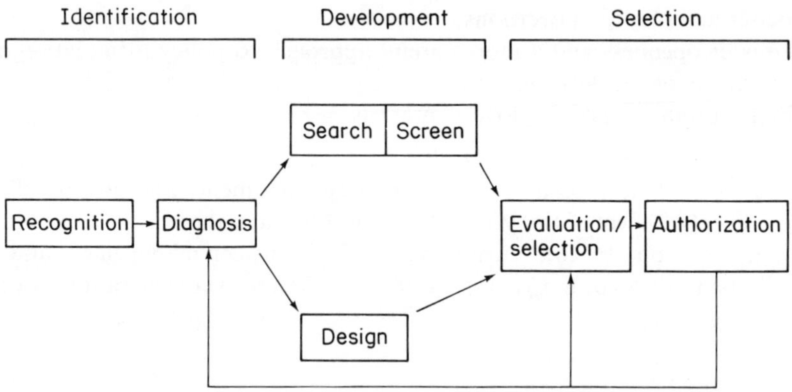

Figure 2. Simplified phases model of Mintzberg *et al.* (1976). Reproduced by permission of the *Administrative Science Quarterly*

solution can be found because of conflicts. Also, many processes are prematurely stopped or blocked because of political or technical reasons.

In another study of 217 complex decision-making processes in organizations in England, Yugoslavia and the Netherlands, empirical support was found for such phases as 'start, development, finalization, implementation' (Heller *et al.*, 1988). However, this study also showed that the steps were not always found neatly ordered in this fashion. Many processes were divided into a number of subdecisions in which the main activities of search, evaluation and selection occurred. The nature of these decision-making processes was therefore more circular than sequential. This phenomenon was also found in a study of reallocation decisions in an international concern (Koopman *et al.*, 1984).

Based on these four phases (start, development, finalization, implementation), the question of how to interpret the various phases remains. For this we want to compare two points of view. The first is that of Sfez (1978), who approaches decision making as an integration process of knowledge and power. According to Sfez, the first and the third phases are primarily characterized by power processes. During the second and fourth phases knowledge aspects are central. The second point of view is that of Enderud (1980), who assumes, as does Sfez, that the power game makes up a very essential part of strategic decisions. However, they differ as to the specific stage in which the power struggle predominantly occurs. According to Enderud, this happens as early as the second phase, generally inside a small group that operates behind closed doors. The primary function of the third phase is the official legitimation of decisions. This implies approval by the authorized bodies and the creation of some acceptance among those directly involved (see Table 1).

It is no simple matter to say which view is more correct. The applicability of the two approaches might well depend on certain circumstances, particularly the

Table 1: The phases model of Enderud (1980)

(1) 'Bull session'
—mapping
—diagnosis
—sorting out

(2) 'Negotiations'
—drafting the outline
—initial agreement among the participants most intensively involved
—in small and closed committees
—real-political

(3) 'Persuasion'
—sell the compromise
—quasi-objective criteria
—feedback loops
—no change substance
—ritual elements

(4) 'Bureaucracy'
—supplements and modifications
—subissues

degree to which the decision-making process is formalized, and the problem towards which the decision making is directed. In the democratized decision-making structure at Dutch universities during the 1970s, departmental and university councils, in which all groups of personnel and students were represented, had fairly effective control of all important decisions. This control came about primarily through participation in the first and the third phases: problem identification and the choice of the ultimate solution.

The model of meaning

An aspect of many strategic decision-making processes that has been neglected so far is the ambiguity of the situation, the environment and—in general—of the information relevant to the decision (McCall and Kaplan, 1985). In addition, most 'players' have access to only part of this information. Especially in periods of crisis or uncertainty, managers who know how to create or outline a promising future will dominate the strategic management of the organization, thus strengthening their position.

The model of meaning directs attention to the manner in which problems are defined and the amount of consensus. An automation process can be viewed as a technical problem. The import of such a definition is obvious: place the solution in the hands of technicians. This is exactly what management often does. Works councils and trade unions, on the other hand, have a different definition of the problem. They place emphasis on important consequences for the organization, the quality of the work and employment opportunity. In this way, they protect their right to be taken seriously as a bargaining partner.

The model of meaning reflects the renewed attention to cultural processes in organizations. The social psychologist, Weick (1979), has given this great impetus, as has experience with Japanese management. In recent books such as Morgan's *Images of Organization* (1986) the creation of a social environs is seen as a central management task. In the Netherlands, Van der Krogt and Vroom (1988) gave a fascinating description of this approach to organizational issues. This revolves around the question of how organizations change and learn from their past experiences.

CONTINGENCIES

In the previous section we reviewed several decision-making models. The strength, but also the weakness, of a model is that it highlights a certain aspect of the object of study. This shifts other characteristics somewhat to the background. According to the concrete case with which we are dealing, one model or another offers a more true-to-life or useful description of reality. This depends on the nature of the problem in question as well as the context (organization, environment) in which it occurs. A few of these contingencies and their influence on the manner of structuring decision-making processes will now be explored.

Type of subject matter

Novelty and complexity

Depending on the novelty and complexity of the problem, higher and more creative investments will have to be made in a variety of search behaviours. When problems are more familiar and surveyable, the organization can rely more strongly upon 'schedules' which were effective in the past.

As research has repeatedly borne out, the logical rule 'the more complex the problem, the more analysis is necessary' is seldom put into practice (Beach and Mitchell, 1978). This can partly be explained by the fact that analysis activities are viewed as cost items. People are not always willing to pay these costs. In part, it also depends on the presence of other strategic factors, particularly the amount of conflict.

The way in which the search process takes place is often entirely different from the assumptions made by the classical model. In 233 decision-making processes relating to the purchase of a computer, Witte (1972) registered the frequency with which the activities 'seeking information, developing alternatives, evaluation of alternatives' occurred in ten different time intervals. The frequencies found differed greatly from the assumed frequencies (see Figure 3). The most

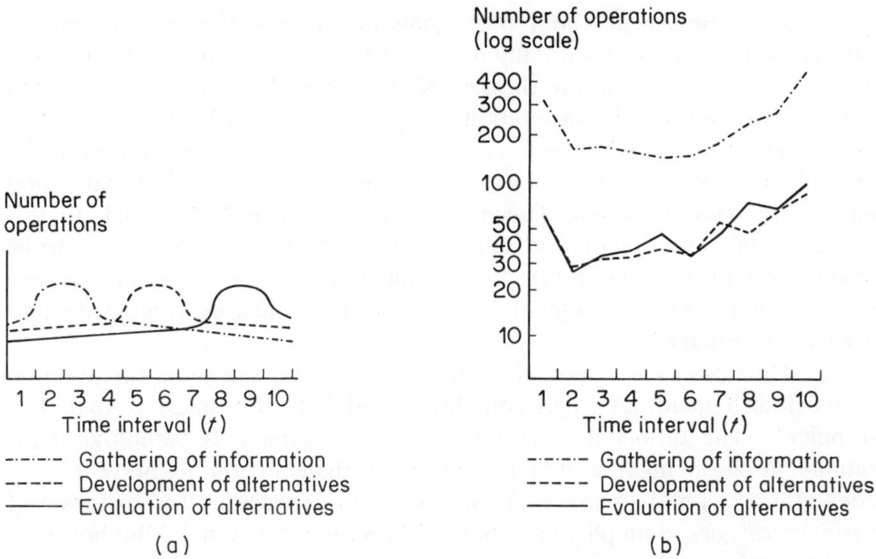

Figure 3. (a) Prediction of the phase model (Witte, 1972, p. 169); (b) results with relation to the phase model (Witte, 1972, p. 170). Reproduced by permission

striking conclusion was that 'seeking information' was the most frequent activity during all time intervals.

However, according to other studies (Nutt, 1984), 'solutions' are often imitated or borrowed from the neighbours or the competition, without a thorough analysis. Many 'happy-hour computers' have been put in cold storage: they were found out not to be the solution to the company problem.

Amount of agreement about goals and means

As early as 1959 Thompson and Tuden developed a typology based on the amount of agreement about goals and means (ways in which the goals are to be achieved). According to these authors, there is a best-fitting 'strategy' for each of the four types of problems (see Figure 4).

		Preferences about possible outcomes: Agreement	Preferences about possible outcomes: Disagreement
Beliefs about causation	Agreement	Computation	Compromise
	Disagreement	Majority judgement	Inspiration

Figure 4. The typology of Thompson and Tuden

If there is agreement about both goals and means, the decision can be calculated. In practice this usually means delegating it to experts (Vroom and Yetton, 1973). If the means to the desired end are unclear, experts will have to reach a solution through consultation ('majority judgement'). If there is conflict about the goals, consultation between the parties involved is necessary (for example, via a representative body). If agreement is lacking on both goals and means, say Thompson and Tuden, the organization is endangered. In this situation, only charismatic leadership ('decision by inspiration') is said to be able to prevent the organization from disintegrating. Axelsson and Rosenberg (1979) used a similar typology of decisions based on the axes 'complexity' and 'dynamics' (Figure 5).

Like Thompson and Tuden, all these authors have to say about the situation in the fourth quadrant (high complexity and high dynamics) is that it is turbulent: 'The turbulent situation is usually regarded as pathological for rational decision making, and organizations therefore try to prevent it or convert it into a more manageable situation. This is accomplished by means of various strategies to simplify or stabilize the decision situation... ' But how they go about this remains unclear.

According to some authors, the number of cells can even be reduced to two: goals and means sometimes overlap. Means often form intermediate steps or subgoals. So the amount of 'conflict' can be reduced to one dimension. Pinfield (1986) distinguished 'structured, orderly but iterative' processes and more unpredictable 'anarchical' ones. The explanatory value of these process types, he stated, depends on whether or not there is consensus on the goals to be achieved.

Fahey (1981), using a study of six strategic decisions, also reduced reality to two contrasting types: 'rational-analytical' and 'behavioural-political'. However, this author saw the amount of complexity (uncertainty, novelty) as the primary factor in determining the decision-making process. Grandori (1984) combined the factors of uncertainty and conflict on one continuum, and distinguished six process types on this basis. As uncertainty and conflict increase, people will turn more to heuristic techniques.

An extensive study of strategic decision making was performed at Bradford University (Hickson *et al.*, 1986). The conclusions based on 150 'top decisions'

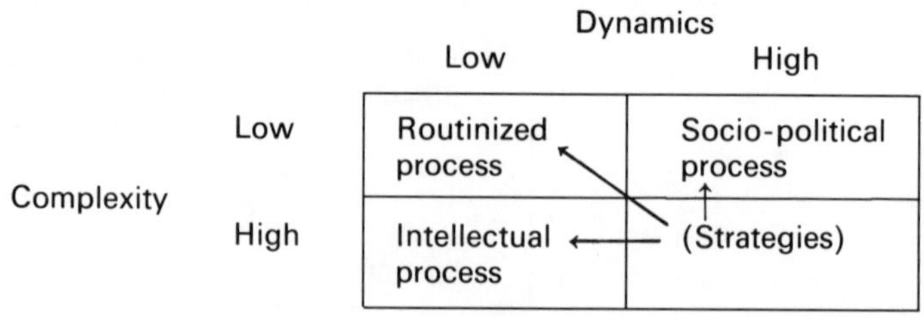

Figure 5. The typology of Axelsson and Rosenberg

in 30 very different organizations are of importance for both this and the following section. As in other studies, two questions were central: *how* do strategic decisions take place and *why* do they take place like that?

To answer the question of how, the researchers classified each decision-making process using twelve process categories such as: duration, formal and informal interaction, negotiating scope, interruptions and delays in the process. Two fundamental process dimensions were distilled from these process variables: discontinuity and dispersion. The discontinuity dimension indicates whether a process has many delays and interruptions, resulting in a longer duration. The second dimension, dispersion, indicates how many groups are involved in the process. If the cases studied are classified according to their scores on these two dimensions, a typology of three process types results: sporadic, fluid and constricted processes (Figure 6).

Sporadic processes are characterized by bursts of activity alternated by still periods, a lengthy duration and much informal contact. They have delays and obstacles, for example, because a report must be awaited or because of resistance. Information of varying quality and from various parts of the organization is used. Sporadic decisions are authorized at the highest level. *Fluid* processes are more regular and linear. They take place mostly in committees, project groups and meetings. The duration is shorter, in terms of months rather than years. The information used comes from fewer sources and is less ambiguous. *Constricted* processes are characterized by more delays, more information sources and less formal communication than fluid processes. On the other hand, the decision has undergone more preparation (less negotiating scope) and less activity is unleashed in the organization. We might even ask whether these are strategic decisions after all, in view of the fact that this type of decision is not authorized at the highest level.

Subsequently, the authors explored the question of *why* strategic decisions take such different courses. They sought explanations in subject matter and type

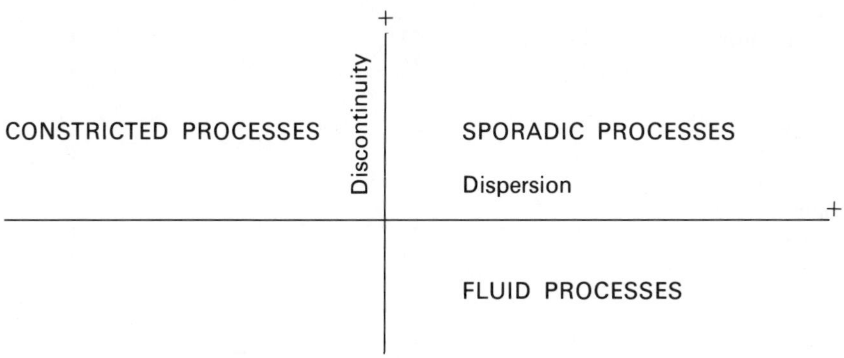

Figure 6. The typology of Hickson *et al.* (1986)

of organization. Two factors are considered important to the *subject*: complexity and politicality. The combination of these factors makes it possible to classify the 150 decisions into three categories, which the researchers entitled 'vortex', 'tractable' and 'familiar'. Vortex topics are both complex and political. Several parties are involved, both inside and outside the organization, and the consequences are serious. The 'tractable' topics are less controversial, but they do set the stage for coming decisions. 'Familiar' topics come up regularly and their consequences are limited. If the 150 cases are classified on the basis of cluster analysis into the type of decision-making process as well as of subject matter, these classifications overlap by two-thirds. Vortex topics usually take a sporadic course, tractable topics show more of a fluid pattern and familiar topics are mostly characterized by a constricted process.

Type of organization

In addition to the type of topic, the type of organization determines in part the course of the process, although in a less consistent manner (Hickson *et al.*, 1986). The 30 organizations studied were classified on the dimensions profit versus non-profit, production versus service and private versus state-owned company (see Table 2). Combinations were also considered. The most remarkable finding was that state-owned production organizations exhibited the most sporadic

Table 2: Differences between organizations in types of decision-making processes (Hickson *et al.*, 1986, p. 199; reproduced by permission)

Classification of organizations	Number of decisions	Type of decision		
		Sporadic (%)	Fluid (%)	Constricted (%)
Commercial	98	38	31	31
Non-commercial	38	39	32	29
Manufacturing	45	49	15	35
Services	91	34	38	28
Privately owned	74	32	34	34
State-owned	62	47	27	26
Manufacturing				
—public	9	78	0	22
—private	36	42	19	40
Services				
—public	53	41	32	26
—private	38	24	47	29

processes, while private service organizations (banks, insurance companies) showed the most fluid ones. Private producers (industry) and government services (hospitals, universities) occupied an intermediate position.

Other authors assumed a more direct relationship between organizational characteristics and the course of decision-making processes. Fredrickson (1986) and Hall and Saias (1980) reversed the traditional statement of Chandler that 'structure follows strategy'. In this view, strategic decision-making processes are largely determined by structural characteristics of the organization in which they take place. Fredrickson cited centralization, formalization and complexity as structure variables. In his view, these characteristics were best represented by three of Mintzberg's (1979) structural configurations, the simple structure, the machine bureaucracy and the professional bureaucracy. Subsequently, Fredrickson assumed that decision-making processes would take different courses in the types of organizations distinguished. Decision making in the centralist, simple structure will be more proactive and innovative, in the formalized machine bureaucracy more problem linked and incremental, while in the complex professional bureaucracy it will be of a political nature. Unfortunately, no research results on these assumptions are available.

Miller (1987) expanded on Fredrickson's work. In almost a hundred small and medium-size companies, Miller researched the relation between organizational structure (formalization, integration, centralization and complexity) and characteristics of decision-making processes (rationality, interaction and assertiveness). Rationality here means the extent to which attention is paid to analysis of the problem and of alternatives and the extent to which there is explicit policy, an orientation to the future and an active attitude towards the environment. Interaction means the extent to which decision making is individual or by consensus and to the scope of negotiation. Finally, assertiveness means whether behaviour is proactive and how far risks are taken in decisions.

From Miller's study it appeared that formal integration (formalization and integration together were found to form one structural factor) primarily went along with the rationality characteristics and, to a lesser extent, with interaction and assertiveness. The presence of 'horizontal ties' (committees, project groups and liaison officers) showed a particularly strong positive correlation with the rationality characteristics.

In addition to the structure, other organizational characteristics play a role. A very important factor is the power constellation in the organization. Is power concentrated in one or a few players (dominant coalition) or is it spread over the organization (e.g. due to the expertise of the employees)? The superior authority of management largely determines its room to manoeuvre, and thus the strategy to be taken. Another characteristic is the prevailing culture in the organization.

An important factor at the level of the organization is the prevailing pattern of ideas and convictions. This is viewed by the top as the organization's *identity*. Donaldson and Lorsch (1983) spoke of 'belief systems'. The most important question here is what the organization sees as its field of activity or its objective, and what its strong points are (distinctive competence). In addition, ideas about what are acceptable risks and the importance attached to self-sufficiency make up an independent part of this 'corporate belief system'. This pattern of ideas and convictions 'sets important limits on the strategic choices managers are willing to make', thus creating a certain stability and certainty. 'Without these belief systems, managers would be adrift in a turbulent sea, without charts'. Fundamental changes in these more or less stable patterns occur if changes take place at the top of the organization (new top managers with fresh ideas) or during crises.

The environment

The type of organization is sometimes difficult to separate from the nature of the environment. The pressure exerted on the organization from outside has important consequences for the internal power relations and—more in general—for the possibilities and limitations of the organization (Jemison, 1981; Mintzberg, 1983). The question whether the external powers are diffused or concentrated is especially important to the autonomy of the organization. This, again, has consequences for the manner of decision making.

In an international study of 217 complex organizational decisions in England, Yugoslavia and the Netherlands (Heller *et al.*, 1988) it appeared that 'meta-power'—that is, influence on the decision-making process by external powers (e.g. the mother company)—was one of the most important determinants of the process structure. Legislation also exerted great influence. It appeared that in the Dutch and English companies the lowest amount of participation (by the various groups in the organization) was found in the first and third phases, the highest in the second and fourth. In the terms of Sfez (1978), in the power phases the degree of participation was lower than in the knowledge phases.

In Yugoslavia the opposite was true: the greatest amount of participation was observed in the first and the third phases. This suggests that, when decision making is more formalized and public (Yugoslavia), it should follow the classical phase model, because it forms a better guarantee for the legitimation of the process. In principle, the worker's council has a grasp on the diagnosis of the problem via the first phase and on the choice of the ultimate solution via the third. Whether this legal power base is effectively converted into actual power depends strongly on what happens in phase two, in which middle management and staff groups play an important role. In the Netherlands, the grasp of the Works Council on the first phase is fairly small (it is entitled to information and may initiate action). In theory, its influence in the third phase is larger (depending on the topic, it is entitled to give advice or to endorse a decison). We will return to the question under what conditions these rights are (or can be) exercised in the third section of this Chapter.

Various authors (Stein, 1981; Pettigrew, 1986) emphasized the effect of a crisis situation on the manner of decision making. Periods of relative calm and stability are alternated by phases in which large changes take place. The latter may accompany a change at the top of the organization (Donaldson and Lorsch, 1983). Often, too, the need for change results from a shift in the environment, which confronts the organization with a new dominant problem. The external threat can become so great that management can push through changes for which insufficient legitimation would have been found during more stable periods.

The strong manager?

How dependent is management on the environment? How much leeway is there for its own policy? What are the possibilities to implement this policy internally? This discussion has been going on in the literature for years (Pfeffer, 1981) and was recently intensified by the vogue of 'no-nonsense management'. Success stories about strong managers are on everyone's lips.

Outcomes of the most serious studies of actual behaviour in strategic management suggest that the power position of the top is often overestimated. Furthermore, this position depends on certain organizational characteristics, such as size. In small companies the influence of top management is more outspoken than in complex organizations. Long-term developments are often more the product of gradual adaptation to changing circumstances than of consistent plans or decisions (March and Olsen, 1983). It is generally a cautious step-by-step process, in which analytical and political elements are interwoven (Lindblom, 1959; Quinn, 1980, 1988). Steering such a process is often done by intuition. The list of agenda items may be left unwritten or formulated in vague terms, depending on the estimated acceptance (Kotter, 1982; Wrapp, 1988).

Innovators must not only compete on a market for new ideas but also on a market for resources and for political support (Kanter, 1983). The outcomes are therefore not only a product of (partly) rational discussions but also of interests of individuals and groups, bureaucratic rules, and of manipulation of the structural context (Bower, 1970).

According to Pettigrew (1986) and Mintzberg (1988), strategic management as a 'continuous process' merely exists as a reconstruction in retrospect. Only in true crisis situations can fundamental changes be implemented. In such a case, the threat, real or imagined, from the environment compensates the limited possibilities of management. In less extreme situations the following description by Quinn (1980) is probably more applicable: 'Strategic management is a logical–political process, running flexibly and experimentally, leading from broad ideas to specific commitments, slowly creating need for change, legitimating new starting points, taking tactical steps, finding subsolutions, acquiring support, neutralizing opposition, formalizing commitment.'

Depending on the type of problem and the organizational context, subaspects become dominant in a certain order. Sometimes power aspects will thrust aside factual arguments, as in restructuring situations. Often the technical aspects are so penetrating that management tends to leave everything to the experts, as with automation.

STRATEGIES

Several decision-making models have been discussed as well as situational factors which must be taken into account in choosing the approach. But what is a good decision-making strategy? In answering this question the management responsible for this process finds itself faced with a number of dilemmas (Koopman *et al.*, 1986). Examples are:

(1) How much openness in the direction?
(problem-oriented versus solution-oriented)
(2) How rigorous?
(gradual versus integral)
(3) How much participation?
(bottom-up versus top-down)
(4) How highly structured and formalized?
(general decision-making design versus detailed design)
(5) How much time pressure and control?
(flexible norms versus precise norms)
(6) When and how to negotiate?
(open facing of problems versus covering up, smoothing)

We assume that a good strategy is generally characterized by a certain amount of internal coherence (that is the choices on the individual dilemmas are not too much in opposition) and that it is sufficiently attuned to the relevant situational factors (cf. Mintzberg, 1979). A systematic combination of choices leads to at least two basic, contrasting management strategies, a linear-integrative approach and an incremental-iterative one (Table 3).

Table 4 shows under what conditions one of the two management strategies is to be preferred in the case of an automation project. A linear-integrative approach requires that the change process can be fairly well overseen beforehand and that it can be steered and coordinated from one point. Therefore predictability must be large (no new problems) and potential resistance slight (no autonomous opponents). Another argument in favour of a linear-integrative approach might be the scale or complexity of the problem. Surely when the matter is interdependent with other policy fields in the organization, an integral approach is often necessary. We might think of the automation of mail sorting in the large Dutch post offices. Demands of uniformity in handling complaints may sometimes also point to an integral approach. An example is the way in which

Table 3: Two management strategies (Koopman, 1989)

Incremental-Iterative	Linear-Integrative
Problem-oriented	Solution-oriented
Goals central	Means central
Gradual	Integral
Bottom-up	Top-down
General design (informal, flexible)	Detailed design (formalized)
Frequent consultation with those involved	Central coordination and control
Flexible norms, adjustment along the way	Precise norms, stringent control
Differences of opinion are discussed	Differences of opinion are denied/covered up

counter terminals are introduced at banks. In both examples, one or two branches are used to test the new system. Once the growing pains are over, it becomes standard in all other branches. At this point, there is not much room left for participation by those directly involved (Algera and Koopman, 1984; Child, 1988).

However, whether or not to utilize potential variety and scope in the organization for a more open consultative strategy is partly a question of policy (Walton, 1985). Is the personnel strategy primarily aimed at greater commitment or at greater control? Does the company see automation as a new means of better utilizing human capacities or primarily as a means of being less dependent on the 'labour factor' (Blackler and Brown, 1986)? Recognized expertise of organization members can be an important argument in this consideration. So, too, can be the attitude of personnel representatives in works councils and trade unions. If there are truly autonomous opponents (for example, in an inter-organizational innovation process) one may be forced to adopt an incremental-iterative strategy. Finally, there are several external circumstances which are an inducement in the direction of one approach or the other. For example, think of the amount of time pressure and of external influence—distributed or concentrated—on the organization (Mintzberg 1983), the stringency of legislation, rules and regulations and the prevailing mood of society at the time.

Table 4: Situational characteristics as stimulating or inhibiting circumstances in management strategies (Koopman, 1989)

	Type of strategy	
Situational Characteristics	Incremental-iterative	Linear-integral
Type of problem		
Newness	New	Familiar
Scale, complexity, interdependence	Limited	Large
Consensus on goals	Moderate	Slight or great
Organizational policy		
Demand for uniformity	Slight	Large
Decision-making structure	Not fixed	Clear-cut
Personnel strategy aimed at	Commitment	Control
Coordination via	Decentralization	Centralization
Distance of designers to location	Small	Large
Opponents		
Autonomy of users (user organization)	Large	Small
Recognized expertise of users	Large	Slight
Attitude of works council and trade unions	Proactive, aimed at contents	Reactive, aimed at compensation
Circumstances		
Time pressure	Slight	Great
Mood in society, culture	Participative	No-nonsense
Legislation	Regulations for automation	Regulations are lacking or unclear
External power	Spread	Concentrated

Address for Correspondence:

Professor Paul Koopman, Vrije Universiteit, Faculty of Psychology and Pedagogics, Dept of Work and Organizational Psychology, De Boelelaan 1081, NL-1081 HV Amsterdam, The Netherlands.

REFERENCES

Aken, J. E. van, and Matzinger, B. (1983) Een neo-rationeel model van besluitvorming. *M&O, Tijdschrift voor Organisatiekunde en Sociaal Beleid*, **37**, 478–93.
Algera, J. A., and Koopman, P. L. (1984) Automation: Design process and implementation. In P. J. D. Drenth, Hk. Thierry, P. J. Willems and Ch. J. de Wolff (eds), *Handbook of Work and Organizational Psychology*. Chichester: John Wiley.
Allison, G. T. (1971) *Essence of Decision: Explaining the Cuban missile crisis*. Boston: Little, Brown.
Andriessen, J. H. T. H., Drenth, P. J. D., and Lammers, C. J. (1984) *Medezeggenschap in Nederlandse Bedrijven. Verslag van een onderzoek naar participatie- en invloedsverhoudingen*. Amsterdam: Noord-Hollandse Uitgevers Maatschappij.
Axelsson, R., and Rosenberg, L. (1979) Decision making and organizational turbulence. *Acta Sociologica*, **22**, 45–62.
Bacharach, S. B., and Lawler, E. J. (1986) Power dependence and power paradoxes in bargaining. *Negotiation Journal*, **2**, 167–74.
Beach, L. R., and Mitchell, T. R. (1978) A contingency model for the selection of decision strategies. *Academy of Management Review*, **3**, 439–44.
Blackler, F., and Brown, C. (1986) Alternative models to guide the design and introduction of the new information technologies into work organizations. *Journal of Occupational Psychology*, **59**, 287–313.
Bobbitt, H. R., and Ford, J. D. (1980) Decision maker choice as a determinant of organizational structure. *Academy of Management Journal*, **5**, 13–23.
Bower, J. L. (1970) *Managing the Reallocation Process: A study of planning and investment*. Boston: Harvard University School.
Brim, O., Glass, D. C., Larvin, D. E., and Goodman, N. E. (1962) *Personality and Decision Process*. Stanford: Stanford University Press.
Child, J. (1972) Organization structure and strategies of control: A replication of the Aston study. *Administrative Science Quarterly*, **17**, 163–77.
Child, J. (1988) *Participation in the Introduction of New Technology into Organisations*. Aston University: Work Organisation Research Centre.
Clegg, S. R. (1987) The language of power and the power of language. *Organization Studies*, **8**, 61–70.
Cohen, M. D., March, J. G., and Olsen, J. P. (1972) A garbage can model of organizational choice. *Administrative Science Quarterly*, **17**, 1–25.
Cyert, R. M., and March, J. G. (1963) *A Behavioral Theory of the Firm*. Englewood Cliffs, NJ: Prentice-Hall.
Donaldson, G., and Lorsch, J. W. (1983) *Decision Making at the Top: The shaping of strategic direction*. New York: Basic Books.
Emerson, R. M. (1962) Power-dependence relations. *American Sociological Review*, **27**, 31–41.
Enderud, H. (1980) Administrative leadership in organized anarchies. *International Journal of Management in Higher Education*, 235–253.
Etzioni, A. (1967) Mixed-scanning: A 'third' approach to decision-making. *Public Administration Review*, **27**, 385–92.
Fahey, L. (1981) On strategic management decision processes. *Strategic Management Journal*, **2**, 43–60.
Fredrickson, J. W. (1986) The strategic decision process and organizational structure. *Academy of Management Review*, **11**, 280–97.
French, J. R. P., and Raven, B. (1959) The bases of social power. In D. Cartwright (ed.),

Studies in Social Power. University of Michigan, Ann Arbor: Institute for Social Research, pp. 150–67.

Grandori, A. (1984) A prescriptive contingency view of organizational decision making. *Administrative Science Quarterly*, **29**, 192–209.

Hall, D., and Saias, M. A. (1980) Strategy follows structure! *Strategic Management Journal*, **1**, 149–63.

Harrison, E. F. (1987) *The Managerial Decision-making Process*. Boston: Houghton Mifflin.

Heller, F. A., Drenth, P. J. D., Koopman, P. L., and Rus, V. (1988) *Decisions in Organizations: A three-country comparative study*. London: Sage.

Hickson, D. J., Hinnings, C. R., Lee, A. C., Schneck, R. E., and Pennings, J. M. (1971) A strategic contingency theory of intra-organizational power. *Administrative Science Quarterly*, **16**, 216–29.

Hickson, D. J., Butler, R. J., Cray, D., Mallory, G. R., and Wilson, D. C. (1986) *Top Decisions: Strategic decision-making in organizations*. Oxford: Blackwell.

IDE-International Research Group (1981) *Industrial Democracy in Europe*. Oxford: Clarendon Press.

Jemison, D. B. (1981) Organizational versus environmental sources of influence in strategic decision making. *Strategic Management Journal*, **2**, 77–89.

Janis, I. L. (1982) *Groupthink*, (2nd edn). Boston: Houghton Mifflin.

Jongh, E. D. J. de (1987) *Commissarissen, Directeuren, OR-leden: Verhoudingen en Verwachtingen*. Leiden/Antwerp: Stenfert Kroese.

Kanter, R. M. (1983) *The Change Masters: Innovation for productivity in the American corporation*. New York: Simon and Schuster.

Kickert, W. J. M. (1979) Rationaliteit en structuur van organisatorische besluitvormingsprocessen. *Bestuurswetenschappen*, **33**, 21–30.

Koopman, P. L. (1980) *Besluitvorming in Organisaties*. Assen: Van Gorcum.

Koopman P. L. (1989) Between control and commitment. *4th West European Congress on the Psychology of Work and Organizations*, 10–12 April, Cambridge.

Koopman, P. L., and Algera, J. A. (1987) Formalization and delegation: Two management dilemmas in automation design processes. *Third European Congress on the Psychology of Work and Organization*, 13–15 April, Antwerp.

Koopman, P. L., Kamerbeek, E., and Pool, J. (1986) Management dilemmas in organizations. *21st International Congress of Applied Psychology*, 13–18 July, Jerusalem.

Koopman, P. L., Kroese, H. A. F. M., and Drenth, P. J. D. (1984) Rationaliteit bij reallocatie. *M&O, Tijdschrift voor Organisatiekunde en Sociaal Beleid*, **38**, 151–70.

Kotter, J. P. (1982) *The General Managers*. New York: Free Press.

Krogt, Th. van der and Vroom, C. (1988) *Organisatie is beweging*. Culemborg: Lemma.

Lindblom, Ch.E. (1959) The science of 'muddling through'. *Public Administration Review*, **19**, 79–88.

Locke, E. A., and Schweiger, D. M. (1979) Participation in decision-making. One more look. In B. M. Shaw (ed.), *Research in Organizational Behavior*, Greenwich, Conn: JAI Press, pp. 265–339.

Looise, J. C., and De Lange, F. G. M. (1987) *Ondernemingsraden, Bestuurders en Besluitvorming*. Nijmegen: ITS.

March, J. G., and Olsen, J. P. (1983) Organizing political life: What administrative reorganization tells us about government. *American Political Science Review*, **77**, 281–96.

March, J. G., and Simon, H. A. (1958) *Organizations*. New York: John Wiley.

McCall, M. W., and Kaplan, R. E. (1985) *Whatever it Takes: Decision makers at work*. Englewood Cliffs, NJ: Prentice-Hall.

Miller, D. (1987) Strategy making and structure: Analysis and implications for performance. *Academy of Management Journal*, **30**, 7–32.
Mintzberg, H., Raisinghani, D., and Théorêt, A. (1976) The structure of 'unstructured' decision processes. *Administrative Science Quarterly*, **21**, 246–75.
Mintzberg, H. (1979) *The Structuring of Organizations: A synthesis of the research*. Englewood Cliffs, NJ: Prentice-Hall.
Mintzberg, H. (1983) *Power in and around Organizations*. Englewood Cliffs, NJ: Prentice-Hall.
Mintzberg, H. (1988) Opening up the definition of strategy. In J. B. Quinn, H. Mintzberg and R. M. James (eds) *The Strategy Process: Concepts, contexts and cases*. Hemel Hempstead: Prentice-Hall.
Morgan, G. (1986) *Images of Organization*. London: Sage.
Nutt, P. C. (1976) Models for decision making in organizations and some contextual variables which stipulate optimal use. *Academy of Management Review*, **1**, 84–98.
Nutt, P. C. (1984) Types of organizational decision processes. *Administrative Science Quarterly*, **29**, 414–50.
O'Reilly, Ch.A. (1983) The use of information in organizational decision making: A model and some propositions. In L. L. Cummings and B. M. Shaw (eds), *Research in Organizational Behavior* Vol. 5. Greenwich, Conn: JAI Press, pp. 103–39.
Pettigrew, A. M. (1973) *The Politics of Organizational Decision Making*. London: Tavistock.
Pettigrew, A. M. (1986) Some limits of executive power in creating strategic change. In S. Srivastva (ed.), *The Functioning of Executive Power*. London: Jossey-Bass.
Pfeffer, J., and Salancik, G. R. (1978) *The External Control of Organizations*. New York: Harper and Row.
Pfeffer, J. (1981) *Power in Organizations*. Boston: Pitman.
Pinfield, L. T. (1986) A field evaluation of perspectives on organizational decision making. *Administrative Science Quarterly*, **31**, 365–88.
Pool, J., Drenth, P. J. D., Koopman, P. L. and Lammers, C. J. (1988) De volwassenwording van de medezeggenschap. *Gedrag en Organisatie*, **1**, 37–57.
Poole, M. (1986) *Towards a New Industrial Democracy: Workers' participation in industry*. London: Routledge and Kegan Paul.
Quinn, J. B. (1978) Strategic change: 'Logical incrementalism.' *Sloan Management Review*, **20**, 7–21.
Quinn, J. B. (1980) *Strategies for Change: Logical incrementalism*. Homewood, Ill: Irwin.
Quinn, J. B. (1988) Managing strategies incrementally. In J. B. Quinn, H. Mintzberg and R. M. James (eds), *The Strategy Process: Concepts, contexts, and cases*. Englewood Cliffs, NJ: Prentice-Hall.
Schwenk, Ch.R. (1984) Cognitive simplification processes in strategic decision-making. *Strategic Management Journal*, **5**, 111–28.
Sfez, L. (1978) Existe-t-il des decisions democratiques? *Dialectiques*, **22**, 59–72.
Simon, H. A. (1947) *Administrative Behavior*. New York: Free Press.
Simon, H. A. (1957) *Models of Man*. New York: John Wiley.
Stein, J. (1981) Contextual factors in the selection of strategic decision methods. *Human Relations*, **34**, 819–34.
Thompson, J. D. (1967) *Organizations in Action*. New York: McGraw-Hill.
Thompson, J. D., and Tuden, A. (1959) Strategies, structures, and processes of organizational decision. In J. D. Thompson, P. B. Hammond, R. W. Hawkes, B. H. Junker and A. Tuden (eds), *Comparative Studies in Administration*. Pittsburgh: Pittsburgh University Press.
Tversky, A., and Kahneman, D. (1974) Judgement under uncertainty: Heuristics and biases. *Science*, **185**, 1124–31.

Vroom, V. H., and Yetton, P. W. (1973) *Leadership and Decision-making*. Pittsburgh: University of Pittsburgh Press.

Wagner III, J. A., and Gooding, R. Z. (1987) Shared influence and organizational behavior: A meta-analysis of situational variables expected to moderate participation-outcome relationships. *Academy of Management Journal*, **30**, 524–41.

Walton, R. E. (1985) From control to commitment: Transforming work force management in the United States. In K. B. Clark, R. H. Hayes and C. Lorenz (eds), *The Uneasy Alliance*. Boston: Harvard Business School Press.

Weick, K. (1979) *The Social Psychology of Organizing*. Reading, Mass: Addison-Wesley.

Wilson, D. C., Butler, R. J., Cray, D., Hickson, D. J., and Mallory, G. R. (1986) Breaking the bounds of organization in strategic decision making. *Human Relations*, **39**, 309–32.

Witte, E. (1972) Field research on complex decision making processes. The phase theorem. *International Studies of Management and Organization*, **2**, 156–82.

Wrapp, H. E. (1988) Good managers don't make policy decisions. In J. B. Quinn, H. Mintzberg and R. M. James (eds), *The Strategy Process: Concepts, contexts and cases*. Englewood Cliffs, NJ: Prentice-Hall.

Part 2.2

Taxonomy of Work Domains

In the following chapters, Leplat, Schmidt and Rasmussen present a discussion of distributed decision making explicitly formulated from the point of view of requirements in cooperative work, as perceived from the perspectives of work psychology, sociology and control theory, respectively.

First, Leplat prepares the ground in Chapter 3, reviewing the problems in task analysis and design, clarifying the differences between prescribed tasks and the actual work activity. He then extends the discussion to cover 'collective activities', and gives an important clarification of terms: decision making is considered to be the control of activity, and it is stressed that the usual connotation of the term 'decision' should not lead to the exclusion of the role of automated, subconscious processes of highly skilled activities. With an emphasis on task allocation and control of collective and cooperative activity, Leplat reviews the concepts and models developed in work psychology. The distinctions made and the focus on relationships between task structure, control of activities, and the structure of working groups make the chapter very useful for modelling distributed decision making in a particular work domain, and as discussed below, they make the concepts derived from work psychology and control systems analysis immediately compatible.

In Chapter 4, on forms of cooperative work, Schmidt, in a very similar way but from a sociological point of view, characterizes forms of cooperative work from an analysis of the different reasons for cooperation: whether cooperation is necessary in order to augment resources, to facilitate differentiation of tools and skills, or because different 'perspectives' of work should be taken into account. Organizations are seen as stabilized patterns of cooperation and the generative mechanisms of organizations are related to articulation of recurrent patterns of work, of meshed efforts of individuals and ensembles having their individual interests and motives. This, in fact, means that organizations are dynamic coalitions of diverging and often-conflicting interests evolving from the basic features of the actual work conditions.

In Rasmussen's approach (Chapter 5), different aspects of distributed decision making are modelled separately, such as: (1) the 'work space' of an organization; (2) the decision making of the individual actors who are in control of only a part of this work space; and, finally, (3) the social organization of the agents necessary for coordination of their activities. The framework is based on a system control point of view. According to this, decision making cannot be considered a sequence of separate decisions but is a continuous control task. In the chapter the approach is compared to similar developments within hierarchical control of complex systems, and it is concluded that formalisms from control engineering can support a development of models suited for experimental test by simulation. The approach appears also to be immediately compatible with the work on management and organization by Thompson, in particular with his emphasis on the significance of an organization's technology for its social structure, and his analysis of heuristics controlling organizational evolution 'under the norm of rationality.' Also this evolutionary approach to representation of organizations can have important implications for development of simulation models (cf. Chapter 20).

Discussion during and following the workshop elaborated on the apparent compatibility of the concepts of these three chapters. Briefly, the conclusions from this discussion were:

(1) Any model of distributed decision making or cooperative work should be expressed with reference to the intrinsic properties of the actual work domain. Therefore in order to be able to generalize, a taxonomy of real-life work domains should be established.
(2) Work activities should not be represented by normative procedures, but instead by means of the network of potential relations among purposes and goals, functions and processes, and material resources of the work domain. Only then is it possible to grasp the discretionary nature of modern work conditions.

Three levels of model appear to be necessary for the activities in the work domain, corresponding to the traditional task and organization models (both, however, are derived from the control required by the work domain):

(1) The role of the individual agents (i.e. the 'role allocation') should be expressed with respect to the work domain by statement of the means–ends relations they manage and their control requirements for meeting the ultimate goals and constraints;
(2) The immediate work organization derived from the mutual communication necessary to coordinate the activities for concerted action; and

(3) The longer-term models of the social organization of the agents representing the evolution of the cooperative structure, depending on human values and cultures, in addition to the requirements for control of relocation of roles and workload in response to changes of values and goals and of material system conditions.

3. Organization of Activity in Collective Tasks

J. Leplat
Ecole Pratique des Hautes Etudes, Laboratoire de Psychologie du Travail, Paris

Performing a collective task requires an organization of activity just as does carrying out an individual task. In this case, however, the organization must take into consideration another dimension, as it is determined not only by its object but also by its relation to the activities of others. When a job which was previously performed alone is now carried out by several persons, the work is determined not only by the previous goal but also by the acts of the other participants with which one has to coordinate.

We shall speak here of activity rather than decision. The distribution of decision is only one side of the distribution of activity. Decision has connotations with activities that are consciously organized, whereas the organization of activity can be based on automatized procedures where the notion of decision is not very relevant.

Collective tasks require, in principle, two types of activity which are sometimes directly linked but which can be dissociated. These are (1) allocating the tasks to the individuals involved in the collective task (which task will be given to whom?) and (2) the modalities of performing the ascribed functions (how will each individual perform his or her task to achieve the goal of the collective task?).

As Savoyant (1984) rightly noted, social psychology has been principally concerned with the first of these aspects, considering that 'the group solves its problems once the tasks have been divided among its members and it is precisely this process of partition and allocation of the tasks that is the principal object of research' (p. 274). However, in work situations, it is in general not the group that decides on how the tasks are allocated; rather, this is imposed by the division of labour. What is therefore essential is the actual performing of acquired experience. This chapter will deal more particularly with the second aspect

Distributed Decision Making: Cognitive Models for Cooperative Work
Edited by J. Rasmussen, B. Brehmer and J. Leplat

mentioned, that is, the modalities of execution in an already determined repartition. Little research has been carried out on this point, which deserves a better understanding for an improved organization of collective work and also greater knowledge of the mechanisms of individual activity.

This chapter does not attempt to provide a systematic view of this theme but rather to briefly show how it is or could be studied within different theoretical frameworks, and to raise some general problems for which these theories must provide a coherent answer. This choice must involve a number of ambiguities, resulting in particular from the fact that the basic notions do not have exactly the same meaning in the different approaches (e.g. action, operation). Some distinguishing features of the collective task, prescribed as such, will be proposed and we shall examine how the activity in response to these tasks is organized, insisting on the use of certain theoretical frameworks and on the forms and means of coordination.

DISTINGUISHING FEATURES OF COLLECTIVE TASKS

First, let us remind the reader of a distinction whose importance for work analysis has already been emphasized (Leplat and Hoc, 1983; Leplat, 1988a, b). The task can be defined as a goal to be realized under given conditions. The activity consists of those processes used by the individual to perform the task. The task itself must be precisely described. The *prescribed* task is the one that the organization and those in charge of the work assign to the subject. The *real* task is the one the subject actually performs and which can be induced from an analysis of the subject's activity. The real task can be considered as a model of the activity elaborated by the analyst—the prescribed task therefore being the organization's model of the activity. These two types of task often differ, and Hackman (1969) has identified some of the sources of these differences, particularly the degree to which the operator understands and accepts the task.

A collective task is one whose execution requires several operators. This necessity can be the result of the means available for executing the task (e.g. sawyers) or of organizational constraints (e.g. one or two operators to accomplish a monitoring task). A prescribed collective task will not necessarily produce a collective activity, and conversely, a collective activity could occur without a prescribed collective task. The differences between the prescribed and real tasks will always be useful to identify in relation with the collective aspect. These differences indicate insufficiencies in the organizational model of the task, particularly concerning the group. They can be related to modifications in the distribution of tasks and in the means of executing these tasks. Here we shall examine several features that are often used to characterize prescribed collective tasks.

Features concerning task distribution

Herbst (1974) suggested describing this distribution within a group by constructing the matrix of correspondences between the members of the group and the tasks (Figure 1). Figure 1(a) represents the case where each individual is allocated a very precise task and Figure 1(b) the case where each task can be performed by all the operators who must therefore decide who will perform which task. In the latter, as each operator can perform each task, it could be said that there is flexibility in the distribution, and one could define degrees of flexibility. The greater the flexibility (that is, the more freedom the organization leaves the group in distributing the tasks), the greater the load imposed on the group for managing this distribution.

Each couple in the group can be characterized on the bases of the tasks which they have been allocated. Herbst (1974) proposed four variables for this description, which we shall adapt after simplification to the description of the global task:

(1) Task relationship: tasks are carried out together or separately (a, $\bar{a}$);
(2) Role differentiation: tasks carried out are identical or different (i, $\bar{\imath}$);
(3) Task dependence: tasks may be dependent, interdependent or independent (d, d^*, $\bar{d}$);
(4) Goal dependence: goals are shared, independent or unreciprocated supporting (g, $\bar{g}$, g^*) (p. 126).

By combining these variables (e.g. $\bar{a}$, $\bar{\imath}$, d, g) one defines the types of work relationship structure for each couple. One can then characterize the work of a team by the types of relationship that exist between all the team members.

It is also possible to define the relations between individual and collective tasks. Swap (1984) differentiates four different group tasks:

	T1	T2	T3
01	I		
02		I	
03			I

(a)

	T1	T2	T3
01	I	I	I
02	I	I	I
03	I	I	I

(b)

Figure 1. Extreme examples of matrices for task (T*i*) allocations to the operators (O*j*) from a group. (a) Rigid allocation; (b) flexible allocation

(1) Additive tasks, in which the members' contributions are simply summed to obtain the final result;
(2) Conjunctive tasks, in which the group outcome is dependent on the least proficient member (the group cannot work faster than the slowest member);
(3) Disjunctive tasks, in which the outcome is dependent on the most expert member;
(4) Discretionary or divisible tasks, in which the members' contributions must be integrated by the group.

The *variety* of subtasks comprising the collective task is often mentioned as an important characteristic of the collective task. This relates to the skills of the group members but also contributes to skill development and coping with uncertain task conditions. Pierce and Ravlin (1987, p. 773) emphasize this factor and note that maintaining variety within the system is particularly useful for the groups confronted with changing environments.

Some authors introduce the notion of divisibility of the task. This can be thought of as the possibility of separating the task into subtasks, or of distinguishing different ways of analyzing the task, with the need to combine the results to perform the task (for example, a synthesis of mechanical, electronic, and psychological points of view to provide a solution to an operational malfunction). These divisible—as opposed to monolithic—tasks lend themselves far better to utilization of the multiple talents and areas of expertise that may exist among a group's members (Rubin, 1984, p. 35).

The task distribution can be characterized also by reference to the means–ends space (see Chapter 5). All these different features concerning task distribution are more or less relevant according to the type of task. They are not exclusive and can be combined in the analysis.

Features concerning the execution of tasks

A second type of prescription concerns the execution of work within the prescribed allocation of the tasks. This execution can be prescribed more or less precisely and therefore gives the group members a varying degree of autonomy, particularly concerning coordination activities. This autonomy, considered as an important variable of work, has been the object of much research in organizational psychology. Breaugh and Becker (1987 p. 383) have recently discussed this research and proposed a measure of this autonomy based on three dimensions that are translatable in terms of work:

(1) *The degree of discretion*: the possible choice regarding the procedures, methods of going about the work;
(2) *Work-scheduling autonomy*: the possibility of controlling the scheduling sequencing, timing of work activities;

(3) *Work criteria autonomy*: the degree of ability to modify or choose the criteria used to modify the performance.

This autonomy is often largely dependent on how the group is managed, and particularly on the role played by the supervisor(s). Cordery and Wall (1985) have pointed out three dimensions defining the supervisor's effects on autonomy:

(1) *Goal structure*: the extent to which the supervisor provides individuals or work groups with clear attainable goals for task performance.
(2) *Method structure*: the extent to which the supervisor exerts active and direct control over employee's work activities and choice of work methods.
(3) *Boundary protection*: the extent to which the supervisor acts to ensure that employees have appropriate knowledge, skills, and resources to exercise discretion within a given situation (p. 434).

These conclusions, based on work carried out in a socio-technical perspective, raise the important problem of the modalities of task-execution coordination within a work group. We shall return to this problem in the analysis of activity.

The task could also be characterized by the way the subject receives feedback and the possibilities he or she has for interpreting this information. This feedback is related to individual results as well as to the results of several members of the group or the group as a whole. In particular, it should be important to give the subject the possibility of evaluating his or her own role as well as those of the other team members when attempting to reach the task goal (Cordery and Wall, 1985).

The collective task can be characterized by the mechanisms that it provides to ensure the coordination of the subtasks that each member of the team must execute. Stoelwinder and Charns (1981), inspired by the work of several authors, distinguish situations of weak uncertainty and high uncertainty. For the first type of situation they characterize 'three mechanisms to reduce the need to exchange information by programming activities' (p. 752):

(1) *Standardization of work process*—where the activities to be performed are specified or programmed. This includes rules, regulations, schedules, procedures and plans;
(2) *Standardization of skills*—where the training and skills necessary to perform activities are specified;
(3) *Standardization of output*—where the results of the activities are specified (pp. 752–3).

In situations of high uncertainty, exchange of information and feedback are necessary. To facilitate the management of unfamiliar situations, one finds the following mechanisms:

(4) *Supervision*—where one person takes responsibility for the work of others. This is the basis of coordination via an organization's hierarchy;
(5) *Mutual adjustment*—the informal exchange of information about the performance of activities;
(6) *Group coordination*—including formal and informal meetings and the establishment of work groups (p. 753).

All these features that characterize prescribed collective tasks are important to identify for two essential reasons. First, they indicate the many demands that the activity should take into consideration. Second, these features could be used to characterize the real task which, as Hackman (1969) notes, can be described in the same language as the prescribed task.

Task definition

The notions of task and subtask are incessantly used in descriptions of the prescribed collective task. These can be defined in various ways. Rasmussen (1986) suggested distinguishing two dimensions of characterizing the units of analysis chosen for task description. The first, called a dimension of *aggregation* or *refinement* (Hoc, 1987), relates to the dimension of the units and is hierarchical in nature, the units of small dimension being nested within large units. Here we speak of 'whole–part relationships' in this decomposition hierarchy (Rasmussen, 1986). The second dimension, referred to as one of *abstraction* or *implementation* (Hoc, 1987), relates to the level at which the units are described. Rasmussen (1986 and Chapter 5 this volume) describes cause and effect or means–ends relationships. The abstraction hierarchies, so defined, 'describe bottom-up, what components and functions can be used for, how they may serve higher level purposes, and top-down, how purposes can be implemented by functions and components' (Rasmussen, 1986, p. 14).

Prescribed tasks could be situated at different levels on these two dimensions. They could also be defined in a more or less precise way. In certain cases they will only be described in terms of their goal and the global task will be treated as a series or a structure of goals. In other cases, the conditions of execution of these goals will be given more or less precisely. The implicit part of prescriptions of the task is linked to the representation the author has of the task's performers' competence and is also directly related to their degree of autonomy, this being smaller, the more precisely the task is defined.

The collective nature of the task induces additional demands concerning task definition, particularly concerning a coherence in the descriptions of the tasks allocated to the different members of the group.

The situations created by collective tasks

Collective tasks are entrusted to the group members, and this task–group interaction constitutes the collective situation. This situation produces two main types of problem, one involving the relationships between tasks and competence or, more generally, the subjects' characteristics, and the other those between group structure and task structure.

Competence of the group members and task demands

Each individual can be characterized by his or her competence in performing the allocated tasks in the group. For this we can use a matrix similar to that in Figure 1. If we limit ourselves to an all-or-nothing evaluation of subject's competence, we obtain a matrix of the type shown in Figure 2 (b). Comparing this matrix with the allocated matrix in Figure 2(a) can help to evaluate the 'group potential flexibility' (Herbst, 1974, p. 154). This indicates the different possible allocations of each individual to the different tasks. It also reflects the possible underuse of the individual's competence in the work of the group. For example, in Figure 2 the operator 03 could perform all the tasks but is only allocated one. The divergence between the group's competence for the tasks and the possibility of using this competence is, without doubt, an important characteristic of the situation. It deserves systematic investigation, and is probably a determining factor in job satisfaction.

One could also conceive of a finer indicator of the divergences between the task demands and the competence of the operator. The greater this divergence, the more the task is no longer a matter of pure execution but one involving more problem-solving activity. With a greater divergence the tasks' perceptions will have to be more explicit or the operators given more training if one wants to reduce the elaborational effort and therefore the cognitive cost of the task.

In their studies concerning the design of self-regulating work groups Pierce and Ravlin (1987) emphasize the importance of viewing the task as a 'whole' piece of work requiring multiple skills. This completeness or 'wholeness' of the

	T1	T2	T3
01	1		
02		1	1
03	1		1

(a)

	T1	T2	T3
01	1	1	
02		1	1
03	1	1	1

(b)

Figure 2. Matrices of allocations and competences. (a) Tasks (T*i*) to be carried out by the operators (O*j*); (b) tasks the operators are able to carry out

task can be defined not only at the individual level but also at the group level. This characteristic is not easy to describe, and is necessarily dependent on the level of competence of the group members, which varies with work experience.

Within an organization, goals can be defined at different levels corresponding to situations of varying dimensions. The goals of collective tasks can be characterized not only by a dimensional hierarchy but also by their nature.

Stoelwinder and Charns (1981 p. 748) note that 'as there are multiple goals, so are there multiple task systems'. They distinguish three main categories of goals or components of the task field, defined by the relationship of the tasks in the category with production processes: production tasks, production assistance, and management. An operator can take part in different collective tasks according to the phases of his or her work (e.g. performing production and maintenance tasks with different people). Being administratively attached to a group does not always mean that one's collective activities take place only within this group.

Relationship between task structure and group structure

The group is not a simple agglomeration of individuals, as the previous descriptions might have suggested. Group members are related in a way that is determined, for a large part, by the organization. These relations can be generally defined by professional status, but they can also be described relative to the execution of a given task—by appointing different people in charge, for example.

The same is true for the tasks which can also be related in different ways, as has been shown above. The task structure is determined by technical and organizational demands (a given subtask must be executed after or at the same time as another because this is technically necessary or because the organizational has decided so, taking other task fields into consideration).

The relationships between group structure and task structure are an essential aspect of the collective situation. The importance of this situation has been underlined by several studies in experimental social psychology. Von Cranach *et al.* (1986), following Faucheux and Moscovici (1960), stressed the hypothesis that 'it is only matching of task and group structure which enables a group to resolve a given task. If either structure is missing or minimal, it must be elaborated during task resolution...' (p. 211). According to these authors, there is a group action structure which directly interacts with group and task structure. In complex tasks, a difficult problem is to define and operationalize these structures.

COLLECTIVE ACTIVITY

We shall now examine how subjects respond to the collective tasks they have to perform and how they deal with the tasks' demands. What will be the real task that corresponds to the prescribed collective task? There are no simple answers to this question, and this section will be devoted to examining some approaches to research in this area.

General features of collective activities

Savoyant (1984) used two conditions to define collective activity: 'The subjects must have *the same goal* ... and each subject must see the final product as the sum, composition or combination of the partial products of his or her own action and those of the other subjects (p. 277). We shall therefore define the group or the team by the subjects which are associated with this collective activity. This definition of the group is justified, according to Savoyant, when one is more interested in the group's activity than in the group itself. From this psychological point of view it can be seen that the activities of formal groups are not always collective activities, but also that, according to the definition of the goal, the group's contour can be different.

Collective activity can be approached in two different ways. First, one can examine how the collective dimension is integrated into individual activity. One can then try to discover how the subject takes this particular demand of the activity into account, that is, how it manifests itself in the activity. Second, one can consider collective activity as the group's activity, the group being conceived as a unit with its own laws of functioning.

This last point was developed by Von Cranach *et al.* (1986), according to whom the 'groups are self-active systems. They rely on a directive behaviour as an indispensable means of adaptation. We name their directed behaviour "action" because it possesses the characteristics of human individual goal-directed action on which it is based, but in addition, it shows features which stem from its group nature, such as communication or cooperation and conflict' (p. 206).

Whatever our conception of collective activity, this activity implies that each individual's actions cannot be performed independently and must be coordinated. The conditions and means of this coordination represent, therefore, a central problem in the study of collective activity.

Collective activity and models of activity

An initial approach to the study of collective activity will be to characterize it relative to models proposed for activity analysis. Two types of model will be discussed here: one developed on the basis of Leontiev's work, the other describing stages of information processing.

Leontiev's model

Savoyant (1979, 1981) has used Leontiev's model in the study of collective activities, and we shall lean heavily here on this work. The model itself is described in the work of Leontiev (1972, 1975) and has been recently refined by Brushlinskii (1987) and Radzikhovskii (1987). Only the main points will be mentioned here. Three notions are distinguished in the model: activity, action, and operation. *Activity* is defining its motive, 'object (material) or idea that arouses and orientates the activity towards it' (Leontiev 1975, p. 113). 'The essential components of human activities are the actions that actualize them. *An action* is a process submitted to a conscious goal'. This action is performed by operations. *An operation* is defined as a means of performing the action. Actions are related to the goal. Operations are related to the conditions. The same action can be performed under different conditions. During learning, action is transformed into operation, integrating itself into a wider action of which it becomes a means of execution. This process could be compared to analyses of skill acquisition which have stressed the hierarchical nature of this acquisition (Leplat, 1988a, b).

In the analysis of collective activities these notions provoke the distinction between true *collective activities*, where the individuals share the same motive, and *co-activity*, where the individuals work together (in the same place, for example) but have different motives (e.g. production management and security guard). One could also dinstinguish situations of *collective action* where the individuals have the same general goal (e.g. pilot and co-pilot) from situations of *co-action* where the individuals have different goals (pilot and ground controller) subordinate to the same general goal. Vandevyver (1986), following Cuny (Leplat and Cuny, 1979), has used these distinctions in the analysis of accidents at work and identified several classes of accident due to coactivity in the case of 'interaction between teams of the intervening and utilizing companies'.

In collective action, coordination concerns the operations, and since the goal is the same, it is the means of execution that must be coordinated. In co-action, coordination concerns the subgoals and therefore the elementary actions. With practice, and inasmuch as the tasks are stable, the coordination of subgoals becomes automatic, is transformed and is increasingly concerned with operations. In this way, the part of collective action in the global activity will grow at the expense of co-action. In other words, the units of collective action increase in dimension and those of co-action decrease in number. One problem here concerns the possibilities of hierarchically organizing goals. Savoyant (1979) correctly distinguishes situations of stabilized co-action where actions are not transformed into operations from situations of co-action which are only steps in the formation of collective actions. Defining the categories of actions involved in a collective action requires detailed analyses in the field and cannot generally be given immediately (Savoyant, 1985). Besides, these different categories could coexist in the execution and the subjects could, as in individual activity, change their means of regulation as a function of the situations and move from one category of action to another.

Within this same theoretical perspective one can distinguish three parts of action (Galperine, 1966; Savoyant, 1984). The *orientation* or planification part concerns the analysis of the conditions of action, determining a system of reference points and a model of execution or a procedure. The representation of the task that the subject elaborates in order to guide his or her performance is referred to as the 'orientation base'. This orientation base can be more or less complete and systematic, and one can improve its development by providing the subject with the necessary elements. The second part of action is the *execution* part, which involves the transformation of the material or symbolic objects that the action is aimed at. Finally, the *control* part of action checks that the goal is in fact reached and the execution conditions respected. These distinctions will be used to analyse the process of action coordination (see below). One could examine, for example, the way in which these different parts are distributed and coordinated within the collective activity at the moment of action.

Stage models

These models have in common the definition of a certain number of stages in the operator's information process. The most well-known models of this type are those of Rasmussen (1986) and Norman (1986). The stages in these two models are fairly similar, although Rasmussen's model is described in more detail. However, as Norman (1986) has noted, 'I do not believe that there really are clean separable stages. However, for practical application, approximating activity into stages should be made, however it seems reasonable and useful. Just what division of stages should be made, however, seems less clear' (p. 41).

Each stage of the model is not involved in every activity and the short-cuts that are used allow us to distinguish between three major types of activity: knowledge, rule- and skill-based activities.

The type of collective activity analysis suggested by such a model consists of determining who associates the different stages of processing in collective activity and how they are associated. Some examples of the use of schemas proposed for this have been provided by Rasmussen (1986), when he defines, on the basis of these schemas, the specific roles of the designer, the operator, and the process computer in a 'control decision' (p. 464) (Figure 3). When analysing the development of activity, the categories of processing represented in such schemas could be specified.

The analytical methodology proposed by Herbst (1974) could serve as inspiration here. This author distinguished six phases in the sequence of the control process: detection, diagnosis, planning, decision, performance, inspection. The flow of these control operations was analysed using a diagram and an example is given in Figure 4. The persons executing the different control phases are given in this figure: the individual, the team, the person in charge, people

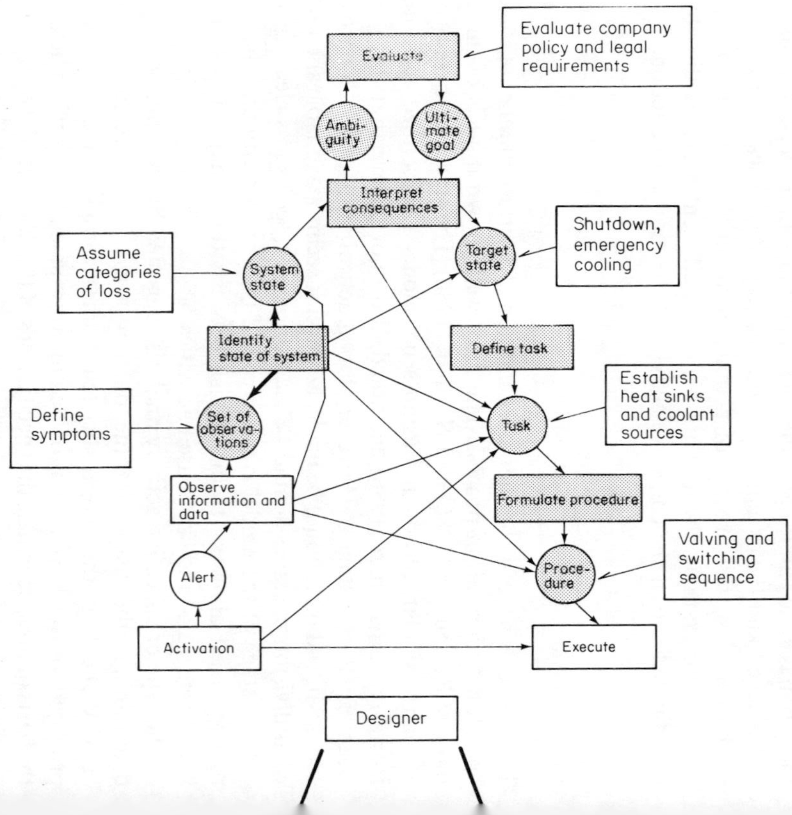
Evaluate
Evaluate company policy and legal requirements
Ambi-guity
Ulti-mate goal
Interpret consequences
Shutdown, emergency cooling
Target state
Assume categories of loss
System state
Identify state of system
Define task
Establish heat sinks and coolant sources
Task
Define symptoms
Set of observa-tions
Observe information and data
Formulate procedure
Valving and switching sequence
Proce-dure
Alert
Activation
Execute
Designer

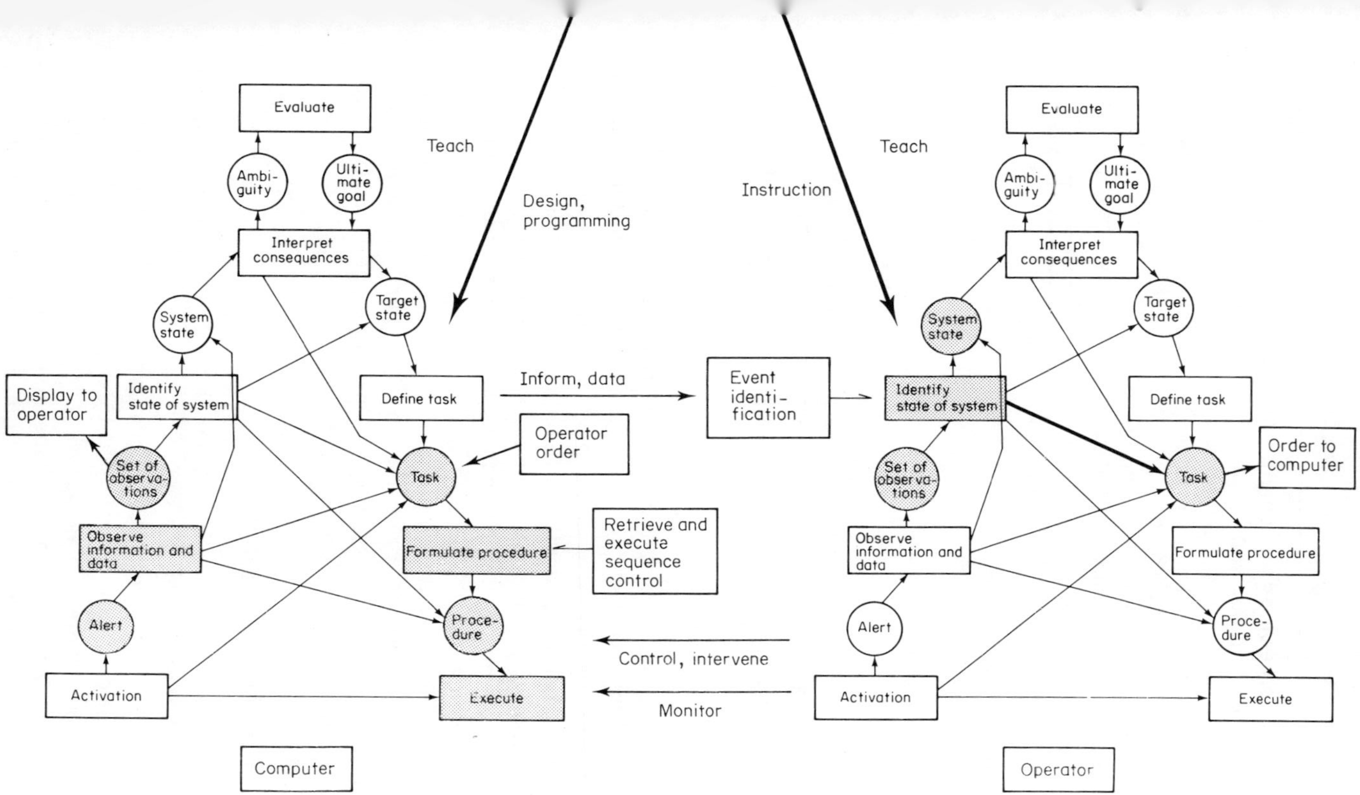

Figure 3. An example of the ladder model used to define the roles of different participants. A similar use can be made with collective work. This figure illustrates the role of the designer, the operator and a computer in a control decision related to protection of a nuclear reactor during a loss-of-coolant accident that has not been fully automated; i.e the operator and computer act in series. The designer has automated a repertoire of protective sequences, but left the diagnosis to an operator. In addition to the decision function, the designer, operator and computer support each other in different inform–teach–learn functions, as discussed by Sheridan (1982). Reprinted from Rasmussen (1986) by permission of Elsevier Science Publishers.

Phase	Description
1. Detection	Perceiving that something is wrong
2. Diagnosis	Finding out what is wrong
3. Planning	Evolving possible methods for getting rid of the trouble
4. Decision	Deciding on method to be used and the allocation of staff and resources
5. Performance	Implementing the decision
6. Inspection	Checking whether the variance has been removed

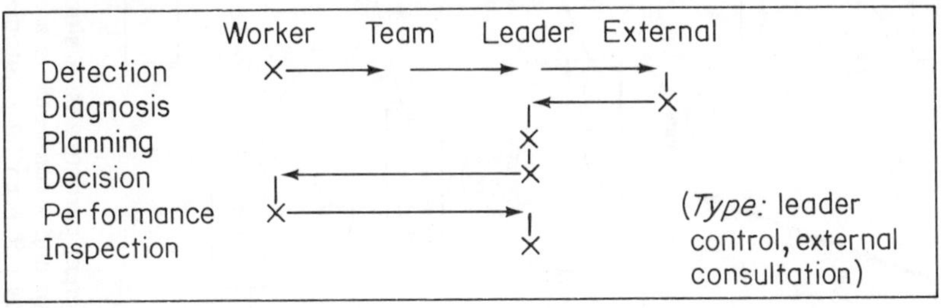

Figure 4. Phase sequence of the control process and diagram (after Herbst, 1974, pp. 140–41).

from outside the team. As emphasized by Herbst, this method 'enables the theoretically possible types of process to be determined and may suggest in specific cases better methods of control' (p. 141). Herbst gives some examples of the type 'variance-control patterns' (p. 142). Such a figure could be completed with an indication of the times corresponding to each phase.

The models of Rasmussen and Norman could be used in analyses of this type where the individuals and groups responsible for the different phases of the action would be determined during this action. The types of action control and distribution of the decisions would then be identifiable using the obtained schemas which could be deployed in time. One important difficulty remaining here concerns the definition of the unit of action.

Coordination: mechanisms and means

All collective activity requires a coordination of individual activities. As previously noted, this coordination can adopt various modalities according to the characteristics of the tasks and the groups in which it occurs. When analyzing the collective task we were led to examine how coordination was arranged by the person prescribing the task. The point of view adopted now is a psychological one: it involves determining how subjects actually coordinate their actions, the mechanisms of this coordination and the means it requires.

Only those aspects of the coordination that appear to be of particular importance for an analysis of collective activity will be discussed here.

Coordination of goals

One of the first questions to be asked in the analysis concerns each subject's representation of the goal and subgoals of his or her activity. In individual activity, a poor representation of the goal can lead to 'mistake' types of errors. In collective activity another source of error lies in the possible divergences in the representations that the different individuals have of their goals and subgoals. These divergences can be the result of a lack of precision in the definition of the prescribed goal. They can also be due to a lack of knowledge of goal-evaluation criteria or poorly interpreted information concerning this goal. A *coherence* in the representations of the goals is one of the essential conditions for effective collective action.

Difficult problems sometimes arise when the actions are multifinalized and when several evaluation criteria must be taken into consideration (e.g. speed–accuracy, production, security, comfort). In this case, the divergences in representations between individuals can arise from the different weights allocated to these criteria. One can also encounter different evaluations of the importance of subgoals leading to conflicts in the organization of collective action.

The choice of a common system of weighting for the different goals (quality of production, load, safety, comfort, etc) can have different consequences for individual activities and an acceptable compromise can be difficult to find.

The coordination of individual representation

The planning and orientation of collective action, like individual activity, is guided by a representation of the conditions of execution of this action. In the case of individual activity, this representation orientated towards achieving the goal of the action is referred to as a functional representation (Leplat, 1985) or mental model (Norman, 1983), and its properties have been described (finality, selectivity, deformation, etc.). In collective activity, the functional representation shared by the individuals who perform the same collective activity constitutes the common referential. This common referential defines the task conditions: the properties of objects, allowable operations actually taken into consideration by the individuals in the collective activity. This common referential is a representation elaborated during the action from the prescriptions given to the operators and from their own competence and practice (learning by action). The referential can vary in terms of how complete it is. At the beginning of training it will be very incomplete, thus obliging individuals to communicate in order to determine the useful conditions. With experience, the common referential becomes more complete in that the functional representations of the individuals in the group become increasingly homogeneous relative to a given task.

This description of the common referential is often linked to the acquisition of a common competence. Navarro (1984) rightly noted that it is 'the widening of the subject's cognitive field, the enriching of his or her operational modalities that make it possible for cooperative behaviour to emerge' (p. 109). The same author has given examples of this phenomenon, noting that the tasks performed by an operator in a group become more diversified with experience as this operator shifts from dependence to a more egalitarian status in the group. The enriching of the common referential can also be marked by the acquisition of a common language particularly adapted to the collective action, and Falzon (1987) showed the characteristics and efficacy of this 'operative language'.

Insufficiencies in the referential are a source of error and, conversely, errors are a means of identifying the characteristics of the referential. The common referential only includes a part of the individual functional representations. Indeed, particularly in co-action, some parts of task execution remain strictly individual. Moreover, individuals can integrate into the common referential the representations they have elaborated of their co-worker and of their methods.

The development of a common referential is of prime importance when the group members must organize the task themselves without any one person taking on a particular role in the coordination. The situation will be different in the following case.

Situations of guidance

This is how Savoyant (1981) termed situations where there is a division of labour and where important decisions are undertaken by a given individual. These situations are encountered in two cases: (1) when the task executer cannot objectively 'identify the relevant properties of the object' (situations where information is centralized) and (2) when the hierarchical division of labour imposes an individual to guide the others (Savoyant, 1981, p. 52). 'In these guidance situations, the essential problem with respect to interindividual coordination concerns the 'orientation–execution' relation' (p. 52). The common referential of the individuals performing the task will, at least partly, be provided by the managing subject. 'The coordination will be effective when the subjects performing the task correctly execute the operations of the task' on the basis of the managing subject's guidance.

This guidance can be given in various forms in the same way as a prescribed task can be described more or less precisely. Guidance can be given concerning the goals, subgoals or, more strictly, a particular procedure. As a starting point of analysis, one can use here what has already been said above concerning autonomy. One should note Savoyant's (1981) comment that 'a strict orientation–execution distribution based on a hierarchical division would lead rather to a definition of individual actions and not the coordination relationships between these actions, but subordination relationships' (p. 55). A study of the true nature of guidance, however, can only be carried out in the field. One must determine the influence of guidance on the development of the common referential. This referential often contains what is implicitly assumed by the instructions and organization of the managing individual. Thus annex activities are often collective ones, where one operator helps another to solve an incident, this help not having been foreseen in the prescribed task.

Lacoste (1983) has described several situations where task-sharing instructions are not respected. For example, in a workshop for automatic conditioning she noted that this could sometimes occur between the functions of the regulator and the operators. It is likely that this phenomenon is due to the development of a referential that goes beyond the strictly official function of these workers, and new solutions are negotiated among themselves. What holds for task distribution can also apply to task execution, and it is possible to observe unforeseen modalities of collective action appearing in execution.

The role of workload in coordination

The individual regulates his or her work, taking into account not only effectiveness but also efficiency. He or she tries not simply to achieve the goal of the action but also to do so with the least possible cost. Several authors have described this regulatory loop in terms of load (Leplat, 1975; Welford, 1977; Bainbridge 1977; Sperandio, 1977). Experimental research has investigated the nature of such a load under various terminologies: effort, cognitive cost, human resources etc. (Navon and Gopher, 1979; Wickens, 1984; among many others). However, very little work has been explicitly directed to the study of workload as an element of the regulation of collective activity. As stressed by Navarro (1980), this is nevertheless an interesting line of research. Marine and Navarro (1980) have shown, on the basis of a study carried out in a pulp-rolling workshop, that operators' activities were aimed at stopping not only their own workload from increasing but also not to increase the workload of following operators too much. Dorel and Queinnec (1980) have also shown that in a shiftwork situation with a process control task, jobs were distributed between operators in a team such that the highest workload was given to the operator due for a three-day rest after the night shift.

The notion of workload is related to that of competence, since the load will always be smaller for an experienced operator compared to a beginner in a given task. This relationship reinforces the role of inexperience and demonstrates the difficulty involved in managing the work of beginners in a group.

The role of workload in the regulation of collective activities has only been touched upon here, and it deserves to be the subject of further study. It will be especially important to be able to answer the following questions. How is the load perceived? On the basis of what principles is it distributed? How is the cost of various possible modes of coordination evaluated? Do phenomena of regulation by workload exist between teams? What is the timescale of this regulation?

The function of communication in coordination.

Coordination requires the exchange of information between group members which occurs via communication. In their conception of the group as a 'self-active system', Von Cranach *et al.* (1986) thus distinguish two modes for information processing: the primary processing mode, corresponding to 'individual cognition', and the secondary processing mode, corresponding to 'intragroup communication'. 'In group communications, individual ideas are discussed, elaborated, changed and enhanced, and through group communications they are finally fed back into individual cognitions' (p. 211). For these authors there is 'a veritable nested order of acts, namely: individual cognitive acts → communicative acts → individual concrete acts → group acts' (p. 216). Therefore they consider 'conscious cognition as an analogue of intragroup communication' (p. 217).

From this particular model will be remembered here that communication plays a capital role in coordination, and its analysis constitutes an important means of approach for the study of collective activity. We will now indicate ways that this analysis will reveal the different dimensions of this activity.

The quantitative analysis of communication. One way of analysing communication consists of noting its volume and duration in different conditions. Conrad (1960), Leplat and Browaeys (1965) and Sperandio (1969) have studied the effects of increasing task demands on communication. One can also study in the same way the effects of variations in the conditions of team work. Thus Siegel *et al.* (1986) examined whether computer-mediated communications can change group decision making (p. 158). To do this, they recorded 'the number of remarks exchanged by group members', 'the number of task-oriented remarks as a fraction of total remarks' and the time of decision as characterizing 'communication efficiency' in a problem to be solved in different settings.

Functional and social communication. One can distinguish communication that is directly linked to execution of the collective task from communication that is not directly related to this but which concerns social exchanges between operators (e.g. exchange of personal information or information concerning the company that is not related to the current activity). This distinction can be found in several studies. De Keyser (1983) and Cellier and Marine (1984) consider that the second type of communication plays the role of social regulation. Cellier and Marine note that this type of communication increases with experience.

Classifying functional communication. This classification can be carried out on the basis of various principles related to theories of collective action described above or to the concrete content of the actions being studied. Using the distinction between planification, execution and control, Savoyant (Savoyant and Leplat, 1983; Savoyant, 1985) analysed the communicational exchanges in a team of electrician fitters in distinguishing:

(1) General orientation communication prior to the actual performance of the action (defining operations, execution conditions and necessary coordination relations);
(2) Limited orientation communication occurring during the action to trigger and guide operations before their execution;
(3) Execution communication which guides or interrupts the execution of action;
(4) Control communication ensuring that certain conditions are or are not achieved.

Within the framework of stage models, categorization could be carried out on the phase processing involved in communication: communication for arousal, observation, identification or interpretation, etc.

Von Cranach *et al.* (1986) have proposed three main categories of communication according to whether it aims at '1. Organization and improvement of difficult acts. 2. Improvement of complex acts. 3. Construction of act-systems' (pp. 218–19). Each of these categories is described by Von Cranach in more detail.

The automatization of coordination

It has been shown that, with practice, individual actions become automatized and adopt a certain number of properties (Shiffrin and Schneider, 1977) and no longer require capacity in working memory. The automatization of collective actions could be conceived, by analogy, as disposing of certain properties, the most characteristic being the absence of communication. Von Cranach tackles the same problem in a similar form: 'what remains open is the question whether we can conceive of on-going information-processing without communication as a strict analogy to non-conscious cognition' (p. 217).

It seems likely that functional communication is reduced with practice (see, for example, Cellier and Marine, 1984). It would be useful to have a better understanding of the mechanisms governing this reduction. They are probably linked to a stability in the conditions of action and also to an improvement in the common referential. Among such mechanisms one could therefore mention:

(1) The use of *temporal references* based on regularities in the course of action. If operator X performed operation 0 at time t, then we expect operation $0'$ at time $t + 1$ without any need for operator X to inform us of this.
(2) Resorting to *external references*, especially environmental signals used by a co-worker and interpreted on the basis of a more developed common referential. This would especially be the case with an extension of the control field—an extension of the temporal field. As the events could be better anticipated, the coordination demands are sometimes less strict (Cellier and Marine, 1984).
(3) *Categorization of the situations*: the operators form the same code of situations or elements of situations, allowing them to simplify their messages and send large quantities of information in a very brief form (Cuny, 1971).

As with individual activity, the incidents that invalidate automatization are sometimes never perceived or are perceived only after a delay. Their processing causes a return to controlled activity, where coordination is once again important for elaborating the solution and executing the task. Here is one source of error in collective activity: incident not perceived, triggering of an automatized procedure inappropriate to the incident, controlled solution not relevant or put into operation too late. Once again, the use of analogies with error analysis of individual activity can suggest possible mechanisms underlying these errors.

CONCLUSION

This chapter is aimed at outlining concepts and indicating some areas for future research. The task-activity distinction on which it is based should help to define coherent perspectives of analysis and to ask the appropriate questions.

For analysis of existing collective work it is necessary to examine, together with the collective task, demands reflecting the organization's representation of the task, and the activities responding to these demands and eventually modifying them. These two types of analysis shed light on each other, and it would be useful to have joint taxonomies associating the characteristics of collective activities to the types of task (and vice versa). This ambitious goal has been only mentioned here, but the proposed framework of studies should prepare the way. The divergences between the prescribed collective task and the effective task that applies to this prescription are an index of the lack of adaptation of the organization's model and provide particularly useful elements for guiding more detailed analyses of activity and sources of dysfunctioning.

For the conception of future collective work it is essential to plan conjointly the characteristics of the collective activity and the structures and modes of functioning concerning the task to be designed. The modalities of coordination and communication that allows them to be achieved are determining factors in the design of systems and system aids.

The study of collective tasks and activities shows that the problem of decision is found at several levels. It is situated at the organizational level where task distribution is prescribed to varying degrees of precision. These first decisions are of capital importance, but this chapter has concentrated on situations in which the group organizes its activity to respond to the tasks fixed by the organization. In the study of collective work it will always be important to carry out an analysis at several levels. Indeed, the distribution and execution of collective tasks are often determined by individual, technical, organizational and even social factors that must be coordinated in order to understand the mechanisms of individual and collective activity.

Decisions are intertwined in the course of collective action. By indicating their place during this collective action one becomes aware of their totally dynamic nature in that they cannot be separated from other moments of the action and from other actions of the individual and the group.

If 'decision' can be characterized as the conscious choice between various alternatives, it is perhaps preferable to maintain the use of the term 'activity' to cover a large field, including actions organized in an automatized way. If one uses the term 'decision' in one of its widest meanings, defined as every process leading to execution (as Rasmussen, 1986, seems to have done) then the concept of decision almost covers that of activity. This therefore justifies having devoted the concept of activity in work written for a workshop on distributed decision making!

Address for Correspondence:

Professor Jacques Leplat, Ecole Pratique des Hautes Etudes, Laboratoire de Psychologie du Travail, 41 rue Gay-Lussac, F-75005 Paris, France.

REFERENCES

Bainbridge, L. (1977) Possibilités oubliées en matière d'habileté et de charge de travail. *Le Travail Humain*, **40**, 203–24.

Breaugh, J. A., and Becker, A. S. (1987) Further examination of the work autonomy scales: three studies. *Human Relations*, **40**, 6, 381–400.

Brushlinskii, A. V. (1987) Activity, action and mind as process. *Soviet Psych.*, **25**, 4, 59–81.

Cellier, J. M., and Marine, C. (1984) Expérience professionnelle et gestion des communications dans une tâche de régulation de trafic. *Psychologie et Education*, 21–40.

Conrad, R. (1960) Letter sorting machines—Paced, 'lagged' or unspaced? *Ergonomics*, **3**, 2, 149–58.

Cordery, J. L., and Wall, T. D. (1985) Work design and supervisory practice: a model. *Human Relations*, **38**, 5, 425–41.

Cuny, X. (1971) Perspectives sémiologiques en psychologie du travail. *Cahiers de Linguistique théorique et appliquée*, **8**, 53–72.

De Keyser, V. (1983) Communications sociales et charge mentale dans les postes automatisés. *Psychologie Française*, **28**, 239–53.

Dorel, M., and Queinnec, Y. (1980) Régulation individuelle en situations d'horaires alternants. *Bull. de. Psychol.*, **33**, 465–72.

Falzon, P. (1987) Langages opératifs et compréhension opérative. *Le Travail Humain*, **50**, 3, 281–6.

Faucheux, C., and Moscovici, S. (1960) Etude sur la créativite des groupes; II—Tâches structure des communications et réussite. *Bulletin du CERP*, **9**, 11–22.

Galperine, P. (1966) Essai sur la formation par étapes des actions et des concepts. In *Recherches psychologiques en U.R.S.S.*, Moscow: Editions du Progrès.

Hackman, J. R. (1969) Toward understanding the role of tasks in behavioral research. *Acta Psychologica*, **31**, 97–128.

Herbst, P. G. (1974) *Socio-technical Design: strategies in multi-disciplinary research.* London: Tavistock Publications.

Hoc, J. M. (1987) *Psychologie cognitive de la planification.* Presses Universitaires de Grenoble.

Lacoste, M. (1983) Des situations de parole aux activités interprétatives. *Psychologie Française*, **28**, 3–4, 231–8.

Leontiev, A. (1972) *Le développement du psychisme*, Paris: Editions Sociales.

Leontiev, A. (1975) *Activité, conscience, personnalité.* Moscow: Editions du Progrès.

Leplat, J. (1975) La charge de travail dans la régulation de l'activité: quelques applications pour les opérateurs vieillissants. In A. Laville., C. Teiger., and A. Wisner (eds), *Age et contraintes de travail.* Paris: NEB, pp. 209–23.

Leplat, J. (1985) Les représentations fonctionnèlles dans le travail. *Psychologie Française*, **30**, 3–4, 269–72.

Leplat, J. (1988a) Les habiletés cognitives dans le travail. In Perruchet (ed.), *Les automatismes cognitifs.* Bruxelles: Mardaga, pp.139–72.

Leplat, J. (1988b) Relations between task and activity in training. Internal report. To be published.

Leplat, J., and Browaeys, R. (1965) Analyse et mesure de la charge de travail du contrôleur du trafic aérien. *Bull. du CERP*, XIV, 1.2, 69–80.

Leplat, J., and Cuny, X. (1979) *Les Accidents du Travail.* 2nd ed. Paris: Presses Universitaires de France.

Leplat, J., and Hoc, J. M. (1983) Tâche et activité dans l'analyse psychologique des situations. *Cahiers de Psychologie cognitive*, **3**, 1, 49–64.

Leplat, J., and Savoyant, A. (1984) Ordonnancement et coordination des activités dans les travaux individuels et collectifs. *Bull. de Psychol.*, **364**, 271–8.

Marine, C., and Navarro, C. (1980) Rôle de l'organisation informelle du travail en équipe lors d'un dysfonctionnement technique. *Bull. de Psychol.*, **344**, 311–16.

Navarro, C. (1980) Quelques reflexions sur la régulation de la charge de travail. *Psychologie et Education*, **4**, 3, 31–42.

Navarro, C. (1984) L'acquisition des modes opératoires en situation de coactivité: étude de cas. *Psychologie et Education*, **8**, 99–113.

Navon, D., and Gopher, D. (1979) On the economy of the human-processing system. *Psychol. Rev.*, **86**, 3, 214–55.

Norman, D. A. (1983) Some observations on mental models. In J. Gentner and A. L. Stevens (eds), *Mental Models.* London: Lawrence Erlbaum, pp. 7–14.

Norman, D. A. (1986) Cognitive engineering in D. A. Norman and S. W. Drapers, *User Centered System Design.* Hillsdale, NJ: Lawrence Erlbaum, pp. 31–62.

Pierce, J. A., and Ravlin, E. C. (1987) The design and activation of self-regulating work groups. *Human Relations*, **40**, 11, 751–82.

Radzikhovskii, L. A. (1987) Activity: structure, genesis and unit of analysis. *Soviet Psychol.*, **25**, 4, 82–98.

Rasmussen, J. (1986) *Information Processing and Human-Machine Interaction.* Amsterdam: North Holland.

Rubin, J. Z. (1984) Introduction, In W. C. Swap and associate, *Group Decision Making.* London: Sage Publications, pp. 15–44.

Savoyant, A. (1979) Elément d'un cadre d'analyse de l'activité. *Cahiers de Psychologie,* **22**, 1-2, 17–28.

Savoyant, A. (1981) *La coordination inter-individuelle dans l'activité des équipes de travail.* Thése de 3éme cycle, Paris V, EPHE.

Savoyant, A. (1984) Définition et voies d'analyse de l'activité collective des équipes de travail. *Cahiers de Psychologie cognitive,* **4**, 3, 273–84.

Savoyant, A. (1985) Conditions et moyens de la coordination inter-individuelle d'opérations d'exécution sensori-motrices. *Le Travail Humain,* **48**, 1, 59–80.

Savoyant, A. and Leplat, J. (1983) Statut et fonction des communications dans l'activité des équipes de travail. *Psychologie Française,* **28**, 3, 247–53.

Sheridan, T. B. (1982) Supervisory Control: Theory and Experiment for Application to Human-Computer Interaction in Undersea Remote Systems. MIT Technical Report, March 1982. Cambridge, Mass.: MIT Press.

Shiffrin, R. M., and Schneider, W. (1977) Controlled and automatic human information processing: II Perceptual learning, automatic attending, and a general theory. *Psychol. Rev.,* **84**, 2, 127–90.

Siegel, J., Dubrovsky, V., Kiesler, S., and McGuire, T. W. (1986) Group processes in computer mediated communication. *Org. Beh. and Human Decision Processes,* **37**, 156–87.

Sperandio, J. C. (1969) Les variations du partage des tâches entre un opérateur et son assistant, en fonction de la charge de travail du système. *Bull. du CERP,* **18**, 2, 81–98.

Sperandio, J. C. (1977) La régulation des modes opératoires en fonction de la charge de travail chez les contrôleurs de trafic aérien. *Le Travail Humain,* **40**, 2, 249–56.

Stoelwinder, J. V., and Charns, M. P. (1981) The task field model of organisation analysis and design. *Human Relations,* **34**, 9, 743–62.

Swap, W. C. (1984) How groups make decisions: a social psychological perspective. In W. C. Swap and associate, *Group Decision Making.* London: Sage Publications, pp. 45–68.

Vandevyver, B. (1986) Intervention d'entreprises extérieures: la co-activité: est-elle un facteur de risque dominant? *Le Travail Humain,* **49**, 3, 195–208.

Von Cranach, M., Ochsenbein, G., and Valach, L. (1986) The group as a self-active system: outline of a theory of group action. *European Journal of Social Psychology,* **16**, 193–229.

Welford, A. T. (1977) La charge mentale de travail comme fonction des exigences, de la capacité, de la stratégie et de l'habileté. *Le Travail Humain,* **40**, 2, 283–304.

Wickens, C. D. (1984) *Engineering Psychology and Human Performance.* Columbus, Ohio: Merril Publishing Co.

4. Cooperative Work: A Conceptual Framework

Kjeld Schmidt
Risø National Laboratory, Denmark

INTRODUCTION

For years, human factors research has been focusing on the interaction between the individual user and a computer-based system. On the basis of this paradigm, considerable progress has been made in the design of man machine interfaces. However, the individualistic presupposition of this paradigm is obviously invalid (Bannon *et al.*, 1988).

Work is a highly social phenomenon. The subject of the production process, human kind, is a *zóon politikón.* Human adults entering the workforce of society arrive fully equipped with language; logical categories and inference rules; concepts and other developed cognitive structures; general and domain-specific knowledge acquired in the process of socialization; ideological notions such as moral and esthetic norms, beliefs, prejudices, etc. These abilities (and, in some cases, liabilities) are of a profoundly social nature.

Not only that, production processes belong to the system of social division of labor. As vividly described by Mandeville (1724), myriads of relations connect each and every production process in the universal commonwealth of production:

> What a Bustle there is to be made in several Parts of the World, before a Fine Scarlet or Crimson Cloth can be produced, what a multiplicity of Trades and Artificers must be employ'd! Not only such as are obvious, as Woolcombers, Spinners, the Weaver, the Clothworker, the Scowrer, the Dier, the Setter, the Drawer and the Packer; but others that are more remote and might seem Foreign to it; as the Millwright, the Pewterer and the Chymist, which yet are all necessary as well as a great Number of other Handicrafts to have the Tools, Utensils and other Implements belonging to the Trades already named.

Distributed Decision Making: Cognitive Models for Cooperative Work
Edited by J. Rasmussen, B. Brehmer and J. Leplat

More than that, each node in this universal network of interdependent production processes constitutes a small social world of its own, that is, each of these production processes normally involve the concerted effort of many people.

Considering the profound social nature of work, the attention attracted in recent years to the prospect of designing computer systems enhancing the ability of people to cooperate is fully justified. Designing systems supporting work in cooperative environments is not a new issue however. While human factors research have been ignoring the collaborative aspects of work, computer-based systems have long been designed and implemented in cooperative work settings such as power stations, factories, offices, and stores. However, to the surprise of designers and the dismay of users, these systems, more often than not, have proved themselves inadequate with respect to matching the cooperative and organizational aspects of work. These experiences should be studied carefully.

As a scientific field, computer-supported cooperative work is still immature, and theoretical problems abound. The following are but a few of the pressing problems:

(1) In a way, designing computer-based systems for cooperative work environments such as organizational decision making is like writing on water. While the information system may be designed to match the current social structure of the labor processes, this change of technology, conversely, induces a change in the social structure of the labor processes. This has been the bitter experience of a plethora of office-automation projects and installations, designed to match the traditional allocation of tasks in the office. The office-automation experience has unequivocally demonstrated that the potentials in terms of productivity, flexibility, product quality, etc. of information technology in the office cannot be realized without a corresponding change in the allocation of tasks among staff (Hammer, 1984; Skousen, 1986; Hedberg *et al.*, 1987; Schmidt, 1987). The lesson has general validity, and calls for a theoretical framework for predicting the development of the forms of cooperation and organization in the course of technological development.

(2) In current research on computer-supported cooperative work it is generally assumed that the cooperating ensemble of people is a 'group' or a 'team,' that is, a relatively closed and fixed collective, sharing the same goal and engaged in incessant and direct communication. Hence the focus on electronic blackboards and electronic mail systems. But the concept of 'the group' is far too blurred to be of scientific utility. The notion of a shared goal, in particular, is murky and dubious. The cooperative process of decision making in a group is a very differentiated process, involving the interaction of multiple goals of different scope and nature as well as different heuristics, conceptual frameworks, etc. Furthermore, the notion of group work does not encompass the rich and complex reality of cooperative work.

As pointed out by Popitz and associates in their classic study (1957), the group is not the specific unit of cooperation in modern industrial plants. Here, cooperation is typically mediated by complex machine systems and often does not involve direct communication between agents. Likewise, in various domains (for instance, administrative work, engineering design, and scientific research), agents often cooperate via a more or less common information space (data, beliefs, concepts, heuristics, etc.), that is, without direct communication and not necessarily knowing each other or knowing of each other. Computer systems meant to support cooperative work must therefore support retrieval of information filed by other workers, perhaps unknown, in another work context, perhaps also unknown. The prevailing group work-oriented paradigm evades this problem. Cooperative work embodies *indirect* as well as *direct* and *distributed* as well as *collective* modes of interaction. Accordingly, the present focus on group work as prototypical cooperative work is misdirected as a general approach to computer-supported cooperative work. A far more rich and subtle conceptual framework is needed to apprehend the complex reality of cooperative work.

(3) In the design of information systems for cooperative decision making the prevalent approach is data-oriented. It is the presupposition of this approach that information is something innocent and neutral. Consequently, it is the ultimate aim of the efforts following this approach to design a Grand Database containing all the relevant data from different parts of the organization so as to provide managers with a unified data model of the organization. In the words of Ciborra (1985), hard reality has condemned this idea to the reign of utopia. In fact, the underlying conventional notion of organizations as being monolithic entities is quite naive. Organizations are not perfectly collaborative systems. Rather, an organization is a mixture of collaboration and conflict. Most information generated and processed in organizations is subject to misrepresentation, because it has been generated, gathered and communicated in a context of goal incongruence and discord of interests and motives. These realities of organizational life must be investigated seriously if computer-supported cooperative work is to be turned from a fascinating research program into useful systems in the real world.

In short, problems abound. What are the real issues in cooperative decision making? Why do people engage in cooperative decision making in the first place? Which knowledge is required of individuals engaged in *cooperative* decision making as opposed to decision making performed in seclusion? What do cooperating partners need to know of each other? How do they interrelate their different strategies and frames of reference? How do they collate their partial and parochial domain knowledge? How do the specific functional requirements and constraints of a cooperative effort affect the pattern of cooperation? And so on. In other words, a theoretical framework for analyzing and modelling cooperative work and specifying requirements to computer-based systems supporting cooperative work is needed.

Fortunately, we are not starting from scratch. Though cooperative work as a distinct research area is quite new and fairly immature, research pertaining to cooperative work has been going on for years, in some areas for centuries. Various important aspects of cooperative work are objects of investigation of multiple scientific specialties and research areas, e.g. political economy, business economics, anthropology, organizational sociology, sociology of science, industrial sociology, labor process studies, management theory, decision theory, psychological theories of human information processing, psychology of learning, cognitive psychology, cognitive science, AI theories of distributed problem solving, human–computer interaction research, control engineering, and industrial engineering. By assessing and collating the different contributions of the various specialties and research areas we will probably be able to perceive the outlines of a conceptual reconstruction of the social system of work and, hence, a theory of cooperative work.

Cooperative work, as used here, is constituted by *work processes that are related as to content*, that is, processes pertaining to the production of a particular product or type of products. Cooperative work, then, is a far more specific concept than social interaction in the system of work in general. The concept pertains to the sphere of production. It does not apply to every social encounter occurring during business hours nor to every interaction pertaining to the running of, say, a company.

The concept, as defined here, does not presuppose any specific organizational setting or form. First, the concept does not imply a specific degree of regularity, nor does it imply group work, face-to-face communication, acquaintance, etc. Second, a specific corporation may have multiple cooperative work processes with no mutual interference. Third, cooperative work processes may cross corporate boundaries. For example, a cooperative work process may involve partners in different companies at different sites, each of the partners producing only one component of the finished product. But, as stated initially, production processes are universally interdependent; where, then, does cooperation stop? First, cooperation pertains to production, that is, it stops where consumption begins. Second, though cooperative work does not presuppose any specific organizational setting or form it does need an organizational form, i.e. it requires that the cooperative relations be established deliberately as opposed to accidentally. In other words, the relations between interdependent production processes that are merely connected via an anonymous market are not cooperative ones.

This conception of cooperative work corresponds to the definition suggested by Marx (1867), according to which cooperation denotes 'multiple individuals working together in a planned way in the same production process or in different but connected production processes'.

METHODOLOGICAL CONSIDERATIONS

Work is an extremely complex social phenomenon involving multitude forms of social interaction, of which some of the most obvious are:

(1) The forms of interaction in the labor process itself as determined by the natural and technical resources available;
(2) The organizational setting of the interaction. Does it take place within an organization in the juridical sense of a corporate body or across corporate boundaries?
(3) The customary privileges and prejudices of task allocation. Does the specific allocation of tasks and the concomitant pattern of interaction reflect specific professional or individual privileges? One type of task may be felt, by an elevated category of workers, to be an insult while another category may defend the same task as their prerogative (that is, their meal ticket);
(4) Institutional forms of manifestation and regulation of conflicts of interest, etc. Labor organizations such as trade unions and workplace organizations like shop steward committees may exert massive impact on the allocation of tasks to various categories of workers. A class of tasks such as CNC programming may be monopolized by the members of one labor organization, thereby generating a specific pattern of social interaction in the labor process. That is, the competitive and collaborative relations of the various labor organizations may affect the structure of social interactions;
(5) The forms of social control in the workplace. For example, to what extent is horizontal information flow among the collaborators regulated, inhibited or impeded by preordained hierarchical lines of communication, that is, to what extent is the cooperative process mediated by a superimposed structure?
(6) The forms of allocation of power and authority. For instance, is a person provided with authority by his or her peers in recognition of his or her contribution to the accomplishment of the objectives of the collective, or is authority given by investiture by some extrinsic power?

Leaving, for a moment, the confines of the system of work directly related to the labor process and addressing the socio-economic system at large, we discern a new, more distant galaxy of forms of social interaction also affecting the kinds of interaction in the social system of work in the narrow sense:

(1) The function of the enterprise in the socio-economic system. Is it a business corporation, an educational facility, or a police force? The system of social control in the workplace is, to a great extent, derived from those functions;
(2) The general structure and state of the labor market (e.g. mass unemployment, immigration, etc.) has profound impact on the actual appearance of the social system of work;
(3) By providing employers with an ample supply of qualified workers, governmental policy on the rights of access to education and vocational training,

economic support of popular education, etc. may have tangible impact on the composition of the workforce in the enterprises in terms of qualifications, and may thereby affect the forms of interaction in the workplace;

(4) The socio-economic system at large is the ultimate seat of the power structure of the enterprise. Is the enterprise owned privately, like, for instance, a corporation? Is it owned by the government, by associations of workers or by the workers of the enterprise themselves?

Certainly, the various forms of interaction in the social system of work do not exist as discrete and easily identifiable entities. On the contrary, they are highly interrelated and appear totally entwined to the empirical apprehension.

Analyzing social work is like reading a palimpsest. Thus, one may look upon these forms of social interaction in the social system of work as so many superposed layers of writing. In order to understand cooperative work one must conceptually separate these layers, and then, by identifying the specific relationships and forms of development of each of the forms of interaction to the other forms, gradually create a conceptual reconstruction of the social system of work.

The first requirement, then, is systematic analytic distinctions to overcome the confusion of the concepts of cooperative work, division of labor, organization, allocation of tasks and responsibilities, profession, management strategy, collaborative styles, labor market structures, class, ideology, etc. (Strauss, 1985).

Now, how to proceed? Since each and every form of social interaction in the system of work is related, directly or indirectly, to every other form, in our analysis we will constantly come across imprints of the other forms. To which form should this imprint be traced? How do we avoid going in circles? We may avoid this by applying a genetic approach (Iljenkow, 1960), that is, by beginning with the most simple and yet all-pervasive form, the 'elemental and general' form (for example, the hydrogen atom in chemistry, the cell in biology, etc.).

Of the web of interrelated forms of interaction, one category of forms stands out as crucial, namely, the forms of interaction determined by the production process itself, i.e. cooperation. The form of cooperation is the interface between the transformation process and the social system of work. The specific configuration of cooperative work relations directly reflects the specific configuration of natural, technical and human resources. Thus, the form of cooperation plays the mediating role of a vehicle conveying the impact of technological development on the social system of work at large. The form of cooperation (i.e. the methodological contention of this chapter) is the generative mechanism of the entire edifice of the social system of work. Therefore, the forms of cooperation may be considered the 'category of origin' (Iljenkow, 1960) of our investigation.

FORMS OF COOPERATION

Let us discuss the simple question: Why do people cooperate? Or, more succinctly: Why are production processes performed cooperatively? Humans cooperate because of the limited capabilities of human individuals. We cooperate because we could not accomplish the task individually, or at least we could not accomplish the task as quickly, as efficiently, as well, etc if we were to do it individually.

If we examine the question more closely it becomes evident that cooperation is evoked by different requirements and, hence, serves different functions. The different functions correspond to different forms of cooperation. Thus, we are able to distinguish at least three forms of cooperation, namely 'augmentative cooperation', 'integrative cooperation' and 'debative cooperation'.

These forms are, so to speak, different answers to the question '*Why* do people cooperate?' This question should be discussed before we embark on the next question: '*How* do people cooperate?'

Augmentative cooperation

We all know that the mechanical and physiological capacities of the human individual are quite restricted. We are all constantly made aware of anatomical limitations in terms of, for instance, payload; operational radius; the number and position of hands, fingers and feet; the angle of vision, etc., not to mention physiologically determined limitations of operational speed and endurance.

Likewise, we are constantly, and painfully, made aware of our bounded information-processing capacities. More precisely, human information-processing capacity appears to be severely restricted by the limited capacity of short-term memory (7 ± 2 'chunks') and by the time required to fixate and retrieve information from long-term memory (of the magnitude of 5 and 0.5 seconds, respectively). Summarizing the massive empirical evidence of the 'bounded rationality' (Simon, 1957) of human information processors, Inbar (1979) arrives at a somewhat disillusioned conclusion:

> If one takes into account the size and time constraints of human-information processing, as well as the fact that the slightest interruption or interference destroys the subject's train of thoughts, a dismal image of man as an information processor emerges. Mentally, he appears to be a peculiar biological computer, characterized by slow, limited, and serial information-processing capability.

The limited mechanical and information-processing capacities of human individuals are compensated by means of 'augmentative cooperation'. By combining their capacities and aggregating their efforts, an ensemble of individuals can perform a task that would have been absolutely impossible to each and every one of them individually. Collectively, they may, for instance, be able to remove a stone that one individual could not move one iota: 'As one man cannot, and 10 men must strain, to lift a tun of weight, yet one hundred men can do it only by the strength of a finger of each of them' (Bellers, 1696).

Now, there is a time to sow and a time to reap. That is, every task has to be accomplished within a certain time horizon, or the purpose is forfeited and the entire effort becomes futile. Again, by aggregating their efforts, an ensemble of workers can perform a task that would have been impossible to each and every one of them individually, not absolutely impossible but impossible within a satisfactory time horizon. Finally, by aggregating their efforts and dividing subtasks and activities between them, an ensemble may simply perform more efficiently.

In the very simple case of augmentative cooperation the task being conducted is unitary and indivisible, and the activities necessary to conduct the task are tightly coupled. In the other cases, however, the task is not unitary. In fact, it has to be decomposed into subtasks that can be conducted separately and concurrently.

The activities or subtasks may be identical. However, this is not a necessary condition. The subtasks may be different according to the nature of the task. It may, for example, be mandatory to perform two different operations simultaneously at different locations. However, in augmentative cooperation the differentiation of activities and subtasks is incidental. That is, the differentiation of activities and subtasks is not essential for augmenting the capacities; it merely mirrors specific requirements of the environment or the equipment. Thus, task allocation may be changed without substantial effect on performance.

In the typical case of a unitary task, the aggregated operations are tightly coupled and their synchronization requires an open channel. Conversely, in the case of a task that can be decomposed and conducted concurrently, the subtasks may be very loosely coupled; in this case the communication channel does not need to be continuously open. For example, in the administrative domain multiple cases of the same type must be processed more or less simultaneously. To cope with this, multiple workers are concurrently engaged in processing the same type of decisions.

By augmenting the physical and information-processing power of the individual worker, technological innovations may significantly reduce the need for and the scope of cooperation required to perform a given task. Thus, one man, when equipped with a bulldozer, is capable of removing loads far beyond the capacity of an individual or even a handful of individuals equipped with shovels. Hence, augmentative cooperation is being eroded by the augmentation of the physical and information-processing capacities of individuals. For example, in a study of the impact of technology on cooperative work among the Orokaiva, New Guinea, Newton (1985) concludes: 'Technological innovations such as shotguns, iron, torches, rubber-propelled spears and goggles have in the short term made individual hunting and fishing more successful, so that large-scale cooperative ventures are no longer more economical... or more efficient.'

Of course, augmenting the material and information-processing capacities of individuals may simultaneously inflate the scope of the tasks undertaken and may thus reproduce the need for augmentative cooperation at a higher level.

Integrative cooperation

The environment confronting human kind in the sphere of production is infinitely diverse. Man adapts to this environment by transforming the environment according to human needs, i.e. by the process of production. Production is a peculiar kind of adaptation. It is a very active and dynamic kind of adaptation and, more importantly in our context, it is a process of adaptation by means of contriving artifacts adapted to the diverse requirements of the environment, i.e. by making *tools*.

A tool is an objectification of the knowledge of a specific transformation process or subprocess. It may be objectified in the form of an ordinary material tool or in the form of a 'mental tool'.

The notion of a mental tool may require some elaboration. Skills and rules, as discussed by Rasmussen (1983), may be interpreted as two categories of mental tools. Sensori-motor skills are based on a repertoire of automated subroutines controlling the movements of the natural tools of human anatomy and, by extension, the material tools created artificially. Thus, these automated subroutines are indispensable corollaries to material tools and they appear as objectified as any of these tools.

Rules, on the other hand, are cognitive representations in the form of discrete statements of particular correlations, a simple conditional statement (Newell and Simon, 1972) derived empirically from experience. They are, in a way, the by-product of problem solving. In a problem-solving task the specific combination and sequence of actions constituting the path to the goal state is not known prior to the actual performance. After the task has been accomplished, however, the path taken is a known fact. In the case of repeated occurrence of the same problem, or the same class of problems, a rule stating the correlation may be derived empirically and revoked should the problem occur henceforth.

A production system is a representation of empirically derived knowledge, or, so to speak, a perfect model of the empirical mind. Because of the high degree of modularity of production systems, the assimilated information can be accessed and modified relatively easily, and competence can be acquired incrementally. Accordingly, a rule-based production system seems to be a representation very fit for spontaneous adaptation to an infinitely diversified environment:

> What makes production systems especially attractive for modeling is that it is relatively easy to endow them with learning capabilities—to build so called *adaptive production systems*. Since production systems are simple sets of productions, they can be modified by deleting productions or by inserting new ones (Simon, 1969).

However, exactly because rules are discrete statements of particular correlations, a representation of a complex environment in production rule format requires a large number of rules. As pointed out by McCarthy (1987), rule-based adaptation is really not very intelligent. 'Production systems do not infer general propositions.'

Adaptation by means of a spontaneous and incremental development of specialized tools, material or mental, is effective in the sense that it actually produces structures matching the particularities and peculiarities of the task environment. But it is adaptation by painstakingly recording and matching each and every peculiar characteristic of the task environment. The approach is empirical.

Rules are the skills of cognition. They are *objectified knowledge* in the sense that they are applied stereotypically. The umbilical cord connecting a rule to conceptual knowledge of the problem domain has been severed. In short, it seems legitimate to conceptualize skills and rules as 'mental tools' and to conceptualize the material and mental aspects of work in identical terms.

Human kind adapts to the diversity of the environment by contriving tools, material as well as mental. To cater for the variety and diversity of the environment, tools are adapted to increasingly specialized purposes and, consequently, the stock of tools is subject to a perpetual process of differentiation (Babbage, 1832; Marx, 1861–3) analogous to the process of differentiation in biological evolution:

> I presume that lowness in this case means that the several parts of the organization have been but little specialised for particular functions; and as long as the same part has to perform diversified work, we can perhaps see why it should remain variable, that is, why natural selection should have preserved or rejected each little deviation of form less carefully than when the part has to serve for one special purpose alone. In the same way that a knife which has to cut all sorts of things may be of almost any shape; whilst a tool for some particular object had better be of some particular shape. Natural selection, it should never be forgotten, can act on each part of each being, solely through and for its advantages (Darwin, 1859).

The statement that tools are adapted to increasingly specialized purposes applies to cognitive as well as to material tools.

The number of different tools that a human individual can handle skillfully and diligently is severely limited for the simple reason that the required abilities are to be acquired through a taxing and time-consuming training process. As observed by Charles Babbage (1832):

> It will readily be admitted, that the portion of time occupied in the acquisition of any art will depend on the difficulty of its execution; and that the greater the number of distinct processes, the longer will be the time which the apprentice must

> employ in acquiring it... If, however, instead of learning *all* the different processes for making a needle, for instance, his attention be confined to one operation, the portion of time consumed unprofitably at the commencement of his apprenticeship will be small, and all the rest of it will be beneficial to his master...

Therefore, the ongoing process of differentiation of the stock of tools generates a corollary differentiation of work, i.e. a process of *specialization.* As opposed to the incidental and reversible differentiation of tasks that may accompany augmentative cooperation, specialization is based on an *exclusive* devotion to a repertoire of activities. This applies to intellectual production as well as material production (Babbage, 1832).

The differentiation of work requires the concerted cooperation of multiple workers representing the different specialities. That is, *differentiation of work requires integrative cooperation.* The higher the degree of differentiation, the greater the scope of the integrative cooperative network.

The process of tool-based specialization culminates in the fragmentation of work that characterizes the proto-industrial organization of large-scale production, often referred to as 'manufactories', of which Adam Smith has given the classic description.[1] According to Smith (1776), in his days 'the trade of the pin-maker' had become subdivided into 'a number of branches, of which the greater part are likewise peculiar trades'.

> One man draws out the wire, another straights it, a third cuts it, a fourth points it, a fifth grinds it at the top for receiving the head; to make the head requires two or three distinct operations; to put it on is a peculiar business, to whiten the pins is another, it is even a trade by itself to put them into the paper; and the important business of making a pin is, in this manner, divided into about eighteen distinct operations, which, in some manufactories, are all performed by distinct hands, though in others the same man will sometimes perform two or three of them.

In fact, the 'scientific management' campaign launched by Frederick W. Taylor at the turn of the century essentially re-enacted within other industries the fragmentation of work experienced by the textile industry in England in the eighteenth century. 'Taylorism' takes to the extreme the tool-based specialization that has been going on since the emergence of *Homo habilis.*

Before the advent of computers, tool-based specialization was prevalent in most work domains. In administrative areas dealing with mass transactions such as banks, insurance companies, governmental agencies, etc. the extreme fragmentation of work of the 'manufactory' type was reproduced (Wright Mills, 1951; Bahrdt, 1958). Mass transaction processing was decomposed into an aggregate of discrete tasks, each of which was described in minute detail by 'procedures'. Each clerk was trained to wield a narrow set of rules. Even the assembly line type of work layout was introduced in administrative work. Witness the following case, observed in 1929:

> Orders are passed along by means of a belt and lights from a chief clerk to a series of checkers and typists, each of whom does one operation. The girl at the head of the line interprets the order, puts down the number and indicates the trade discount; the second girl prices the order, takes off the discount, adds carriage charges and totals; the third girl gives the order a number and makes a daily record; the fourth girl puts this information on an alphabetical index; the fifth girl time-stamps it; it next goes along the belt to one of several typists, who makes a copy in sextuplicate and puts on address labels; the seventh girl checks it and sends it to the storeroom (Wright Mills, 1951).

The fragmentation of work caused by the differentiation of tools is reversed by the introduction of a control system relieving the worker of the task of real-time operation of the tool, i.e. by transferring that function to a machine system.

A machine system consists of three basic elements: a set of tools, a power system, and a control system. It is fairly trivial that a CNC machining center consists of a set of tools, a power supply and a control system. The subsystems even appear as distinct subsystems. It is also fairly trivial that the CNC machine performs control functions formerly performed by human operators. However, in a host of machines the control system is not immediately apparent as a distinct subsystem but is embedded in the physical form of the device (Hirschhorn, 1984). Likewise, in a conventional, procedurally oriented computer application program the tools and control system are not readily discernible subsystems. Knowledge-based systems are, however, designed on the basis of a clear-cut and explicit separation of tools ('production rules') and control system ('interpreter', 'inference engine', 'control') (Davis and King, 1977).

The control system may be mechanical or electronic, of course, but it is indispensable. Otherwise, the system is not a machine, merely a power tool like, for example, a motor drill or an electric typewriter. The machine wields the tool and, consequently, with the introduction of machinery the process of differentiation of work is reversed. Note that the differentiation of tools is not reversed. On the contrary, it is bound to continue indefinitely. Instead, the direct coupling from the tool to the human operator and, hence, the coupling from differentiation of tools to differentiation of work is severed by the introduction of an intermediate control system. Thus, the development of machine systems reduces the need for, and the scope of, integrative cooperation.

This reversal was first observed by Andrew Ure (1835) in the cotton industry during the Industrial Revolution:

> When Adam Smith wrote his immortal elements of economics, automatic machinery being hardly known, he was properly led to regard the division of labour as the grand principle of manufacturing improvement... But what was in Dr Smith's time a topic of useful illustration, cannot now be used without risk of misleading the public mind as to the right principle of manufacturing industry. In fact, the division, or rather adaptation of labour to the different talents of men, is little thought of in factory employment. On the contrary, whenever a process requires

> peculiar dexterity and steadiness of hand, it is withdrawn as soon as possible from the cunning workman, who is prone to irregularities of many kinds, and it is placed in charge of a particular mechanism, so self-regulating, that a child may superintend it.

Following Ure, Marx (1857–8) went even further:

> Labour no longer appears to be included within the production process; rather, the human being comes to relate more as watchman and regulator to the production process itself... No longer does the worker insert a modified natural thing [i.e. a tool] as middle link between the object and himself; rather, he inserts the process of nature, transformed into an industrial process, as a means between himself and inorganic nature, mastering it. He steps to the side of the production process, instead of being its chief actor.

It should be noted that Marx, building on Babbage (1832), does not explicitly include the control system in his definition of machinery, but he does imply the control system and its crucial role by stating very strongly that machinery is endowed with skills that formerly were in the human realm (Marx, 1857–8, 1861–3).

In recent years a number of authors have challenged Ure's statement (e.g. Braverman, 1974).[2] A conspicuous and critical flaw in the reasoning of these authors is that they mistake the proto-industrial organization of work for the industrial organization (based on machine systems). The real distinction between proto-industrial and industrial organization of work is whether the operation of the tool is controlled by the human operator or whether that control function has been transferred to some mechanical or electronic control system. In this context it is of no consequence whether the force being applied to effectuate the transformation of the object is provided by a horse, an engine or a worker. The crucial question is: Which agent of production wields the tool, man or machine?

Proto-industrial organization of work has been prevalent since the Industrial Revolution in spite of great advances in mechanization by means of power tools such as lathes, drills, sewing machines and electric typewriters, and by means of highly mechanized systems of transportation of parts and part-assemblies. Assembly line work, for instance, the putative archetype of modern industrial organization of work, is typically primarily tool-based specialization taken to the extreme.[3] It goes without saying that evidence from studies of proto-industrial work organizations does not disprove Ure's statement concerning the changing role of the worker in industrial work organizations.

Another critical flaw is of a methodological nature. The authors confound technological and socio-economic aspects of the problem. For instance, they raise no questions as to the different causes of the apparent fragmentation and de-skilling. One should keep in mind, however, that the general structure of the labor market has a profound impact on the actual appearance of the social system of work. Mass unemployment, immigration, etc. may provide employers with a reservoir of cheap labor. In order to be able to exploit this reservoir of cheap labor and replace well-paid workers by low-paid ones (e.g. young women, children, illiterate immigrants, etc.) employers must redesign jobs so that the required qualifications are reduced to a minimum. Thus, competitive relations on the labor market may motivate a radical fragmentation of work and a concomitant process of de-skilling. The fragmentation of work caused by competitive relations on the labor market, that is, the fragmentation of work generated by the socio-economic system, may reinforce the fragmentation caused by the perpetual differentiation of tools. Likewise, the fragmentation of work generated by the socio-economic system may counteract the reversal of the fragmentation of work heralded by the introduction of machine systems.

Ure's observation has been confirmed by a wealth of conceptually sound and careful empirical studies of the transformation of the character of work in various industries, e.g. chemicals, power plants, metallurgy, automobiles (Mickler *et al.*, 1976, 1980; Mickler, 1981; Kern and Schumann, 1984; Hirschhorn, 1984).

The introduction of a machine system augments the capacity of the individual worker and transfers control of the operations of tools to the machine system. Execution of the automatic routines of skill-based work and of the rules of rule-based work are delegated to the machine system, leaving workers in charge of such functions as planning, supervision and fault diagnosis. The individual worker must attend to a wider segment of the total transformation process; that is, the required domain knowledge becomes more extensive and more complex. Furthermore, workers must control the behavior of the machine system itself. Accordingly, workers in modern industrial settings must cope with very complex environments where disturbances and accidents are not linear courses of events released by only one cause, and the potential ramifications of any intervention are immense (Rasmussen, 1987b, 1988). However, skill- and rule-based work cannot cope effectively with high degrees of complexity, unexpected contingencies, etc. Accordingly, workers in charge of operating large-scale industrial plants possess *conceptual knowledge* of the domain and the machine system as opposed to skills or rules directly derived from empirical experience. As a result of the introduction of machine systems, then, work in areas of production formerly characterized by predominance of skill- and rule-based work is being transformed into knowledge-based work.

Debative cooperation

The validity and veracity of a decision arrived at by knowledge-based work processes is fragile and contestable (Inbar, 1979). The function of debative cooperation is to alleviate this deficiency.

The social construction of knowledge: 'bias discount'

In knowledge-based work, multiple problem-solving strategies are possible. From analysis of verbal protocols from real-life work situations, Rasmussen and associates have shown that in a mental task a satisfactory result can be reached by very different information processes (Rasmussen, 1987a).

On the other hand, a plurality of viewpoints is a prerequisite to effective knowledge-based work. Viewpoints originating from accidental individual preferences, strategies and propensities provide a rich, random variation of views.

Debative cooperation serves the function of selecting the 'fits' from the 'misfits'. This point was brought home very eloquently by Cyert and March (1963) in their classic study:

> For the bulk of our subjects in both experiments, the idea that estimates communicated from other individuals should be taken at face value (or that their own estimates would be so taken) was not really viewed as reasonable. For every bias, there was a bias discount.

In cooperative discretionary decision making, 'bias discount' serves the function of 'natural selection' of the 'fits' among the kaleidoscopic variation of views.

Accordingly, even though dubious assessments and erroneous decisions are transmitted to other decision makers, this does not entail a diffusion or accumulation of mistakes, misrepresentations and misconceptions within the decision-making ensemble. In other words, by debating the reasoning to fellow workers in problem-solving tasks cooperating individuals may, as an ensemble, arrive at relatively balanced and objective decisions in very complex environments. The cooperating ensemble establishes a negotiated order.

Orr (1986) gives an illustrative account of this kind of debative cooperation among technicians:

> Whenever technicians gather, much of the conversation consists of anecdotes of their experiences with machines and customers. During their working day, technicians will meet at particular restaurants and coffee shops at breakfast, lunch, or for coffee when things are slow; the conversation always includes the latest stories of machine behavior.

In a particular cooperative troubleshooting task analysed by Orr, a dozen anecdotes were told in the course of the session. According to Orr, war stories

> are told as part of the process of considering possibilities, to refresh one's memory of the contextual details of earlier encounters with the machines and to aid in examining the applicability of that experience to the current problem context. [The] stories serve both to advance an idea and to provide an illustrative context for the other to consider.

The most striking example of 'bias discount' is the mode of operation of scientific communities (Hagstrom, 1965). Ideas, suggestions, assumptions, conjectures, experimental results, definitions, generalizations, deductions, theorems, laws, etc. are duly scrutinized by colleagues in the community. In recent years, an abundance of sociological studies of science has illuminated the social processes transforming local knowledge into scientific 'facts' (e.g. Latour and Woolgar, 1979; Brannigan, 1981; Knorr-Cetina, 1981; Collins, 1985; Gerson and Star 1986).

In some environments 'bias discount' has been institutionalized. In parts of the Danish civil service, for example, no official may dispatch a document unless it has been controlled and endorsed by a colleague. Again, the most obvious example of institutionalized 'bias discount' is scientific communities, characterized as they are by specialized institutions serving the function of 'bias discount' (e.g. refereeing, reviews, replication of experiments, etc.).

For 'bias discount' to be exercised in cooperative decision-making processes several preconditions must be met. First, 'bias discount' requires redundant processing capacity in the cooperating ensemble; replication of actors is a prerequisite. Second, by requiring ample time for mutual critique and adjustment, 'bias discount' may proceed at a leisurely pace.

Third, the identity of the originator of decisions and information must be known to the eventual users. Information produced by discretionary decision making, like, for instance, a medical diagnosis or an evaluation of a job applicant, will only be taken as being reliable by professionals if the originator is known. Knowledge of the professional capabilities and individual propensities of the originator is an important part of the contextual knowledge in cooperative decision making. For example, in his decision of the role of war stories in cooperative fault diagnosis Orr (1986) observes that 'a technician knows the expertise of other technicians and so whether to believe their stories or not'. Likewise, from a field study of a biological laboratory, Latour and Woolgar (1979) reported a kind of conversational exchange that featured discussion by participants about other researchers:

> Sometimes this consisted of reminiscences about who had done what in the past, usually after lunch or in the evening when the pressure of work was relaxed. More common were discussions in which particular individuals were evaluated. This was often the case when reference was made to the argument of a particular paper. Instead of assessing the statement itself, participants tended to talk about its author and to account for the statement either in terms of authors' social strategy or their psychological make-up... This kind of reference to the human agency involved in the production of statements was very common. Indeed, it was clear from participants' discussions that *who* had made a claim was as important as the claim itself.

Fourth, a social system of work warped by relations of domination cannot exercise 'bias discount' effectively. As an inherently and strongly biased system, it does not properly impede diffusion and accumulation of mistakes, misrepresentations and misconceptions within the system. On the contrary, it may function as an amplifier, resulting in Lysenko-like affairs.

In fact, knowledge-based work is inherently cooperative. As demonstrated by Piaget (1947), an individual not engaged in exchange of thought and collaboration with others would never be able to conceptualize ('group') his or her thoughts into a coherent whole. The function of this conceptualization is to liberate the spontaneous perception and intuition of the individual from the 'egocentric' viewpoint, and in its place construct a system of relations that makes it possible to shift freely from one relation to others, that is, without being restrained by the viewpoint. Conceptualization is, in principle, a coordination of viewpoints, that is, a collaboration of multiple individuals. Conceptual thinking is a cooperative effort. Seemingly, then, the apparent deficiencies of human decision making claimed to be demonstrated by an array of psychological investigations (Einhorn and Hogarth, 1982) should not be attributed to some inherent deficiency with *Homo sapiens*. The findings may rather be attributed to the individualistic paradigm prevailing in psychological research and, in consequence of these presuppositions, the spurious settings of the experiments: individuals engaged in conceptual thinking in enforced isolation.

The ontological structure of the work space: perspectives

The notion of a complex work environment, as applied above, is far too shallow. Decision making in complex environments requires 'deep knowledge'. Not only does the work space exceed the information-processing capacity of an individual problem solver, but it is a complex of multiple, ontologically distinct, though interrelated, object domains. This multiplicity of distinct object domains must be matched by a concomitant multiplicity of perspectives on the part of the decision maker to enable the apprehension of the diverse and contradictory aspects of the work as a whole.

A perspective is a conceptualization of the object domain, i.e. a conceptual reproduction of the essential structural and behavioral properties of the object (e.g. generative mechanisms, causal laws, and taxonomies, and a concomitant body of representations—models, notations, etc.).

A conceptualization should not be conceived as a collection of production rules. It apprehends the essential properties of the object as opposed to its incidental properties. Conceptual thinking goes beyond the boundaries of common sense thinking, i.e. direct generalization from empirical apprehension. In some parts of the AI community, however, 'commonsense reasoning' has been elevated to a model deserving to be emulated (McCarthy, 1987). In some cases it would presumably be beneficial if knowledge-based systems commanded the large repertoire of factual knowledge acquired by any normal human adult raised in advanced industrial society. It would 'know', for instance, that a cup will fall to the ground because of gravity, and it would know that an ostrich is as much a bird as a penguin or a sparrow. Human adults know this, not because of some mysterious faculty for commonsense reasoning but because they have undergone a comprehensive and intensive training and education process, day in and day out, for decades. In another era, it would have been common sense that a whale is a fish, that a load of 5 kg will fall faster than a load of 1 kg, or that the Earth is flat.

The relationship between conceptual knowledge and knowledge of particular instances is complex, and conceptual knowledge cannot be applied directly to particular instances. If, for example, we subscribe to Benjamin Franklin's definition of human kind as 'a tool-making animal' we would not consider Einstein an animal due to the fact that he was not, as a particular individual, creating any tools. The statement should not be interpreted as an abstract-general statement of an attribute common to each and every individual member of the class. Rather, it should be seen as a statement of the specific generative mechanism of human kind as a totality (Iljenkow, 1960). To model conceptual thinking, then, the simple deductive inheritance principle of the object-oriented paradigm should be supplanted by a much more powerful paradigm mirroring the complex relationship between general, specific and particular statements in conceptual thinking.

The obvious example of conceptualizations is, of course, the body of scientific knowledge. The object domains of the different sciences and scientific specialities are ontologically distinct. As observed by Bhaskar (1975), most scientific research proceeds from identification of invariances in nature to the explanation of these invariances in terms of enduring mechanisms. Thus, the reactions of chemistry, which are represented by a formula such as $2Na + 2HCl = 2NaCl + H_2$, are explained by reference to the atomic hypothesis and the theory of valency and chemical bonding. In turn, chemical bonding and valency has been explained in terms of the electronic theory of atomic structure, etc. In the case of chemistry the structure of knowledge may be represented as a hierarchy of representations, of which the lower stratum constitutes the explanation of the stratum immediately above (Bhaskar, 1975):

Stratum I $2Na + 2HCl = 2NaCl + H_2$
explained by:
Stratum II Theory of atomic number and valency
explained by:
Stratum III Theory of electrons and atomic structure
explained by:
Stratum IV Competing theories of subatomic structure...

This stratification can be observed in the total body of scientific knowledge, from quasars to quarks.

The task of attending to different perspectives may be performed by the joint effort of multiple individuals (or groups of individuals), each attending to one specific perspective. In this case, we are dealing with a systematic cooperation of specialized guardians of explicit perspectives, i.e. a form of cooperation based on *perspective-based specialization.* Thus, in addition to debative cooperation serving the function of facilitating 'bias discount', debative cooperation also encompasses cooperation required for integrating the different contributions of specialists attending to different perspectives on a given problem or class of problems.

Of course, to apply a particular perspective is to be biased. However, there is an essential difference between 'bias discount' and application of multiple perspectives. In the case of perspectives, the bias does not reflect accidental individual preferences, strategies and propensities. On the contrary, the bias of a perspective is deliberately and systematically cultured to match the properties of the object domain, It is an objective bias, not a subjective one.

Perspective-based specialization is also fundamentally different from tool-based specialization. As stated above, a perspective is not a collection of production rules but a conceptualization and a concomitant body of representations. Of course, perspectives are implemented in a large repertoire of tools, material and mental, applied on a daily basis without recurrent invocation of deep conceptual structures. Thus, a cooperative arrangement of specialties embodying different perspectives may appear to be tool-based. However, as opposed to workers involved in tool-based specialization proper, those involved in a perspective-based speciality do, contingently, revoke the deep conceptual structures of the perspective. In tool-based specialization the deep conceptual structures are not accessible. Either the tool does not embody a perspective, merely a spontaneously acquired empirical representation in production rule format, or the workers have not been given access to revocation of the conceptual origins.

The function of debative cooperation based on perspective-based specialization is to facilitate the application of multiple pertinent perspectives on a given problem to match the multifarious nature of the work environment. The crux of this form of cooperative work, then, is to interrelate and compile the partial and parochial perspectives. Again, the cooperating ensemble establishes a negotiated order, not merely an order transcending the accidental biases of different individuals but one transcending the systematic biases of different perspectives.

In a discussion of engineering design, based on two years of field research, Bucciarelli (1984) observed:

> Different participants in the design process have different perceptions of the design, the intended artefact, in process. What an engineer in the Systems Group calls an interconnection scheme, another in Production calls a junction box. To the former, unit cost and ease of interconnection weigh most heavily; to the latter, appearance and geometric compatibility with the module frame, as well as unit cost, are

> critical. The task of design is then as much a matter of getting different people to share a common perspective, to agree on the most significant issues, and to shape consensus on what must be done next, as it is a matter for concept formation, evaluation of alternative, costing and sizing—all the things we teach.

Again, science epitomizes perspective-based specialization. The different pertinent perspectives on nature, as embodied in the stratification of scientific knowledge and, concomitantly, in the different scientific disciplines and specialties, are applied by specialized guardians in the shape of the different scientific communities. As pointed out by Whitley (1974), scientific specialties in general are 'built around a set of cognitive structures which order and interpret a particular, restricted aspect of reality.' Thus, cross-disciplinary research is an application of different perspectives to a particular problem and, hence, a case of debating cooperation based on perspective-based specialization. In the wordsof Chubin (1985), interdisciplinarity implies 'complementary perspectives onmutual research problems that insure new approaches and collaborative efforts'.

While perspective-based specialties in general are 'cognitive structures which order and interpret a particular, restricted aspect of reality', research areas are defined by *problem situations*: 'A research area can be said to exist when scientists concur on the nature of the uncertainty common to a set of problem situations' (Whitley, 1974). A problem situation may be ordered on the basis of different principles. The phenomena under investigation may be similar (e.g. superconductivity), or an object may be common (e.g. amorphous materials). Obviously, these ordering principles are emerging perspectives on the world. However, 'the common use of a particular instrumentarium with its associated rules for obtaining meaningful information' may also act as an ordering principle. In the words of Whitley, this

> usually occurs when the technique is comparatively complex and its use requires expertise. The acquisition of the cognitive and technical skills necessary to operate a complex piece of apparatus may require lengthy training; thus it acts as a demarcation criterion for the research area.

Consider, for example, techniques based on reactor physics, the use of helium in low-temperature physics, radiation techniques in radiobiology, or high-voltage electron microscopy. In these instances, the specialization at hand might be classified as tool-based. However, these techniques imply a complex set of theories in producing information. But

> this is often relegated to the category of 'background knowledge' which is assumed as non-problematic for the immediate purposes and will only become a source of concern if substantial difficulties are encountered. When a technique becomes so accepted that it is generally included in the scientists' basic intellectual equipment without further thought, it ceases to be a meaningful demarcatory device for current work.

That is, when a technique is transmuted into a tool and the umbilical cord has been cut, then the technique ceases to be a meaningful demarcation device of specialization. In other words, it is not tools but problem situations related by 'common preceptions of cognitive uncertainty' of phenomena or objects that constitute research areas. In these cases, specialization is basically perspective-based, not tool-based.

The different perspectives in science are incongruent but not incompatible; that is, they may be related but not collapsed. Incompatible perspectives do, however, exist in scientific research. In the case of contending paradigms, the different paradigms may represent alternative methodologies. They are, so to speak, rivalling emerging perspectives. The conflict is most likely solved, eventually, either because one of the paradigms emerges victorious from the dispute or because they are both united on a more general foundation. However, the contending paradigms may in fact be revealed to relate to different object domains, in which case the former contenders may co-exist peacefully once the border dispute has been settled and the implicit perspectives have been established.

Perspectives need not be easily reconcilable. In fact, they may be irreconcilable and may even be antagonistic. The conflict of perspectives need not be a sign of some mistake in the structuring of work and its distribution; it may be perfectly functional in the sense that it mirrors conflicting forces in the domain. Thus, debative cooperation may acquire a quality of antagonism. But however heated the debate, it is still a debate.

Incongruent and incompatible perspectives are frequent occurrences in the administrative domain. Administrative work mediates and controls the myriad of transactions of goods and services that connect the nodes of this universal network and make it buzz and bustle (Schmidt, 1986). It is, in the words of Wright Mills (1951), the Unseen Hand become visible. Hence, the field of work of administrative agencies is characterized by incongruent or even conflicting interests and motives. Administrative decision making requires apprehension of the interests and motives operating in the field of work. Administrative workers must know of the *stakeholders* in the social system whose economic activities are being mediated and controlled. Thus, the domain of administrative decision making encompasses a set of subordinate object domains corresponding to the relations of interests in the social field, each identifiable interest in the social field, or cluster of interests, constituting a distinct object domain. Often, the clustering of divergent and conflicting interests in the object domain is reflected in the structure of task allocation in the cooperating ensemble. That is, the major conflicting clusters of interests in the field of work are represented by actors negotiating, as it were, as their advocates.

In a study of a case-tracking system in a US court, Albrecht has presented an interesting picture of conflicting perspectives in operation. Two different perspectives were active, each of which was attended to by a specialized guardian:

the legal staff and the probation officers. In the words of the résumé given by Kling (1980):

> Each of the two groups brought a different orientation to its work with defendants and convicts, and each was able to exercise moderate autonomy in its control over the meaning of its work. The legal staff members were concerned that cases be processed through the courts in an orderly manner and emphasized due process. In contrast, the probation staff emphasized rehabilitating individuals to become productive and trusted members of the community.

One day, a computer-based case-tracking system was introduced on the staff of the court. The antagonistic nature of the two perspectives was not, however, appreciated in the design. The information system failed and was eventually discarded. It failed, presumably, because the perspectives could not be reconciled, at least not in a system as tightly coupled as a shared database. Albrecht, however, interprets the failure of the information system as a result of a power struggle in the organization. Apparently, a power struggle did take place, but the *content* of the struggle was clearly the antagonistic nature of the perspectives on the same domain.

In another study of a large insurance company that provides health insurances, Gerson and Star (1986) have demonstrated, very eloquently, the complex and comprehensive interaction of conflicting 'viewpoints', or perspectives, in administrative work. They show, for example, that different groups involved in the decision-making process have different 'viewpoints' about how to code medical procedures. In the case reported by Gerson and Star the 'resolution of conflicting viewpoints and continually evolving, inconsistent knowledge bases' was handled by a specialized unit. This unit used 'a repertoire of strategies to reconcile viewpoints, decompose the fuzzy and complex procedures, and bring temporary local closure to the open information system in order to produce its single representation'.

MODES OF COOPERATION

Having outlined different answers to the question 'Why do people cooperate?' we can now turn to the next question' '*How* do people cooperate?' That is, we can now discuss the different *modes of cooperation.* First, cooperative work relations may extend across distances in space and time.

Remote or proximate cooperation. Workers cooperating at the same location (in the same room, for instance) are able to interact freely, whereas those cooperating remotely are constrained in their interaction by the availability, bandwidth and response time of the communication medium.

Synchronous or asynchronous cooperation. The different subtasks of a cooperative effort may be performed simultaneously or delayed. The duration of the interval between cooperative acts varies as well. The subtasks may be performed as a closely coupled sequence or as a protracted series of interconnected acts. In some domains the chain of interconnected acts may last for years: for example, in scientific research when a scientist reverts to an idea of a predecessor, in administrative work when a decision maker retrieves information that was filed years ago by a colleague, and in design when an engineer retrieves a mathematical model of a component, developed previously by a colleague, in order to apply it to a modification of that component. In rare cases cooperative endeavors have lasted for centuries (e.g. the construction of the cathedral in Cologne).

Other modes of cooperative work can be distinguished as well.

Collective and distributed cooperation. In the collective mode of cooperative work, multiple workers cooperate overtly and consciously. As a collective, the workers constitute a group with a common responsibility. None of the workers can pursue a strategy until that strategy has been endorsed by the other workers. By contrast, in the distributed mode workers are semi-autonomous. Each worker can modify his or her behavior as circumstances change and devise his or her own strategies (Lesser and Corkill, 1987). That is, in the distributed mode of cooperative work the different workers are not necessarily aware of the existence of the other workers or informed of their activities. They cooperate by means of a shared information space.

Direct or mediated cooperation. In direct cooperation, workers interact by exchanging symbolic information; they communicate. By contrast, in mediated cooperation, workers cooperate via a technical system, typically a machine system. This mode of cooperation has been described by Popitz *et al.* (1957) in a classic study of cooperative work processes in a West German steel plant. The cooperating workers attend to different functions in relation to the process. In response to the state of the system, e.g. to control some likely disturbance, one operator takes appropriate action, thereby, however, changing the state of the system. Perceiving this state change, another operator, with other responsibilities and perhaps at another location, is prompted to take appropriate action of a different kind. They do not necessarily communicate; nevertheless, they cooperate.

WORK ORGANIZATION

Any cooperative effort involves a number of secondary tasks of mediating and controlling the association of individuals. First, tasks are to be allocated to different members of the cooperating ensemble: which worker is to do what, where, when? Second, by assigning a task to a worker, that worker is rendered accountable for accomplishing that task according to certain criteria: when, where, how, how soon, level of quality? Accountability requires reporting and controlling accountability (Strauss, 1985). Finally, again in the terminology suggested by Strauss, cooperative work requires 'articulation work'. The numerous tasks, clusters of tasks and segments of the trajectory of tasks are to be meshed. Likewise, the efforts of individuals and ensembles are to be meshed. In the words of Gerson and Star (1986), articulation work consists of all the tasks needed 'to coordinate a particular task, including scheduling subtasks, recovering from errors, and assembling resources'.

Again, task allocation and articulation may have different forms and modes: tasks may be prescribed, requested or assumed (Strauss, 1985). Likewise, task articulation may be performed as part and parcel of the task, or it may be performed by a specialized category of workers; it may be planned in advance, or it may be done contingently.

In the real world, the different forms and modes of cooperative work and of task allocation and articulation do not exist as separate entities. They co-exist in every cooperative work setting and are meshed into a specific configuration, the *work organization.*

The specific configuration of the work organization in a given setting is determined by the specific characteristics of the work environment. For instance:

(1) The nature of the object system, i.e. of the system to be transformed or controlled. Is the object system primarily intentional or causal?
(2) The degree of stability and predictability of the work environment. Are tasks recurring? Are product requirements stable or predictable? Are operational conditions stable or predictable?
(3) Consistency of product requirements. Are product requirements consistent or inconsistent? Are requirements irreconcilable?
(4) The dynamic character of the object system. Is it turbulent or static?
(5) The structure of the work space. Is interaction of multiple perspectives required? Are the different perspectives reconcilable?
(6) The potential danger to the environment of the process.
(7) Requirements in terms of lead time.
(8) Requirements in terms of product quality.
(9) Requirements in terms of process and product documentation.

Some brief examples follow:

(1) In the organization of scientific research, the position of debative cooperation is in no way monopolistic. The performance of the scientific worker is as constrained by bounded rationality as that of any other worker. Thus, augmentative cooperation is required. In addition, the development of

scientific production is as dependent on the development of appropriate specialized tools as any other branch of production. Accordingly, tool-based specialization and integrative cooperation figure prominently in the social system of scientific work. But, because of the very high degree of task uncertainty distinguishing scientific work, augmentative and integrative cooperation are subordinate to debative cooperation. However, the degree of task uncertainty varies between disciplines and fields. Thus, the various scientific fields are characterized by different work organizations (Whitley, 1984).

(2) The ontological structure of the domain may call for an isomorphous structure of the cooperating ensemble. For example, portfolio management is characterized by two distinct object domains: knowledge of the structure and behavior of the markets on the one hand, and knowledge of the economic position of the client, his propensity to take risks, etc. on the other. In a portfolio management agency investigated by the author this dichotomy of the work domain was reflected in the structure of specialization. The employees were divided into two categories corresponding to the two subdomains: analysts and consultants. The analysts would be supervising the behavior of the markets, watching out for profitable opportunities. Coming across 'attractive stock', they would alert the attention of the consultants. However, in the words of one of the analysts, 'it takes a hard fight to convince the consultants that the stock is worth buying'. In fact, the consultants were quite frequently exposed to the needs and anxieties of the clients and should—at any time—be able to legitimize to the client the actions taken or not taken. Faced with new schemes from the analysts, they would represent the interests of the clients. Accordingly, daily work in the department appeared as a continuous debate between analysts and consultants. The debate was of a dual character. On the one hand, the consultants challenged the reasoning of the analysts so as to avoid biased judgments. On the other, two different perspectives were applied and interrelated.

(3) Manufacturing companies have successfully been reducing task complexity and uncertainty by enforcing simplicity, stability and predictability on the environment by numerous means, e.g. by reducing the range of products and models, by reducing the variety of parts (e.g. group technology), by assuring that parts and materials adhere to specifications, by maintaining buffer stocks of parts, etc. Likewise, in the administrative domain an identical strategy has been implemented by imposing strict procedures on acceptable applications or inquiries, by ordaining certain channels, hours and time limits, by making use of predesigned forms mandatory, and by the many other ingenious inventions of red tape. This strategy is the foundation for a work organization characterized by comprehensive tool-based specialization combined with hierarchical systems of planning, allocation and supervision.

This strategy has been effective in reducing complexity and uncertainty, but at the cost of loss of flexibility. During the last decade an opposite trend has become visible in management thinking, probably primarily spurred by decreasing product lifecycles. In the emerging business environment, parameters such as minimal lead time and response time, product diversity, and production to customer-defined specifications are becoming more important than price. In this emerging environment, work organizations characterized by tool-based specialization and hierarchical control systems are receding into the background while self-organizing ensembles of workers equipped with flexible manufacturing systems, etc. are coming to the fore.

(4) The transformation process may be hazardous to the environment, as in the case of nuclear power plants, chemical plants, etc. Labor processes may also be explosive in the social sense. The decisions to be taken in administrative work may be highly sensitive and controversial, as is often the case with decision making in political bodies such as governmental bureaucracies, political parties, pressure groups and law-enforcement agencies. This may enhance the need for debative cooperation and may, in addition, call for strict procedures of authorization. For instance, the higher echelons of the organization might become involved in decision making pertaining to certain delicate matters to avoid risks of, for instance, public scandal. As a precautionary measure, enforcement of strict regulation of the flow of information may be attempted. Thus, the constraints imposed by the risks involved in the domain modifies the pattern of cooperative relations within the ensemble.

SOCIAL ORGANIZATION

Until now, we have been discussing cooperative work *sub specie* its content, i.e. the transformation process. Let us now examine its specific social form, the *social organization.*

The emergence of social organization

The regularity of cooperative relations varies immensely. In some cases the cooperating ensemble is merely a transient formation, assembled in a particular situation to carry out a particular task and then dissolved. In other cases, the cooperating ensemble assumes the character of a stable formation.

Cooperative relations stabilize because of the requirements of the work being done. First, the task itself may be a perpetual or a perpetually recurring phenomenon. Second, the work environment and the technical and human resources available at any given time may be relatively stable. Third, relative stability of the workforce may be a requirement. Normally, specific domain knowledge is required and must be acquired by means of participation in the work process; socialization of new members of the cooperating ensemble may be a prerequisite to effective cooperative decision making, etc. Finally, stability of cooperative work patterns may also arise from the economics of cooperative work. Specifically, the overhead costs of articulation in cooperative work may be reduced by entering stable relations of cooperation.

In so far as the relations of cooperation becomes stable, cooperative work acquires an *organizational form.* That is, an organization is a stable pattern of cooperative relations.

By defining an organization as a stable pattern of cooperative relations the organization is demarcated by actual cooperative behavior, not by legal criteria such as ownership. For example, if a stable pattern of cooperative relations is established between a manufacturing company and its subcontractors this pattern is as much an organization as the patterns of cooperative relations between, say, the different departments of the manufacturing company, provided that the latter patterns exhibit the same degree of stability as the former. Thus, the degree of organization is the corollary of the degree of stability of cooperative relations.

Ouchi (1980) has advocated a somewhat similar understanding of organizations. A proponent of the Transactions Cost approach, however, Ouchi presents the reduction of the costs of mediating and controlling exchange transactions as the exclusive generative mechanism of organizations. Thus he does not distinguish between *cooperative work* and *exchange transactions*, and defines an organization 'as any stable pattern of transactions'. This definition is definitely not tenable. The concept of transactions does not apply to the sphere of production but to that of exchange of commodities. A transaction occurs when a commodity is transferred from one possessor to another. Renting a hotel room is not an act of cooperative work. Conversely operators running a rolling mill in a steel plant are not exchanging commodities between themselves. The steel plate is conveyed from one operator to another as an object of work; it is not transferred from one possessor to another as a commodity. According to Ouchi, however:

> The 10,000 individuals who comprise the workforce of a steel mill could be individual entrepreneurs whose interpersonal transactions are mediated entirely through a network of market and contractual relationships.

But the transfer of a steel plate from one manned station to another is not an 'interpersonal transaction'. It is a cooperative act. Ouchi proceeds by arguing that in this case the market forces have failed as the governance structure because the determination of value contributed by one worker is highly ambiguous in the integrated steelmaking process. That is indeed the reason why cooperative relations in modern industrial environments are not mediated by market relations, as pointed out by Hodgskin (1825): 'Each labourer produces only some part of a whole, and each part having no value or utility of itself, there is nothing on which the labourer can seize, and say: "This is my product, this I keep to myself." '

As argued in the preceding sections of this chapter, the nature of the production process may require the cooperative effort of many people. Thus, the process is performed as a cooperative effort, or it is not performed at all. In an attempt to refute this, Ouchi (1980) argues that 'cooperation need not take the form of a formal organization'. Indeed not! But the question explicitly addressed by Ouchi is not that of the reasons for the emergence of *formal* organizations but that of the reasons for the emergence of organizations in general. The question is not why a steel plant is a unitary corporate body but why the cooperative relations stabilize in the first place. The crux of the story being that it would be technically impossible to run a modern integrated steel mill in any way other than a fairly stable cooperative network of individuals.

It should also be noted that Ouchi contradicts his own definition of an organization by stating: 'In this definition, a market is as much an organization as is a bureaucracy or a clan.' The market, *per se*, is not an organization. Of course, an organization may exist in the form of a stable pattern of cooperative relations mediated by market transactions. Typically, however, the patterns of transactions in markets are not particularly stable; on the contrary, they are typically volatile and transient. If the pattern of transactions is not stable then, according to Ouchi's own definition, there is no organization, market or no market.

By defining organization in terms of patterns of transactions Ouchi is unable to transcend the conventional formal notion of organizations. Formal organization is to be defined in terms of ownership and liability as opposed to the dynamic patterns of actual cooperative work reflecting the requirements of the work environment and the technical and human resources available.

Real work is not done by formal organizations but by real ones, i.e. by ensembles of workers engaged in more or less stable patterns of cooperative relations. By conceiving an organization as a stable pattern of cooperative relations we are able to conceptualize organizations as emerging formations of cooperating workers that, by entering into stable cooperative arrangements, adapt to the requirements of the work environment. As emerging formations, organizations are susceptible to changes in the work environment, to variations in the technical and human resources at hand, etc. Real organizations, then, are complex formations of cooperative relations of different degrees of stability. In a given organizational setting, highly stable structures are punctuated by transient cooperative patterns, called forth by the requirements of a novel task in a particular situation. The definition suggested above allows us to conceive organizations as complex hierarchical systems of cooperative networks. Multiple cooperative networks of different degrees of stability may be nodes of wider cooperative networks.

In this conceptualization of organizations nothing is implied in terms of formalization of the cooperative pattern. Formal organization is a superimposed structure safeguarding the interests of the owner and regulatory bodies. Accordingly, formal organization reflects the relations of property and codifies the cooperative relations in a legally valid form (e.g. by contract, statute, authorization), thus serving the function of allocation of resources, responsibilities, and, when appropriate, disciplinary measures. In some very special cases where the work environment is characterized by a high degree of stability and tasks are highly routinized, the real organization may appear as being congruent with the formal organization. In most domains, however, the actual pattern of cooperation changes dynamically, according to the requirements of the situation. In these cases the formal organization is only faintly congruent with the real organization.

Williamson (1975) has attempted to turn mediation of transactions at lower costs into the generative mechanism that explains the emergence of formal organizations. For instance, according to Williamson a formal organization such as a corporation exists because it can mediate economic transactions between its members at lower costs than a market mechanism can. That is evidently a reason for the formation of corporations. But it cannot be taken as the exclusive explanation. Factors other than the costs of transactions are involved in the formation of corporations. For example, first, the scale of formal organization is determined by the scale of real organization emerging from the production process. At a given stage of the development of technology in a given domain, a certain configuration of the technical and human resources is a prerequisite. A given stage, then, is characterized by a minimum level of capital investment and a corollary scope of formal organization. Second, the technical and human resources may be utilized more efficiently and flexibly by having a large but diversified mix of products. Again, this requires a certain level of capital investment. Third, corporations may be able to establish and defend dominant positions in the market by being able to mobilize large amounts of capital for research and development, marketing, aggressive pricing, etc. None of these alternative reasons for the formation of formal organizations can be derived from the ability of formal organization to mediate transactions at lower costs.

The dialectics of organization and the individual

Labor power is an attribute of human individuals and, hence, cannot be separated from the individual. A cooperative work process, then, is performed by individuals with individual interests and motives.

Because of that, organizations must be regarded as coalitions of diverging and even conflicting interests rather than perfectly collaborative systems. An organization is not an entity acting as if guided by a single will. This point was brought home by the so-called Carnegie School in organizational theory (Simon, 1945; March and Simon, 1958; Cyert and March, 1963; Thompson, 1967). An organization is not characterized by unity of interests; it is not monolithic. On the contrary, it is a 'coalition' of individuals motivated by individual interests and aspirations and pursuing individual goals (Cyert and March, 1963).

This understanding has been continued forcefully by the Transactions Costs school. In the words of Ciborra (1985):

> Organizations are seen as networks of contractual arrangements to govern exchange transactions among members having only partially overlapping goals. Conflict of interests is explicitly admitted as a factor affecting information and exchange costs.[4]

Thus, according to Ciborra, this approach allows us to grasp 'the daily use of information for misrepresentation purposes in partially conflictual organizational settings'. The Russian proverb saying that 'Man was given the ability of speech so that he could conceal his thoughts' applies perfectly to the use of information in organizations.

In accordance with the prevalence of goal incongruence in organizations and the partially conflictual nature of organizations, allocation of tasks is just as controversial. As pointed out by Strauss (1985), a wide variety of social modes of task allocation can be observed:

> Tasks can be imposed; they can be requested; also they can just be assumed without request or command; but they can also be delegated or proffered, and accepted or rejected. Often they are negotiated. And of course actors can manipulate openly or covertly to get tasks, or even have entire kinds of work allocated to themselves.

Workers may agree or disagree with the allocation. But they may also conceal their disagreement. They may reject it but not reveal their rejection, or they may reject it and act on that basis but conceal their rejection. They may also agree or disagree to the criteria of the tasks for which they are made accountable, and they may again disagree overtly or covertly.

In sum, then, on the top of the discords stemming from random variation of individual problem-solving strategies and the discords stemming from different or even contending perspectives on the domain, we have a whole new level of discord of interests and motives. These levels of discord may interact so that they mutually reinforce each other.

It is beyond the scope of this chapter but should be noted that organizations are not only subjected to disturbances emanating from partially conflictual individual interests and motives. Cooperative work is always performed in the wider context of a socio-economic system. Accordingly, organizations are subjected to the general conflicts of interests derived from the social relations of production of the wider socio-economic and political system. The individuals involved in cooperative production may have conflicting economic interests and ideological allegiances. That is, an organization is a system of interaction warped by the conflicting impact of contending social forces. Consequently, the structure of interaction of the basic forms of cooperation is modified radically. For instance, horizontal information flow may be curtailed and military forms of organization emulated as a means of social control to such an extent that it becomes dysfunctional.

Congruence of motives in the organization is highly dependent on the climate of the wider socio-economic system in general and the specific position of the organization within this context. If, for example, the organization is situated in an expanding market it may have room for handsome wages and relative open career opportunities. In this instance, motives are more likely to converge compared to an organization in adverse conditions. The collaborative climate of a particular organization may also be affected by managerial strategies. An organization that systematically exploits an external reservoir of labor power at the detriment of a policy of internal training, education and promotion will have a high frequency of manpower turnover and, hence, a low degree of congruence of motives. Conversely, a managerial strategy of job recruitment based on an internal system of training, education and promotion may be conducive for congruence of motives in the organization (Littler, 1982; Gospel and Littler, 1983).

The different forms of organization are resultants of the interaction of multiple forces: the forms of cooperation, the modes of cooperation, the forms and modes of task allocation and articulation as meshed by the specific requirements of the work environment, the degree of organization, the degree of formalization of organization, the varying degrees of competition and collaboration, the impact of the wider socio-economic and political system, etc. An analysis of a particular cooperative arrangement must meticulously distinguish the different forces involved.

The bureaucratic form of organization, for example, may be regarded as a specific form created by the conflicting impacts of different requirements:

(1) The domain is that of administrative work; the work environment is politically and ideologically charged and hazardous; decision making is discretionary, and decisions are potentially controversial; accountability is a hot issue.
(2) The administrative agency exercises functions of social control within the socio-political system at large; it tends to insulate itself in relation to the social subsystem being controlled (e.g. the clientele), and the clientele is in no position to demand effectively that applications are processed rapidly, flexibly, etc.

(3) Thus, the individual decision maker is inclined to guard his or her individual interests by mechanical adherence to regulations, needless duplication of records, and compilation of an excessive amount of extraneous information, and by 'passing the buck', i.e. to involve colleagues, preferably at a higher level of authority, in making or certifying the decision. Hence the 'red tape' and the ensuing delays and inactions distinguishing the bureaucratic phenomenon (Crozier, 1963; Lee, 1984).

CONCLUSION

This chapter has outlined a conceptual framework that will enable us to distinguish different pertinent aspects of cooperative work and analyse specific characteristics of these aspects and their interplay. It seems feasible to develop a 'generative' theory of cooperative work, that is, a theory explaining specific work organizations in terms of the domain characteristics and the technical and human resources available. By identifying the generative mechanism of organizational formations, we are then able to predict organizational changes stemming from technological development.

Finally, a conceptual framework like the one outlined in this chapter allows us to identify and discuss design requirements to computer-based information systems for cooperative work settings in terms of different work environments and work organizations.

Address for Correspondence:

Dr Kjeld Schmidt, Cognitive Systems Group, Risø National Laboratory, DK-4000 Roskilde, Denmark.

NOTES

---

[1] The term proto-industrialization as defined by Mendels (1972) denotes market-oriented forms of production based on craft specialization. That is, denotes cottage production as well as manufactories, i.e. factory production based on craft specialization. On the concept of manufactories, cf. Marx (1867), Forberger (1962) and Wolf (1963).

[2] For an overview of the debate triggered by Braverman's book, cf. Wood (1982) and Thompson (1983).

[3] Of course, this statement applies to mass production systems *prior* to the advent of NC technology and its application to machining, joining and materials handling.

[4] Some reservation is required. The form adopted by arrangements governing transactions, or cooperative relations, is not necessarily that of the specific legal form of a *contract*. Evidently, some form of tacit or explicit agreement on the terms of cooperation is mandatory in any stable pattern of cooperative relations, but the agreement need not take the form of a contract.

REFERENCES

Babbage, C. (1832) *On the Economy of Machinery and Manufactures.* London.

Bahrdt, H. P. (1958) *Industriebürokratie. Versuch einer Soziologie des Industrialisierten Bürobetriebes und seiner Angestelten.* Stuttgart: Ferdinand Enke Verlag.

Bannon, L. Bjørn-Andersen, N., and Due-Thomsen, B. (1988) Computer support for cooperative work: an appraisal and critique, *EURINFO '88, First European Conference on Information Technology for Organisational Systems,* Athens, 16–20 May.

Bellers, J. (1696) *Proposals for raising a colledge of industry of all useful trades and husbandry, with profit for the rich, a plentiful living for the poor, and a good education for youth.* London (Quoted in Marx, 1867).

Bhaskar, R. (1975) *A Realist Theory of Science.* Leeds: Leeds Books.

Brannigan, A. (1981) *The Social Basis of Scientific Discoveries.* Cambridge: Cambridge University Press.

Braverman, H. (1974) *Labor and Monopoly Capital. The degradation of work in the twentieth century.* New York: Monthly Review Press.

Bucciarelli, L. L. (1984) Reflective practice in engineering design. *Design Studies,* **5**, No. 3, July, 185–90.

Chubin, D. E. (1985) Beyond invisible colleges—inspirations and aspirations of post-1972 social studies of science. *Scientometrics,* **7**, Nos 3–6, 221–54.

Ciborra, C. U. (1985) Reframing the role of computers in organizations: the transaction costs approach. *Proceedings of Sixth International Conference on Information Systems,* Indianapolis, 16–18 December.

Collins, H. M. (1985) *Changing Order. Replication and induction in scientific practice.* London: Sage.

Craig, R. L. (1986) *The Development of the Labour Process in Capitalist Societies. A comparative study of the transformation of work organization in Britain, Japan and the USA.* Aldershot: Gower.

Crozier, M. (1963) *The Bureaucratic Phenomenon.* University of Chicago Press.

Cyert, R. M., and March, J. G. (1963) *A Behavioral Theory of the Firm.* Englewood Cliffs, NJ: Prentice-Hall.

Darwin, C. (1859) *On the Origin of Species.* London.

Davis, R., and King, J. (1977) An overview of production systems. In E. W. Elcock and D. Michie (eds) *Machine Intelligence,* Vol. 8. Chichester: Ellis Horwood; New York: John Wiley, pp. 300–32.

Einhorn, H. J., and Hogarth, R. M. (1982) Behavioral decision theory: processes of judgment and choice. In G. R. Ungson and D. N. Braunstein (eds), *Decision Making: An Interdisciplinary Inquiry.* Boston, Mass: Kent Publishing Co., pp. 15–41.

Ferguson, A. (1767) *An Essay on the History of Civil Society.* Edinburgh: Edinburgh University Press 1966.

Forberger, R. (1962) Zur Auseinandersetzung über das Problem des Übergangs von der Manufaktur zur Fabrik. In *Beiträge zur Deutschen Wirtschafts-und Sozialgeschichte des 18. and 19. Jahrhunderts* (Schr. d. Inst. f. Gesch., Dt. Akad. d. Wiss., Series I, **10**). Berlin: Akademie-Verlag.

Gerson, E. M., and Star, S. L. (1986) Analyzing due process in the workplace. *ACM Transactions on Office Information Systems,* **4**, No. 3, July, 257–70.

Gospel, H. F., and Littler, C. R. (1983) *Managerial Strategies and Industrial Relations. An historical and comparative study.* London: Heinemann.

Hagstrom, W. O. (1965) *The Scientific Community.* New York: Basic Books.

Hammer, M. (1984) The OA mirage. *Datamation,* **30**, No. 2, February, 36–46.

Hedberg, B. *et al.* (1987) *Kejsarens nya kontor. Fallstudier om datoranvändning.* Malmö: Liber.

Hirschhorn, L. (1984) *Beyond Mechanization: Work and Technology in a Postindustrial Age*. Cambridge, Mass: MIT Press.

Hodgskin, T. (1825) *Labour Defended Against the Claims of Capital*, New York; Kelley, 1969.

Iljenkow, E. V. (1960) *Die Dialektik des Abstrakten und Konkreten im 'Kapital' von Karl Marx*. West Berlin: Das Europäische Buch, 1979.

Inbar, M. (1979) *Routine Decision-Making. The future of bureaucracy*. Beverly Hills: Sage.

Kern, H., and Schumann, M. (1984) *Das Ende der Arbeitsteilung? Rationalisierung in der industriellen Produktion: Bestandaufnahme, Trendbestimmung*. München.

Kling, R. (1980) Social analyses of computing: theoretical perspectives in recent empirical research. *Computing Surveys*, **12**, No. 1, March, 61–110.

Knorr-Cetina, K. D. (1981) *The Manufacture of Knowledge. An essay on the constructivist and contextual nature of science*. Oxford: Pergamon Press.

Latour, B., and Woolgar, S. (1979) *Laboratory Life. The construction of scientific facts*. Princeton, NJ: Princeton University Press.

Lee, R. M. (1984) Automating red tape: The performative vs. informative roles of bureaucratic documents. *Office: Technology and People*, **2**, 187–204.

Lesser, V., and Corkhill, D. (1987) Distributed problem solving. In S. C. Shapiro and D. Eckroth (eds), *Encyclopedia of Artificial Intelligence*, Vol 1. New York. John Wiley, pp. 245–51.

Littler, C. R. (1986) *The Development of the Labour Process in Capitalist Societies. A Comparative Study of the Transformation of Work Organization in Britain, Japan and the USA (1982)*. London: Gower.

Mandeville, B. de (1724) *The Fable of the Bees*. Harmondsworth: Pelican, 1970.

March, J. G., and Simon, H. A. (1958) *Organizations*. New York: John Wiley.

Marx, K. (1857–8): *Grundrisse der Kritik der politischen Okonomie*, MEGA, Vol. II/1.1–1.2.

Marx, K. (1861–3). *Zur Kritik der politischen Ökonomie* (*Manuskript* 1861–63), MEGA, Vol. II/3.1–II/3.6.

Marx, K. (1867) *Das Kapital. Kritik der politischen Ökonomie*, Vol. 1; MEGA, Vol. II/5.

McCarthy, J. (1987) Generality in artificial intelligence. *Communications of the ACM*, **30**, No. 12, December, 1030–35.

Mendels, F. F. (1972) Proto-industrialization: The first phase of the industrialization process. *Journal of Economic History*, **32**, No. 1, March, 241–61.

Mickler, O. (1981) *Facharbeit im Wandel. Rationalisierung im industriellen Produktionsprozeß*. Frankfurt and New York.

Mickler, O. *et al.* (1976) *Technik, Arbeitsorganisation und Arbeit. Eine empirische Untersuchung in der automatischen Produktion*. Frankfurt am Main.

Mickler, O. *et al.* (1980) *Bedingungen und soziale Folgen des Einsatzes von Industrierobotern. Sozialwissenschaftliche Begleitforschung zum Projekt der Volkswagenwerk AG, Wolfsburg: 'Neue Handhabungssysteme als technische Hilfen für den Arbeitsprozess'*. Göttingen: Soziologisches Forschungsinstitut, and Universität Bremen.

Newell, A., and Simon, H. A. (1972) *Human Information Processing*. Englewood Cliffs, NJ: Prentice-Hall.

Newton, J. (1985) Technology and cooperative labour Among the Orokaiva. *Mankind*, **15**, No. 3, December, 214–22.

Orr, J. E. (1986) Narratives at work. Story telling as cooperative diagnostic activity. *Proceedings of the Conference on Computer Supported Cooperative Work*, Austin, Texas, 3-5 December pp. 62–72.

Ouchi, W. G. (1980) Markets, bureaucracies, and clans. *Administrative Science Quarterly*, **25**, March, 129–41.

Piaget, J. (1947) *La psychologie de l'intelligence*. Paris.

Popitz, H., Bahrdt, H. P., Jüres, E. A., and Kesting, H. (1957) *Technik und Industriearbeit. Soziologische Untersuchungen in der Hüttenindustrie*. Tübingen: J. C. B. Mohr.

Rasmussen, J. (1983) Skills, rules, and knowledge; signals, signs, and symbols, and other distinctions in human performance models. *IEEE Transactions on Systems, Man, and Cybernetics*. **SMC-13**, No. 3, May/June, 257–66.

Rasmussen, J. (1986) *Information Processing and Human-Machine Interaction. An Approach to Cognitive Engineering*. Amsterdam: North-Holland.

Rasmussen, J. (1987a) A cognitive engineering approach to the modelling of decision making and its organization in process control, emergency management, CAD/CAM, office systems, library systems. In W. B. Rouse (ed.), *Advances in Man-Machine Systems Research*, Vol 4. Greenwich, Conn: JAI Press.

Rasmussen, J. (1987b) Approaches to the control of the effects of human error on chemical plant safety. Invited paper for International Symposium on Preventing Major Chemical Accidents, American Institute of Chemical Engineers, February.

Rasmussen, J. (1988) Coping safely with complex systems. Invited paper for American Association for Advancement of Science, Annual Meeting, Boston, 11–15 February.

Schmidt, K. (1986) A dialectical approach to functional analysis of office work. *Proceedings of the IEEE International Conference on Systems, Man, and Cybernetics*, Atlanta, Georgia, 14–17 October, pp. 1586–1591.

Schmidt, K. (1987) *Kontorautomation—realitet eller reklame*? Copenhagen: Kommuninformation.

Simon, H. A. (1945) *Administrative Behavior. A Study of Decision-Making Process in Administrative Organization*, 2nd edn. New York, 1957.

Simon, H. A. (1957) *Model of Man*. New York: John Wiley.

Simon, H. A. (1969) *The Sciences of the Artificial*, 2nd edn. Cambridge, Mass: MIT Press, 1981.

Skousen, T. (1986) *Kontorautomatisering og medarbejderindflydelse. 3 succeshistorier fra erhvervsliv og offentlig sektor*. Copenhagen: Samfundslitteratur.

Smith, A. (1776) *The Wealth of Nations*. London; Dent, 1964–6, Vols 1–2.

Strauss, A. (1985) Work and the division of labor. *The Sociological Quarterly*, **26**, No. 1, 1–19.

Thompson, J. D. (1967) *Organizations in Action. Social science bases of administrative theory*. New York: McGraw-Hill.

Thompson, P. (1983) *The Nature of Work. An introduction to debates on the labour process*. London: Macmillan.

Ure, A. (1835) *The Philosophy of Manufactures: or, an Exposition of the Scientific, Moral, and Commercial Economy of the Factory System of Great Britain*. London.

Whitley, R. (1974) Cognitive and social institutionalization of scientific specialties and research areas. In R. Whitley (ed.), *Social Processes of Scientific Development*. London: Routledge and Kegan Paul, pp. 69–95.

Whitley, R. D. (1983) From the sociology of scientific communities to the study of scientists' negotiations and beyond. *Social Science Information*, **22**, Nos 4–5, 681–720.

Whitley, R. D. (1984) *The Intellectual and Social Organization of the Sciences*. Oxford: Clarendon Press.

Williamson, O. E. (1975) *Markets and Hierarchies: A transactional and antitrust analysis of the firm*. New York: Free Press.

Williamson, O. E. (1981) The economics of organization: the transaction cost approach. *American Journal of Sociology*, **87**, No. 3, November, 548–77.

Wolf, K. (1963) Stages in industrial organization. *Explorations in Entrepreneurial History*, 2nd Series, **1**, No 1, Fall, 125–44.

Wood, S. (ed.) (1982) *The Degradation of Work? Skill, deskilling and the labour process.* London: Hutchinson.
Wright Mills, C. (1951) *White Collar. The American Middle Classes.* New York: Oxford University Press.

5. Modelling Distributed Decision Making

Jens Rasmussen
Risø National Laboratory, Denmark

INTRODUCTION

Design of decision support systems for modern work environments can be based neither on normative, proceduralized descriptions of transactions nor on normative models of a formal organizational structure. Tasks will typically be discretionary, depending on improvization, judgement and problem solving. Design, therefore, should be focused on the creation of an envelope including system resources which allows users to perform according to their 'style' without violating resource constraints. In addition, means should be found for prediction of the actual organization as evolving from the requirements of work content and from the means of communication available to decision makers. A framework for systems analysis along these lines is given elsewhere (Rasmussen, 1986, 1988a).

In this chapter a comparison is in focus of the approaches to models of distributed decision making as they are presently found within cognitive science, control and system engineering, and management science. A pronounced convergence is found in the recent modelling efforts within these different professions. This convergence has probably been supported by the present interest in information system design and the consequent need for descriptive models derived from field studies of the behaviour of skilled people in 'real-life' systems in contrast to the traditional interest in normative models for training and instruction of novices. In addition, an increased interest in cognitive phenomena has replaced the more behavioristic point of view.

Topics such as *decision making*, *systems control* and *organization and management* have long been established academic research fields. In the following sections the aim is to demonstrate that these topics, when considered with reference to complex, integrated systems, tend to merge into a unified framework which can be covered by the term *distributed decision making* or the wider concept of *cooperative work*. In modern work environments, in which manual work has been taken over by mechanized and automated tools, the difference

Distributed Decision Making: Cognitive Models for Cooperative Work
Edited by J. Rasmussen, B. Brehmer and J. Leplat

between cooperative work and distributed decision making appears to be a reflection of the route taken into the area rather than of basic conceptual differences.

DISTRIBUTED DECISION MAKING: A COGNITIVE ENGINEERING APPROACH

The cognitive engineering approach to modelling distributed decision making is aiming at a model of human cognitive functioning in a complex cooperative work setting to serve as a basis for design of information and decision support systems. For modern work, advanced information technology is the origin of many fundamental and simultaneous changes. Increasing automation and replacement of humans in the physical work process by robots implies that new skills and competence is required by agents, that is, knowledge and skill in the physical work process will be replaced by skills in diagnosis, operations analysis and planning of contingency control. Computer integration of entire manufacturing systems will offer a high degree of flexibility of manufacturing systems, which are able to respond quickly and effectively to specific customer requirements. That is, design, production planning and production can no longer be a rather slow sequence of separate processes in different departments, but will be simultaneous, integrated activities of a task force oriented, high-tempo organization and, consequently, require *distributed decision making*. Such organizations will require decision support systems, centralization of databases and advanced communication systems which can only be designed from a reliable model of the needs of the individual agent in the *new* organization and, notably, in the actual work organization, not the one found in formal organization charts representing legal and economic responsibility. In such systems, the effects of one significant technological change have not stabilized before another change appears, and the many influences of the technological developments can no longer be considered to appear separate in an otherwise stable system. We are no longer faced with the application of new technological means for solving problems which are empirically identified in the present systems. Instead, a continuous flux of simultaneous changes is found from introduction of new tools which place established functions in completely new relationships, together with changes caused by dynamic markets and legal environments.

In most work environments, a large variety of opportunities and alternatives are found for the accomplishment of all functions of work. However, in stable work environments only a few alternatives are normally considered in normal performance. Many degrees of freedom are neglected due to the habits and practice of the individual actor or to company and branch standards, practices and traditions. It is a general finding that organizations do not explore adequately the degrees of freedom for restructuring business when advanced information technology is introduced. This follows naturally from the fact that explicit criteria of choice during normal operation are replaced by tradition and practices. New technology means new ways of doing things. If, however, the degrees of freedom offered by such new technology is not identified and formulated explicitly together with the necessary set of criteria of choice, there is a severe danger that the blindness from tradition and practice will prevent proper exploitation of the potential of improvement actually present.

In this situation there is a severe need for strategical planning tools, adequate for the design of new workplaces, including the work organization. This is stressed also by the fact that modern enterprises will be complex and have very individual characteristics. The organizations and manufacturing systems will be custom designed to a particular market and line of unique products to the same degree as the products will have to match the requirements of individual customers.

System design, consequently, cannot be based on analysis of the work procedures in the present system and its established structure and practices. In order to identify the actually existing degrees of freedom to change and to adopt new means in the system, an analysis is required in terms of company goals and constraints, the *potential relationships* among goals, functions and processes, the criteria available for allocation of roles to individual agents, and the coordination needed, i.e. the work organization and management structure. From here, a predictive model of the distributed decision-making structure needed to control the state of affairs in the intended, future system is needed.

The behaviour in work of individuals (and, consequently, also of organizations) is, by definition, oriented towards the requirements of the work environment as perceived by the individual. Work requirements, *what* should be done, will normally be perceived in terms of control of the state of affairs in the work environment according to a goal, i.e. *why* it should be done. *How* these changes are made to a certain degree is a matter of discretion of the agent.

The *alternative, acceptable work activities*, how to work, will be shaped by the work environment which defines the boundaries of the space of *possibilities*, i.e. acceptable work strategies. This space of possibilities will be further bounded by the resource profile of the particular agent in terms of tools available, knowledge (competence), information about state of affairs, and processing capacity. The presence of alternatives for action depends on a many-to-many mapping between means and ends present in the work situation as perceived by the individual. In general, several functions can serve the individual goals and each of the functions can be implemented by different tools and physical processes. If this were not the case, the work environment would be totally predetermined and there would be no need for human choice or decision.

The conclusion of this introduction is that a modelling framework which is useful for design of information systems for advanced socio-technical systems cannot be based on analysis of work in procedural terms. It should, instead, serve the identification of a resource envelope within which an agent can navigate also in unforeseen situations. The identification of such an envelope depends on separate representation of the work domain, the generic cognitive decision tasks, and the useful strategies for such decision tasks together with the subjective criteria of choice. In consequence, for design of decision support systems, the structure of complex socio-technical systems should be modelled from at least four different points of view:

(1) The content and structure of the basic *work domain*;
(2) The structure of the decision-making task, i.e. the *control function*, implemented to obtain concerted functions in this work domain;
(3) The level of cognitive control of the decision agents and their cognitive resource profile; and,
(4) The structure of the *work organization*, i.e. of the allocation of control functions to decision-making agents and the resulting *social organization*.

When, for instance, referring to 'hierarchical organization' it is necessary to make explicit whether the work domain, the control structure or the social organization is considered, since frequently there will be no simple mapping between the structures as seen from the different points of view. In the following sections the four aspects will be discussed in more detail to outline an approach to a model of distributed decision making which can serve as a specification and design of information and decision support systems.

Work domain

When decision making is considered a systems control problem it follows immediately that the architecture of the necessary decision-making function will depend on the nature and degree of internal coupling within the work domain to be controlled. To serve the design of decision support systems, the representation of a work domain must also be adequate for situations and tasks not known at the time of design and, therefore, it should be described in situation- and task-independent terms. The representation adapted in our framework of analysis depends on analysis along the means–ends and part–whole dimensions. Means–ends relations are important for analysis of the state of affairs, for setting priorities, and for planning in any work situation involving resource management and adaptation to changing conditions. Decisions, in general, are not based on primary data about the state of affairs and on consideration of the ultimate goal. Rather, goals have to be interpreted and made concrete in order to be operational and primary data must be integrated and generalized before they can be related to goals. For effective support of decision processes, therefore, information about the substance matter of a work domain should be accessible in the 'knowledge base' of the system at several levels of abstraction, representing goals and requirements, general functions, physical processes and activities, as well as material resources. The need for decisions is basically caused by the many-to-many mapping found among these levels. Any function in a work domain (what should be used) can be seen both as a goal (why it is relevant) for a function at a lower level, and as a means for a function at a higher level (how it is realized). It is a basic feature that any work content can be described in very different terms, related to different levels of abstraction and decomposition, and any element can be described in terms of 'what' it is, 'why' and 'when' it can be useful, and 'how' it can be implemented. An explicit formulation of the work space in these terms is necessary for support of any attempt to improvize and to find solution of new demands. In Ashby's (1962) terms, the representation of the work domain constitutes the space of *possibilities* from which the *actualities* are selected in a particular situation (see the discussion below).

The different levels of representation along the means–end dimension reflects the different categories of functions used to describe the work domain (see Table 1 and the example in Table 2), while the part–whole dimension reflects the decomposition applied at the various levels to identify the elements to consider for coordination by the control functions. For a discussion of the characteristics of different work domains, see Rasmussen (1986, 1988).

Control and decision tasks

The control requirements of a work domain which ultimately determine the decision and control task of the agents of the system depend on the internal functional structure, the system and the coupling among elements necessary for coordinated function. This coupling can be described with reference to the level in the means–end hierarchy at which the effects of the functioning of the individual parts of the system must be coordinated with respect to temporal synchronization. In highly structured causal systems such as, for instance, some industrial process plants, the functioning in time at the level of physical processes needs to be effectively coordinated, and so tight coupling between control decisions must be established at this level. The decision making at the lowest level must meet the requirements for data capacity and response times posed by system dynamics (and, consequently, will normally be automated in technical systems). In less-structured and more loosely coupled systems, such as, for instance, a production department, the effects of activities will have to be coordinated only at the level of general function, e.g. in terms of the outcome of 'production' not of the production process itself. Consequently, the decision task will be coordination between different separate physical processes and activities to meet production targets. This implies that coordination depends on less detailed status information and lower data rates, and has a longer time horizon. In other systems, coordination is only necessary at the abstract functional level, for instance, in economic terms. Finally, systems can be envisaged which only have couplings at the highest level of system goals and purposes, e.g. the group of companies of a trust (see Table 3).

Table 1: Description of a system depends on categories of concepts which constitute the elements of the relational networks of the representation. System properties can be categorized in several different ways depending on the conventions chosen for description and the language of representation available. The Table lists different levels of descriptions commonly applied for analysis of complex systems

Means–ends relations	Properties represented
Purposes and constraints	Properties necessary and sufficient to establish relations between the performance of the system and the reasons for its design, i.e. the purposes and constraints of its coupling to the environment. Categories are in terms referring to properties of environment
Abstract functions	Properties necessary and sufficient to establish priorities according to the intention behind design and operation: Topology of flow and accumulation of mass, energy, information, people, monetary value. Categories in abstract terms, referring neither to system nor environment
General functions	Properties necessary and sufficient to identify the 'functions' which are to be coordinated irrespective of their underlying physical processes. Categories according to recurrent, familiar input–output relationships
Physical processes and activities	Properties necessary and sufficient for use of equipment; to adjust operation to match specifications or limits; to predict response to control actions; to maintain and repair equipment. Categories according to underlying physical processes and equipment
Physical form and configuration	Properties necessary and sufficient for classification, identification and recognition of particular material objects and their configuration; for navigation in the system. Categories in terms of objects, their appearance and location

The structure of the control requirement in a given situation, i.e. the structure of the distributed decision-making task, depends very much on the actual operating condition. During control of disturbances and adjustment of the activities in a system to new circumstances, exploration of the available means–ends relationships as illustrated by Table 2 will be necessary for planning of the relevant control actions, and the structure of the control requirements will be closely related to that of the work domain (see Tables 4 and 5). It will be necessary explicitly to consider the various goals and constraints of the system as determined by the coupling to the environment, and the propagation of values and goals as well as constraints and side-effects down through the system is important for control of such situations.

Table 2: The problem space in which a decision maker has to navigate in supervisory process control has two principle dimensions. One is the means–ends dimension representing the level of abstraction in the decision process, i.e. the level of generality considered for selection of solution. The table illustrates the levels normally used for representation of technical systems. Another dimension of the problem space is the part–whole dimension representing the span of attention necessary for the particular problem, i.e. the part of the system considered. Normally, there is no simple mapping between the whole–part decomposition used at the different levels

Means–ends relations	Properties of the system selected for representation
Goals and purposes, constraints	Customer and market relations; competitors; production volume requirements; legal requirements for financial relations and environmental protection; work safety legislation; workers' union agreements
Priority measures; flow and accumulation topology of mass, energy, information, people and money	Topology of flow of products, energy, and various forms of material, (losses, contaminants, raw material, etc); sources and sinks of funds; flow through the system of monetary values; manpower turnover
General functions and activities	Production functions; such as cooling, heating, purification, material conversion, control functions, feedback loops, etc.
Physical processes in work and equipment	Physical processes and characteristics of equipment, machinery, tools, and components; capabilities and limitations; control characteristics; content of manuals and technical specifications; maintenance properties
Appearance, location, and configuration of material objects	Material characteristics, shape, size, weight, appearance, location; anatomy and configuration of equipment and installations; building layout; drawings; access roads and site topography

During normal situations, however, goals, values and constraints are only implicitly represented in the established practice and the rules of conduct which have evolved. In this case, the structure of the necessary distributed decision function will take the shape of a rather shallow 'management hierarchy'. In a process system, for instance, such a flat hierarchy can be based on control algorithms for which all control 'set-points' at the level of physical function are derived in advance from the higher-level goals. The co-ordinating decision making will be made by the designer, and the supervisory control task during normal operation will be to adjust the controller setpoints to pre-programmed values, i.e. the control decisions have been made in advance by the systems designer. Also in stable organizations, coordination of the basic physical

Table 3: The coordination of functions required by a control function for concerted system function depend very much upon the intrinsic coupling within the work domain. The lowest level at which coordination of the entire system is required depends upon the nature of the activities in the system

Means–ends relations	Intrinsic coupling within basic work domain
Goals and purposes, constraints	Coupling only on the level of goals and values without considering coordination within the system itself is found in some systems. Examples can be political campaigns, religious movements, etc.
Priority measures; flow and accumulation topology of mass, energy, information, people and money	Loose coupling depending only on abstract value measures such as economy without consideration of the underlying functionality or content is adequate for systems such as commercial outlet chains, industrial corporations, etc.
General functions and activities	In some systems, such as offices, manual production workshops, etc., physical processes need not be synchronized. Coupling is necessary only in terms of their longer-term effects i.e. coupling is only required in terms of general functions; depending on decoupling by storage facilities, queues, piles, etc.
Physical processes in work and equipment	Integrated technical systems such as industrial process plants need tight coordination at the physical process level. Physical variables must be closely controlled and coordinated for proper system function. Temporal synchronization is essential
Appearance, location, and configuration of material objects	Coupling at this level is essential for structural support systems, such as bridges, scaffolding, buildings, etc.

activities can be based on preplanned procedures and coordination taken care by a 'flat' bureaucratic decision layer (see Figure 1). In such cases, the different means–ends levels of the work domain need not be reflected in the structure of the control requirements faced by the controlling agent because many control decisions have been taken by the control system designer, based on his or her knowledge of this structure, and embedded implicitly in the physical implementation of the control strategy (see Figure 1). In contrast, the control requirements to be met during situations calling for more drastic system restructuring and changes of resource allocation will reflect more closely the structure of the work domain.

Consider the control requirements during start-up of a process system. Fo

Table 4: The means–ends space is useful for representation of the roles and tasks of decision makers. In bureaucratic organizations different people are normally assigned the tasks at different levels, whereas in process control, the operating staff in a control room during disturbances will have to take care of all levels, including high-level priority choice, e.g. production versus safety

Means–ends relations	Actors	Decision task
Goals and purposes, constraints	Chairman of board; president	Value analysis; goal setting; policy making
Priority measures; flow and accumulation topology of mass, energy, information, people and money	Vice presidents; department heads	Strategical planning; priority judgments
General functions and activities	Department heads; office and group leaders	Resource allocation and function coordination
Physical processes in work and equipment	Skilled staff; workers	Control and execute work procedures; control and monitor equipment operation
Appearance, location, and configuration of material objects	Skilled and unskilled staff	Find and identify work items; move things; plan navigation and transport

this, components have to be connected in a way which supports the required physical processes. When the individual physical processes are operating, their input–output relations have to be adjusted to enable the interconnection of several process systems, etc. In this case, the functional structure of the system will be reflected in the control structure, as shown in Table 5. The structure behind the decomposition of the system elements suitable for control is to be determined at each of the means–ends levels separately. The basic principle will be to identify aggregates which can be separated and controlled as a unit with a minimum of interaction and communication across their boundaries. (This problem is discussed in more detail in the section on allocation of roles to agents.)

The conclusion is that the structure of the control requirements which must be met by the distributed decision-making function depends dynamically on the actual state of affairs in the system, as well as on the control decisions which are already considered during system design and, consequently, embedded in the system (in the actual physical equipment, in normative work procedures, or in automatic control algorithms).

Table 5: This illustrates the control tasks at the different levels of the work domain in supervisory process control. During plant start-up and disturbance control, the operating staff in the control room will have to take care of decision making at all levels, depending upon the situation and the phase of a decision task. During normal operation the control task is focused on the adjustment of the automatic controllers at the lower levels (see Figure 1)

Means-ends relations	Typical control tasks in process control
Goals and purposes, constraints	Explore relevance of goals and targets with respect to environmental conditions; define constraints and penalties of violation; define control variables for coordination at the functional level
Priority measures; flow and accumulation topology of mass, energy, information, people and money	Derive operational specifications and measures necessary to coordinate functions and activities to match system purposes and constraints; resolve conflicts; coordinate experiments to optimize, maximize or minimize performance in case of conflicts or unresolved degrees of freedom
General functions and activities	Adjust input required by and output rendered by general functions for overall coordination according to priorities defined by higher-level criteria; select processes and activities to serve the functions required according to priorities
Physical processes in work and equipment	Adjust process parameters in order to align operational states of components, equipment and systems to match requirements and limitations; adjust process variables to production targets and align process variables as required for system start-up or for contribution to and/or conditioning of higher-level functions
Appearance, location, and configuration of material objects	Move parts and equipment to proper locations; replace and connect components; change anatomy and configuration of equipment and installations to match requirements of physical processes and activities

Cognitive control and resources

This level of analysis is aimed at an identification of the cognitive control structure an agent can apply to the task, depending on background and expertise. The resources available to an agent depend very much on the cognitive control structure in action, and an analysis in this domain can serve as a basis for allocation of decision roles to individual agents. When we distinguish categories of human behavior according to basically different ways of representing the properties of a deterministic environment as a basis for control of actions, three typical levels of performance emerge: skill-, rule- and knowledge-

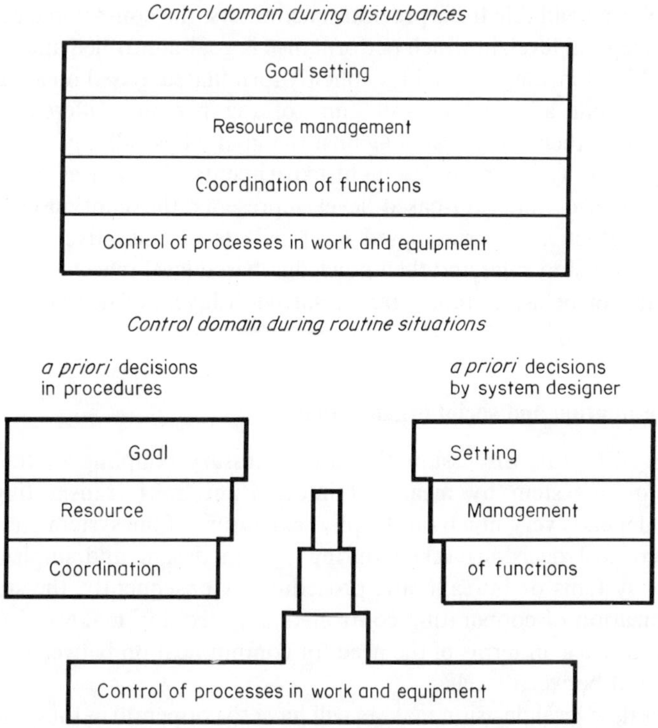

Figure 1. During unusual situations calling for improvisation and design of new work procedures, the domain to consider for decision making can reflect the entire structure of the work domain. This is not the case during normal, routine situations in which higher-level goals and constraints are embedded in the established practice and the adopted rules of conduct and standard work procedures

based performance. This distinction has been discussed in detail elsewhere (Rasmussen, 1983), and here only a brief recapitulation will be given for comparison with concepts mentioned in the following sections.

Skill-based behavior represents sensori-motor performance during acts or activities that, after a statement of an intention, take place without conscious control as smooth, automated, and highly integrated patterns of behavior. The person is not consciously choosing among alternative action courses. At the next level of *rule-based* behavior the composition of a sequence of subroutines in a familiar work situation is typically consciously controlled by empirical cue–action correlation. The person is aware that alternative actions are possible and has to make a *choice*. For this choice, no more information will normally be considered than is necessary to choose between the perceived alternatives of action. The context will make it unnecessary to consult detailed information or higher-level goals. During unfamiliar situations for which no knowhow or rules for control are available from previous encounters, the control must move to a higher conceptual level, in which performance is goal-controlled and *knowledge-based*. In this situation, the goal is explicitly formulated, based on an analysis of the environment and the overall aims of the person. Different plans are considered and their effect tested against the goal, physically by trial and error or conceptually by means of 'thought experiments'. Viewed as a hierarchical control structure, the skill-based level represents the continuous real-time control of activities, the rule-based level reflects the adaptive choice among preplanned decision rules and the knowledge-based level reflects intelligent self-organization of behavior (compare Mesarovic's layers of decision complexity below).

Work coordination and social organization

It follows from this discussion that the necessary coupling of the different elements of a system by means of information links transmitting control decisions depends very much on the physical nature of the system and upon the *a priori* control decisions taken during system design and implemented in automatic systems or bureaucratic procedures. Consequently, the structure of the organization of cooperating controllers and decision makers also depends on this nature, e.g. in terms of the need for communication between elements at one level and between levels.

In general, several decision makers will have to cooperate in the control of the system represented by the problem space, and decision making at a level above the primary decision makers can be necessary for coordination of decision making in order to assign decision functions and workload, depending on the changing conditions and requirements of the system (see Figure 2). This meta-level is necessary execept in stable systems, in which control decisions can be entirely and deterministically data driven and allocated to fixed roles (in which case, they hardly can be characterized as decision makers but instead are merely 'automatic' controllers). Here they have no degrees of freedom and coupling among them is entirely dependent upon fixed rules and communication through the work content or primary system function (cf. Figure 1).

Normally, however, the control requirements have to be decomposed into sets of tasks which can be handled by individual, cooperating agents. In other words, the large number of elementary control tasks are aggregated into task repertoires suited for allocation to the individual agents.

Different principles of allocation will result in different architectures of coordination. Since control requirements are defined with reference to particular work scenarios and situations, this architecture can change dynamically through time. Within the architecture several (sometimes conflicting) criteria will be determining the decomposition suitable to define the role of individual agents.

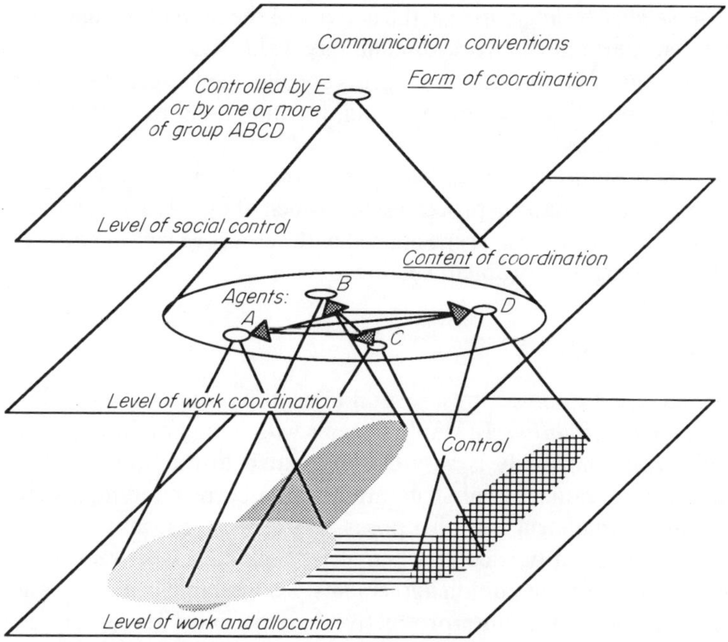

Figure 2. This illustrates four agents or decision makers each allocated particular but overlapping 'activity windows' giving access to a part of the overall work domain. The concerted action within this (normally rather loosely coupled) work domain requires inter-agent coordination and communication. The structure of the communication net and content of the communication and, therefore, the actual work organization is determined by the control requirements of the work domain. The social organization, in contrast, is determined by the conventions chosen for the form of the communication, which depends on the 'management school' or 'culture'. This, in turn, determines whether the decision making at the level of social control involves another agent E or one particular agent of the group ABCD in a hierarchical organization, or them all, in a democratic coordination process

Role-allocation principles

The allocation of roles to individual members of a work team can be made in different ways, resulting in different architectures of the work organization:

(1) *Individual work*: An individual agent can be assigned to cope with the entire problem space of a particular work scenario, irrespective of the decision functions and information processes the work implies.
(2) *Collective work*: In collective work a group of people acts together, pooling their resources and knowledge.
(3) *Cooperative work*: In an organization of cooperating agents control tasks can be allocated according to different principles.

(4) *Domain-related architecture*, i.e. the activity of the individual agent is related to different parts of the work domain (see Table 4).
(5) *Function-related architecture*, i.e. agents are allocated selected functions such as analysis and diagnosis, goal setting, planning, and execution, for which they are specialized.
(6) *Process-related architecture*, i.e. agents are allocated only a particular selection of information processes for which they have specialized tools. Agents can, for instance, be specialized with respect to routine operations or troubleshooting and problem solving.

Role-allocation criteria

Within the different architectures, several allocation criteria are possible:
(1) *Organizational tradition*: In stable systems with a long prehistory the formal role allocation normally is very closely related to the adopted, frequently hierarchical, organizational structure and the corresponding social status. Often this formal structure also poses very strict constraints on the actual work allocation, in particular when strict boundaries between professions are established through union agreements. Such established work-allocation criteria can be very counterproductive in a period with rapidly changing technology and, consequently, changing control requirements from the work domain. (See, for instance Drucker, 1988; Savage, 1987.)

For a discussion of the requirements, when changes in system environment, and in technological basis has to be considered, some more functional criteria are relevant.
(2) *Functional decoupling* can serve to minimize the necessary exchange of information among agents. The basic principle will be to identify aggregates which can be separated and controlled as a unit with a minimum of interaction and communication across their boundaries. Within control engineering, special tools are available for system decomposition, generally based on matrix manipulation of a connectivity matrix (state-space representation; see, for instance, Himmelblau, 1973). This technique can be used also to define teams of tightly coupled agents to be organized in groups which are mutually more loosely coupled (see Figure 2).
(3) *Load-sharing*: Frequently, the partitioning of the control structure in several levels along the means–ends dimension of the work domain will be determined from controller capacity considerations. Control at the physical process level needs real-time, synchronous information processing, which requires large data-processing and communication capacity but frequently rather simple processing and decision rules. At higher levels, decision problems become more complex and response times will be slower.
(4) *Agent competency* required for different decision tasks often determines role allocation. In this case the allocation does not follow the levels of the

means–ends hierarchy. This, however, can be the case if different acquired skills and decision strategies are the basis for role allocation, as, for instance, in an office management organization, for which the tools and strategies at the various levels are very different (see Table 4).

(5) *Allocation for problem solving*: The information needed to plan and control an activity depends very much on the role allocation, and the difficulty of a decision task depends on the width of the information window. If the window is too narrow and limited to one level of the means–ends hierarchy, improvisation and problem solving will be difficult. The effectiveness and ease with which practical reasoning can serve problem solving depend very much on the opportunity to draw on analogies, to judge whether solutions are reasonable, and to interpret ambiguous messages from other actors from a perception of their motives and opportunities which, in turn, depend entirely on the access to information from several levels of the means–ends hierarchy (see Rasmussen, 1985). This alone is an argument against the effectiveness of step-hierarchical role allocation in a system which has to survive in a changing environment and to adapt to rapid internal technological change (Drucker, 1988).

Several criteria for role allocation are possible, and in any organization the actual, informal role allocation will reflect the immediate attempt to match requirements with resources. Shifts in role allocation can be expected to play the same role in demand/resource matching of a group as do the alterations in cognitive strategies for the individual. This, in turn, implies that the *architecture of actual distribution of roles will be very dynamic.*

Social organization

In the present context it is important to develop a framework for the discussion of the organizational and management aspects which, on the one hand, is compatible with the cognitive, information-processing point of view and, consequently, can be used to support system design and, on the other, maps well onto the frameworks available from social and organizational sciences. The following discussion is intended for this purpose.

The typical work domain will be rather loosely coupled, that is, only in special cases (for example, assembly line work) will the work domain be able to pace the agents directly in a coordinated way. In most cases, communication among agents is necessary for coordination. In the present context, *organization* does not refer to stable groups of people as seen in organizational charts but to the relational structure necessary to coordinate the work activities of several individuals. In contrast to the *formal organization* which reflects the allocation of economic and legal responsibility to groups and individuals, the *actual organization* of work and social relations shows very dynamic relationships.

The discussion by Ashby (1962) of the nature of organization and self-organization is very relevant in this context. According to Ashby, the core of the concept of organization is that of 'conditionality'. 'As soon as the relation between two entities A and B becomes conditional on C's value or state then a necessary component of "organization" is present. *Thus the theory of organization is partly co-extensive with the theory of functions of more than one variable*' (Ashby's emphasis). He goes on: 'The converse of "conditional on" is "not conditional on", so the converse of "organization" must therefore be, as the mathematical theory shows as clearly, the concept of "reducibility". (It is also called separability).' This definition of organization is very compatible with the definition underlying the use of communication analysis used in the previous section for the identification of the actual work organization. Ashby continues:

> The treatment of 'conditionality'... makes us realize that the essential idea is that there is first a product space—that of *possibilities*—within which some subset of points indicates the actualities. This way of looking at 'conditionality' makes us realize that it is related to that of 'communication', and it is, of course, quite plausible that we should define parts as being 'organized' when 'communication (in some general sense) occurs between them,'... Thus the presence of 'organization' between variables is equivalent to the existence of a *constraint* in the product-space of possibilities. I stress this point because while, in the past, biologists have tended to think of the organization as something extra, something *added* to the elementary variables, the modern theory, based on the logic of communication, regards organization as a restriction, a constraint.

Another point, raised by Ashby, is that of good and bad organization. His conclusion, which supports the definition of the dynamic work organization in the previous section, is the following: '*There is no such thing as a good organization in any absolute sense.* Always it is relative; and an organization that is good in one context or under one criterion may be bad under another.' In conclusion, if the organization is allowed to adapt to the requirements of a changing environment, a very flexible and variate work organization will evolve.

Following this point of view, we will have to consider organizational aspects at two different levels of analysis. The *work organization* will be determined by the control requirements of the work domain and by the task-allocation architecture, and the necessary coordination of the cooperating agents will specify the *content* of communication. On the other hand, the architecture of the *social organization* will depend very much on the *form* of the communication, i.e. on the conventions and constraints chosen for this communication (see Figure 2).

In other words, a particular task allocation and, consequently, work organization will evolve for each situation guided by the competence of the actors and the 'technology' of the work domain and will determine the content of inter-agent communication. The social interaction among the agents, on the other hand, depends on the form of the communication which, in turn, depends on the coordination strategy adopted. The work organization is determined by the work domain and the role allocation, while the social organization is evolving from the coordinating control requirements and the strategy adopted for this purpose.

Independent of the task and role-allocation principle adopted and the characteristics of the work domain, different structures of the social organization are possible for coordination of activities:

(1) *Autocratic coordination*: One decision maker is responsible for the coordination of the activities of all other agents.
(2) *Hierarchic coordination*: Coordination is distributed in the organization which is stratified such that one level of decision makers evaluates and plans the activities at the next lower level.
(3) *Heterarchic planning*: In bureaucratic organizations, however, the stratification is less pronounced, and decision makers frequently invade the domain of subordinates and superiors for advice and monitoring.
(4) *Anarchistic planning*: Each agent plans his or her own activity without interaction with other decision makers on the meta-level. Communication is entirely through the work content.
(5) *Democratic planning*: Coordination involves interaction and negotiation among all decision makers of the organization (worker participation committees).
(6) *Diplomatic planning*: The individual decision makers negotiate only with the neighbors' involved and the information traffic is locally planned.

It will be evident that these different architectures will imply, or evolve from, different forms of communication among agents, i.e. whether information is passed as neutral information, advice, instructions or orders. The effective way of influencing the social organization independent of the work organization will be through constraints and conventions for communication.

CONTROL: A SYSTEM-THEORETIC APPROACH

The structure of distributed decision making in action in control of cooperative work discussed in the previous section can be conceived as a hierarchical, distributed and self-organizing control system. It is, therefore, of interest to compare the concepts involved in the cognitive approach to those of control theory. The role of multilevel representation and hierarchical organization of complex control systems have been discussed by Mesarovic and his group from Case Western Reserve University in a number of papers and books through the late 1960s and early 1970s (see Mesarovic, 1970a,b). In this theoretical framework special emphasis is on the formulation of the hierarchical concepts from a variety of approaches 'which are termed hierarchical with more or less justification'. Later, this interest in basic structural system problems seems to have decayed considerably in the control-theoretic literature.

The essential characteristics of hierarchies are taken to be: vertical decomposition, priority of action or right of intervention and (vertical) performance dependence. These distinctions are closely related to the classical notion of a command hierarchy:

> Any hierarchy involves a vertical arrangement of subsystems.... The operation at any level is influenced directly and explicitly from the higher levels. ... The influence is binding for the lower levels, reflecting a priority in importance of actions and goals of the higher levels...

Different notions of hierarchies of importance for process control are discussed which are similar in nature to the distinctions described in the previous sections. Distinctions are made between (1) levels of description or abstraction, (2) levels of decision complexity and (3) organizational levels. In order to keep the different hierarchical descriptions separate, Mesarovic introduces different terms for the levels: strata, layers and echelons, respectively. This terminology is not, however, maintained consistently by the various authors in the field.

Levels of description: strata

According to Mesarovic (1970), 'an effective method to describe a complex system is in terms of a hierarchy of models referred to as a stratified description of the system. Each stratum refers to a different aspect of system operation and for a complete description one has to consider the totality of all strata.' This stratification has many aspects in common with the means–ends level discussed in the previous section. One major difference is, however, that Mesarovic does not define explicitly the dimension along which 'abstraction' takes place and in the examples given, abstraction in terms of part–whole relations and in terms of the language chosen for description are not kept separate:

> Several features of a stratified description are particularly important in the process control area; they are: 1. For each strata there usually exists a different set of rules, principles, and laws in terms of which the system operation is described; this contributes to reducing the coupling between strata. 2. On the lower strata the description is more detailed than on the higher strata.

In general, there is an emphasis on the part–whole abstraction: 'On any strata one concentrates on the functioning of a subsystem while the effects of interactions between subsystems are considered on the higher strata.' This point of view reflects the requirements during control system design for a representation structured according to the basic physical functioning. Note that in the cognitive framework proposed in the previous section, the part–whole decomposition is considered to be orthogonal to the abstraction (means–ends) dimension.

Levels of decision complexity: layers

For advanced control systems, particularly computer-based ones, the objective is to

> Maximize profit by taking into account both economic and technological factors and in reference to both short term and long term effects in a changeable environment. ... In practice, there is no solution method which will accomplish such a global objective because of both complexity and lack of knowledge and information. A method of approaching such a solution, however, can be designed based on constructing a hierarchy of subgoals defined in practical operational terms and which then will enable synthesis of the corresponding decision-making units arranged in a hierarchical fashion and charged with pursuing the respective subgoals. ... In other words, the solution of the overall problem results from the solution of the hierarchically arranged subproblems which are simpler and for which solution methods and algorithms already exists.

The levels in this type of hierarchy are called layers.

As being of special interest to process control are mentioned the 'three fundamental aspects of the general control (decision) problem under conditions of true uncertainties', and the corresponding three layers of control: the lowest layer, the selection layer determining the control to be actually applied to the physical process and which can actually be divided into two layers, the regulator layer (including feedback control) and the optimizing layer. The next layer is adaptation and learning (including statistical and logical techniques), and the highest layer is self-organizing control (e.g. based on heuristics). Note that these three levels are similar in nature to the skill-, rule- and knowledge-based levels of cognitive control mentioned above.

Levels of the organizational hierarchy: echelons

'For a variety of practical and conceptual reasons... a vertical decomposition is accompanied by a horizontal decomposition' forming an organizational hierarchy. On each level a decision unit (controller) is concerned with a larger portion of the system and its primary task is to coordinate the actions of the subordinate units. The difference between this organization in echelons and that in decision layers is not defined explicitly. Organization in echelons, however, appears to be related to decomposition of a complex task for allocation to a number of similar functional units, whereas the layered decision structure is related to basically different decision functions.

Relationships between the different notions

In practice, a multilevel system may be described in reference to all three notions. For example, in a system with organizational hierarchy the tasks of the decision units on different levels can be specified in terms of a stratified description of the system or in reference to decision layers of the overall problem (see Figure 3). Another example (Figure 4) illustrates how the layered organization of control functions can be found embedded in an organizational echelon. Furthermore, any decision unit in an organizational hierarchy can use a stratified description for the model of the system under its control. In other words, each of the notions are related to a particular aspect of control system design. The different notions are not conceptually related in a consistent framework, and their use for a theoretical discussion of the properties of different types of complex systems and their organization is not feasible. This is

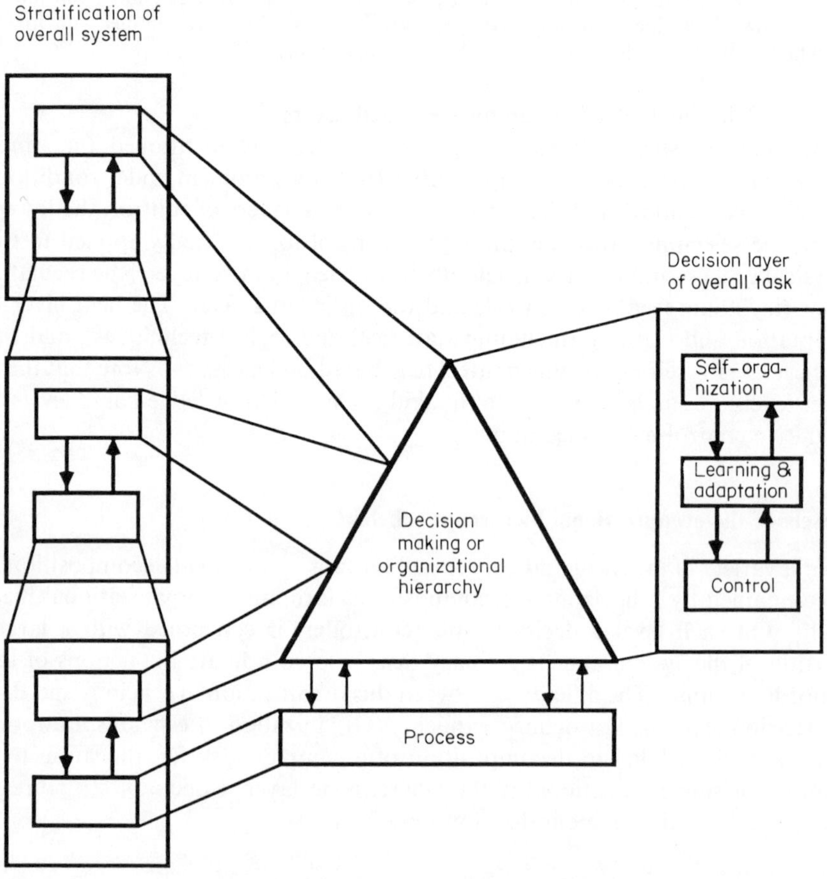

Figure 3. In a system with an organizational hierarchy, the tasks of the decision units on different levels can be specified in terms of a stratified description of the system as well as with reference to decision layers of the overall problem (reproduced from Mesarovic, 1970a, by permission of Academic Press)

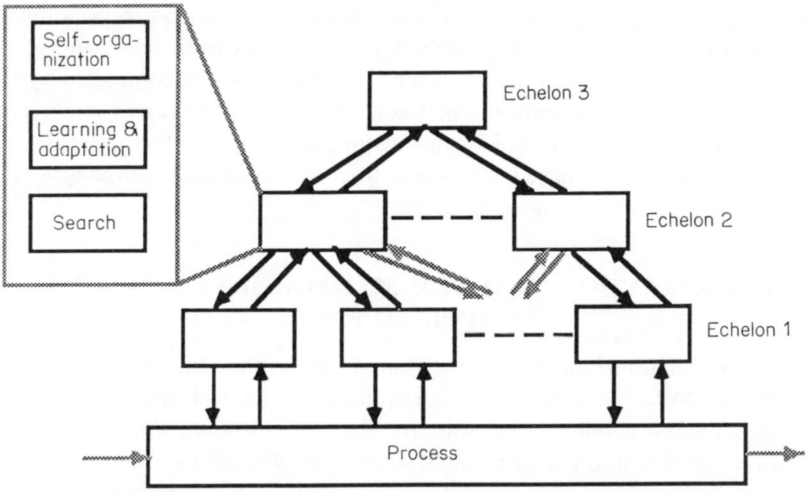

Figure 4. This illustrates how the layered organization of control functions can be found embedded in an organizational echelon. Furthermore, any decision unit in an organizational hierarchy can use a stratified description for the model of the system under its control (reproduced from Mesarovic, 1970a, by permission of Academic Press)

probably the reason why the theoretical analysis proposed by Mesarovic is focused only on mathematical algorithms for coordination of a number of similar units in organizational echelons (e.g. for control of electric power dispatch in a pool consisting of a number of similar power plants).

Coordination strategies

In control theory, distinction is frequently made between several different strategies for coordination of hierarchical systems, depending on the decomposition approach (Schoeffler, 1969). Coordination can be obtained through:

(1) Manipulation of *goals* of lower levels or parameters of these goals;
(2) Manipulation of *constraints* of lower levels, i.e. restriction of the domain of their control actions;
(3) Manipulation of *interaction variables* between units from estimation or prediction; or
(4) Manipulations of the *information* available to the units at lower levels.

It appears to be possible to apply similar distinctions for a formalization of the coordination of the social organization of decision makers and, thereby, to develop simplified models suited for experiments with the structure of distributed decision making. The experimental hypothesis being that the evolution of the various role allocations illustrated in Figure 2 can be controlled by constraints on the communication between decision makers corresponding to the different coordination strategies. Such experiments can include laboratory tasks in which the interaction between several subjects can be controlled by the conventions for communications between their work stations, as well as simulation experiments in which the strategies used by the subjects are implemented in models based on object-oriented simulation languages (e.g. Smalltalk).

ORGANIZATION AND THE MANAGEMENT SCIENCE APPROACH

The two approaches to modelling distributed decision making discussed so far as a central topic considered the organization of 'decision makers' and 'controllers', and it will be illuminating to relate them to the theories developed within management and organizational science. In general, two lines of reasoning seem to underly most of the literature. Gouldner (1959) distinguished clearly between two fundamental models, the 'rational' and the 'natural system' models, which Thompson (1967) later related to 'closed-system' and 'open-system' strategies of analysis. Much of the literature about organizations has, however, been focused on a search for improved efficiency and performance and, consequently, it is based on closed-system assumptions (employing the rational model) about organizations.

Closed-system models

Thompson (1967) discusses the three major closed-system strategies of analysis:

(1) Scientific Management (Taylor, 1911), which is focused primarily on manufacturing and similar production activities, and which employs economic efficiency as ultimate criterion and seeks to maximize efficiency by rational planning procedures. Conceptual closure is obtained by assuming that goals are known, tasks are repetitive, output of the production processes will 'somehow disappear' and resources are available in uniform qualities.
(2) Administrative Management (Gulick and Urwick, 1937), which is focused on structural relationships among production, personnel, supply, and other service units of the organization. Administrative management achieves closure by assuming that ultimately a master plan is known, against which specialization, departmentalization and control are determined.
(3) Bureaucracy (Weber, 1947), follows similar patterns, focusing on staffing and structure as a means of handling clients and disposing of cases. Efficiency is maximized by defining offices according to jurisdiction and place in a hierarchy, by appointing experts to offices, establishing rules for

categories of activities and clients and by motivating proper performance of expert officials by providing salaries and patterns of career advancement. Closure of the bureaucratic concept is obtained: the possible influence of policy makers above the bureaucracy is 'set aside'; the complexity of human components is controlled by divorcing private life and office roles by means of rules, salary and career, effects of outsiders, 'clientele', are nullified by depersonalization and categorization.

Open-system models

Thompson illustrates two examples of open-system strategies of analysis: the informal organization view, with attention focused on sentiments, cliques and social control by informal norms seen as patterned, adaptive responses in problematic situations (Roethlisberger and Dickson, 1939), and the interaction view, in which organizations are not autonomous entities but interacting intimately with other organizations and the public. Even the best-laid plans of managers have unintended consequences and are conditioned or upset by other social units (Barnard, 1938; Selznick, 1949; Clark, 1956).

In reality, this dichotomy is artificial. Both points of view are necessary together, and an elaboration of Barnard's work by Simon, Cyert and March (Simon 1957a, March and Simon, 1958, Cyert and March, 1963) have produced a newer tradition which evades the dilemma. To cope with complexity, organizations must develop processes for searching and learning as well as for deciding; decisions are satisficing rather than maximizing, and are based on 'bounded rationality' (Simon, 1957b). In his book, Thompson 'seeks to extend this newer tradition', but asks why so many people maintain the older, more extreme strategies of analysis, and he therefore tries to combine rather than compromise.

Thompson's approach

The basis of Thompson's approach is Parson's (1960) suggestion that organizations exhibit three distinct levels of responsibility and control: technical, managerial and institutional. This distinction is very similar to the stratification in terms of means–ends relations proposed in the previous sections. Thompson argues that every formal organization has suborganizations whose 'problems' are focused around effective performance of the technical functions—teachers conduct classes, the bureau processes income tax and handles recalcitrants, workshops process material and supervise operations. The managerial level services the technical suborganizations. It mediates between them and their customers, pupils, etc., and procures the resources and supplies. The managerial level controls (i.e. administers) the technical level. Finally, the institutional level is the source of the 'meaning' of the entire enterprise. It supplies the higher-level support to make the organization's goals possible. Parson's reasoning leads to the expectation that different technical functions or technologies cause significant differences among organizations and, consequently, Thompson stresses the need to include the control of the physical work domain in the organizational model: 'The technical parts of the system provide a major orientation for the social structure. There are both instrumental and economic reasons but the instrumental question is prior to that of efficiency.'

Technical rationality can be evaluated by two criteria: instrumental and economic. Instrumental is concerned whether an action does in fact result in the desired output, the economic whether the most beneficial way is in fact chosen. The present literature on organizations gives considerable attention to the economic criteria, 'but hides the importance of the instrumental question, which in fact takes priority. Complex organizations are built to operate technologies which are impossible or impractical for individuals to operate. The instrumentally perfect technology would produce the desired outcome inevitably. Less perfect technologies need organizations.' (Compare the discussion of intrinsic coupling in Table 3.)

Corresponding to the way in which the means–ends levels in Tables 1 and 2 represent qualitatively different system properties, Parson stresses the qualitative break in the simple continuity of 'line' authority because the functions at each level are qualitatively different:

> Those on the lower levels are not simply lower-order spellings-out of the higher level functions. The articulation of levels and of functions rest on a two-way interaction with each side, withholding its important contribution, in a position to interfere with the function of the other and of the larger organization.

The idea of Thompson's approach is to combine all this. It will be advantageous for an organization subject to the criteria of rationality to remove uncertainty from its technical core. Hence, if both resource-acquisition and output-disposal problems (which are in part controlled by environmental elements) can be removed from the technical core, the logic can be brought closer to closure. Uncertainty would appear to be greatest at the institutional level. At this level, the closed system of logic is inappropriate.

Since technology is an important variable in understanding the actions of complex organizations a typology of work domains is necessary. Thompson applies only a rather crude distinction:

(1) 'Long-linked technology' covers sequentially dependent acts, e.g. assembly line technology for standard products, based on repetitive processes. This is the domain of scientific management.

(2) 'Mediating technology' serving a population of clients; insurance companies, banks, etc., requiring operating in standardized ways, i.e. bureaucratic techniques of categorization and impersonal application of rules.

(3) 'Intensive technology', in which a variety of techniques are brought into action on some specific object—hospital, construction industry, military combat teams, etc. (A more differentiated typology of work domains is being developed from the framework for analysis of cognitive work described in Rasmussen, 1986, 1989.)

Technical rationality is an abstraction only perfect in closed systems. The closure varies in the three categories and is most perfect in the first. Under the norms of rationality, organizations seek to seal off their core technologies from environmental influences. This is done by different means: buffering with input and output components, by smoothing transactions, by forecasting and planning, and, when none of these works, by rationing. (Note: these are all control-theoretic measures.)

Relationships with control theory and cognitive science

The approach to organizational and management models represented by Thompson is compatible with the framework discussed in the two previous sections. In order to characterize the adaptive behaviour of an organization Thompson finds the most important characteristics of task environments along dimensions in terms of degree of homogeneity and stability. During adaptation, homogeneity influences organization structure in the following way:

> Under norms of rationality,
> —organizations facing heterogeneous task environments seek to identify homogeneous segments and to establish structural units to deal with each.
> —boundary-spanning components facing homogeneous segments are further sub-divided to match surveillance capacity with environmental action.

In the discussion of the influence of environmental stability on the adaptation of an organization to the environment, distinctions are made which have many parallels to the previously mentioned distinction between skill-, rule- and knowledge-based control of individual behaviour and Mesarovic's levels of decision complexity (see Table 6):

> —The organization component facing a stable task environment will rely on rules to achieve its adaptation to that environment.
> —When the range of variation presented by the task environment segment is known, the organization component will treat this as a constraint and adapt by standardizing sets of rules. (This is an empirical categorization routine typically used by bureaucratic organizations: bureaucratic procedures are based on categorizing events and selecting appropriate responses.)

Table 6: Two distinctions in the characteristics of the task environment are important for the adoption of coping strategies by an organization, i.e. whether the task environment is stable or shifting, and whether it is homo- or heterogeneous. (Adopted from Thompson, 1967)

Environment	Stable	Shifting
Homogeneous	Simple structure, few functional divisions. Departments are rule-applying agencies, Administration rule-enforcing	Rules inadequate, subdivisions only to extent required for capacity. Administration decentralized
Heterogeneous	Variety of functional divisions, each relying primarily on rules	Rules inadequate, functional differentiation and decentralization

—When the range of task-environment variations is large or unpredictable, the responsible organization component must achieve the necessary adaptation by monitoring that environment and planning responses, and this calls for localized units.

The close relationship with the evolution of work organization discussed earlier is clear when Thompson describes how the actual, informal organization evolves as a joint result of the attempt to cope with a task environment:

> The basis for grass-root groups, and for successive combinations of groups into clusters, clusters into larger clusters, etc., eventually result in an overall structural pattern for the complex organization.... To a large extent they [the organizational varieties] can be accounted for as attempts to solve the problems of concerted action under different conditions, especially conditions of technological and environmental constraints and contingencies (p. 74).

As an example of the evolution of an organization, Thompson mentions the synthetic organization emerging for emergency management after a major accident:

> In a surprisingly short time and with little of the random, aimless behaviour sometimes attributed to disasters, resources designed for other purposes are disengaged from their normal employment and adapted to disaster-recovery activities.... Initial efforts at disaster recovery occur whenever resources and an obvious need or use for them occur simultaneously.... In a relatively short time, usually, two things happen... and bring about a synthetic organization: (1)

> uncommitted resources arrive... and (2) information regarding need for additional resources begins to circulate. When knowledge of needs and resources coincide at a point in space, the headquarters of the synthetic organization has been established. Such headquarters only occasionally emerge around previously designated officers, indicating that their power rests not on authority in any formal sense but on scarce capacity to coordinate.... Authority to coordinate is attributed to the individual or group which by happenstance is at the crossroads of the two kinds of necessary information, resources available and need.... What it does have, compared with normal organizations, is (1) consensus among participants about the state of affairs to be achieved and (2) great freedom to acquire and deploy resources, since the normal institutions of authority, property and contract are not operating (p. 52).

This example of an organization evolving by a process controlled by (1) the information available to decision makers and (2) the part of the work domain under their control illustrates the approach suggested for an evolutionary simulation model described in the section below.

Thompson's presentation of principles and heuristics representing the mechanisms behind the self-organization evolution of an organization appears to be a useful source of rules and criteria for the development of a simulation model, which will not only be able to simulate organizational behaviour in terms of production-rules based scenario models but also generate new scenarios by adaptive search to meet higher-level performance criteria, derived from Thompson's principles.

Two examples will illustrate the close relationship between Thompson's formulations and control considerations. System interdependence is discussed in terms of:

(1) *Pooled interdependence*: Each part is not dependent on others in any direct way, but they support the same whole and are dependent on the same whole;
(2) *Sequential interdependence*: output of one part is the input of another;
(3) *Reciprocal interdependence*: mutual coupling (e.g. operations and maintenance of an airline).

All organizations have pooled interdependence; more complicated organizations have sequential as well, and the most complex also have reciprocal. Different types of interdependence require different devices for coordination:

(1) *Standardization*: This involves the establishment of routines or rules which constrain the action of each unit or position into paths consistent with those taken by others in the interdependent relationship (corresponds to control decoupling). Typical for pooled interdependence;

(2) *Coordination by plan*: This involves the establishment of schedules governing the actions of the interdependent units. Better suited for a dynamic environment (that is, standardization). Typical for sequential interdependence;
(3) *Coordination by mutual adjustment*: This involves the transmission of new information during the course of action. The more variable and unpredictable the situation, the greater the reliance on mutual adjustment. Typical for reciprocal interdependence.

In turn, these lead to organizations employing:

(1) Standardization, relying on liaison groups to link groups with a rule-making agency (p. 61) (staff positions);
(2) Sequential interdependence not contained by departmentalization relying on committees;
(3) Reciprocal interdependence not contained by departmentalization relying on task forces and project groupings.

Self-designing organizations

Self-organizing features of organizations similar in nature to Thompson's synthetic organizations have been studied by Rochlin *et al.* (1987) on board aircraft carriers. This organization was chosen because of the very high reliability in performance records. Analysis is based on very careful field studies, with the team participating in lengthy missions. In conclusion, the high reliability is explained by a high degree of learning and self-organization which is facilitated by the rapid turn-over of staff in the navy in contrast to prior expectations.

In spite of the formal, hierarchical organization task

> decomposition rules are often *ad hoc* and circumstantial: some tasks are organized by technical function (Navigation, Weapons), some by unit (Squadron), some by activity (Combat, Strike). Men may belong to and be evaluated by one unit (e.g. one of the squadrons), yet be assigned to another (e.g. aircraft maintenance). In order to keep this network alive and coordinated, it must be kept connected and integrated horizontally (e.g. across squadrons), vertically (from maintenance and fuel up through operations), and across command structures (Battle Group–Ship–Airwing).

Note that the work domain representation proposed in the previous section is well suited to map these complex relationships. This organizational structure is probably very similar to the one we have found in general hospitals, where a task force-like organization is oriented towards treatment of patients, while a departmentalized organization takes care of the resource management (cf. also Thompson, 1967, p.80). The modern hospital includes specialized groups for housekeeping; for purchasing, billing, etc.; for pharmaceutical supplies; for nursing, medicine and surgery. Some of these groups, such as the administrative offices and the pharmacy, perform their activities as groups. But in those areas where professional knowledge and skills are brought to bear on particular individual cases, the task force structure is employed.

The naval operations manuals are

> full of details of specific tasks at the micro level, but rarely discuss integration into the whole. There are other written rules and procedures, from training manuals through Standard Operating Procedures (SOPs), that describe and standardize the process of integration. None of them explain how to make the whole system operate smoothly, let alone to the level of performance that we have observed.

The high turnover rate in naval systems is discussed in detail, and the conclusion is that

> the ship appears to us as one gigantic school, not in the sense of rote learning, but in the positive sense of genuine search for acquisition and improvement of skills. One of the great enemies of high reliability is the usual 'civilian' combination of stability, routinization, and lack of challenge and variety that predispose an organization to relax vigilance and sink into a dangerous complacency that leads to carelessness and error.

The difference between the formal and actual organization is analysed in detail:

> Our team noted with some surprise the adaptability and flexibility of what is, after all, a military organization in the day-to-day performance of its task. On the paper, the ship is formally organized in a steep hierarchy rank with clear chains of command and means to enforce authority far beyond that of any civilian organization.... Flight operations and planning are usually conducted as if the organization were relatively 'flat' and 'collegial' because events of the flight deck, for instance, can happen too quickly to allow for appeals through a chain of command. 'Planning' is largely done by a process of ongoing and continuing argument and negotiation among personnel from many units, in person and via phone, which tend to be resolved by direct order only when the rare impasse develops that requires an appeal to higher authority.
>
> Operational redundancy—the ability to provide for the execution of a task if the primary unit fails or falters—is necessary for high-reliability organizations to manage activities that are sufficiently dangerous to cause serious consequences in the event of operational failure. In the classical organizational theory, redundancy is provided by some combination of duplication (two units performing the same function) and overlap (two functional units with functional areas in common). Its enemies are mechanistic management models that seek to eliminate these valuable modes in the name of efficiency.

The high reliability found at the flight deck is contributed to decision/management redundancy in terms of internal cross-check on decisions even at the micro level:

> Almost everyone involved in bringing the aircraft on board is part of a constant loop of conversation and verification taking place over several different channels at once. At first, little of this chatter seems coherent, let alone substantive, to the outside observer. With experience, one discovers that seasoned personnel do not 'listen' so much as monitor for deviations, reacting almost instantaneously to anything that does not fit their expectations of the correct routine.

The findings of Rochlin *et al.* have been discussed in some detail in the present context because they support the point of view that models of distributed decision making cannot be based on those of stable organizational structures, nor on normative task procedures or decision scenarios. The only reliable kind of model appears to be a self-organizing simulation model that can be tested experimentally. For the development of such a model, Thompson's book offers a wealth of organizing principles that can be used to guide the selection of adaptive features to include in the model structure.

CONCLUSION

The conclusion of the discussion in this chapter is that development of a kind of self-organizing model of the organization of distributed decision making should be attempted. The basis can be the framework for analysis of cognitive work, in which the work domain, the requirements for control decisions and the organization of the decision makers are represented by separate domains.

Support for the modelling effort can be found in the results of organization and management research focusing on self-organizing features of organizations, such as the work by Thompson, and Rochlin *et al.* This research can supply adaptation heuristics guiding the formation of organizational structures in response to requirements from the environment and the task content.

In addition, the interaction between decision makers and the allocation of roles to individuals will depend on the conventions and 'protocols' that are adopted for communication between the various decision makers, and reflecting the organizational 'culture'. As a source of concepts for systematic formulation of these communication conventions, modern theories for complex multilevel control systems should be considered.

Finally, methods and concepts for simulation of complex decision-making organizations should be critically reviewed and developed. An equivalent to statistical significance of results from measurements in controlled experiments must be developed for the qualitative results from 'object-oriented' simulations of complex, real-life scenarios which cannot meaningfully be repeated many times under controlled conditions.

Address for Correspondence:

Professor Jens Rasmussen, Risø National Laboratory, PO Box 49, DK-4000 Roskilde, Denmark.

REFERENCES

Ashby, W. R. (1962) Principles of the self-organizing system. In H. von Foerster, and G. W. Zopf (eds), *Principles of Self-Organizing*. New York: Pergamon Press.

Barnard, C. I. (1938) *The Function of the Executive*. Cambridge, Mass.: Harvard University Press.

Brehmer, B. (1984) Brunswikian psychology for the 1990s, In K. M. J. Lagerspetz and P. Niemi (eds). *Psychology in the 1990s*. New York: Elsevier.

Clark, B. R., (1956) *Adult Education in Transition*. Berkeley: University of California Press.

Cyert, R. M., and March, J. G. (1963) *A Behavioral Theory of the Firm*. Englewood Cliffs, NJ: Prentice-Hall.

Davidson, D. (1967) Causal relations. *Journal of Philosophy*, **64**, 691–703. Reprinted in E. Sosa (ed.), *Causation and Conditionals*. Oxford: Oxford University Press.

Drucker, P. F. (1988) The coming of the new organization. *Harvard Business Review*, January-February, 45–53.

Gouldner, A. W. (1959) Organizational analysis. In R. K. Merton, L. Broom and L. S. Cottrell, Jr (eds), *Sociology Today*, New York: Basic Books.

Gulick, L., and Urwick, L. (eds) (1937) *Papers on the Science of Administration*. New York: Institute of Public Administration.

Himmelblau, D. M. (ed.) (1973) *Decomposition of Large-Scale Problems*. Amsterdam: North-Holland.

La Porte, T. R. (1982) On the design and management of nearly error-free organizational control systems. In D. L. Sills, C. P. Wolf, and V. B. Shelanski (eds), *Accident at Three Mile Island—The Human Dimension*. New York: Westview.

March, J. G., and Simon, H. A. (1958) *Organizations*. New York: John Wiley.

Mesarovic, M. D. (1970a) *Theory of Multi-Level, Hierarchical Systems*. New York: Academic Press.

Mesarovic, M. D. (1970b) Multilevel systems and concepts in process control. *Proceedings of the IEEE*, **58**, No. 1, New York: Free Press.

Parsons, T. (1960) *Structure and Process in Modern Society*. New York: Free Press.

Rasmussen, J. (1983) Skill, rules and knowledge; signals, signs, and symbols, and other distinctions in human performance models. *IEEE Transactions on Systems, Man and Cybernetics*, **SMC-13** , No. 3.

Rasmussen, J. (1985) The role of hierarchical knowledge representation in decision making and system management. *IEEE Transactions on Systems, Man and Cybernetics*. **SMC-15**, No. 2, 234–43.

Rasmussen, J. (1986) Comparison of models needed for conceptual design of man–machine systems in different application domains. In *Proceedings of the 1986 IEEE International Conference on Systems, Man and Cybernetics*, Atlanta, 14–17 October, Vol. 1 New York: IEEE, pp. 412–17.

Rasmussen, J. (1988a) A cognitive engineering approach to the modelling of decision making and its organization in process control, emergency management, CAD/CAM, office systems, library systems. In W. B. Rouse (ed.), *Advances in Man–Machine System Research*, Vol. 4. Greenwich, Conn: JAI Press.

Rasmussen, J. (1988b) Coping safely with complex systems. AAAS Annual Meeting, Boston, February 11/15, 1988.

Rasmussen, J. (1989) *Concepts for Analysis of Cooperative Work*. To be published.

Rochlin, G. I., La Porte, T. R., and Roberts, K. H. (1987) The self-designing high-reliability organization: aircraft carrier flight operations at sea, *Naval War College Review*, Autumn.

Roethlisberger, F. J., and Dickson, W. J. (1939) *Management and the Worker*. Cambridge, Mass: Harvard University Press.

Rosch, E. (1975) Human categorization. In N. Warren (ed.), *Advances in Cross-Cultural Psychology*. New York: Halsted Press.

Russell, B. (1913) On the notion of cause. *Proc. Aristot. Soc.*, **13**, 1–25.

Savage, C. M. (1987) *Fifth Generation Management for Fifth Generation Technology*. SME Blue Book Series, Dearborn, MI: Society of Manufacturing Engineers.

Schoeffler, J. D. (1969) Decomposition and multilevel methods for on-line computer control of industrial processes. *Technical Report*; Systems Research Center, Case Western Reserve University.

Selznick, P. (1949) *TVA and the Grass Roots*. Berkeley, CA: University of California Press.

Simon, H. A. (1957a) *Administrative Behavior*. New York: Macmillan.

Simon, H. A. (1957b) *Models of Man, Social and Rational*. New York: John Wiley.

Taylor, F. W. (1911) *Scientific Management*. New York: Harper and Row.

Thompson, J. D. (1967) *Organizations in Action*. New York: McGraw-Hill.

Weber, M. (1947) *The Theory of Social and Economic Organization*. A. M. Henderson and Talcott Parsons (trans.) and Talcott Parsons (ed.), New York: Free Press.

Part 2.3

Cooperative Dialogues

One prerequisite for modelling cooperative work will be studies of communication among cooperative decision makers. Such a review is presented by Falzon, who has analyzed the 'operative' language of communication in different domains and the change of the form of communication depending on the actual situations, such as, for instance, in response to disturbances. To study further the distinction made in Chapter 5 between constraints shaping the content and form of communication in cooperative work, studies such as those of Falzon are very important.

6. Cooperative Dialogues

Pierre Falzon
INRIA, France

This chapter deals with a specific activity within collective work: goal-oriented dialogues between two interlocutors. These situations are obviously simpler than many considered by other contributors in this book: first, because collective work (and cooperative dialogues) may involve far more actors than two; second, because dialogue is not the only aspect of collective work. However, cooperative dialogues are, in general, necessary in collective work.

Only functional dialogues will be considered here (in the rest of this text, 'dialogue' will always mean 'functional dialogue'). A definition of functional dialogues has been proposed by Savoyant and Leplat (1983): 'Communications dealing directly with the task content, thus excluding those that mostly focus on human relationships within the team, on cohesion, on influence processes, etc.' However, we will include in functional dialogues (contrary to Savoyant and Leplat) the communications concerning the activity which occur while the operators are not actually performing the task.

A dialogue typology appears in Figure 1. It differentiates between two large classes of dialogues: dialogues between experts, and expert/non-expert dialogues. Some of the subclasses—such as those taking place during design, multi-expert problem solving and knowledge elicitation—have not extensively been studied. This does not mean, of course, that these *situations* have not been considered but only that studies of *dialogues* in these situations are scarce. These dialogue subclasses will be considered in the final section.

The first section of this chapter focuses on expert/expert dialogues and introduces the notion of operative languages, their characteristics and their description. The second section presents the notion of operative understanding, and applies it to both expert/expert and expert/non-expert dialogues. A third section is dedicated to the limits of operative languages and operative understanding. Variations in situation complexity modify both the content of the dialogues and the language used, especially in communication between experts. The conclusion first considers interlocutor modelling, an important aspect of

Distributed Decision Making: Cognitive Models for Cooperative Work
Edited by J. Rasmussen, B. Brehmer and J. Leplat

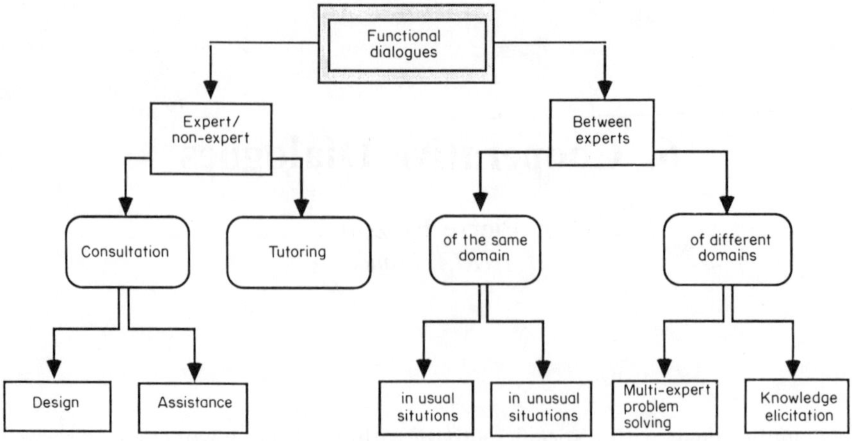

Figure 1. A dialogue typology

operative understanding, then examines some categories of cooperative dialogues that have received little attention, and finally presents the benefits that can be expected from the study of cooperative dialogues.

OPERATIVE LANGUAGES

Expert–expert dialogues and operative languages

Expert–expert dialogues are characterized by the use of specific languages, derived from natural language, understandable by and efficient for specialists in the domain but more or less unintelligible for the layman. These specialized languages do not appear only in work contexts. All subjects involved in a repeated way in the practice of some activity tend to construct specific languages. Cooking recipes, knitting instructions, communications between people involved in some sports (e.g. sailing) or games (e.g. chess) make use of specialized languages that are obscure for the non-specialist. These languages appear, and are efficient, in all situations in which the interlocutors share a common domain knowledge: when used with a non-specialist interlocutor, a technical language becomes a jargon.

Specialized languages constitute representation systems more compatible with the schemata acquired through experience. They are the result of the adaptation, by the operators themselves, of a general system of representation: natural language. We will use the term 'operative languages' to refer to these languages directly molded by domain-specific knowledge. The choice of the word 'operative' is intentional, and refers to Ochanine's (1978) theory of cognitive functioning.

Ochanine describes the mental representations used by operators when processing a situation. He indicates that experience allows the operators to build operative images of the object to be processed. These operative images are partial representations of the environment, 'partial' being used in both senses of the term: selective and biased. Only some of the elements of the environment are selected, and distortions tend to occur, emphasizing the task-relevant aspects of these selected items of information. Operative representations are particularly efficient when operators have to process usual situations but may be detrimental if used for the processing of unusual problems.

As operative images, operative languages stem from experience in a domain. Just as operative images are partial representations of the object of the activity, so operative languages are restricted and distorted tools of representation.

The characteristics of operative languages

The characteristics described below are taken from different sources:

(1) *Studies of specific operative languages.* Such studies are still not numerous, but do exist.

(2) *Presentations of dedicated interactive systems.* Dedicated interactive systems are not assumed to be able to understand language in general but only communications in a given domain. In many cases, a study of the target language has been made before design. This preliminary study allows simplification of language processing. These restricted means are significant: they indicate characteristics of the language or characteristics of the comprehension of these languages. Therefore although these texts do not deal directly with the study of operative languages, they do provide information about these languages.

(3) *Experiments on natural-language human–computer dialogues.* Human–computer interactions are a specific class of functional dialogues. Several experiments (e.g. Scapin, 1985) have demonstrated that subject interacting with computers tended to restrict their expression. However, the results of these experiments have to be considered with caution. It is sometimes difficult to distinguish the effects caused by restrictions of the subjects' goals from those provoked by the subjects' representations of the capabilities of computers. In order to minimize this problem, only those experiments in which subjects were explicitly told that the computer understood natural language (the 'Wizard of Oz' method) are reported here. (*The Wizard of Oz* is a children's story in which the characters are terrified by the appearance of a wizard until they discover that he is a scared old man with a loudspeaker. The Wizard of Oz method consists of having an experimenter simulate a machine capable of performing complex human activities, such as under-

standing natural language without any restriction. Subjects believe that they are interacting with a machine (and not another human).)

Lexical aspects

The important question here is the relation between the vocabulary of the language as a whole and those of operative languages. In brief, the lexical characteristics of operative languages are the following:

(1) Operative languages use restricted vocabularies; this restriction does not hinder communication.
(2) The words of these vocabularies may be rare, or unknown, in the general language (the vocabulary is not a representative sample nor a subset of the vocabulary of general language).

Vocabulary size. The first property of the vocabularies of operative languages is to be restricted (Phal, 1968; Malhotra, 1975; Lehrberger, 1982; Grosz, 1982). Cuny (1971), in a study of the vocabulary of users of an intercom network, concludes that vocabulary size is an aspect of a more general tendency of professional communication towards limiting linguistic means. The vocabularies of operative languages are 'embedded in situations' (Gregory and Carroll, 1978), in the sense that their words allow reference to all the objects, events or situations important in situations, and only to these.

The size of the vocabularies of operative languages can also be studied by considering the vocabularies necessary to issue commands to dedicated computer systems. These are often very restricted. Moyne (1977) notes, for instance, that the vocabulary of a robot cook amounts to only 150 words. The vocabulary, defined by experiment, of a graphics editor designed by Hauptmann and Green (1983) amounts to 189 words (however, these do not represent the total number of words that can be used but only the number necessary to understand users' commands; unrecognized words are ignored by the system). According to Moskovich (1982), operative vocabularies have another characteristic: they are finite, in the sense that they can be counted.

Monolexemy. Lexical restrictions can be made deliberately. Meyer (1985), for instance, has described rules for the writing of technical specifications. He notes that the rules applicable to literature do not apply to technical writing. In literature, the novelist attempts to minimize repetitions by using several referents for the same object. On the contrary, one rule of technical writing is to minimize diversity by always using the same word for the same object. This rule can be found in many handbooks for technical writing (e.g. Bell, 1985). One consequence of its application is, of course, a restriction on the size of the vocabulary of technical texts.

Vocabulary size and communication efficiency. Lexical limitations do not lower communication efficiency if the vocabulary is adapted to the task. Kelly and Chapanis (1977) have studied the effect of several levels of lexical restriction on performance in a problem-solving task. Subjects were communicating by teletype. Three experimental conditions were studied: no lexical restriction, an imposed vocabulary of 500 words and an imposed one of 300 words. Imposed vocabularies were composed of a general vocabulary (of 225 words) to which was added, for each problem, a specific vocabulary.

The main result indicates that the time needed to solve the problems is not affected by vocabulary restrictions. An explanation for this absence of handicap can be found in the fact that the imposed vocabularies have not been arbitrarily elaborated by the experimenters. They have been defined from the vocabularies used by subjects of previous studies, working on the same experimental tasks. The imposed vocabularies were thus operative, adequate to the task.

Rare or specific words. The vocabularies of operative languages are not a statistically representative sample of the general vocabulary of the language. Michaelis *et al.* (1977) have compared the 225 words of the general vocabulary of the Kelly and Chapanis (1977) experiment to the data provided by two tables of word frequencies (one for spoken English, the other for written English). The observed frequencies in the experiment differ from those of the tables. The words of the experiment are often rare words in the 'general' English of the tables. A very similar result is reported by Thomas (1976) in unrestricted natural-language dialogues with a computer (Wizard of Oz method).

The vocabularies of operative languages are not a subset of the general vocabulary of the language since they include words that do not belong to the dictionary of the language. For instance, British legal language is characterized by the use of words or expressions pertaining to other modern languages (e.g. French) or to older ones such as Latin, Old English or Middle English (Charrow *et al.*, 1982).

Syntactic aspects

The syntactic characteristics of operative languages are the following:

(1) Some syntactic rules are privileged, and appear preferentially.
(2) These grammars are more restricted than the general grammar of the language; they include fewer rules.
(3) These grammars are not a subset of the grammar of the language as a whole: some rules are specific to the operative language.
(4) These grammars vary from one operative language to the other.

A privileged syntax

Operative languages tend to privilege some syntactic structures:

(1) Because the dialogue situation implied by the task may lead to a more frequent use of some syntactic means. For instance, subjects interacting with a database will often use the interrogative form.
(2) Because linguistic habits will be adopted by operators while completing the task.

Conventionality. This last point is related to the question of the conventionality of the forms of expression. The conventionality phenomenon can be described as a tendency to associate specific forms of expression to specific contexts (Gibbs, 1979, 1981).

According to Gibbs' observations, a given form of expression is not conventional in itself (i.e. it is not a generally preferred syntactic structure) but in reference to a context. Some syntactic structures can be very conventional in some contexts and very unconventional in others. Gibbs' results indicate that understanding a conventional request (in its context) is always quicker than understanding unconventional requests, whatever the syntactic structure. This means, in particular, that, in context, an indirect form may be processed quicker than a direct form if the indirect form is the conventional one. (For example, the indirect form for a request to close a window can be 'Must you open the window?', the direct form can be 'Close the window'.) This modifies the general thought that indirect forms take longer to process.

The syntax of the expert. Preference for some syntactic means has been clearly demonstrated by the evaluation of the LUNAR system by its author (Woods, 1973). LUNAR is the consultation interface of a database (dealing with lunar geology) which can be queried in natural language. The system was designed following analysis of the language of experts in geology.

The very interesting result reported by Woods is that the performances of the system vary as a function of the competence in the domain of its users. The experts are better understood than non-experts (geology students). According to the author, this difference in performance is caused not only by the fact that the experts use a technical vocabulary but also by the fact that they have adopted some syntactic habits that do not cover the full range of possibilities of the language as a whole. During design, efforts have been directed towards those expressions really used by the experts. Since non-experts tend to use non-standard expressions, they are not always understood.

The observations reported by Rialle (1985) support the idea of syntactic preferences in the language of experts in a domain. This author presents a program of consultation of a medical expert system. This program was written after an analysis of the language of the specialists (the prospective users). The author notes that the language uses short and simple sentences, with few pronominal or elliptic references and few metaphors. According to Rialle, the use of nominal groups in order to express descriptions or factual knowledge characterizes the language of the experts. Verbal groups are mostly used for the expression of inferences.

A restricted syntax

Many experimental results indicate restrictions in the number of syntactic structures used in goal-oriented situations (Moskovich, 1982; Rialle, 1985). The grammar of an operative language includes only a subset of the total grammar of the language. As a consequence, operative languages are less flexible than natural language, since they allow fewer syntactic structures than natural language. For instance, Hendler and Michaelis (1983), analyzing the natural language communications recorded in a cooperative problem-solving task, point out that the grammar of these communications is restricted (14 rules and 11 symbols), can be processed easily by usual systems, and is sufficient to take into account most of the observed syntactic forms. A similar result is reported by Malhotra (1975). This author has analyzed the commands issued by subjects querying a supposedly very intelligent database (Wizard of Oz method). The subjects' utterances can be classified in a limited number of grammatical classes (each class represents a syntactic pattern): 78 % of the utterances can be classified in only ten classes. Moreover, some classes are much more used than others: three classes account for 81 % of the utterances of the same ten classes. In an experiment using the same method, Malhotra and Sheridan (1976) note that only five syntactic classes are necessary to account for 50 % of the commands (63.4 % if minor alterations of the pattern are tolerated).

According to Phal (1968), the origins of the syntactic limitations of scientific and technical languages lie first in the fact that 'expression needs (defined more in terms of the procedures used in the domain than in terms of the objects under study) are finite in the scientific field, by opposition to everyday life', second in the objective of rigour and precision of the users of these languages.

Domain-specific grammars

The above observations may lead to the idea of trying to define an all-purpose, universal grammar by studying a variety of operative languages and describing their grammars. This research framework hypothesizes that the grammars of operative languages are a subset of natural-language grammar, and that grammars of different operative languages are similar. As will be seen, experimental results contradict both hypotheses.

Grammars that differ from natural-language grammar. Kittredge (1979, 1982) has studied a body of 11 specialized languages and has compared the French and English versions of these languages between themselves and with language as a whole. He gives the following results:

(1) Operative languages can be described with a smaller number of grammatical rules than natural language;
(2) The grammar of operative languages cannot be reduced to a subset of the grammar of the language as a whole: some rules are specific to the operative languages and do not exist in the grammar of the language.

This characteristic is also stressed by Lehrberger (1982) and de Heaulme (1982). The latter has studied the language of medical reports (in French). He notes that this language differs from standard French in a number of ways:

(1) A frequent absence of verbs.
(2) An accumulation of cascaded adjectival forms (e.g. 'atteinte neurogène périphérique discrète).
(3) The use of notations such as ':', ' = ' or of parentheses for different purposes. These notations may mean 'is present', or 'shows that', or they may indicate a numerical result or a comment.
(4) 'Strong' ellipses, i.e. ellipses assuming an important professional competence and a large intermediate reasoning process: e.g. 'the rest is normal'.

Grammars that differ between themselves. Operative languages grammars not only differ from the grammar of language as a whole but also between themselves. Kittredge (1979), comparing the French and English versions of 11 operative languages, observes that:

(1) There are more differences between two operative languages of the same language than between the two versions (French and English) of the same operative language. Syntactic rules are common to the two versions, this being more true when the text is more technical. However, it must be noted that French and English are languages of the same family. Different results might be obtained if comparing more distant languages (e.g. French and Chinese).
(2) Grammatical differences exist not only between operative languages and natural language but also between operative languages: a specific grammar must be built for each operative language.

Comparable observations are made by Kelley (1983). The language-understanding interface designed by this author is not based on an *a priori* grammar of the language but on an empirically derived grammar. This kind of grammar, as the author points out, cannot be generalized: it is efficient only for a specific sublanguage. (However, the design methodology is a general one, and has been used for the design of other systems; cf. Wixon *et al.*, 1983.) This is a disadvantage from the point of view of system design (since the method cannot yield a universal grammar) but it confirms that each task is characterized by a specific set of grammatical rules.

However, it may be the case that, within a category of tasks, the structure of the language remains constant, in spite of the surface variations between different sublanguages. The results presented by de Heaulme and Frutiger (1984) support this idea. These authors have designed an artificial language (REMEDE), starting from the study of clinical reports in a specific medical specialty. REMEDE was then applied to a dozen other specialties. The interesting point is that it is not necessary to modify REMEDE for these other specialties: conceptual and syntactic structures remain constant from one specialty to the other. Vocabulary changes, but not concepts and relations between concepts.

Semantic and pragmatic aspects

Semantic and pragmatic aspects are difficult to separate from comprehension processes and from understanding difficulties. Many semantic or pragmatic difficulties disappear in operative languages, and allow simplification of language processing. In operative languages interpretation is restricted because:

(1) Words tend to be monosemous.
(2) Interpretation is constrained by the task.
(3) Interpretation occurs within a restricted universe.
(4) The intentions of the dialogue partners are clear and restricted.
(5) This type of dialogue is characterized by a tighter application of communication rules.

Monosemy

Lexical monosemy has two aspects:

(1) The vocabularies of operative languages may include specific words: these words are monosemous.
(2) The vocabularies may include non-specific words (i.e. words that appear in a non-specialized dictionary): these words will be monosemous within the universe of the operative language.

Guilbert (1973) has published a study of the relations between the general vocabulary and technical and scientific vocabularies (for French). In particular, he points out that:

(1) The modifications of the French vocabulary (analyzed through successive modifications of the dictionary) suggest that technical vocabularies have a much quicker evolution. Words referring to tools, techniques and concepts that have grown out of date disappear.
(2) The general vocabulary is characterized by a constant increase in the number of possible meanings of each single word (i.e. a constant increase of polysemy). On the contrary, words of specialized languages tend to be monosemous, not because the word in itself is monosemous but because it is used in a given context by a given speaker. The same word, used by the same speaker but in a non-specialized context, or used by a non-specialist in the same context, will lose its specialized meaning.
(3) Words that appear in several technical languages should be considered as homonyms rather than as a single, polysemous, word. Guilbert gives the example of the word 'charbon', which belongs to the vocabularies of art, of the mining industry and of medicine, with very different meanings: (kind of) pencil, coal, a specific illness.

Different observations give credit to this idea. Rialle (1985), analyzing the language of the future users of a medical expert system, stresses the almost total absence of polysemy: words are almost never ambiguous. Thomas (1976) has studied dialogues in a task where subjects had to order stationery. The meanings of the words in these dialogues are restricted. The word 'order', for instance, has 14 meanings in the dictionary: 48 times (out of 50), 'order' is used to refer to a single meaning— 'request that something be supplied'. In the same way, 'price' has seven meanings in the dictionary: only one of them is used.

As was seen above, some authors have proposed that, in technical languages, each object is represented by a single word. If this characteristic is combined with monosemy, there exists a bijective relation between the set of meanings and the set of words. Words are monosemous and objects and concepts are monolexemous.

Goal-oriented semantics

Meanings of the words of operative languages are restricted and adequate to the task. This observation will be illustrated by a comment made by Rich (1984), dealing with the dictionaries to be used by natural-language interfaces. She considers that it is not useful to use a total dictionary of the language, first, because the vocabulary of an application is generally a subset of the total vocabulary of the language, and second, because the information that should be associated with each word and the way this information should be represented depend on the functioning of the understanding program and on the goals of the application program.

It is impossible to speak of the meaning of a word independently of the task to be performed. Even if some words seem to possess a core significance, they may take very different meanings according to the context in which they will appear. Context imposes an interpretation on the words in terms of relationships with other words. Other contexts require other relationships (Anderson and Ortony, 1975). This is particularly clear when relevant meanings are not stored in memory but have to be constructed. Clark (1983) provides examples of situations in which a word takes on an occasional meaning, linked to a particular experience. As the author points out, some occasional meanings may become conventional for speakers of a specific community. The processes of elaboration of task-oriented vocabularies are described in Krauss and Weinheimer (1964) and Clark and Wilkes-Gibbs (1986).

The simplification of the semantics of quantifiers. The determination of the meaning of quantifiers is a complex problem in language understanding, for machines as well as for humans. The difficulty is not so much in ordering possible quantifiers (subjects agree on the order) but rather in evaluating the quantities implied (Hammerton, 1976).

Quantification problems are very much simplified within an operative language. It is then much easier to give a meaning to the couple quantifier–quantified object. For instance, 'little' in the sentence 'Buy butter if there is little left' will mean different things for the average consumer and for the manager of a large restaurant. The quantity can be determined only if the universe is known (of course, quantity varies also according to the object to which the quantifier is applied).

Rare or specific meanings. In the same way as the words of an operative language may be rare or unknown in the general language, the meanings of these words may also be rare or unknown in that language. For instance, the word 'rare' if interpreted by a robot cook, will mean 'raw' and not 'infrequent', although this last meaning is probably the most frequent use of the word (Moyne, 1977). Charrow *et al.* (1982) provide other examples, taken from legal language. They add that operative meanings may differ widely from usual meanings. The fresh fish of the lawyer is not the fresh fish of the layman: in legal language, 'fresh' means 'never having been frozen', whatever the date the fish was caught.

The semantics of a limited universe

The restriction of semantic dimensions limit the number of possible interpretations. The restriction of the semantic universe results in a limitation of possible ambiguities in word meaning (Kittredge, 1979). In order for a word or a sentence to be ambiguous the dimensions that structure the reference universe have to allow for at least two interpretations. Since the number of dimensions is limited in the universe in which each operative language functions, very few ambiguities are possible.

This aspect is well illustrated by a study of a non-verbal language, the gesture language of crane operators (Cuny, 1971). This is structured by a small number of dimensions (high versus low, quick versus slow, movement versus stop, horizontal versus vertical, etc.). These dimensions correspond to a goal-oriented representation of space and time, i.e. a representation limited to the dimensions useful for the task.

This restriction in semantic dimensions can facilitate comprehension processes. What is considered as an ambiguity by linguists may very well not be one for a comprehension system functioning in a limited domain. For example, in the request 'Are there any books on computers?' the interpretation of 'on' as 'above' is impossible if the request is sent to a database (Moyne, 1977).

The restriction of the universe makes it unnecessary to distinguish between some interpretations. In the above example, ambiguity disappears because the absence of a semantic dimension prohibits one interpretation. Semantic simplification may take a different form. A word may refer to objects that are differentiated in the 'general' world but undifferentiated in the domain of the operative language.

Kittredge and Mel'Cuk (1983), in a study of the language of stock market reports, note that some words refer to identities that are distinct in general but not in this operative language. 'IBM', for instance, refers to the company, its spokesman, its stock, or the price of its stock. The fact of not distinguishing these four meanings does not affect understanding.

This observation is interesting, since this kind of question has often been presented as a difficulty for natural-language understanding. A classical example is the meaning of 'Nobel prize' in sentences such as:

The Nobel prize has been attributed (= the award)
The Nobel prize has allowed me to buy (= the money)
The Nobel prize said (= the winner)

This example is often given to demonstrate that only context can allow the meaning of the expression 'Nobel prize' to be found. According to Kittredge and Mel'Cuk, the sentence context is not useful, not because the general context (the stock market universe) allows us to choose the relevant meaning but because the general context eliminates the necessity of this choice. 'IBM' is not ambiguous because the dimensions that allow us to choose between the different meanings are absent from the universe of stock market reports and are irrelevant in this universe.

A strict application of conversational rules

The strategies above rely on the assumption that the speaker is cooperative and attempts to obtain something that the addressee can provide. They rely on conversational conventions, comparable to those developed by Grice (1975), that can be summarized as: be informative, be brief, be relevant, be sincere. Each dialogue partner assumes that the other is attempting to convey relevant and true information, and this as concisely as possible.

Bunt (1981) has studied the applicability of these principles in the framework of human–machine dialogues, and in this perspective has researched dialogues between users and a very intelligent information-providing computer (Wizard of Oz method). Results indicate that Gricean principles apply even more to this kind of dialogue than to human–human dialogues.

In fact, the difference between the situations described by Grice and those studied by Bunt is not the fact that one is dealing with human–human dialogues and the other with human–machine dialogues, but rather the fact that Grice is interested in conversations 'in general' and not in dialogues with restricted goals (as is Bunt). In other words, Bunt's results about the particular relevance of Gricean principles may be caused more by task orientation than by the effect of having a machine as a dialogue partner.

In this sense, Bunt's results indicate that pragmatic constraints used in goal-oriented dialogues are applied in a tighter way than in the general case. Consequently, the comprehension of goal-oriented dialogues does not require us to process extensively the interlocutor's intentions. Most of the time, interlocutors will comply with Gricean conversational principles.

Description of operative languages

Description of the vocabulary

It is sometimes interesting (e.g. when designing an interactive language) to be able to determine a vocabulary that is really useful in a specific objective and context. This means selecting, in the set of words used by the subjects, a subset considered as the core vocabulary of the task. Different criteria can be used in this purpose: frequency, occurrence and commonness.

Frequency. Miller (1981) uses frequencies in order to define a core vocabulary. Subjects have to specify, in natural language, procedures for sorting, selecting or calculating. The total vocabulary amounts to 610 words; the frequencies of use of these words vary greatly. For example, the words used less than three times (pooling all subject's utterances) represent 4.3% of the words spoken but 50% of the vocabulary. Thus, even if the number of acceptable words was limited to 300 (half of the total vocabulary), 96% of the subjects' utterances would remain intact. In addition, these 300 words include many synonyms. If these synonyms were eliminated, the vocabulary would be restricted to 100 words.

Commonness. The commonness of a word is a measure of the number of subjects (in a given population) who use this word at least once. (Miller, 1981, has proposed another method for evaluating commonness, which seems less easy to use than the one proposed here.) Word commonness has been studied by Michaelis *et al.* (1977), who have considered data collected by Kelly and Chapanis (1977). Results indicate that the vocabulary shared by the 36 subjects of the experiment (i.e. words of maximum commonness, words for which $c = 36$) is very small: only four words.

Michaelis *et al.* then considered the number of words corresponding to lower levels of commonness (c-1, c-2, etc.) and the cumulative distributions of the words, i.e. the words used by at least c-1, c-2, ... subjects. The cumulative distributions indicate a very slow increase of the vocabulary common to progressively smaller samples of subjects. Words used by at least half of the subjects (i.e. words for which $c = 18$ at least) represent only 40% of the total vocabulary (i.e. the vocabulary that could be used in any experimental condition or problem). Data suggest that an even more restricted vocabulary could have been proposed. This vocabulary can be defined by considering the measure of commonness.

Occurrence. The third measure that can be taken into account in order to define the core vocabulary is occurrence. Occurrence is defined here as the number of different expressions in which a word appears. It is then a measure of its usefulness as a communication tool. Occurrence differs from frequency.

Measures of occurrence are particularly important in some cases. Notably, the habitability (Woods, 1973) of an interactive system is strongly dependent on the use of this measure. If the only criterion is word frequency, the result will be a system which will understand the most frequent words but which will not allow any flexibility in expression.

These three measures—frequency, commonness and occurrence—can be combined in order to determine the core vocabulary of a language (Falzon, 1982).

Description of grammatical structures

Different authors have proposed methods for the determination of the preferred syntactic rules of the target language. That suggested by Ogden and Brooks (1983) in order to design query languages is based on the study of the verbal productions of a group of subjects to whom no language constraints are imposed. Three constituent elements are identified in the queries: command phrases (C: imperative verb or wh-pronoun), missing element phrase (M: the information sought), qualifying phrase (Q: specifiers of the missing element). These constituent elements are found in various orders: C-M-Q, C-Q-M, C-Q-M-Q, with C being optional. The order C-M-Q is the most frequent one, so that a preferred form of expression can be derived from the subjects' productions.

A parent method is presented by Malhotra (1975) and Malhotra and Sheridan (1976). The idea is to define basic sentence types, capable of accounting for most of the subjects' utterances. Each sentence type may have several templates associated with it, i.e. several orders in which words and word groups may occur. In addition, some elements of the templates may take on special features or may be combined (conjunctions) or modified (e.g. by prepositions) in specified ways. Figure 2 provides an illustration of a basic sentence type, with its templates and examples of utterances.

An iterative methodology is advocated by Kelley (1983). The objective of this author is the design of a language-understanding interface for an electronic agenda. A first subject allows the definition of a tentative grammar, which is then implemented. Ten subjects then use the system (for one hour each). After each subject, new rules and new words are added to the grammar and vocabulary. The increase in rules and words is asymptotic: after ten subjects, the increase is almost nil. In a similar way, Wixon *et al.* (1983) build the grammar of an electronic mail interface through iteration. Their methodology consists of having an experimenter backing up the system. When a command issued by a subject cannot be parsed, the experimenter is alerted and translates the user expression into a command that the system can accept. At the end of each session the system is modified in order to integrate new rules or to alter existing ones.

Description of semantic structures

The research efforts presented below assume that, in operative languages, the structure of verbal productions corresponds to the structure of the knowledge of the users of these languages. The analysis of these operative languages then allows the description of the knowledge of their users.

Wh-questions
Template: Wh-word Verbphrase Nounphrase n[Prepositionalphrase]
Example: What are valid terms?
Template: Wh-word Nounphrase Verbphrase n[Prepositionalphrase]
Example: What items are related to the customers?
'n[Prepositionalphrase]' denotes any number of prepositional phrases including none.

Figure 2. A basic sentence type: Wh-questions (from Malhotra and Sheridan, 1976, reproduced by permission of IBM Watson Research Center)

Functional analyses. Several methodologies make use of the analysis of paraphrases and near-paraphrases. Such a methodology has been used to describe the schemata underlying the language of air traffic controllers (Falzon, 1983, 1984). The method consists first of classifying the messages of the controllers in functional categories. Within each category, messages are then considered as instances of a single schema, which can be described by comparing the messages of the category.

Consider, for instance, some messages belonging to the 'flight-level modifications' category, for which the schema is built step by step (see Figure 3):

(1) Climb level 330
(2) Descend level 330
(3) Leave 290 for 330
(4) Climb level 330 at pilot's discretion
(5) Climb to the flight level 330
(6) Climb 330

Step 1. The schema is named CHLVL (for Change Level). By category definition, the action (Act) concerns the vertical dimension (VE) and the nature of the action (Nat) concerns the level (LVL), and not the rate of climb or descent.

Step 2. The comparison of messages (1) and (2) indicates that the schema has to mention the level to be reached, which will be coded as P (for parameter). Moreover, messages (1) and (2) do not indicate the same kind of relation between the present level and the level to be reached. The schema must include two possibilities: a positive or a negative relation between the levels.

Step 1	((Act: VE) (Nat: LVL))
Step 2	((Act: VE) (Nat: LVL) (Rel: (+ −)) (To: P))
Step 3	((Act: VE) (Nat: LVL) (Rel: (+ −)) (From: (PV P)) (To: P))
Step 4	((Act: VE) (Nat: LVL) (Rel: (+ −)) (From: (PV P)) (To: P) (Time: (def NOW PV)))

Figure 3. Successive versions of the CHLVL schema (flight-level modifications category)

Step 3. In message (3) a new element of information appears: the present level. This information was omitted in messages (1) and (2), which could be rewritten: 'From your present level, climb/descend level 330'. A 'From' slot is then added to the schema to include this item of information. This slot can be filled either with the present value (coded PV) or with a P parameter (as in message (3)).

Step 4. In message (4) the expression 'at pilot's discretion' has several implications concerning the time of execution of the action and the way in which the action should be performed. If this information is not specified, the pilot must assume by default that the action must take place now. The schema is modified accordingly. The filler 'def' stands for 'default', meaning that the default value of the 'Time' slot is the following element.

All the category schemata are built using this method. An extension of the technique allows elaboration of the dictionary of the language of air traffic control. This means both selecting the words that need to be in the dictionary and providing definitions of these words.

Messages (5) and (6) are strict paraphrases. From their study it can be inferred that some words are not necessary in order to understand the messages of this category. The information provided by 'to the flight level' (message (5)) is null: the word 'climb' is enough to evoke an instruction of modification of the flight level. Therefore analysis of the different forms of expression allows the definition of the words that need to be included in the dictionary. Word definitions can make use of the same elements of schema definition. For instance, 'climb' may be defined as: ((Act: VE) (Nat: LVL) (Rel: (+)) (From: (PV))).

Some of the words are given a special property: they are able to trigger a specific schema. Words like 'climb', 'descend' and 'leave' evoke the CHLVL schema.

Analysis of paraphrases has also been used by Kittredge and Mel'Cuk (1983) to elaborate a system for understanding the language of stock exchange reports. The aim of the analysis is the description of semantic primitives; these represent the main action of each message, and compose the nodes of a semantic network. For instance, the CHANGE primitive indicates a change in state and admits six arguments:

(1) The price of a stock;
(2) The initial value;
(3) The final value;
(4) The sign (positive or negative) of the difference;
(5) The subjective importance of the difference;
(6) The speed of the modification.

A method of comprehension of the language of meteorological bulletins is presented by Moskovich (1982). The sentences of this sublanguage are analyzed on the basis of the functional characteristics of their constituent words. A system built following these principles can use two types of information: a dictionary of the words of this sublanguage and a graph of a 'maximum sentence'.

The program retrieves the functional definitions of the words and inserts them into the graph. Three subprograms assist this process:

(1) One is in charge of the cases when several elements compete for the same slot of the graph; the case in which they cannot both be placed in the same slot is considered as an indication for triggering a new graph.
(2) Another subprogram takes decisions on the limits of the segments and on the triggering of new graphs.
(3) A third subprogram processes ellipses, on the basis of the empty slots of the graph when it is to be closed.

Moskovich stresses that the same general procedure can be, and has been, applied successfully to other sublanguages (e.g. military dispatches).

Syntaxico-semantic analyses. In the above methodologies the definition of the schemata or graphs is based on a functional categorization of the messages and words. Other authors have claimed that the description of knowledge structures of operative languages can be based on a purely linguistic analysis.

For Sager (1981), semantic processing relies on the use of 'information formats'. The elaboration of these formats is made as follows:

(1) In a body of texts using the sublanguage under study, and for each word of these texts, the environment in which the word is found is examined in order to identify classes of words. These classes reflect the specialized use of the language. For instance, in the medical domain words like 'X-rays', 'radio' and 'mammography' are often found in similar environments. These words belong to the TEST class in medical texts.
(2) Going up a level, associations between classes of words are detected. For instance, a frequent association in radiology is: noun of the TEST class + verb of the INDICATE class + noun of the RESULT class. These patterns are the backbone of the information formats.
(3) Additional classes (modifiers) are added to these patterns: negations, temporal modifiers, quantitative expressions. Patterns plus modifiers constitute the information formats.

In a given instantiation of a format only some of the slots will be filled. In most cases the instantiated slots will be enough to identify the pattern.

According to Sager, this procedure of elaboration of the formats does not require consultation by experts. Formats are deduced from an analysis of the language of the specialists and reflect their knowledge in the domain. In particular, grammatical classes are entirely dependent on the domain. This is quite different from more traditional grammars, in which grammatical categories—verbs, nouns, adjectives, etc—are stable whatever the domain, and depend on a theory of the structure of the language as a whole.

Dachelet and Normier (1982) have studied the language of medical reports in order to design a language-understanding system. The authors note that this language is not standard French: words have specific meanings, syntax differs from the usual syntax of French. It is then of no value to use results obtained with standard French.

The analytic tool used by the authors is the commutation test, which includes two operations: segmentation, then substitution. The principle is the following. Messages are first segmented, then a segment is replaced by another. If the new message is possible in the sublanguage and if meaning has changed, it means that the segments which have been commuted are relevant and distinctive units of the sublanguage. In order to reach the minimal distinctive units one must make sure that no part of the segment that had been commuted can be involved in another commutation test.

As in Sager's method, this test leads to the definition of classes of segments and, for each class, to a list of the possible linguistic realizations. This defines a grammar, which has the form of a hierarchical decomposition into classes down to the linguistic realizations. For instance, the EXAMEN class is decomposed in EXAM + RESULTAT. The EXAM class is represented directly in lexical form, or is further decomposed in TYPE + OBJET, each of these classes being represented in lexical form (cf. Figure 4).

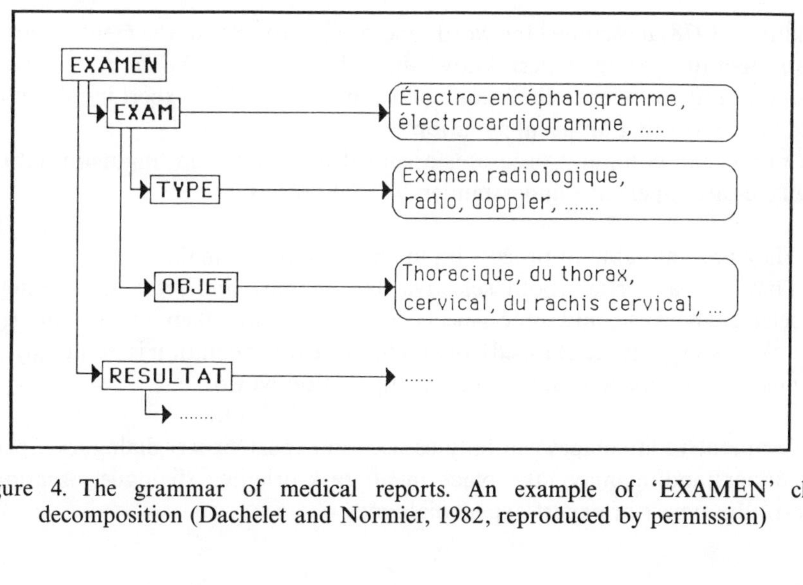

Figure 4. The grammar of medical reports. An example of 'EXAMEN' class decomposition (Dachelet and Normier, 1982, reproduced by permission)

OPERATIVE UNDERSTANDING

Expert/non-expert dialogues and operative understanding

Expert/non-expert dialogues occur in a wide variety of situations, which encompass both simple information queries ('What time is the next train to London?') and complex requests of expertise ('Doctor, I've got these terrible headaches...'). These dialogues are characterized by differences in the knowledge of each dialogue partner. In order for them to be able to communicate they have to use a neutral, non-specialized language. Natural language meets these requirements: it is 'a universal tool of representation and of communication' (Bisseret, 1983). We should in fact speak of 'general' language rather than of 'natural' language, since this language corresponds to the manipulation of general, non-specialized elements of knowledge.

Different results indicate that the experts rarely need to process intensively the requests they receive, for two reasons:

(1) The discourse domain is restricted and constant, so that the search for signification is *a priori* limited to a well-specified universe.
(2) Most of the time these requests are not new. Experience (repetition of similar situations) has allowed the expert to define classes of problems for which mental processing procedures have been elaborated. Activity is thus simplified, sometimes automatized, for the most frequent requests. The expert will have to elaborate new procedures only when facing totally new situations, using domain knowledge and general problem-solving processes for this purpose.

Ochanine (1978) has coined the word 'operativity' to refer to the mental activity of an operator using expert knowledge. We will use the term 'operative understanding' to refer to the comprehension activity of an expert involved in a dialogue concerning an usual situation.

A number of computer programs assumed to understand 'inputs in natural language' are 'operative understanders' in the sense that:

(1) They are only able to process inputs in a limited domain.
(2) They use a partial (both selective and biased) understanding strategy: selective because only some aspects of the inputs are taken into account (e.g. unknown words are skipped), biased because interpretation is limited by the possible actions and objects of the application world.

While operative languages can only be used in expert–expert dialogues, operative understanding may take place in all task-oriented dialogue situations: expert/non-expert or expert/expert dialogues.

Characteristics of operative understanding

A partial syntactic analysis

Syntactic analysis is partial in two ways:

(1) Selection of task-relevant parts of the communication;
(2) Focused analysis of some parts.

Selection of relevant communications. Hayes and Reddy (1983) provide several examples (in human–computer interaction) of heuristics allowing us to focus syntactic analysis on specific parts of communications. It is often possible to neglect parts of the users' communications by locating some linguistic marks. For instance, novice users tend to justify their requests. Consequently, utterances beginning with 'because' may be skipped, since this system is generally not interested in knowing the users' motives.

However, this depends on the dialogue situation. Luzzati (1984), who also proposes the use of 'because' as a mark, notes that one should consider what appears before 'because' if the utterance is an answer to a direct question, and what appears after 'because' if the utterance is an answer to a request for explanation. In both cases, locating the mark allows us to skip parts of the communications.

Focused analysis. The dialogue module of an expert system (for medical diagnosis) designed by Rialle (1985) illustrates the simplifications allowed by the characteristics of the operative language to be understood and by the goal of the expert system. Rialle notes that the language of the experts is characterized by the use of nominal groups to express factual knowledge; verbal groups are used in most cases to express inferential knowledge. Because of the goals of the system, the dialogue module focuses on the analysis of nominal groups.

Another illustration is provided by a study of telephone queries to the information center of the French railway system (Leroy, 1985). This study was made within research dealing with the variations of the language according to the type of interlocutor (human or machine; Wizard of Oz method). Leroy considered only the queries addressed to the (supposed) machine. She notes that most (80%) of the queries use a single structure (with two variants: queries concerning timetables or fares), that can be derived from the user's utterances. This structure can guide understanding. The elements of this structure appear in a preferential order, but this order, which is not always respected, is not necessary for understanding. Thus, a 'global' syntactic analysis (meaning an analysis of the total utterance) can be avoided. A 'local' syntax is enough to specify the elements of the structure which are to be activated, on the basis of the detection of prepositions. This local syntax and the use of some heuristics lead to the definition of rules, which avoid the use of a global syntax and allow us to restrict the size of the dictionary. The author proposes the following rules:

(1) Any place name will be considered as the destination if only one place name appears in the utterance.
(2) Any place name will be considered as the destination if it is the second of a group of two place names, consecutive or not, except if it is preceded by the preposition 'au départ de' ('starting from').

In the same way, the choice of a variant is determined by the presence or absence of a keyword (e.g. 'fare'). Some heuristics allow us to fill in the empty slots. For instance, absence of the station of departure means that departure takes place in the town where the call has been received.

A simplified syntactic analysis

The effect of semantic restrictions. The characteristics of operative languages allow us to simplify the processing of some potentially ambiguous utterances. Oden (1983) explains that two strategies can be used to process these:

(1) The one-meaning strategy: a single interpretation is considered; other possible interpretations are considered only if the first proves to be inconsistent.
(2) The many-meanings strategy: all possible meanings are considered, and one of them is selected as soon as possible.

From the point of view of understanding language, the first strategy is more economical, since it allows us to restrict the number of meanings considered simultaneously. If it is also possible to select immediately the appropriate meaning among all possible meanings, the strategy becomes even more powerful.

Operative understanding applies particularly well to operative languages. We have seen that, in the case of these languages, three factors contribute to reducing semantic ambiguity: the trend towards monosemy (which eliminates the choice between alternatives), the preferential use of some meanings in some contexts (which allows us to select a plausible meaning), and the limitations of the dimensions which allow ambiguity. An important consequence of semantic restrictions is that syntax is not necessary in order to solve lexical ambiguities (Guilbert, 1973). In this perspective, Lehrberger (1982) stresses that semantic restrictions have two consequences:

(1) *Limitations of lexical ambiguities*: this relates to homonyms of the same grammatical class. In the sublanguage studied by Lehrberger (aviation maintenance manuals) the word 'eccentric' may not apply to an animate subject (one cannot find 'an eccentric pilot').

(2) *Limitations of structural ambiguities*: this concerns homonyms belonging to different grammatical categories. Some grammatical categories are prohibited to some words. For instance, the word 'fine' can only be an adjective, not a noun, in aviation maintenance manuals, although a general English dictionary provides two entries for this word: adjective and noun.

The effect of pragmatic restrictions. Syntactic variability is often of no use when comprehension has restricted goals (Rich, 1984). Consider the following queries, sent to an imaginary database:

(1) How many references are there in the database?
(2) What is the number of references in the database?
(3) I want to know the number of references in the database.

These different expressions must result in the same semantic representation and the same pragmatic interpretation. Variability in expression must not be considered, within this application, as informative.

On the other hand, other contexts may require the processing of syntactic variations, in the sense that different syntactic structures would correspond to the fulfilment of different goals. Hobbs (1979) has studied the relations between planning and verbal productions in a natural-dialogue situation. He notes that, contrary to planning for a robot (in which a single goal requires the accomplishment of several actions), conversation is characterized by the fact that a single utterance corresponds to the fulfilment of multiple goals, i.e. that the decisions concerning the expression are a function of the set of active goals at a given instant.

The dialogue studied by Hobbs takes place in the context of a job-applicant interview. This context is complex, as far as the structure of the goals of both interlocutors are concerned. In operative dialogues, goals are far more restricted. Operators often attempt to fulfil a single goal; when goals are multiple, they are stable. The consequence is that operative languages make use of a limited number of syntactic structures, and that syntactic variations (when they appear) may often be neglected, considered as irrelevant in the context of the task.

According to Coulon and Kayser (1982), two dimensions are involved in text understanding: on the one hand, processing depth (at which level does one stop?), and, on the other, processing direction (which branch is to be explored?) These authors propose that processing depth and direction vary according to the subjects' goals at a given instant, in a given situation. In the case of goal-oriented situations, goals are stable, determined by the characteristics of the task. In such situations, processing depth and direction tend to remain constant, at least for standard situations.

A partial semantic analysis

Task orientation. Operative understanding is limited in its objects and objectives. It is limited in its objects in the sense that it is only applicable to a specific type of communication, those that may appear in the universe of the task. Its purpose is not to understand everything that can be said but only what can be said in a given context. Operative understanding is limited in its objectives in the sense that understanding is defined in relation to the possible objects and actions of a domain.

This applies particularly well to human–computer interaction. Rich (1984) notes that a message can only be understood with reference to a particular language and set of possible actions. This observation has two consequences:

(1) In designing an interface, the first aim of the designer should be the determination of the sublanguage appropriate to a target program. In fact, when designers use the term 'natural language interface' they do not mean that natural language as a whole would have to be understood, but only a subset of natural language.
(2) Understanding of the users' inputs should be oriented by the objectives of the application, i.e. by the possible actions of the program. Rewriting rules (i.e. rules that transform the users' messages into commands to the system) should be such that:
    (a) The resulting structure corresponds to the structure of the inputs of the target program.
    (b) The set of messages for which the syntactic and semantic analysis is successful corresponds to the set of possible actions of the domain.

In short, rewriting rules should allow the elaboration of representations adapted to the task, and only to this task. An illustration of this point is provided by Moyne (1977), in his presentation of the language analysis of a robot cook. In his system, the word 'raw' is associated with a procedure indicating 'three-minute cooking', i.e. the representation that will be elaborated will correspond to the task of the robot, and not to the task of the client ordering the meal. One orders a raw steak because of its taste, not because it is cooked for only three minutes.

This limitation in the objectives of operative understanding will limit the evaluation of interpretation hypotheses. In fact, each time a reasonable interpretation (i.e. one which makes sense in the universe of the application) can be elaborated from what has been understood, then the system's answer should be based on this interpretation, without trying to validate it (Hayes and Reddy, 1983). This strategy has two advantages. If the interlocutor does not react negatively, the interpretation hypothesis is implicitly verified. If the interlocutor reacts negatively, the hypothesis is rejected, without having been explicitly validated by the interlocutor (which would have handicapped the dialogue).

This dialogue strategy, suggested by Hayes and Reddy in the context of human–computer communication, has been observed in human–human dialogues (Falzon *et al.*, 1986). These authors have analyzed the dialogue strategies used by secretaries of a medical centre, in charge of taking appointments for some services. The operators use a model of a standard client in order to interpret the queries. The model postulates that:

(1) The client wants an appointment.
(2) The appointment concerns the caller or a close relative.
(3) The appointment is wanted as soon as possible.
(4) The client is in a standard situation as regards Social Security.

The use of this model allows quick interpretations of the requests, with the risk of errors if the call is non-standard. In fact, the secretary assumes the client to be a standard case: she does not verify it through direct questioning. In most cases, this is verified indirectly by the simple fact that the client does not object to the interpretation. In this sense, the use of the model speeds up the dialogue by skipping two steps:

(1) The validation of the hypothesis according to which the client wants an appointment.
(2) A request for the desired dates of the appointment.

If an appointment is not wanted, or if the proposed date is not convenient, the client will mention it, focusing on the way in which the operator's answer does not fit his or her needs. If the client wants an appointment, and if the proposed date is convenient, the task of the operator is nearly completed.

This mechanism is, of course, efficient only if the 'appointment request' hypothesis is plausible and if the proposed date of appointment is likely to be accepted. The model of the client takes care of these points. Most clients call to ask for an appointment, and they generally want it to be as soon as possible.

A restricted model of the interlocutor's intentions. Interpretation of the utterances of the dialogue partner is thus made on the grounds of a model of the interlocutor and of his or her goals. In the case of goal-oriented dialogues this model is better specified and more constraining. For these reasons, it allows us to eliminate some decision processes by using the standard (default) values of the model.

Lubonski (1985) gives the example of a railway database that can be consulted by the public. This system may have to process inputs such as 'I want to go to Rome'. Obviously, a system that would consider this input solely as a piece of information and that would answer 'Have a good trip' would not be judged satisfactory by its users! The message must be considered as equivalent to 'Give me the timetable of the trains for Rome', i.e. interpreted as an order. The system must assume that users are seeking information.

This model of the user prevents the direct interpretation (i.e. information providing) and favors the indirect interpretation (i.e. information request). Leroy (1985), studying telephone requests to a railway station information center, concludes that all expressions by the clients have to be interpreted as requests. This direct access to the relevant interpretation is in close relationship with Gibbs' results, reported earlier in this chapter.

Shapiro and Kwasny (1975) have designed the help program of an operating system which can be consulted in natural language. Understanding of user's inputs is facilitated by the restriction of the application domain and by the use of a model of the user, which makes the following assumptions:

(1) The user is seeking information.
(2) The information sought concerns system commands. Consequently, if the name of a command, or a synonym, or a word that implies the use of a command is recognized in the request, information on this command must be provided.
(3) Request formulations will refer to the operations that commands can execute (and not to the commands themselves).
(4) Details can be neglected; the only important thing is to discover the user's goal.
(5) The user's goal, and the context of this goal, is constant throughout the dialogue.

The system designed by Shapiro and Kwasny is a version of ELIZA (Weizenbaum, 1966). However, ELIZA's capacity to understand is very incomplete. It makes no attempt at parsing or at elaborating a representation of the input. The interest in Shapiro and Kwasny's program is its demonstration that this very simple analysis is enough to fulfil the goals, if it employs an appropriate model of the user.

The restriction of the universe of the interpreter. The above text concerned pragmatic restrictions on the interlocutor's universe. The following deals with pragmatic restrictions of the universe of the receiver of the communication, the interpreter. These restrictions are due to the fact that the interpreter also has limited goals and possibilities.

Hayes and Reddy (1983) consider the problem of the interpretation of sentences such as 'Can you give me Fred's number?' Is it an indirect request (i.e. 'Give me Fred's number') or a direct query about the system's abilities (i.e.

'Have you access to Fred's number in your database?')? They suggest that the system should consider these messages as requests if it can answer them, as queries about abilities if it cannot. It is interesting to note that where the objectives of the dialogue partners are clear, it is possible to provide a simple answer to a question that is, in general, a difficult pragmatic problem.

A similar issue is mentioned by Moyne (1977). The author gives the example of an indirect request to a database: 'Can you tell me if you have books about computers?' Moyne notes that the request is not ambiguous if the database has no means of examining its own abilities. The message is then systematically interpreted as an indirect request. More generally, it is not necessary to give the machine more information than that necessary for the goals of its users (Addis, 1977). Limiting the universe also means limiting the interpretation of the messages to a subset relevant for the goals of the task.

OPERATIVE LANGUAGES, OPERATIVE UNDERSTANDING AND UNUSUAL SITUATIONS

Operative languages and unusual situations

The existence of an operative language does not mean that everything said by experts in a domain while they are performing their activity will be said using the operative language of the domain. Most of the communication between experts takes place during the processing of usual situations, for which they have evolved an operative knowledge and for which they have elaborated a simplified and well-adapted language. Unusual situations, when recognized as such by the operators, require the abandoning of routine or rule-based behavior. Operators must attempt to generate a new procedure, using for this purpose all the knowledge available. This can be done on-line (e.g. incident processing in a process control room) or off-line (e.g. debriefing of that same incident, days or weeks later). Meta-functional dialogues, in which operators process not the environment but their own knowledge and procedures are examples of off-line processing.

When unusual situations occur, experts do not dispose of any operative knowledge nor of any specialized language. They must then make use of a non-specialized language, i.e. natural language. As Rich (1984) notes, 'natural languages are concise and efficient when the universe of possible messages is large', which is the case when experts face new, unpredictable situations.

The processing of unusual situations thus modifies the communications:

(1) On the one hand, the content of communications is altered: discussions concern the preconditions of the interpretation of the situations, the status and origin of the mental models, the relevance of past experience, etc. (Rasmussen, 1985).

(2) On the other (and consequently), operators return to the use of a non-specialized language, which is less concise but more flexible than their operative language.

Several examples will be given here, taken from the world of ATC (air traffic control). As will be seen the situations may be unusual in different ways.

An incidental dialogue

The first example (Figure 5) is borrowed from Mell (1987), and involves a French air traffic controller and an English pilot. When the conversation begins, the pilot has committed several offences according to the rules of air traffic control:

(1) He entered the zone (20 minutes ago) without calling the controller. Since then, he has not replied to the controller's calls.
(2) He is following a forbidden route, and has created several risks of collision with other aircraft.
(3) His silence could be caused by a radio failure, but then he should have followed the last clearances that were given or his original flight plan.

The operative language is totally abandoned by the controller, and this continues until the situation has been normalized. Mell points out several characteristics of this conversation:

(1) It is abnormally long compared to usual ATC dialogues.
(2) Speech turns are longer (more words, more dialogue acts).
(3) Illocutory acts differ from those used in routine situations (in particular: no commands at all).
(4) The thematic and notional content is diversified (reference to past events, causal relations, sequential relations, evaluative comments, etc). In routine situations, most conversations are monothematic.

This example dealt with a 'true' incident, in which a real danger existed. But this characteristic need not appear. Even in non-dangerous incidents, communication is altered, as the next example will show.

An incidental dialogue involving no danger

This dialogue (Figure 6) takes place in the context of airport control. An aircraft is about to take off. The first communications are routine ones, using the ATC operative language. At the fifth communication, the pilot warns the controller that a warning on the cockpit's control panel prohibits his taking off. The plane

C—Seven two one four, France control, do you read me?
[...]
C—Seven two one four, France
P—Seven two one four, bonjour. We checked LOUT at three seven, passing three two zero for three five zero, estimating CANG at five seven
C—Yes sir. I'm very glad to speak with you now, but will you please remind that when you are getting a radio failure the squawk is seven six zero zero
P—What radio failure? We were ... we were in contact with France on one two six two five, we called them. They didn't reply to us, we heard other aircraft
C—I'm sorry, but all the centres are calling you for twenty minutes and no reply, so I guess you're under radio failure. So I would appreciate you squawk seven six zero zero. I made two radar separations with two other aircraft with you because I had no contact with you
P—Will you contact SEIL then? Because they gave us frequencies and we went one two eight eight five. We went across to one two six two five and we were working SEIL on those frequencies and they did not give us a frequency change
C—Yes sir but your previous clearance certified your climb to maintain three five zero on course to MEND Mike Echo November, and from your present position you are ten miles north of Alpha Golf November. There is a real mistake
P—Yes, our flight plan that we put in was PENG, LOUT, GANE, CANG, and that was a flight plan that fitted at GERO
C—Yes sir, but your clearance ... your clearance ... your clearance provided by SEIL centre specified to climb level three five zero on course to Mike Echo November, so this clearance ... this clearance is very strict and you must adhere with this clearance, not with your flight plan sir
P—That's clear, I'm sorry, and we gave our position reports as we went along which were acknowledged
C—Yes but I think this is a very dangerous position for you and the other aircraft all over you
P—Well, why didn't someone tell us before?
C—I'm sorry, but I must file an official report about this incident sir.
[...]

Figure 5. An incidental ATC dialogue (taken from Mell, 1987, by permission)

is on the runway at that time. The controller must ask the pilot to get out of the way, in order for the other aircraft to be able to take off.

The following speech is characteristic of unusual situations: again, the controller switches back to natural language. This is all the more surprising since, contrary to the previous case, the commands to be issued could have been expressed through the ATC operative language. After all, they concern movements on the runways and taxiways which are routinely issued by the controller.

C—TWA 122 heavy, 28 left, position and hold
P—Position and hold, 28 left, TWA 122
[..]
C—TWA 122, 28 left, cleared for take-off
P—Clear for take-off, 28 left, 122 heavy
[..]
P—TWA 122 heavy, we've got an N1 indication and that was not acceptable for take-off. We'll have to taxi clear and take a look at it, hold on
C—Roger. Make a left turn next taxiway and you can taxi back
P—Okay, we'll take the left turn and get well out of the way and then we'll hold just off the runway and I'll lock into a taxi back, okay
[..]
C—TWA 122, I tell you what, why don't you just taxi down on the runway 19 left, make a left turn on 19 left, that way you could run your engine without bothering anybody if you want, and then you can make right or left turn at Fox, whatever
P—Aaah, we're committed to this turn, well go over to ground and then we'll do that as necessary, okay
C—Alright
P—TWA 122 heavy
C—TWA 122 heavy, easy on the power, there'll be departing traffic behind you

Figure 6. An incidental ATC dialogue involving no danger

But the fact that the situation script is not strictly complied with is sufficient to modify the language used.

An unequal-knowledge dialogue

A third example (Figure 7. This dialogue is translated from French) concerns a very rare situation within expert–expert dialogues: a situation in which knowledge is not equal on both sides. Operative languages are developed in situations in which the shared knowledge is large. If the ATC language (and operative languages in general) are difficult to understand for the layman, it is because they are elaborated in addition to a knowledge base that is foreign to the non-specialist.

What happens in this dialogue is that the pilot is not aware of a modification of an approach procedure in the Paris area. The controller realizes this, and begins a long explanation of the procedure. Here again, the language used is closer to natural language than to the ATC operative language.

What the examples above teach us is that the processing of unusual situations may involve using a language more complex than the one used in routine situations. This finding has direct implications for the design of interactive

C—601 Q, you will proceed ROLEX after Luxeuil
P—Ah. If your wish ...
P—You did say ROLEX after Luxeuil, is that correct?
C—ROLEX
P—... I didn't find it
C—601 Q, I confirm: you proceed ROLEX after Luxeuil
P—Yes, I am looking for it, I don't find this point
C—601 Q?
P—Yes?
C—Yes, then ROLEX exists since about one month Sir, a note of information has been issued. You should have had it ... since April 15
P—Yes but you confirm it is Romeo Oscar Lima Alpha Tango?
C—Romeo Oscar Lima Echo X-ray. It is an intersection point which ... you proceed your route after Luxeuil on the 273 radial 273 from Luxeuil to intercept the 153 of Rolampont, and then, if you go to Orly, you go direct to Melun, and if you go to Roissy, you go to Troyes
P—Alright, thank you

Figure 7. A dialogue caused by unequal knowledge

systems. System designers cannot expect users to behave in the same way when they are confronted with unexpected or new situations: the linguistic behavior will vary.

Operative understanding and unusual situations

The occurrence of unusual situations affects also operative understanding. The speaker must first note that the usual assumptions about the characteristics of the interlocutor or of the situation are not applicable, and must adapt his or her behavior accordingly. This is not always easily done. As Ochanine (1978) points out, operative behavior, which is very efficient in known situations, can be a nuisance in unusual ones. Subjects may well fail to notice that the situation is a non-routine one: even contradictory information will pass unnoticed. Even if they are able to identify the situation as new, they may experience difficulty in getting rid of their usual processing activity.

The following illustration of these difficulties is borrowed from Falzon *et al.* (1986). It has been explained earlier how the secretaries studied by these authors used a canonical model of the client in order to maximize communication efficiency. Their use of a canonical model is not obvious when everything goes well, i.e. when the client corresponds to the model. It can be detected when clients differ significantly from the model. Secretaries may experience some difficulty in noticing these differences and in recovering from the model failure. The dialogue in Figure 8 provides an example (this dialogue is translated from French).

S—Medical centre, good morning
C—Well, my son had an appointment on May 24, at 18:30
S—Who's calling
C—With the ophthalmologist and his file number is 17416
S—This is kind of you, very kind of you Madam
C—Well you know we did not have the number this morning
S—Well yes, hold on, hold on until I find it. Excuse me
C—The 24th ... Laurent Fanier
S—June 24? No it's a Sunday
C—No no, not June 24, May 24. Today is the 7th
S—No, today is June 7
C—Yes, but then it was May 24
S—He had an appointment, yes, and he did not turn up?
C—I would like to know if he came
S—Oh, alright, yes alright. Hold on, so you said the number is ...
C—17416, the file
S—17416 then, well hold on, I look for it
C—It is important for me
S—Here it is, yes
C—Yes
S—Well yes he did come Madam
C—He came
S—Yes yes yes
C—[...]

Figure 8. An incidental appointment dialogue (from Falzon *et al.*, 1986, reproduced by permission of Elsevier Science Publishers)

In this dialogue, a client (C) is calling to check whether her son turned up at an appointment he had on 24 May (the date is 7 June). As soon as the word 'appointment' is mentioned the secretary (S) assumes that the client is calling to obtain or modify an appointment, because this is what clients usually want. Starting from this assumption, she understands (wrongly) that the appointment is on 24 June (although the client said '24 May'), since the date of a requested appointment is always in the future. Then she consults the appointment's diary and discovers that 24 June is a Sunday. The client realizes the mistake at this point and attempts to correct it, with some difficulty.

This example shows how operative understanding can lead to a false interpretation of the interlocutor's words. In this example, the client's request, although non-standard, does not differ very widely from usual requests. More unusual situations lead to far longer recovery dialogues.

Situation complexity and dialogue processes

In both situations (expert–expert dialogues and expert/non-expert dialogues) variations in the complexity of the situations lead to variations in dialogue processes. In expert–expert dialogues non-routine situations result in the abandoning of the operative language of the domain and a switch towards natural language. In consultation dialogues, the detection of a non-routine situation causes a switch towards a more complex processing of the request.

CONCLUSION

Here we consider three points that have been omitted from the above sections. First, we develop one aspect of cooperative dialogues that deserves specific attention: interlocutor modelling. Second, we describe some categories of dialogues on which little research has been conducted and the benefits one can expect from their study. Finally, we insist on the importance of studies of cooperative dialogues for a better understanding of collective activities.

Interlocutor modelling

Interlocutor modelling has already appeared several times in this chapter. It has been seen that dialogues between experts do not require us to build a model of the interlocutor's knowledge. In these dialogues, interlocutors are assumed to share a common knowledge. Thus they do not have to *elaborate* a model of the interlocutor (except perhaps for minor aspects). Communication operates assuming the veracity of a predefined model. For instance, dialogues between air traffic controllers and pilots function on the basis of a shared knowledge of the rules of civil aviation. The existence of this underlying implicit model is demonstrated by the modifications that occur in verbal interactions when one of the interlocutors ignores a fact. The modelling activity is only concerned with minor aspects, e.g. the ease of a pilot in using English (the international language of air traffic control).

The use of an interlocutor model is one aspect of operative understanding. The aim of this section is to show how interlocutor modelling plays a central part in various task-oriented dialogues. Two large classes of situations will be differentiated: tutoring situations and assistance situations.

Interlocutor modelling in tutoring dialogues

Tutoring dialogues occur in situations in which the goal is explicitly pedagogical. The objective of the expert is not to provide a solution to the non-expert (although he or she may occasionally do this) but rather to help the novice in finding a solution. In that sense, tutoring situations differ from consultation situations, in which the expert's activity is focused on providing a solution. In tutoring dialogues the task of the expert does not consist of solving the problem processed by the novice but in assessing the gaps and misconceptions in the novice's knowledge, i.e. in elaborating a model of that knowledge.

The fundamental activity of the expert is thus a modelling one. Several formalizations of this activity have been implemented in intelligent tutoring systems (ITS). All involve a mapping of the novice's knowledge on a representation of expert knowledge. Three categories of models have been proposed.

(1) *Overlay models*: novice knowledge is defined as a subset of the expert knowledge (e.g. Carr and Goldstein, 1977). The problem with these models is that they indicate the items of knowledge that have actually been used by the novice but not what should have been used.
(2) *Differential models*: novice knowledge is defined with reference to the subset of the expert domain knowledge that an expert would have actually used in a similar situation (e.g. Burton and Brown, 1982). The secret is to have the ITS solve the same problem and mark all knowledge units it uses. This is used to focus subsequent learning.
(3) *Perturbation models*: overlay models and differential models assume that novice knowledge is a subset of expert knowledge. In fact, novice knowledge may include aspects that are beyond the scope of the expert domain knowledge, e.g. erroneous beliefs, misconceptions, bugs, etc. Perturbation models attempt to describe these aspects (Stevens *et al.*, 1982; Burton, 1982; Sleeman, 1982).

There is no point in providing examples of tutoring situations, but it may be worth giving some references about studies of real tutoring dialogues, since these are not so numerous. Such studies have been conducted in learning a programming language (McKendree *et al.*, 1984) and in studying meteorology (Stevens *et al.*, 1982). A synthesis on user modelling in ITSs can be found in Kass (1987).

Interlocutor modelling in assistance dialogues

Assistance dialogues occur when a non-expert requires the advice of an expert on a relevant problem. The expert has to provide a diagnosis of the problem met by the non-expert. The characteristic of these dialogues is to be oriented towards a solution to the problem met by the non-expert, and not towards the teaching of the domain to the non-expert, although these dialogues often include phases in which the expert transfers some items of knowledge.

Assistance dialogues vary greatly in complexity, since they cover not only very simple situations of information request (e.g. flight timetable dialogues) but also more complex diagnosis situations such as medical interviews (Evans,

1976), or dialogues with computer experts (Alty and Coombs, 1980; Aaronson and Carroll, 1986).

It must first be noted that in many of these situations the interlocutor model is not elaborated but only applied: the expert uses a predefined model of the typical interlocutor. An example of such a situation has been developed earlier in this chapter, taken from a study of the activity of secretaries at a medical centre (Falzon *et al.*, 1986). We have been able to show that the secretaries make use of a canonical model of the typical client, which allows us to speed up the dialogue by avoiding some conversation steps.

Canonical models have two characteristics. First, they do not have to be built during dialogue; they pre-exist. Second, they are very often used implicitly. This is especially true of computer systems. All computer systems make use of a user model, but this model is very often not explicit. The interpretation rules of Lubonski's system (1985), which have been presented above, are a good example of the use of an implicit model. Another example of implicit modelling can be found in Hayes and Reddy (1983).

Although the object of the expert's task is not the transfer of knowledge, interlocutor modelling plays an important part in assistance dialogues, as the examples below will show. We will differentiate between interlocutor modelling as an intermediate step in problem solving and interlocutor modelling as a tool for dialogue management.

Interlocutor modelling as an intermediate step in problem solving

Interlocutor modelling may intervene as an intermediate (and essential) step in problem solving. A general framework for these situations is provided by Clancey (1984). Clancey presents the expert system MYCIN as an example of heuristic classification. Starting from the patient data, and through a process of data abstraction, a model of the patient is elaborated. The model is then 'heuristically classified', i.e. matched with a classification of disease classes. Finally, a refinement process leads to a diagnosis of a specific illness within a class.

The general idea is thus that the interlocutor's model is, in some situations, an intermediate step in a problem-solving activity. The content of the model varies according to the type of classification problem. In MYCIN's perspective, the content of the model deals with the patient's symptoms, but it may be quite different in other situations.

Another example is provided by Rich (1979) in her work on GRUNDY. This is a system that attempts to simulate the behavior of a librarian. During dialogue, it elaborates a model of the user which is then used to select a book in GRUNDY's database. As in MYCIN, the user model is thus matched with a classification of solutions (a classification of books) in order to reach a solution (a specific book). Here, the content of the model deals with the user's personality traits.

Interlocutor modelling as a tool for dialogue management

In the above situations the interlocutor model plays a necessary part, either as the object of the activity (tutoring systems) or as an intermediate step in reasoning. In other situations, the interlocutor model may be used 'additionally', in the sense that the model is not necessary for the task to be fulfilled but that it helps in fulfilling the task. Two examples will be provided. In the first, interlocutor modelling is used for dialogue adaptation; in the second, it is employed for dialogue adaptation and problem solving.

Interlocutor modelling and dialogue adaptation. The first example comes from a study by Isaacs and Clark (1987). The authors use a modified replication of a method designed by Krauss and Weinheimer (1964) in which two subjects collaborate to fulfil a matching task. In Isaacs and Clark's experiment the subjects are given a set of cards depicting the sights of New York. One of the partners (the director) is given these pictures arranged in a specific order. The other partner (the matcher) is given the picture set and has to arrange them in the same order, with the help of the director. The two partners have to execute this task several times (the order of the pictures varies each time). They communicate only by voice (they do not see each other).

Subjects vary in their knowledge of New York. Four conditions are tested, corresponding to four director-matcher pairs: expert-expert, expert-novice, novice-expert, novice-novice. Recordings of the sessions are made. Data analysis is focused on the way the places appearing on the pictures are referenced in each type of pair, and how reference varies along trials.

Results indicate first that the findings of previous studies are confirmed (e.g. whatever the pair, there is a decrease along trials in the number of words necessary to refer to the pictures). However, for our purpose, the interesting result is that partners are able to see very early during dialogues the level of knowledge of New York of their interlocutor, and to adapt their behavior accordingly. Novice directors learn the names of the sights (through the cooperative answers of the experts) and expert directors learn to use them less. Each partner may evaluate the level of competence of the interlocutor by analyzing their interventions. For instance:

(1) The director gives a name and the matcher agrees = expert/expert.
(2) The director gives a name and the matcher answers a description or refuses = expert/novice.
(3) The director gives a description and the matcher provides a name = novice/expert.

(4) The director gives a description and the matcher agrees = novice/novice.
(5) The director gives a description and a name and the matcher provides a description or a request for clarification = expert/novice.

Other clues may be used, such as:
(1) Use of definite or indefinite articles (*the* flea market versus *a* flea market).
(2) Experts refer to the place pictured, novices to the picture itself.
(3) Experts consider the place (independently of its specific representation on the picture), novices consider the representation provided, including irrelevant details.

Interlocutor modelling and diagnosis. We have been able to describe a very similar modelling situation in a field study of diagnosis by telephone (Falzon, 1987). The study was conducted in a firm which constructs and sells programmable controllers. Some of the firm's engineers are in charge of answering telephone queries from clients who find difficulties in using the equipment they have bought. The equipment is of varying complexity, and the callers have various levels of competence in the domain. The task of the engineers is to diagnose the origin of the client's problem.

Telephone conversations have been recorded and transcribed. Interviews have taken place with the engineers, focusing on the way they handled these conversations. A second interview was conducted, at least two months after the recordings, using the following method. The engineer had to read, line by line, the transcription of his conversations and was asked to verbalize all he could say about the dialogue.

The object of this procedure was originally to gain some insight into the way the diagnosis was performed. The striking result is that many of the verbalizations do not concern the problem but the level of competence of the client. These evaluative remarks occur very early, after having read a few lines of transcription. Evaluation sems to be made using two kinds of information:

(1) The content of the client's speech: the technical concepts mentioned by the client, the correctness of the links between concepts, the relevance of the level of description of the problem, etc.
(2) The way these concepts are expressed by the client: hesitations, for example, are noted.

Evaluation is then made both on the grounds of technical knowledge and verbal behavior. This evaluative activity has consequences on both diagnosis and dialogue management, as Figure 9 shows.

These observations also indicate how modelling the interlocutor's domain knowledge helps in choosing an appropriate level of processing. In the case of a 'low domain knowledge' evaluation of the request will probably require only a

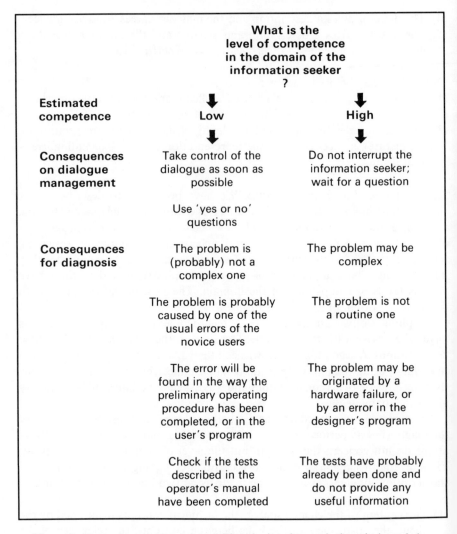

	What is the level of competence in the domain of the information seeker ?	
Estimated competence	**Low**	**High**
Consequences on dialogue management	Take control of the dialogue as soon as possible	Do not interrupt the information seeker; wait for a question
	Use 'yes or no' questions	
Consequences for diagnosis	The problem is (probably) not a complex one	The problem may be complex
	The problem is probably caused by one of the usual errors of the novice users	The problem is not a routine one
	The error will be found in the way the preliminary operating procedure has been completed, or in the user's program	The problem may be originated by a hardware failure, or by an error in the designer's program
	Check if the tests described in the operator's manual have been completed	The tests have probably already been done and do not provide any useful information

Figure 9. Some consequences of modelling the interlocutor's domain knowledge

minimum of processing. A 'high domain knowledge' evaluation implies a non-routine problem, thus a more complex processing. Interlocutor modelling plays a part in regulating the cognitive implication of the expert.

Further explorations in cooperative dialogues

Three types of dialogues will be considered here: consultation interaction in design, multi-expert problem solving, and knowledge elicitation.

Design

Design dialogues are a specific class of consultation dialogues, in which a non-expert requires some expert advice on a relevant problem (i.e. a problem that belongs to the domain of competence of the expert). The expert has to design a solution, starting from the information provided by the non-expert. The task for the expert consists of eliciting the necessary information and translating it into terms that are meaningful within the task context (i.e. in terms of functional constraints). Dialogues between clients and architects are good examples of such situations (Lebahar, 1983).

The study of design dialogues would allow a better specification of the interface of expert systems in design when these systems have to be consulted by non-expert users. Very little research has been conducted on this subject (however, see Malhotra *et al.*, 1980).

Multi-expert problem solving

This class of dialogue and the next (knowledge-elicitation dialogues) belong to a more general class: dialogues between experts of different domains. Multi-expert problem-solving dialogues occur in situations in which specialists in different domains have to collaborate in order to reach a solution. The characteristics of these situations are thus:

(1) The expertise domains of the dialogue partners differ.
(2) The problem is common to all dialogue partners.
(3) Its solution requires the knowledge of all dialogue partners.

Such dialogues can be found in large design projects, involving various specialists. In harbour design, for instance, several experts are involved: architects, economists, naval architects, marine specialists, etc. All these specialists have to cooperate in order to reach a solution. However, it is to be noted that dialogues of the same category may also occur in situations of pseudo-sequential design. In many work situations design is assumed to take place sequentially: various actors provide successive specifications, each actor using the output of the preceding one as input data. It is well known (see, for instance, Visser, 1988) that design is only partially sequential. In many cases an actor has to go back to the preceding actor in order to ask for modifications. These dialogues are also examples of multi-expert problem-solving conversations.

To say the least, these dialogues have not been studied extensively. However, they could give interesting indications in at least two domains:

(1) Obviously, for the design of multi-expert systems.
(2) For the design of interfaces of expert systems when these systems are to be consulted by experts in other domains.

This second case is somewhat futuristic at present. Most experts systems are designed in order to help (human) experts in the same domain. There are in fact serious doubts concerning their efficiency in that respect (cf. Bisseret, 1984; Woods, 1986). However, an interface that would allow an expert system to have a dialogue with a (human) expert in another domain would be very beneficial.

Knowledge elicitation

Knowledge-elicitation dialogues are also a particular case of multi-expert dialogues. In these, the expertise of one of the experts (the knowledge engineer) lies in an ability to elicit and formalize the knowledge of the other. These cannot be considered as simple consultation dialogues, since the processed object is the knowledge possessed by the other expert and not the answer to a particular problem. Even if the method of knowledge elicitation consists of observing the expert solving a problem, the knowledge engineer is not in fact interested in the solution to the problem but in what it reveals of the expert knowledge.

For this reason, there is some similarity between elicitation dialogues and tutoring dialogues. The tutor is interested in the problem only as far as its resolution by the trainee gives indications on the trainee's level of knowledge. In both types of dialogues one of the interlocutors (the knowledge engineer or the tutor) attempts to model the knowledge of the other.

However, elicitation dialogues cannot be considered as tutoring dialogues, since the knowledge used for modelling differs. The tutor disposes of a large body of domain knowledge, plus some meta-information dealing with typical misconceptions, usual errors, difficult issues to learn, etc. Knowledge engineers, of course, do not dispose of such elements of information. They 'read' the expert knowledge according to their available modelling tools: formal logic, reasoning models, representation formalisms, etc.

Studies of knowledge-elicitation dialogues are scarce. What exists, of course, is a literature concerning methods of analysis of knowledge-elicitation protocols (e.g. Ericsson and Simon, 1984; Kidd, 1987), but there seems to be little interest in the way in which these dialogues operate. The obvious application of such studies concerns automatic knowledge-acquisition systems, elicitation environments and learning systems.

A plea for the study of cooperative dialogues

This section is devoted to a presentation of the possible benefits of studying dialogue activities in collective tasks.

Dialogue analysis as a tool for task analysis

A first point is that dialogue analysis is a tool for task analysis. Verbal behavior is sensitive to the variations of the situations to be processed. For instance, we have seen above how experts abandoned operative languages when facing unusual situations. Similarly, in consultation dialogues we have seen how recovery activities had to take place when the expert faced an unpredicted request. Thus, variations in dialogue behavior indicate modifications in problem processing.

Dialogue analysis is a prerequisite for training

Operative languages are elaborated while operative knowledge in the domain is being built. Initially, they are not taught during training, although the learning of these languages often becomes, after a while, part of the training. Their acquisition then becomes a prerequisite for action. For instance, Bross (quoted by Argyle *et al.*, 1981) notes that 'underlying the effective action of the surgeon is an effective language', the language of anatomy, which must be learnt by the students before they can be taught surgical procedures.

Consequently, the study of operative languages is necessary for training purposes: novices have to learn the domain language. Another reason for their study is that it may become necessary to adapt existing operative languages or to create new ones. A first point is that operative languages may include undesired features: for instance, there may be a lack of discriminability between some commands. These features should be eliminated, especially when safety is at stake (see Wiener, 1987, for examples). A second point concerns the cases when new technology (and notably computer systems) are introduced within a community which already possesses its own professional language. Nygaard (1984) advocates that this professional language should be carefully adapted in order to integrate the concepts of the new technology. This new, adapted, professional language should be the basis for the design of the language of interaction with the system.

Dialogue analysis as guidelines for interface design

Several lessons can be learnt from the analysis of human–human dialogues. The first is that, in dialogues between experts, natural language is not the natural language of interaction. Experts use operative languages, as least as long as they deal with usual situations. This supports the idea of designing command languages in restricted natural language.

A second lesson is that the use of natural language does not mean that understanding is complex. As can be seen from the analysis of dialogues between expert and non-expert, operative understanding limits the complexity of the comprehension processes. This idea is implicit in a number of interactive systems, which allow the use of natural language but which produce a partial understanding of the user's interventions.

Finally, a third lesson is that the means of dialogue vary according to the characteristics of the situation. Cognitive economy rules the experts' functioning. Operative languages and operative understanding are used in routine activities. As soon as an unusual situation occurs, experts switch to natural language or to a more elaborate processing of the interlocutor's interventions. In terms of system design, this means that systems should function at varying levels of complexity, according to the nature of the situations. When possible, they should accept (and output) operative languages and apply economic procedures of interpretation. However, they also should accept natural language and should be able to use more elaborate processing procedures when needed.

Address for Correspondence:

Dr Pierre Falzon, INRIA, Domaine de Voluceau Rocquencourt, BP105, F78153 Le Chesnay Cedex, France.

REFERENCES

Aaronson, A. and Carroll, J. M. (1986) *The answer is in the question: a protocol study of intelligent help.* Report RC 12034, Yorktown Heights, New York: IBM Watson Research Center.

Addis, T. R. (1977) Machine understanding of natural language. *International Journal of Man–Machine Studies*, **9**, 207–22.

Alty, J. L., and Coombs, M. J. (1980) Face-to-face guidance of university computer users—I. A study of advisory services. *International Journal of Man–Machine Studies*, **12**, 389–405.

Anderson, R. C., and Ortony, A. (1975) On putting apples into bottles. A problem of polysemy. *Cognitive Psychology*, **7**, 167–80.

Argyle, M., Furnham, A., and Graham, J. A. (1981) *Social Situations.* London: Cambridge University Press.

Bell, P. (1985) *Hightech Writing. How to write for the electronics industry.* New York: John Wiley.

Bisseret, A. (1983) Psychology for man–computer cooperation in knowledge processing. In R.F.A. Masson (ed.), *IFIP 83, Information Processing 83.* Amsterdam: Elsevier, North-Holland.

Bisseret, A. (1984) Expert computer-aided decision in supervisory control. *Proceedings of the IFAC Conference (IFAC'84)*, Budapest, 2–6 July.

Bunt, H. (1981) Conversational principles in question–answer dialogues. In D. Krallman and G. Stickel (eds), *Zur Theorie der Frage.* Tübingen: Gunter Narr Verlag.

Burton, R. R. (1982) Diagnosing bugs in a simple procedural skill. In D. Sleeman and J. S. Brown (eds), *Intelligent Tutoring Systems.* London: Academic Press.

Burton, R. R., and Brown, J. S. (1982) An investigation of computer coaching for informal learning activities. In D. Sleeman and J. S. Brown (eds), *Intelligent Tutoring Systems.* London: Academic Press.

Carr, B., and Goldstein, I. P. (1977) *Overlays: a theory of modelling for computer-aided instruction.* Technical report A. I. Memo 406, Cambridge, Mass.: MIT Artificial Intelligence Laboratory.

Charrow, V. R., Crandall, J. A., and Charrow, R. P. (1982) Characteristics and functions of legal language. In R. Kittredge and J. Lehrberger (eds), *Sublanguage. Studies of language in restricted semantic domains*. Berlin: De Gruyter.
Clancey, W. J. (1984) *Classification problem solving*. Report STAN-CS-84-1018, Stanford, CA: Department of Computer Science, Stanford University.
Clark, H. H. (1983) Making sense of nonce sense. In G. B. Flores d'Arcais and R. J. Jarvella (eds), *The Process of Language Understanding*. New York: John Wiley.
Clark, H. H., and Wilkes-Gibbs, D. (1986) Referring as a collaborative process. *Cognition*, **22** (1), 1–39.
Coulon, D., and Kayser, D. (1982) La compréhension: un processus à profondeur variable. *Bulletin de Psychologie*, **35** (11), 815–23.
Cuny, X. (1971) Perspectives sémiologiques en psychologie du travail. *Cahiers de Linguistique Théorique et Appliquée*, **VII**, 53–72.
Dachelet, R., and Normier, B. (1982) *Etude de la langue des comptes rendus d'hospitalisation en vue d'une analyse automatique*. Rapport de fin de contrat ADI 82/042, Paris: ERLI.
de Heaulme, M. (1982) Approche du traitement des données médicales textuelles. *Communication au colloque de l'A.R.C. sur 'Domaines et objectifs de la recherche cognitivé*, Pont-à-Mousson, 21–23 April.
de Heaulme, M., and Frutiger, P. (1984) Analyse du processus cognitif médical. Approche d'une implémentation par la technique des langages contrôlés. *Communication au colloque de l'A.R.C. sur 'Les modes de raisonnement'*, Orsay, 25–27 April.
Ericsson, K. A., and Simon, H. A. (1984) *Protocol Analysis. Verbal reports as data*. Cambridge, Mass.: MIT Press.
Evans, C. R. (1976) Improving the communication between people and computer. In *Proceedings of the NATO ASI on Man–Computer Interaction*, Alphen aan den Rijn, Netherlands.
Falzon, P. (1982) *Les communications verbales en situation de travail. Analyse des restrictions du langage naturel*. Technical Report 19, Projet de Psychologie Ergonomique, Rocquencourt: INRIA.
Falzon, P. (1983) *Understanding a technical language*. Research Report 237, Projet de Psychologie Ergonomique, Rocquencourt: INRIA.
Falzon, P. (1984) The analysis and understanding of an operative language. In *Proceedings of INTERACT'84, 1st IFIP Conference Human–Computer Interaction*, London, 4–7 September.
Falzon, P. (1987) *Les dialogues de diagnostic: L'évaluation des connaissances de l'interlocuteur*. Report 747, Rocquencourt: INRIA.
Falzon, P., Amalberti, R., and Carbonell, N. (1986) Dialogue control strategies in oral communication. In K. Hopper and I. A. Newman (eds), *Foundation for Human–Computer Communication*. Amsterdam: North-Holland.
Gibbs, R. W. (1979) Contextual effects in understanding indirect requests. *Discourse Processes*, **2**, 1–10.
Gibbs, R. W. (1981) Your wish is my command: convention and context in interpreting indirect requests. *Journal of Verbal Learning and Verbal Behavior*, **20**, 431–44.
Gregory, M., and Carroll, S. (1978) *Language and situation: Language varieties and their social contexts*. London: Routledge & Kegan Paul.
Grice, P. (1975) Logic and conversation. In P. Cole and J. C. Morgan (eds), *Syntax and Semantics*, Vol. III, *Speech Acts*. New York: Academic Press.
Grosz, B. (1982) Discourse analysis. In R. Kittredge and J. Lehrberger (eds), *Sublanguage. Studies of language in restricted semantic domains*. Berlin: De Gruyter.
Guilbert, L. (1973) La spécificité du terme scientifique et technique. *Langue Française*, **17**, 5–17.

Hammerton, M. (1976) How much is a large part? *Applied Ergonomics*, **7** (1), 10–12.

Hauptmann, A. G., and Green, B. F. (1983) A comparison of command, menu-selection and natural-language computer programs. *Behaviour and Information Technology*, **2** (2), 163–78.

Hayes, P. J., and Reddy, D. R. (1983) Steps towards graceful interaction in spoken and written man–machine communication. *International Journal of Man–Machine Studies*, **19**, 231–84.

Hendler, J. A., and Michaelis, P. R. (1983) The effects of limited grammar on interactive natural language. In A. Janda (ed.), *Proceedings of the CHI'83 Conference on Human Factors in Computing Systems*, Boston, Mass., 12–15 December.

Hobbs (1979) Conversation as planned behavior. In *Proceedings of the 6th IJCAI*, 390–396, Tokyo.

Isaacs, E. A., and Clark, H. H. (1987) References in conversation between experts and novices. *Journal of Experimental Psychology*, **116** (1), 26–37.

Kass, R. (1987) *The role of user modelling in intelligent tutoring systems.* Report MS-CIS-86-58, LINC LAB 41. Philadelphia, PA: Department of Computer and Information Science, University of Pennsylvania.

Kelley, J. F. (1983) An empirical methodology for writing user-friendly natural language computer applications. In A. Janda (ed.), *Proceedings of the CHI'83 Conference on Human Factors in Computing Systems*, Boston, Mass., 12–15 December.

Kelly, M. J., and Chapanis, A. (1977) Limited vocabulary natural language dialogue. *International Journal of Man–Machine Studies*, **9**, 479–501.

Kidd, A. L. (1987) *Knowledge Acquisition Techniques for Expert Systems.* New York: Plenum.

Kittredge, R. (1979) Textual cohesion within sublanguages: implications for automatic analysis and synthesis. Actes du colloque IRIA-LISH sur *Représentation des connaissances et raisonnement dans les sciences de l'homme*, St Maximin, France, 17–19 September.

Kittredge, R. (1982) Variation and homogeneity of sublanguages. In R. Kittredge and J. Lehrberger (eds), *Sublanguage. Studies of language in restricted semantic domains.* Berlin: De Gruyter.

Kittredge, R., and Mel'Cuk, I. (1983) Towards a computable model of meaning-text relations within a natural sublanguage. *Proceedings of the 8th IJCAI*, Karlsruhe, FRG.

Krauss, R. M., and Weinheimer, S. (1964) Changes in reference phrases as a function of frequency of usage in social interaction: a preliminary study. *Psychonomic Science*, **1**, 113–14.

Lebahar, J.-C. (1983) *Le dessin d'architecte. Simulation graphique et réduction d'incertitude.* Roquevaire: Editions Parenthèses.

Lehrberger, J. (1982) Automatic translation and the concept of sublanguage. In R. Kittredge and J. Lehrberger (eds), *Sublanguage. Studies of language in restricted semantic domains.* Berlin: De Gruyter.

Leroy, C. (1985) Structure des requètes. In *Analyse linguistique d'un corpus d'oral finalisé*, Etude collective sous la direction de M.-A. Morel, Rapport au GRECO Communication Parlée (GRECO No. 39).

Lubonski, P. (1985) Natural language interface for a Polish railway expert system. In V. Dahl and P. Saint-Dizier (eds), *Natural Language Understanding and Logic Programming.* Amsterdam: North-Holland.

Luzzati, D. (1984) Discours et signification dans l'oral-ordinateur. In J. M. Pierrel, N. Carbonell, J. P. Haton and F. Neel (eds), *Dialogue homme–machine à composante orale*, Actes du séminaire GRECO-Communication Parlée, Nancy, 11–12 October.

Malhotra, A. (1975) *Design criteria for a knowledge-based English language system for management: an experimental analysis*, Report TR-146, Cambridge, Mass.: MIT.

Malhotra, A., and Sheridan, P. B. (1976) *Experimental determination of design requirements for a program explanation system.* Report RC 5831. Yorktown Heights: IBM T. J. Watson Research Center.

Malhotra, A., Thomas, J. C., Carroll, J. M., and Miller, L. A. (1980) Cognitive processes in design. *International Journal of Man–Machine Studies*, **12**, 119–40.

McKendree, J. M., Reiser, B. J., and Anderson, J. R. (1984) Tutorial goals and strategies in the instruction of programming skills. *Proceedings of the Cognitive Science Conference*, Boulder, Colorado, June.

Mell, J. (1987) *Les besoins langagiers en anglais des contrôleurs de la Navigation Aérienne en France, et les problèmes de formation.* Document of the Section des Sciences du Langage, Université de Toulouse II, Toulouse, France.

Meyer, B. (1985) On formalism in specifications. *IEEE Software*, **2** (1), 6–26.

Michaelis, P. R., Chapanis, A., Weeks, G. D., and Kelly, M. J. (1977) Word usage in interactive dialog with restricted and unrestricted vocabularies. *IEEE Transactions on Professional Communication*, **PC-20** (4), 214–21.

Miller, L. A. (1981) Natural language programming: Styles, strategies and contrasts. *IBM Systems Journal*, **20** (2), 184–215.

Moskovich, W. (1982) What is a sublanguage? The notion of sublanguage in modern Soviet linguistics. In R. Kittredge and J. Lehrberger (eds), *Sublanguage. Studies of language in restricted semantic domains.* Berlin: De Gruyter.

Moyne, J. A. (1977) Simple English for data base communication. *International Journal of Computer and Information Sciences*, **5** (4), 327–43.

Nygaard, K. (1984) Profession oriented languages. In *Proceedings of the European Congress on Medical Informatics*, Brussels, 10–13 September.

Ochanine, D. (1978) Le rôle des images opératives dans la régulation des activités de travail. *Psychologie et Education*, **3**, 63–5.

Oden, G. C. (1983) On the use of semantic constraints in guiding syntactic analysis. *International Journal of Man–Machine Studies*, **19**, 335–57.

Ogden, W. C., and Brooks, S. R. (1983) Query languages for the casual user: exploring the middle ground between formal and natural languages. In A. Janda (ed.), *Proceedings of the CHI'83 Conference on Human Factors in Computing Systems*, Boston, Mass., 12–15 December.

Phal, A. (1968) De la langue quotidienne à la langue des sciences et des techniques. *Le Français dans le Monde*, **61**, 7–11.

Rasmussen, J. (1985) *A framework for cognitive task analysis in systems design.* Report Risø-M-2519, Roskilde, Denmark: Risø National Laboratory.

Rialle, V. (1985) Du langage naturel spécialisé au système expert. *Actes de Cognitiva 85*, Vol. 1, Paris: CESTA.

Rich, E. (1979) User modeling via stereotypes. *Cognitive Science*, **3** (4), 329–54.

Rich, E. (1984) Natural language interfaces. *Computer*, **17** (9), 30–47.

Sager, N. (1981) *Natural Language Information Processing: a computer grammar of English and its applications.* London: Addison-Wesley.

Savoyant, A., and Leplat, J. (1983) Statut et fonction des communications dans l'activité des équipes de travail. *Psychologie Française*, **28** (3/4), 247–53.

Scapin, D. L. (1985) Intuitive representations and interaction languages: an exploratory experiment. In F. Klix (ed.), *MACINTER I.* Amsterdam: North Holland.

Shapiro, S. C., and Kwasny, S. C. (1975) Interactive consulting via natural language. *Communications of the ACM*, **18** (8), 459–62.

Sleeman, D. (1982) Assessing aspects of competence in basic algebra. In D. Sleeman and J. S. Brown (eds), *Intelligent Tutoring Systems*. London: Academic Press.

Stevens, A., Collins, A., and Goldin, S. E. (1982) Misconceptions in students' understanding. In D. Sleeman and J. S. Brown (eds), *Intelligent Tutoring Systems*. London: Academic Press.

Thomas, J. C. (1976) *A method for studying natural language dialogue*. Report RC 5882, Yorktown Heights, NJ: IBM Watson Research Center.

Visser, W. (1988) *Giving up a hierarchical plan in a design activity*. Research Report 814, Rocquencourt: INRIA.

Weizenbaum, J. (1966) ELIZA—a computer program for the study of natural language communications between man and machine. *Communications of the ACM*, **9**(1), 36–45.

Wiener, E. L. (1987) Fallible humans and vulnerable systems: lessons learned from aviation. In J. A. Wise and A. Debons (eds), *Information Systems: failure analysis*. (NATO ASI series, Vol. F32). Berlin: Springer Verlag.

Wixon, D., Whiteside, J., Gould, M., and Jones, S. (1983) Building a user-defined interface. In A. Janda (ed.), *Proceedings of the CHI'83 Conference on Human Factors in Computing Systems*, Boston, Mass., 12–15 December.

Woods, D. D. (1986) Cognitive technologies: the design of joint human-machine cognitive systems. *AI Magazine*, Winter (6), 86–92.

Woods, W. A. (1973) Progress in natural language understanding—an application to lunar geology. *Proceedings National Computer Conference*, Vol. 42, Montvale, NJ: AFIPS Press.

Part 2.4

Dynamic Decision Making

In Chapter 7, Brehmer discusses the problems which can appear from time delays in organizations, when decision making is involved in real-time control of cooperative work. This raises very explicitly the question of the characteristic of 'dynamic' decision making and the modelling problems involved, which are dealt with in more detail in Section 6.

Part 2

7. Modern Information Technology: Timescales and Distributed Decision Making[1]

Berndt Brehmer
Uppsala University

A system allows distributed decision making to the extent that it permits different persons in the system to function autonomously, without endangering the overall goals of the system. Conversely, a system may be said to require distributed decision making to the extent that its overall purpose can be realized only if some (or all) individuals in the system are required to act on their own.

The military system illustrates the problems facing the designer of a system characterized by distributed decision making. A military system for command and control may be seen as a compromise between a tendency towards distributed decision making and one towards centralized decision making. It is instructive to contemplate why this is the case (see Brehmer, 1988, for a more extensive discussion).

The problem here is a consequence of the dynamic nature of battle. Despite what John Wayne movies might suggest, the goals of a military campaign cannot be achieved by an individual. This is because the object of war, i.e. the domination of area, cannot be achieved by an individual; the areas in question are simply too large for that. Yet battles are fought by individuals. This simple observation has two important consequences: (1) there is a need for coordination of the individuals, and (2) as the individuals are coordinated in, say, platoons, there is a need to consider the problems of coordinating platoons (and so on, up to the army units), and this introduces the problems of time. A platoon requires the consideration of a different scale of time and area, and this, in turn, needs a new level of control. Hence, we arrive at the typical military hierarchical system. This system achieves the important objective of regulating the complexity of the command and control problem (by limiting the number of units that need to be monitored on each level in the command hierarchy). At the same

Distributed Decision Making: Cognitive Models for Cooperative Work
Edited by J. Rasmussen, B. Brehmer and J. Leplat

time, it creates the problem of timescales, i.e. the battle fought at the level of the individual soldier proceeds on a timescale different to that fought by battalions, with an attendant need for different levels of control and coordination of units at a lower level from the level above.

However, the units on a lower level cannot be completely controlled by the level above. This is a consequence of the different timescales. The higher levels cannot (and should not) process information at the rate required for decision making at the lower levels, and if it tried to interfere at the lower level, it would only create confusion. Consequently, decision making must be distributed, and in the military system, this takes the particular form of having the higher levels of command issue goals, which the lower levels are then left to achieve by their own devices. Thus, we arrive at a system characterized by a compromise between distributed and centralized decision making.

The military example also illustrates the intimate connection between the architecture of the system for decision making and the task. The specific hierarchical form of a military system is a consequence of the nature of the decision problem facing it (that of coordinating effort). Thus, the organization of decision making cannot be discussed in the abstract; we also need to consider the nature of the decision task.

The problem of different timescales is, however, a general one. Consider a modern process plant, for example. Running that plant presents problems on very different timescales. On the lowest level we find the problems relating to the minute-by-minute running of the actual process. This is the task of the team of operators. It consists of solving *all* problems that can and must be solved at this lowest level, such as adjusting process parameters and detecting equipment failures. Because only the operators work on this timescale, they must have (and assume) full responsibility for decision making at this level. At higher levels in the hierarchy we find maintenance units. These carry out periodic maintenance on, say, a monthly basis. Still higher up, the marketing department decides upon the kinds of products to be manufactured on, perhaps, a yearly basis, or whatever timescale can be monitored on the basis of the sales figures. Development of new products in the design department takes place at a still higher level, requiring a timescale of many years, perhaps.

Here the hierarchy is not a command hierarchy of the kind found in the military example. While the fate of the plant may be said to be ultimately controlled at some hierarchical level, e.g. the design department, as is the case in the military example, this department generally does not have complete authority over the production department in the way that the battalion level has authority over the company level. (Perhaps the introduction of CAD/CAM will change this.) Instead, there is a separate command and control organization that is not tied to actual production. This is because this organization differs from the military one in one crucial aspect: the goal-setting function is carried out by a separate organization. This is necessary, because the designers generally will not have all the information that is needed to decide what can be sold profitably. This, in turn, is a consequence of the fact that the plant is not a profit-maximizing system, it is production-maximizing, and therefore, the plant cannot be left to control itself. (Of course, this description overstates the differences between the company and the military organization, at least where such an organization exists in the Western democracies and the Soviet Union, where, in the latter, the military forces are subject to political control.)

In hospital intensive-care units, we find another example of a hierarchical organization based on different timescales (A. Brehmer, 1989). In this case, we find three timescales. The lowest is the minute-by-minute supervision and care of the patient. The second level is an approximately 6-hour timescale which involves making various tests on the patient, and, on the basis of these, decisions about the fine tuning of the current treatment program are made. Finally, there is a 24-hour cycle, involving decisions about the treatment program. Different categories of personnel are in charge of the different timescales, junior nurses being in charge at the lowest level, senior nurses at the middle level and physicians at the highest. The personnel on the two lowest levels in this system have two kinds of tasks. The first is to monitor and care for the patient on their assigned timescale; the second is to detect when decisions on a higher level are needed so that they can transfer control to the next category of personnel.

CONTROL STRUCTURES AND ORGANIZATIONS

Few (if any) organizations function only on one timescale. When there are different timescales, (or spatial scales) to consider, different levels of control are needed to monitor these scales, for a system that does not monitor all relevant timescales is subject to what Lanir (Chapter 9, this volume) has called 'fundamental surprises' (such surprises may also happen because the organization monitors the wrong things, of course). Thus, a hierarchical control structure cannot be avoided. Whether this has to be implemented in a hierarchical organization is another matter.

One important aspect here is the sheer magnitude of the control problem. In the military situation this is such that complexity must be regulated by the introduction of a hierarchical organization. This is a consequence of Ashby's law of requisite variety (Ashby, 1956).

In a small manufacturing company there may be less need for such an organization, for there is less need to keep track of and organize the workforce. However, if the company does not make sure that it monitors all relevant timescales it may have a fundamental surprise. This is presumably why companies either grow or die; to survive beyond the circumstances under which they were created, they need to differentiate their monitoring functions. That is, they need to introduce specialist functions, and this requires a higher level of production to support these functions.

Modern information technology may be one means of breaking the connection between organization and control. This problem is discussed below.

PROBLEMS FACED BY A DISTRIBUTED ORGANIZATION

A distributed organization faces two kinds of problems: information and trust. The information problem is that of generating the information needed for different levels of decision in the system. This is discussed in Brehmer (1988) and involves the question of finding information suitable for different levels in the control structure. This usually requires some transformation of information from below. That is, the same basic information may be used at different levels of the system but in different form. Alternatively, different levels may monitor different variables.

Conversely, there is a problem of transforming the information from above to a suitable form for action at the lower level. As noted above, the information from above will be in the form of goals which then have to be transformed into action, taking the actual situation at the lower level into account. The information problem is tied to the control structure, and it is necessary to solve this problem to make the control structure function.

The trust problem, on the other hand, concerns the functioning of the organizational structure. The level of trust determines the need for monitoring in the organization. When there is trust, there will be little need for monitoring the lower levels and for lower levels to monitor higher levels. This enables the organization to use its information-processing capacity for the real task at hand.

Lack of trust is highly disruptive, because it uses up part of the information-processing capacity of the organization for non-essential tasks. In many organizations this need for monitoring creates new levels of control to handle the increased demands for information processing created by lack of trust. One reason for the resistance to modern information technology on the part of the lower levels in an organization is that it introduces increased possibilities for carrying out this monitoring.

Lack of trust seems to have its own dynamics. In an organization characterized by lack of trust with many special monitoring functionaries the monitored levels are likely to rely increasingly upon these functionaries for the monitoring of their performance rather than upon their own monitoring. Thus, the organization confirms the need for monitoring and perpetuates the lack of trust. Note that this will work both ways. It is just as destructive to make the process operator dependent upon the shift supervisor as it is to make the board dependent upon the trade union for monitoring its decisions.

MODERN INFORMATION TECHNOLOGY IN DISTRIBUTED DECISION MAKING

The characteristics and consequences of modern information technology are relevant to the problem of distributed decision making in two different, and somewhat paradoxical, ways. First, it creates new opportunities for distribution of decision making. It does so because it makes information widely available in the system. Therefore, the need for centralization caused by privileged access to information disappears, and it becomes possible to create 'flatter' organizations. This does not, however, eliminate the need for a hierarchical control structure in tasks characterized by different timescales. Nor does it eliminate the need for coordination of individual units in tasks where such coordination is essential because the individual unit cannot carry out the task.

Note, however, that the distribution of information that is to support distributed decision making is possible only with a highly centralized information system. This makes the system very vulnerable.

Behind the positive first consequence of modern information technology, then, is the second consequence: it invites the creation of highly centralized information systems. Such systems need to be used for increasing the possibilities for distributed decision making. They may just as well be used to eliminate decision functions that were formerly distributed in the system. As noted above, the technology also creates new possibilities for monitoring performance throughout the organization.

This raises the problem of which decision functions can be distributed in an organization. Basically, we have three different kinds of functions: monitoring of the task and the need for making decisions, coordination of action, and monitoring of results. We discuss each in turn.

TASK MONITORING IN DIFFERENT FORMS OF ORGANIZATIONS

As noted above, every decision environment will require its own control structure. In so far as the decision problem has different timescales, this control structure must be hierarchical. A completely flat control structure will be possible only if there is one timescale. This requires that the organization functions in a static environment. It is the one characteristic that the environment of an organization is not likely to have.

The military system embodies one solution to this problem: to match the organization to the control structure, leaving each level free to choose whatever action is needed in its timescale and spatial scale while accepting goals from higher levels in the organization that monitor slower timescales and larger spatial areas.

Is there an alternative to this kind of organization? Rasmussen (Chapter 5, this volume) lists two alternatives to hierarchical organizations: autocratic organizations and heterarchic organizations. An autocratic organization is run by a single individual. This involves no distribution of decision making and is likely to work only for very simple organizations designed for simple problems. Modern societies do not provide much opportunity for old-style tyrants.

In a heterarchical organization the levels of the organization are more flexible, so that decision makers from one level can invade other levels. Rasmussen considers three forms of such heterarchical organizations: anarchistic organizations, democratic organizations, and diplomatic organizations. In an anarchistic organization each person plans his or her own work without any consultation with the other decision makers in the organization. A democratic organization, on the other hand, involves interaction and negotiation among all decision makers in the organization. Diplomatic organizations are characterized by restricted communication with local planning of communication between neighbours.

These three forms of organization are not interchangeable, for they imply that different control structures apply. Thus, neither of these organizations involves monitoring of different timescales. Consequently, they are not congruent with a hierarchical control structure. This does not mean that they will not work for such problems; it is possible that monitoring of different levels will occur despite the lack of a formal organization. The three forms of decision also differ with respect to the extent and for which kinds of problems they allow the organization to function as a whole. An anarchistic organization will obviously have considerable problems functioning as a whole for any problem that requires concerted action. A diplomatic organization will allow the organization to function as a whole only for problems that require local coordination and that take place within one timescale. Democratic organizations have the least formal constraints, but there is, of course, no guarantee that such an organization will discover the actual timescales that will need monitoring. This underlines the point above that the organization of a decision-making organization cannot be considered in the abstract; it has to be considered in relation to some specific task. It is clear, however, that the kinds of organization that are discussed as alternatives to a hierarchical organization are mainly alternatives with respect to another form of task. Thus, whereas the hierarchical organization suits the dynamic problems with different timescales, the alternative forms of organization are best suited to static problems, or problems with a single timescale.

HOW WILL PROBLEMS OF COORDINATION BE SOLVED IN DISTRIBUTED DECISION MAKING?

Assuming that we have solved the information problem, we still face the problem of coordination of action. For example, we may have designed and implemented an information system for a truck company that shows the position of every truck and of every customer at a given point in time, leaving it to the truck driver to decide where to go.

Clearly, having just such a representation of the decision task is likely to lead to conflicts, and it requires some mechanism for conflict resolution. One might, for example, institute the rule that every truck must always go to the customer closest to it. Note that this takes away all decision-making elements from the task and transforms it into a simple rule-following task. This seems to hold little advantage over a hierarchical system.

For some tasks there may be no simple rules of the kind applicable in the truck problem. For example, in a military environment it is far from clear how the coordination of units needed for strategic purposes could happen without active coordination. It has been suggested that strategic and tactical doctrines serve as a substitute for hierarchical control (Hamill and Stewart, 1986). This seems to have the same general effect as the introduction of conflict-resolution rules in the truck problem, and it exposes the military system to a serious problem: it becomes predictable by the enemy.

SUMMARY

This chapter has provided a number of examples of systems in which distributed decision making is made necessary (and possible) by the complexity of the system caused by the fact that there are different timescales which need to be monitored, and where this monitoring cannot be made by a single decision maker. One consequence of these different timescales is that the system can be understood in different ways, and in a very real way, decision makers working in different timescales are working on different systems. This creates problems of finding adequate descriptions of the system that shows how different levels are connected. Unless this can be done, there will be a lack of understanding among personnel working on different levels in the hierarchy, with lack of trust as one important consequence. (In hospitals, for example, we find endless discussions about who actually cares for the 'real' patient.) Here is a great challenge for modern information technology to find system representations and forms of information that enable all levels in the hierarchy to both carry out their own job and to understand the system as a whole.

Address for Correspondence:

Professor Berndt Brehmer, Uppsala Universitet, Dept of Psychology, Box 1854, S-751 48 Uppsala, Sweden.

NOTE

[1]This study was supported by a grant from the NKA/INF program.

REFERENCES

Ashby, R. (1956) *Introduction to Cybernetics.* London: Hutchinson.

Brehmer, A. (1989) *Intensivvård som ett hierarkiskt kontrollsystem*, Report No. 4, Uppsala University: Center for Human Computer Studies.

Brehmer, B. (1988) Organization for decision making in complex systems. In L. P. Goodstein, H. Andersen and S. E. Olesen (eds), *Tasks, Errors, and Mental Models.* London: Taylor & Francis.

Hamill, B. W., and Stewart, R. L. (1986) Modelling the acquisition and representation of knowledge for tactical decision making, *Johns Hopkins Technical Digest*, **7**, 31–38.

Section 3

Special Problems in Modelling Decision Making in Social Systems

The term 'distributed decision making' implies the cooperation of several people in the control of the state of affairs in a complex, distributed problem domain. The involvement of several decision-making agents results in a problem domain which displays significant 'intentional' features to each of them. Dealing with a well-structured technical system, a decision maker can base his or her inferences on the assumption that the system consistently respects the laws of nature. In contrast, in social systems, the response to decisions can only be predicted from assumptions about other agents' motives and intentions. Consequently, the development of predictive models to serve decision making raises basic conceptual problems.

The particular view taken in this book is based on the control theory point of view that decision making is management of a flow of events rather than resolution of a choice of dilemmas. In such a view, intentions (which constitute the set points), and mental models of the task (which are necessary for predictive control) become crucial.

Intentionality, together with sheer complexity, also implies great difficulty in explanation of observed chains of events in the usual causal terms. The focus of this section is a discussion of such problems in modelling decision making in complex problem domains, based on examples.

The chapters in this section serve to identify and illustrate the problems which are met when predictive models of decision making in complex systems are needed. Current approaches to such models are discussed in the next section.

Part 3.1

Fallacy of Predictive Models of Intentional Systems

In this part the problems of modelling intentional systems and the consequent difficulties in predicting the behavior of such systems are illustrated by two chapters. Reason (Chapter 8) applies two well-documented cases of military planning for discussion of the difficulty of predictive planning in systems requiring distributed decision making. He compares the German Schlieffen Plan in the First World War and the contemporary French Plan 17. The two cases present very illustrating examples of the difficulties in prediction of the behavior of complex intentional systems, and of different ways to circumvent this problem in actual cases. The Schlieffen Plan was a very thorough and clever attempt to produce a detailed action plan from a basic assumption about the intentional structure and strategy of the opponent, which turned out to be incorrect, being based on conditions from a previous war. Therefore, the detailed plan was found to be wrong and, in addition it prevented proper improvization because it was 'as rigid as a blueprint for a battleship'. The French strategy, in contrast, did not include assumptions about opponents' plans. Instead it focused on the creation of a French value structure, 'a mystique of will was preached', which could provide the necessary drive behind improvization and action under actual conditions. This case illustrates very well the feedback approach to action in intentional environments but, at the same time, shows the resulting difficulty with adequate resource coordination and planning for this strategy.

While Reason's cases illustrate the problem of prediction in intentional systems, Chapter 9, by Lanir, in a similar way exposes the problems of causal explanations of events in intentional systems. Chains of events which, after the fact (not to mention in prediction), appear to be inconceivable (i.e. of extremely low probability) when considered a set of independent events are quite understandable and reasonable when seen in the light of the intentional structure by the people involved. Just one particular change of assumption about the actual perception of the people involved will make the course of events plausible as a human design while it is inconceivable as a probabilistic coincidence.

These analyses of prediction and decision making in complex social domains demonstrate clearly the importance of intentional relations and human value structures for the development of models of distributed decision making.

8. Two Contrasting Military Plans: The Schlieffen Plan and Plan 17

James Reason
University of Manchester

In the absence of empirical data on distributed decision making it is instructive to look at well-documented case studies. Military history provides a rich source of such material. The reality of war has a way of thwarting the 'best-laid plans', throwing the burden of decision onto widely dispersed local commanders.

The German and French plans for waging the First World War offer some interesting contrasts. So also do their sequelae. This chapter presents brief accounts of (1) the German Schlieffen Plan and (2) its French contemporary, Plan 17. It also examines how both coped with the reality of August and September 1914. A brief analysis is made of the decision-making implications of these plans and their consequences. Finally, the chapter comments very briefly on how the lessons of 1914 were implemented by the same antagonists in May 1940.

THE SCHLIEFFEN PLAN

This was the brainchild of Count Alfred von Schlieffen, Chief of the German General Staff from 1891 to 1906. The plan dictated Germany's strategy in the event of a war between the Austro-German and the Franco-Russian alliances. A somewhat watered-down version of it became '... the mainspring which set in motion the hands of the war clock in 1914' (Liddell Hart, 1934).

Background

The plan was formulated on the clear understanding that, in any future European conflict, Germany would have to fight on two fronts against the numerically superior forces of both France and Russia. As a result of the diplomatic manoeuvrings of the late nineteenth century, Germany was obliged

---

Distributed Decision Making: Cognitive Models for Cooperative Work
Edited by J. Rasmussen, B. Brehmer and J. Leplat

to support Austria in any conflict with Russia. Under the terms of the alliance between France and Russia, both countries were committed to support each other if either became engaged in a 'defensive war' with Germany. Great Britain was also likely to become involved as the result of a treaty signed in 1839, and reaffirmed by Gladstone in 1870. Britain, along with four other signatories (France, Russia, Prussia and Austria), guaranteed to preserve Belgium as an 'independent and perpetually neutral state'.

Britain's military power lay predominantly in its navy. In the event of war, Schlieffen anticipated that Britain would field an expeditionary force in support of the French of no more than 100 000 troops, which, in contrast to the large conscript armies of the European powers, was not a major consideration. As it turned out, Schlieffen slightly overestimated the British contingent. The British Expeditionary Force (BEF) that landed at Rouen on 10 August 1914, was made up of only four divisions (as opposed to the intended six), some 80 000 soldiers and 30 000 horses.

The Plan's basic assumptions

Although Germany was committed to the dangerous prospect of a war on two fronts, there were two mitigating factors. First, the country's central position gave it the considerable advantage of interior lines of communication. Second, it was thought unlikely that Russia could fully mobilize in anything less than six weeks. With the memory of Napoleon's Grand Army being swallowed up in the vast Russian interior still fresh in their minds, German war planners were not tempted to strike a major blow towards the east while Russia's unwieldy mobilization machinery creaked into action. Instead, they resolved to deliver a rapid offensive against France, holding the Russians at bay with a skeleton force in East Prussia. Later, when France was defeated, they would reverse the railway schedules and destroy the now-assembled Russian armies in the kind of decisive battle that Clausewitz had ordained as the first object of offensive war.

The major obstacles facing a rapid attack westwards were the natural and man-made barriers which the French frontier presented to the invader. The common frontier was narrow, only some 150 miles across, anchored at either end on the borders of the two neutral countries, Switzerland and Belgium. In between lay 70 miles of the Vosges mountains and an almost continuous French fortress system based on Epinal, Toul and Verdun. Such a frontier offered little space to deploy the million and a half men that Germany planned to launch against France. Faced with this obstacle, the logical course was to go around it, and it was to this end that the Schlieffen Plan was conceived.

The main features of the Plan

The need to avoid large-scale engagements on two fronts simultaneously, as well as Clausewitz's doctrine of the early 'decisive victory', made speed of paramount importance. Frontal attack and the possibility of becoming bogged down in a war of attrition were anathema to Schlieffen. He, like other Prussian military thinkers before him, was obsessed with the idea of the double envelopment, the manoeuvre employed so successfully by Hannibal against the Romans at Cannae 2000 years earlier, and by themselves at Sedan in 1870.

Schlieffen's plan evolved as follows. The mobilization timetables of the opposing armies dictated an early victory against the French and their British allies. Decisive battle and the constraints of the French frontier demanded a flanking movement, and this, in turn, necessitated the invasion of Belgium. Germany did not have enough forces for a classic double envelopment. Consequently, Schlieffen took the bold decision to concentrate the mass of his troops into a heavily one-sided right wing that would envelop the whole of Belgium and cross the Franco-Belgian frontier along its entire width. The left wing, facing the French frontier, would be reduced to the slenderest possible size. The huge right wing, pivoting on the fortified area Metz–Thionville, was to comprise 53 divisions, while the secondary army on the left was to be composed of only eight. Meanwhile, ten divisions were allocated to East Prussia to hold the Russians in check.

The strength of the Plan

The subtlety of the Plan lay not so much in the geographical detour through Belgium as in the deliberate imbalance between the German left and right wings. French fervour to liberate the provinces of Alsace and Lorraine, lost in the débâcle of 1870, as well as the evident weakness of the German left wing would, Schlieffen correctly reasoned, tempt them to launch their main attack against the Alsace-Lorraine frontier. The inevitable early success of this French offensive would ultimately serve the German purpose of drawing the French armies into a 'sack' between Metz and the Vosges, and make it extremely difficult for them to counter the main German blow delivered by the massive right wing. This would swing across Belgium and then into northern France like an enormous hay rake, with its furthest extremes brushing the Channel coast. It would then begin to turn gradually eastwards, engulfing Paris and crossing the Seine to the south near Rouen. Finally, it would fall upon the rear of the main French armies, now lured away from their fortifications by the withdrawal of the German left, and hammer them in a decisive battle of annihilation '... on the anvil formed by the Lorraine fortresses and the Swiss frontier'. Like a revolving door, therefore, French pressure on the German left would enable the strong right wing to swing round and strike them in the back.

The Plan's intrinsic flaws

This was a daring and imaginative plan, and it very nearly succeeded. But with the benefit of hindsight, we see that it contained a number of flaws.

The first was that the assumption of a quick decisive battle, though appropriate to earlier wars, was no longer meaningful in the early twentieth century, when the enormous resources of industrialized nations meant that single battles were unlikely to decide the outcome of a war. Schlieffen's contemporary, the elder Moltke, sensed this in 1890 when he predicted that the next war might last seven years or even 30. His nephew, the younger Moltke, who succeeded Schlieffen as Chief of Staff (and severely weakened the force of the Plan), also knew it when he wrote to the Kaiser in 1906: 'It will be a national war which will not be settled by a decisive battle but by a long wearisome struggle with a country that will not be overcome until its national force is broken ...' But no one would act upon this Clausewitzian heresy, so the doctrine of a decisive battle remained intact in 1914.

The second serious error lay in Schlieffen's underestimation of the consequences of violating Belgian neutrality. He did not believe that Belgium would add its six divisions to the forces opposing Germany's westward and then southward sweep. On the basis of his unsavoury track record, it was thought that Leopold II, King of the Belgians in Schlieffen's time, could be persuaded merely to protest at the passage of German troops through his country by the offer of French territory and the sum of £2 million sterling (to be paid by the defeated French). But by August 1914, Leopold had been succeeded by his nephew Albert, a man of a quite different stamp, and the resistance of the tiny Belgian army caused a significant delay in the German advance. Furthermore, as anticipated, the invasion of Belgium brought Great Britain into the war—'just for a scrap of paper' as the agitated Chancellor Bethmann told the British ambassador in Berlin—and although the BEF was small, Britain's subsequent human and material contribution to the defeat of Germany were not.

A third and, in the event, fatal flaw was that the Plan provided no formula for neutralizing the powerful Paris garrison. Schlieffen recognized this problem, but failed to find a solution.

The younger Moltke's tinkering with the Plan

Sclieffen's successor, General von Moltke, was not a man to put most of his eggs in one basket. A gloomy pessimist, he fretted both about the weakness of his left wing against the French and about the forces defending East Prussia against the Russians. After a moment of crisis when he nearly abandoned the Schlieffen Plan in favour of fighting a defensive war against France, he regained his nerve and stuck by the Plan, or at least by a pallid version of it.

Each year prior to 1914, he gradually whittled away its essential idea by transferring troops from the right to the left wing. Of the nine new divisions formed between 1905 and 1914, Moltke allocated eight to the left wing and only one to the right. The final line-up was thus a left wing of about 320 000 men to hold the Alsace-Lorraine front south of Metz, a centre of 400 000 men to invade France through Luxembourg and the Ardennes, and a right wing of 700 000 to attack through Belgium after first assaulting the strong gateway fortresses of Liège and Namur. This last change was to have enormous political repercussions. Schlieffen had intended the right wing to outflank the Belgian forts. Moltke, however, resolved that they had to be destroyed at the outset. As Liddell Hart put it: '... For a fancied addition to military security he deliberately invited the condemnation of the neutrals, provoked Belgium to resistance, and drew the weight of Britain into the scales against his own forces' (Liddell Hart, 1934, p. 42).

The finishing touches

With these revisions made, the fine details of the Plan were worked out with infinite care and thoroughness by the highly professional officers of the German General Staff, men whose bedside reading consisted of railway timetables and large-scale maps, and who were trained at war college desks and on staff rides to provide for every eventuality. The final plan of campaign was '... as rigid and complete as the blueprint for a battleship'. Every day's schedule of march was established in advance, and the Plan called for decisive victory in the west on the thirty-ninth day following mobilization. The Plan lacked only one essential commodity: flexibility.

PLAN 17

This was the French plan, largely devised by Foch and adopted in May 1913 for victory against Germany in the long-awaited war of 'revanche' to reverse the shaming defeats of 1870. It contrasted with Schlieffen's plan not only in its opposing purpose but also in its structure—or rather in its almost complete lack of structure. It was less a military plan than a mystical expression of the French national spirit as it prevailed in the decade before 1914.

Background

In the years immediately following the disasters of 1870 French military thinking was largely defensive, and gave rise to the fortress system along the Franco-German frontier. But towards the end of the nineteenth century a new school of thought emerged which argued that the offensive was more in tune with French character and tradition. They quoted Napoleon's dictum that 'the moral to the physical are three to one', but they forgot that each is dependent on the other. Élan, rather than careful planning and material strength, was now seen as the key to victory.

Basic assumptions

Foremost among the advocates of the new doctrine of the offensive was General Ferdinand Foch, Director of the Ecole Supérieure de la Guerre, or War College. Foch preached a mystique of will: 'The will to conquer is the first condition of victory' and 'A battle won is a battle in which one will not confess oneself beaten'. Nevertheless, Foch was a practical man and stressed the physical as well as the metaphysical implications of his doctrine. But it was only the latter—the mystique of will—that captured the minds of the French Command, and particularly Colonel Malmaison, Director of the Troisième Bureau (Military Operations). He translated Foch's ideas into the one-sided principle of *offensive à outrance*—offensive to the limit. The crucial factor was '... the will to seize and retain the initiative'. Gaining the initiative demanded flexibility. Preconceived plans based upon assumptions as to what the enemy might do imposed undesirable constraints upon the seizure of this initiative. Defensive thinking was abandoned entirely.

Embodiment in Field Regulations

In 1912, General Joffre was appointed Chief of the General Staff. With his encouragement, the advocates of the *offensive à outrance* gained control of the French military machine, and the doctrine was embodied in the new Field Regulations of 1913. This document, the ultimate authority for the training and conduct of the French Army, consisted of eight commandments, expressed in such stirring phrases as 'offensive without hesitation', 'breaking the will of the adversary' and 'ruthless and tireless pursuit'. No mention is made of the practicalities of material or firepower. Its teaching was summed up in a word favoured by the French officer corps of the time: *le cran*—nerve or guts.

The essence of Plan 17

This doctrine was also the basis for Plan 17, which was elaborated by Foch's disciples from a strategic plan he had left behind on his departure from the War College to command an army corps at Nancy. Its central idea, as expressed by Foch, was to get to Berlin by crossing the Rhine at Mainz, although this was not directly stated in the final version of the plan. After a characteristic opening flourish—'Whatever the circumstances, it is the Commander in Chief's intention to advance with all forces united to the attack of the German armies'—all that the army commanders who were to carry out the plan received in common was a five-sentence directive stating that French action would consist of two major offensives, one to the north and one to the south of the German fortified area of Metz-Thionville. In stark contrast to the Schlieffen Plan, no schedule of operations was provided. Almost everything was left to the initiative of the five army commanders whose forces were deployed along the frontiers from Belfort in the south to one-third of the way along the Franco-Belgian border in the north. The remaining two-thirds of that frontier, from Hirson to the sea, were left undefended.

False premises

From what we already know of the Schlieffen Plan, it is clear that nothing could have served the German purpose better than Plan 17—except perhaps the immediate surrender of the French. It could have been conceived by the German General Staff to mesh in with Schlieffen's grand design. Aside from negating both historical experience and common sense, Plan 17 was based on a double miscalculation—of force and place. French staff officers had always underestimated the strength of the German army in the west, but at the outset of war French Intelligence counted only 45 divisions instead of the actual 83, a miscalculation by half. However, this proved to be less disastrous than their erroneous assumptions about where the German attacks might fall. It had always been recognized by the French that the Germans might move through Belgium, but they were expected to take the difficult short-cut through the Ardennes rather than the broad sweep through Flanders that they actually made.

This mistaken belief could be more readily excused if it were not for the fact that the French General Staff had received numerous intelligence reports indicating a massive German right-wing envelopment through the whole of Belgium. In 1904 a heavily disguised German staff officer handed over to French Intelligence an authentic early version of the Schlieffen Plan that correctly specified the routes to be taken in 1914. But the French rejected the information on three counts. First, they thought it was a trick to draw their forces away from the point of the main attack—which they believed to be coming across the plateau of Lorraine. Second, they did not think that the Germans had sufficient troops to manoeuvre on such a scale. Third, such an extensive violation of Belgian neutrality would, they correctly surmised, be bound to bring Britain into the war against Germany, and it was unlikely that the Germans would go out of their way to provoke such a reaction.

However, in the remote possibility that this information turned out to be true, there was no need to make any moves to counter it, since a strong German right wing would give the French superiority of numbers against the German centre and left. This was summed up in General Castelnau's famous remark, 'So much the better for us!' One is reminded of the last words of the Confederate general who leapt out of his trench and shouted to his reluctant troops: 'Come on men, they couldn't hit a barn door at this dist ...'

AUGUST AND SEPTEMBER 1914: THE REALITY

On 4 August, 70 miles to the east of Brussels, the first detachments of German cavalry crossed into Belgium. By 12 August, ferried by 550 trains a day crossing the Rhine bridges, one and a half million German soldiers were ready to advance. The ring of forts surrounding Liège resisted stubbornly, falling only to the enormous shells delivered by giant howitzers brought up by rail from the German interior. German troops entered Brussels on 20 August, and on the same day appeared before the Namur fortresses, the final obstacle barring the Meuse route into France.

On the south-eastern front, a French offensive into upper Alsace opened on 7 August. This was halted, but was renewed on the 19th when a larger force actually reached the Rhine. But disasters elsewhere compelled the abandonment of the attack, and units of this force were sent westwards to reinforce the hastily assembled French left falling back before von Kluck's First Army on the extreme German right wing.

On 14 August, the French launched their main thrust, totalling 19 divisions, into Lorraine. This attack was shattered on 20 August when the French discovered that *le cran* alone was no match for machine guns and modern artillery. This seesawing was to throw the French back upon their own fortified barrier which so restored their powers of resistance that they were able to send units to reinforce the western flank—a contribution that was to have important results in the critical Battle of the Marne in early September.

At this point it was evident that Schlieffen's aim of falling back before a French offensive had been thwarted both by the reluctance of the German commanders on the left wing to give ground when opportunities presented themselves for attack and by Moltke's dithering. By increasing the size of his left wing, Moltke had made it unnecessarily strong—but not strong enough for a crushing counter-offensive.

Other inconclusive engagements were fought in the Ardennes region between the German and French centres. The French were defeated, but the Germans failed to exploit their advantage.

Meanwhile in Belgium the British were driven back from their exposed forward position at Mons on 24 August, after their French allies had retreated without prior warning during the night of the 23rd. This hurried recoil of the French left wing finally convinced Joffre that Plan 17 had utterly collapsed. He decided to swing back his centre and left with Verdun as a pivot, while drawing troops from the right in Alsace.

Now occurred the fateful manoeuvre known as 'von Kluck's turn', which was to be the final nail in the coffin of the Schlieffen Plan. Tempted by the chance of rolling up the French left wing, von Kluck, commander of the rightmost German army, began to turn eastwards north of Paris—instead of to the south, as dictated by the overall strategic plan. This movement was spotted by an allied airman, and a makeshift French force, assembled by the inspired General Gallieni, composed of Paris garrison troops and refugees from the fighting in the east, was transported in hastily commandeered taxis and buses to the Ourcq, where they struck at the exposed right wing of von Kluck's wheeling army. Joffre then ordered the whole French left wing to turn about and return to the offensive, and the German advance was finally halted at the Battle of the Marne.

Thereafter followed successive attempts by both sides to envelop the other's western flank, resulting in the so-called 'race to the sea', a movement which ended in a trench line stretching from the Belgian coast just south of Ostend to the Swiss border. From then on, the war of mobility ceased until the summer of 1918.

ANALYSIS

The story, then, is full of paradoxes and contrasts. Although lacking in flexibility, the Schlieffen Plan, at least in its original form, was a bold, imaginative and exquisitely tuned conception for fighting a war on two fronts. It almost succeeded. Plan 17, on the other hand, was an ill-conceived piece of gallic nonsense. Yet, in the end—and the end was a long time coming—it achieved some kind of victory. Plans can be assessed by two sets of criteria. Before they are implemented, they can be judged on their thoroughness, foresight, contingency planning, imagination, boldness, technological exploitation, and the like. By these *a priori* standards, Schlieffen is clearly the winner. Yet plans are also measured by results. Do they eventually achieve their objectives? Here, it is Plan 17 that comes out best. Janis (1972, p. 11) put it well: 'Defective decisions based on misinformation and poor judgement sometimes lead to successful outcomes ... we must acknowledge that chance and the stupidity of the enemy can sometimes give a silk-purse ending to command decision worth less than a sow's ear.'

What do these case studies tell us about distributed decision making? One observation, at least, deserves some discussion. The Schlieffen Plan and Plan 17 differed markedly in their respective structures. Schlieffen's plan was classically hierarchical: every foreseeable decision was taken in advance. Plan 17, to the extent that it could be called a plan, was a loose framework for distributed decision making.

It is therefore interesting to note that whenever the decisions of German army commanders deviated significantly from the Plan, they failed. Von Kluck turned left too early, and Prince Rupprecht of Bavaria preferred to attack rather than fall back, drawing the French to the east, as intended by Schlieffen.

By contrast, certain French commanders, notably General Gallieni, the military governor of Paris, performed marvels of on-the-spot improvization. Even the phlegmatic Joffre had the sense to realize that the original conception of Plan 17 was lost, and turned his retreating armies to defeat the Germans on the Marne. Can we infer from this that the quality of distributed decision making by subordinate military commanders is inversely related to the rigidity and detailedness of their governing strategies? Obviously, it depends upon the talents of the general. But are the troubleshooting skills of military commanders stifled by an excess of prior planning? Who knows? But at least we can begin to focus our minds on some of the issues facing would-be investigators of distributed decision making. Also, there is little doubt that a close study of military decision making could yield some important answers ... if only one knew the right questions.

POSTSCRIPT: THE 1940 REPLAY

Military planners, it is said, are prone to learning the wrong lessons of the last war. The events of 1940 suggest that this was true of one side but not the other.

French thinking between the wars was focused on the Maginot Line, a series of fortifications stretching from south of Sedan to the Swiss Frontier. The remaining army strength was placed along the Franco-Belgian border, in anticipation of another Schlieffen-like attack through Belgium. The weakest part of the army was in the Sedan area on the assumption that the German panzers could not attack through the hilly and heavily wooded Ardennes.

The German plan for the invasion of France, *Sichelschnitt* ('the cut of the sickle'), required the main armoured thrust (*Schwerpunkt*) to come through the Ardennes on a 45-mile front. These forces, headed by Guderian's XIX Panzer Corps, would cut through the French defences on the Meuse between Dinant and Sedan, with the main effort being made at Sedan. And this is precisely what happened in May 1940.

Although brilliantly successful, *Sichelschnitt* had its flaws. It was a plan for breakthrough without much thought for the aftermath. The planners little imagined they could be so successful in so short a time. Having broken through at Sedan, Guderian had to decide upon his own objectives as his columns rushed westwards.

Address for Correspondence:

Professor James Reason, Department of Psychology, University of Manchester, Manchester M13 8PL, UK.

REFERENCES

Liddell Hart, B. H. (1934) *The History of the First World War*. London: Pan Books (1979 edition).

Janis, I. (1972) *Victims of Groupthink*. Atlanta: Houghton Mifflin.

Keegan, J., and Wheatcroft, A. (1976) *Who's Who in Military History*. London: Hutchinson.

Tuchman, B. W. (1962) *The Guns of August—August 1914*. London: Four Square.

9. The Reasonable Choice of Disaster

Zvi Lanir
Tel Aviv University

Military command, control, communication and intelligence systems (C3I) come in a variety of types. They differ in the situations and environments they are meant to control, the forces and the level of command they serve—be they tactical or strategic—and consequently, they differ in size and complexity.

What is common to all of them, however, is the belief engendered that complexity and uncertainty can be better controlled by a system that will base its decisions procedures on well-defined distributed decision making responsibilities (DDM), on a variety of predefined scenarios, diagnoses, and solutions (expert systems), that will be capable of simultaneously taking into account the information collected about the environment (intelligence) as well as about the state of the system, and that all that be done in 'real time', which means relying heavily on advanced computers and communication technologies (Athans, 1986).

Although the concepts of the C3I systems are very convincing in theory, most of them have not yet been tested in the field under conditions of war and crisis, relegating their evalution to expert guesswork.

In this regard, the C3I air surveillance early warning systems are interesting exceptions. Although these systems operated long before the term C3I was first suggested, they included all the basic concepts and characteristics of the most advanced complex C3I systems. Such systems contain radar stations and other surveillance facilities, ground-to-air missile batteries, and interception fighters, all controlled by a ground control center.

An air surveillance early warning system is a multi-echelon distributive decision making (DDM) and expert system, highly dependent on the integration in 'real time' between command, control, communication, and intelligence. It is extremely technological, and its success depends heavily on the human–machine interrelationship and between scientific statistical rationality and human cognitive judgment.

Distributed Decision Making: Cognitive Models for Cooperative Work
Edited by J. Rasmussen, B. Brehmer and J. Leplat

The C3I air surveillance early warning systems accentuates the need to 'get it right the first time'. In this sense they confront a critical problem that is becoming more frequent, not only in the military domain, where the speed and lethality of weapons preclude reliance on trial and error for effective response to a threat, but also to large-scale industrial installations.

This chapter summarizes a comparison study of two cases of failure of C3I air surveillance early warning systems: the shooting down of a Korean Boeing 747 on 1 September 1983 by a Soviet Mig fighter and of a Libyan Airline Boeing 727 on 21 February 1973 by an Israeli Phantom F-4.

As will be described later, there are many similarities between the two cases. However, there are two important differences that make the comparison interesting:

(1) Contrary to the Soviet case, the Israelis recovered the plane's 'black box'—its flight recorder. Therefore, we can provide more reliable answers to some critical questions, which in the Soviet case still remain unanswered.
(2) The Korean 747 case revealed many errors and many incompetencies in the Soviet 3CI system performance. The study of the Libyan airliner case reveals that the Israeli 3CI system performed efficiently, although the disaster still could not be prevented. This fact raises what is the most interesting question in this regard. Just how reliable *is* a reliable 3CI early warning system?

At the time, the downing of the Korean plane aroused an immense amount of international interest and threatened to develop into a confrontation between the USSR and the USA. The case was studied carefully by formal and informal commissions and investigators. These studies and other information gathered on this case were analyzed and summarized by Dallin (1985) in a well-documented volume. The following description of this case is based on Dallin's work.

The downing of the Libyan Airlines Boeing 727 by the Israelis in February 1973 attracted less international attention. This may explain why the case has not yet become a subject for academic study, and why, until today, its details have remained relatively little known. Our analysis of this case is based on a transcription of the 'black box', on other documents referring to the case, on interviews with people who took part in the incident and conversations with Israeli air safety experts.

THE SHOOTING DOWN OF KAL 007

A South Korean Boeing 747 on flight KAL 007, from New York, with a stop at Anchorage, Alaska, was scheduled to land in Seoul, South Korea, at 5:53 a.m., on 1 September 1983. On the way from Anchorage to Seoul the plane deviated more than 200 miles north of its preplanned course, a route that took it over Sakhalin Island and Kamchatka, heading straight towards a major base of the

USSR's strategic nuclear forces. Then the aircraft continued for more than an hour over international waters—the Sea of Okhotsk—and finally sharply changed direction, and again approached the Soviet territory of the southern part of Sakhalin Island, flying over Soviet air-defense missile units and other sensitive military facilities. When the Soviet Su-15 missiles were fired at the Korean 747 the plane was within 90 seconds of heading out to sea, leaving Soviet airspace. All 265 passengers and crew members were killed.

What caused the deviation? The hypothesis of equipment failure—while it cannot be ruled out entirely—was regarded by experts as the least likely cause. The Boeing 747 had three back-up inertial navigational systems—Litton LTN-72R INS. The performance record of the INS has been excellent and the likelihood of simultaneous mechanical failure or malfunction of the three independent INS was unlikely. The number of possible cross-checks—both automatic and manual—was simply too great to entertain the hypothesis of inadvertent error.

The International Civil Aviation Organization (ICAO) investigation indicated that the plane crew was experienced, with a good record, and that the possibility of deviation from the flight plan being due to human error was also very unlikely.

The US National Aeronautics and Space Administration (NASA) records show that the likelihood of US pilots finding themselves 50 or more miles off course as a result of human error is less than 1 in 10 000 flights (Dallin, 1985, p. 29). In KAL 007's case, however, the ICAO investigation disclosed no evidence that the crew knew what was taking place at any time during the five hours and 26 minutes of off-course flight.

That left the experts with a list of bizarre speculations as to what could have produced the deviation and the resultant disaster. Many speculations have been suggested. The International Civil Aviation Organization (ICAO) Commission and other aviation experts found all these speculations difficult to validate because each of them contained some features which could not be explained satisfactorily.

They rejected, as very unlikely, American speculations that the Soviets had developed a system to cause planes to lose their direction, as well as Soviet claims that KAL 007 was on an American intelligence surveillance mission through Soviet airspace, and that the crew intentionally deviated from the international route. Thus, the Korean pilots' behavior during the accident remains an unsolved mystery.

As to the Soviet side of the mystery, the USA produced tapes of the recorded communication between the Soviet fighter pilots and the ground stations. These indicated that:

(1) Soviet radar had begun tracking the Korean airliner only over Sakhalin, where Soviet fighters had tried unsuccessfully to intercept it.

(2) There were no indications that the interceptor pilots made any attempt either to communicate with the airliner or to signal it to land in accordance with international regulations. In fact, during the entire incident, at no point did the pilots raise the question of the identity of the aircraft, nor did the ground controllers mention the need for doing so. Both referred to the aircraft as nothing other than 'the target'.
(3) The Soviets claimed that the airliner was flying without aerial navigation lights. This claim was neither verified nor rejected by the investigations.
(4) Before firing the missiles the Soviet pilot sent four tracer shells across the airliner's nose, but it continued to fly on the same course and at the same height, although it is difficult to assume that they did not notice that something unusual was happening.
(5) During the final pursuit which led to the aircraft's destruction the instructions from the ground controllers were clear—to destroy 'the target'.

There is strong evidence indicating that, from the outset, the Soviet regional Air Defense Forces Command mistakenly identified the aircraft as a reconnaissance plane performing a special intelligence mission.

Before the Soviet radar detected the Korean airliner it had picked up an American RC-135, on an intelligence reconnaissance flight in the same area. Thus, although by the time KAL 007 was shot down, the RC-135 had long returned to its base on Shemya Island, it seems that the Soviets had identified KAL 007 as the RC-135 heading towards Soviet secret installations.

It has been the Soviet assertion that they could not tell which was the RC-135 and which was the second unidentified plane. Unbelievable as it may seem, it is possible that the Soviet air-defense radar system made a mistake in identifying the signal-processing 'signature'. From the very beginning, the Soviets assumed that they were dealing with an RC-135, and from this point on there are no indications that they tried to verify this assumption, although they had many opportunities to do so. The Korean aircraft was always referred to in the Soviet communication channels as 'the target', despite the fact that the 747 was flying much too fast to be an RC-135, which typically turns 'lazy eights' while operating its communications gear, and that the airliner was flying in a straight line—something the RC-135 did not usually do for long periods.

The interceptor pilots could have visually sighted the airliner but they never bothered to come near enough, nor were they asked to do so by the ground controller. In fact, the Soviet fighters did not come closer than 2 kilometers to the airliner—and then the fighter pilot was busy following instructions to fire tracer bullets. When he fired the two fatal rockets, a few minutes later, he was 8 kilometers away.

The Soviet interceptors did not go aloft until about 45 minutes after the 'unidentified' plane appeared on Soviet radar. The Soviet ground controllers were encountering difficulties in directing the interceptors on the course tha would intersect with that of the South Korean airliner, and the planes were unable to locate the airliner for 2 hours. This may also provide an explanation as to why the Soviet surface-to-air missiles did not shoot down the unidentified plane. They simply could not find it.

As to the communication between Moscow and the commanders controlling the operation: the event occurred thousands of miles from Moscow, and it was late at night, long after office hours in the capital. On the other hand, the event lasted almost 4 hours, during which time a great deal of 'real-time' information, consultations and instructions could have been exchanged between Moscow and the China Anti-air Defense Command. There are strong indications that the Soviet High Command itself was surprised to learn what really happened only after the event had become a subject of an international crisis and inquiry.

All in all, the KAL 007 accident has remained a fascinating unsolved puzzle. One reasonable explanation for this phenomenon, suggested by Dallin, is that despite the intensive professional investigation that has been carried out, Washington and Moscow are hiding pieces of the mystery from the public.

THE SHOOTING DOWN OF THE LIBYAN AIRLINER

The shooting down of the Libyan airliner occurred during daylight hours, and the distance between the scene and Israeli headquarters was less than 300 kilometers. All the decision makers involved were well acquainted with the terrain, knew each other personally, and had long experience in working together through crises. This may explain why there were no confusion or 'black spots' in the communications between the various Israeli echelons of command and control, despite the fact that the time was very short. The entire incident took less than 15 minutes. Moreover, when it occurred, Major-General Mordechai Hod, the Israeli Air Force Commander, happened to be in the Central Air Operations Headquarters, so he received a first-hand impression of what was going on and heard the communications between the ground controllers and the pilot.

It also happened that the Israeli Chief of Staff, Lieutenant General David Elazar, was at home when the Air Force commander called him. From this moment on, throughout the entire incident, they kept an open line of communication, where consultations and orders took place in 'real time' and the Israeli Chief of Staff personally became an active partner in the operational consultations and decisions.

At the beginning of 1973 Israeli Intelligence received reports indicating that Arab terrorists were planning a suicide mission. A civilian aircraft would try to fly over the Sinai in order to bomb or self-destruct on the Israeli nuclear installation of Dimona and other targets in Beer Sheva.

On 21 February a sandstorm covered the sky of Egypt and the Sinai. At *13.54 hours* an aircraft penetrating the war zone in the Sinai Desert from the Suez Bay (the Ras Sudar area) was picked up on Israeli radar. The plane was flying at 20 000 feet in a general north-easterly course toward the Refidim (Bir Gafgafa) air base and Beer Sheva. The course that the unidentified plane used in its intrusion into the Israeli war zone was the route Egyptian fighters used in their intrusions. It was what the Israelis called a 'hostile route'.

On its way to Israeli territory the aircraft was flying above the most sensitive parts of the Egyptian war zone, yet the Egyptians did not launch fighters to intercept the intruder, nor did they try to fire their ground-to-air missiles, which were supposed to have been on full alert. In their communications there was no reference to an intruding plane. It was known to the Israelis that the Egyptians had a very sensitive early warning system. Only a few months earlier an Ethiopian plane that had mistakenly flown over their war zone was shot down.

At *13.56 hours* two Phantom fighters were sent to intercept the intruder in order to identify it (make and nationality).

At *13.59 hours* they intercepted the plane. The fighter pilots flying only a few hundred meters from it identified it as a Libyan airliner. They reported that they could see the Libyan crew in the cockpit, and that they were certain that the Libyans could see and identify them. (On every Israeli fighter there is a clear marking showing the Shield of King David.)

Libya was known to the Israelis as a state that provided terrorists with means for their activities, and exercised very little self-restraint in violating international law. The fighters were therefore instructed to order the intruder to land at the nearby Refidim air base. According to international practice, the intercepting plane must signal by radio and rock its wings, while the intercepted aircraft must respond with similar signals, follow the instructions given by the interceptor, notify the appropriate air traffic services unit, and establish radio communication with the interceptor. The Libyan aircraft did not respond to the fighters' rocking of their wings nor did they establish radio communication with the interceptors. One of the Israeli pilots reported that he was only few meters from the right side of the airliner, that the pilot (later it became clear that it was the Libyan co-pilot) was looking straight into his eyes, and that the crew in the Libyan airliner's cockpit were signaling by hand that they understood the orders and were going to obey them. It was clear beyond any doubt that the Libyans identified the fighters as Israelis and that they understood their orders. However, the airliner continued its flight toward the north-east.

At *14.01 hours*, only after the fighters had fired tracer shells in front of the airliner's nose, did the Libyan airliner turn down toward the nearby Refidim air base. However, after descending to 5000 feet and lowering its landing gear, it suddenly changed direction toward the west and started to ascend again.

It is well known that a civilian pilot's first priority is the safety of his passengers. A pilot would not endanger his aircraft and his passengers unless there was a higher priority or unless there were no passengers on board.

Therefore, when the airliner, while in the process of landing, suddenly turned and tried to 'escape' it seemed to the Israeli Air Force Commander that the intruder's crew must have a good reason to avoid landing at *any* price, strengthening even more the military reasoning behind forcing the airliner to land. At this stage he suspected that there were no passengers on board. To make sure, he ordered one of the fighters to fly close to the airliner and to identify the faces of any passengers.

At *14.05 hours* the pilot came to within a few meters of the airliner and reported that blinds were drawn on all the windows. In passenger airliners there is never a situation where all the window blinds are drawn, not even during the screening of a movie. In any case, it was not on a long flight, when a movie would be shown.

There was no way of verifying the accuracy of the pilot's report, and no convincing explanation of why the blinds were down, if they were. In any event, the Air Force Commander became even more convinced that he should not let the plane get away, and that if the plane succeeded in escaping, then the mission that the airliner had not accomplished this time may be attempted the next. This had to be avoided.

At *14.08 hours* the fighters received the order to force the airliner to land by firing at the edges of its wings. Nevertheless, even after bullets had hit the edge of the right wing, the airliner still did not obey the orders and continued to fly westward. During these critical moments, the Israelis opened international and Cairo Airport channels—but no communication was identified as referring to the Libyan airliner.

At *14.10 hours* the fighters were ordered to fire at the bases of the wings. The bullets hit a wing and the airliner started to descend for landing on the nearby flat sandy area. It failed to land safely, and after running along the ground for 600 meters, at *14.11 hours* it crashed. One hundred and ten out of the 116 passengers and crew members on board were killed.

When the black box was opened and the recorded communications between the cockpit and the Cairo international airport approach and control were analyzed the almost unbelievable solution to the puzzling behavior of the Libyan airliner was revealed:

(1) There were three crew members in the cockpit of the airliner; a French captain, who was sitting in the left front seat, a Libyan co-pilot, who was sitting in the right front seat, and a French flight engineer, who was sitting behind the captain.
(2) The captain and the engineer were conversing in French. The co-pilot was not proficient enough in the language to take part in the conversation. They were drinking wine, and had not the slightest idea that they had deviated more than 70 miles from the planned route, flying over Egyptian and, later, Israeli war areas.

(3) At *13.44 hours*, when the captain had his first doubts about his correct position, he consulted his flight engineer and not his co-pilot. He did not report his suspicions about his correct position to Cairo Approach and at *13.52 hours* he received Cairo's permission to start a descent toward Cairo International Airport.

(4) At *13.56 hours*, with continuing uncertainty about his actual position and track, the captain tried to receive Cairo VOR and BEACON and got signals from directions contrary to those expected according to his flight plan. Despite that, the captain did not take any decision and continued flying 'as scheduled'. The situation, though, looked strange to him. Cairo Approach was silent and did not take any initiative in order to correct the serious error.

(5) At *13.59 hours* Cairo told the pilot for the first time that he was deviating from his course and ordered him to 'stick to beacon and report position'. The Libyan co-pilot reported for the first time that he was having difficulties with the VOR and radio beacon.

(6) At *14.00 hours* Cairo Approach asked the pilot to switch over to Cairo Control, which meant that it believed that the airliner was close to Cairo Airport.

(7) At *14.02 hours* the pilot reported to Cairo Control, in answer to a specific question, that they were not receiving Cairo NDB (non-directional beacon), but did not say that he had lost his way. Cairo Control asked the pilot to descend to 4000 feet.

(8) When they were intercepted by the Israeli fighters they identified the fighters as Egyptians. The Libyan co-pilot reported: 'Four Migs behind us.'

(9) At *14.04 hours* the captain reported to Cairo Control: 'I guess we have some problems with our heading and we now have four Migs trying to get behind us.' He asked Cairo to get him a 'radar fix' of his position. Cairo answered that the Cairo VOR was working normally, and that they were trying to fix the airliner by radar.

(10) It happened that the Israeli pilot approached the airliner from the side of the Libyan co-pilot, to whom he signaled by hand his instructions to land. When the Libyan co-pilot told them that the fighter pilot was signaling them to land, the captain and the flight engineer tried to explain to each other what was going on. The captain complained angrily: 'Oh, No! I don't understand such a language' (meaning that this is not the way to behave with me). He was sure that the interceptors were Migs. Their conversation was still in French, which the co-pilot did not understand.

(11) From *14.06 hours*, when Cairo Control advised them to climb up to 10 000 feet, until *14.10 hours*, the time of the airliner's second hit, Cairo Control continued to maintain silence and did not fix the airliner's position.

(12) In the Cairo area there were two airfields, Cairo West, the international airport, and Cairo East, a military air base. The crew probably interpreted the fighters' actions as a warning that they may have overshot Cairo West, and were over the military air base. The fighters were therefore escorts to guide them back to Cairo West.
(13) It seems that when they approached the Refidim area and made the final preparations for landing, thinking that it was Cairo West, they suddenly realized that it was a military air base, which they thought to be Cairo East. Once they came to this conclusion, they decided to avoid landing in the military 'Egyptian' air base, and to turn to the other nearby civilian airport—Cairo West.
(14) At *14.09 hours* the captain reported to Cairo Control: 'We are now shot by *your* fighter'. Cairo Control answered: 'We are going to tell them [the military authorities] that you are an unreported aircraft, . . . and we do not know where you are'.
(15) When the airliner was fired at again they became panic-stricken, still talking French. They thought that the Egyptian fighters were crazy; an Egyptian fighter shooting a Libyan civilian airliner? Then suddenly, the Libyan co-pilot finally identified the fighters as Israeli planes.

In the final tragic landing they were totally out of control, and the results were devastating.

Since 1973, when the Israeli case occurred, there have been remarkable improvements in the C3I's sensoring, computerizing and communication technologies. In principle, however, the C3I early warning systems as presented in this case have remained basically the same. The Israeli incident provides an example of how such a system should perform. It demonstrates a well-organized distributed decision making mechanism, based on 'real-time' information, well communicated among all the echelons involved.

It was an expert system wherein the best experts happened to take part in the decision-making process. No surprising malfunctions in the system's expected behavior were discovered during the crisis. The intelligence operational elements of the system were well integrated. Throughout the incident, the system was very active in collecting data from different sources in order to verify the information at hand.

This leaves us with the need to evaluate the quality of the decisions that were taken in this case.

If one follows Bayesian logic as the basis for calculating the likelihood ratio of the two dichotomous alternatives—innocent civilian aircraft versus terrorist aircraft camouflaged as a civilian airliner in a dynamic situation with constantly evolving new information—which C3I's systems are expected to do, then the conclusion can only be that the second alternative is the sound one, and that the likelihood of error in such a conclusion is infinitely small.

In a course on decision making held in Tel Aviv University, the author gave his students the task of making the decisions, *ex post facto*, as if they were the Israeli Chief of Staff or the Air Force Commander, following the Libyan 707 downing case step by step and calculating the odds by the Bayes theorem equation. Each student did the exercise individually, giving his own estimates each time he was faced with new evidence or a new item of information. Even though the results of this case were well known to them, all of them, by following Bayesian logic, became increasingly certain along the axis of time that the airliner was a foe, and should have been forced to land.

THE REASONABLE CHOICE OF DISASTER—THREE EXPLANATIONS

In the case of the Korean airliner the investigators struggled to find the missing piece of the puzzle needed to complete the logical sequence of events. They presented two main puzzles. What was the explanation for the Korean crew's mistake in navigation, and why was the Soviet system not careful enough to identify the aircraft as an airliner carrying civilian passengers unless they were careless, nervous, or eager enough to shoot it down, in spite of everything?

In the Libyan airliner case, if the black box had not revealed what it did and if the Israeli system had not functioned so exceptionally well, or if the Israelis could have been blamed for violating international practice in handling the case, the explanations would have been arrived at by a reasoning similar to that used in the Korean airliner case. It is very rare indeed that in a crisis situation a system does not give any examples that can be explained as a causal factor in the accident. The exceptional feature in this case, however, is that it provides a unique case where none of these 'if's' occurred, evoking questions about 'second order' or 'context of context' types of lessons about safety and risk or the limits of safety we should learn from this 'reasonable choice of disaster' case.

One may claim that no important 'context of context' lessons should be learned. After all, it is well known that even good decisions cannot always be guaranteed to produce good results. They cannot take unreasonable events into consideration.

This idea is demonstrated by the anecdote about the limits of human wisdom in such cases, which has many versions in different languages. In Hebrew it is said that 'what one idiot smashes, a thousand wise men cannot put back together'. Advanced technology systems are designed for reasonable people who may make reasonable mistakes. One cannot and should not design a system that tries to cope with events of such a high degree of unreasonableness, as the Libyan crew demonstrated, even if it means that in those rare cases the reasonable choice may lead to disaster. If we accept this explanation as sufficient then there is very little to learn from these two cases beyond the need to improve regulations and training, and the recognition that new technology has significantly increased the need for better communications facilities and skills for getting on with others, friend or foe.

A second kind of 'context of context' lesson to the 'reasonable choice of disaster' may be presented by the concept of 'inconceivable event', as presented by Ostberg (1984). That is, 'those cases which cannot readily be explained by reference to such deviations from normal performance or demands which can be expected on deterministic or statistical grounds' (p. 88).

The shooting down of the Libyan airliner in 1973 provides a good example to demonstrate this point:

(1) As already mentioned, the probability that the crew of an aircraft will make a mistake of more than fifty miles in navigation without noticing it is not more than 1 in 10 000.
(2) The probability that an air-controlling system will fail to detect intruder aircraft crossing its war area, even in a sandstorm—as the Egyptian C31 air early warning surveillance system, failed to do—is very small. We do not have statistical data about this probability. Some Israeli experts whom the author asked to estimate this probability did not estimate it as more than 5 in 1000. If we accept this estimate, then the probability of the occurrence of (1) *and* (2) is less than 1 in 2 million.

The Libyan airliner incident was characterized by an accumulation of more 'conditional independent' occurrences, each of them *by itself* of a very low probability:

(1) Israeli information about a civilian Libyan airliner which was expected to enter the Sinai war area in order to attack the Dimona installations and the fact that the intruder was a Libyan plane;
(2) Failure of the Egyptian military C3I air surveillance system to detect the plane;
(3) A crew in which the co-pilot, on the one hand, and the captain and the flight engineer, on the other, had command of a mutual language (English) to a degree only sufficient for communicating standard technical terms, and who lost communication when facing a crisis that could not be communicated adequately by their limited technical jargon;
(4) Cairo Approach, which did not take any initiative to correct the airliner's serious error, and Cairo Control, which did not fix the airliner's position, even after being asked to do so by the pilot;
(5) The failure of the crew to distinguish between Phantoms and Migs, and to see the Israelis' Shield of David on their fighters; and
(6) The frame of mind of Cairo West and Cairo East that was so fatally misleading to the Libyan crew.

In retrospect, what is so striking in this case is that so many 'conditional independent' occurrences, each a very small probability, accumulated and led to the disaster.

One may, however, argue that we tend to conceive of events as very rare or inconceivable because of our unsatisfactory measurement tools. We are aware only of those events that these tools detect in the environment, and these tools are not fine or accurate enough.

For example, the classical training exercise of fighter pilots is the 'dog fight'. This starts when two fighters, flying close to each other, separate, and after making a wide loop, return to approach each other 'nose to nose' and narrowly miss each other. The closer they approach each other, the better, but if they come too close, an accident may occur. To observe how close they are, both pilots operate their cannons' cameras that photograph whatever 'enters' their sight field. After the flight, the pictures are analyzed and studied, and the information gathered is used, *inter alia*, for statistical analysis of 'near-miss' cases.

Only recently, after the cameras had been replaced by video equipment, air safety experts learned to their surprise that those 'near-misses' were far more frequent than they realized from their estimations and theories based on statistical data derived from the cameras.

Navigational errors of more than 50 miles may also be much more common than 1 in 10 000. The reason is that most of the evidence collected on such deviations are from those cases where the planes were approaching or supposed to approach an airport or other ground-controller station. There are probably many more cases of such errors in navigation between stations, probably unnoticed even by the pilots. These cases are not reported, and consequently are not included in statistical data.

Some of the occurrences described in this chapter as 'conditional independent' may actually be 'conditional dependent'. Thus the sandstorm may be the common cause not only for the Libyan airliner's deviation from its route but also for the fact that the Egyptian military C3I air surveillance system failed to spot the plane, for the Israeli pilots' failure to see passengers on board, and for the airliner's fatal emergency landing.

Following such explanations for the paradox, the lesson to be learned from this 'reasonable choice of disaster' case is that our measurement tools and theories about the environment lag behind the capabilities we would like to see in our C3I systems in controlling this environment, and that such gaps can lead to disasters.

The author has presented two possible explanations for the 'reasonable choice of disaster' phenomenon. The first refers to the 'state of nature' as one with inherent uncertainties and randomness. The second refers to the incompleteness of our observations and measurement tools.

The first explanation leads to the conclusions that 'inconceivable events' are so rare that they should be treated as negligible. The second suggests that 'inconceivable events' do not exist at all. However, there is also a third 'context of context' explanation to the 'reasonable choice of disaster' paradox—a cognitive one. The argument is that 'inconceivable occurrences' are cognitively unavoidable. If the third explanation is sound, then the conclusion should be that inconceivable events are more common than we realize. They have always been with us and probably always will be.

The fundamental reason for the 'inconceivable occurrences' concerns a basic characteristic of our cognition. The cognitive starting point of any human observer is the imposition of distinctions on the environment in order to observe. Only then can one observe, describe and theorize (Bateson, 1982).

Safety rules are tools for the imposition of distinctions upon the environment. It is the purpose of safety to create distinctions between what is 'safe' and what is not, and this cannot be done without a kind of 'punctuation' of the streams of events. Thus, 'inconceivable occurrences' are those occurrences that lie outside the demarcation lines of the punctuation.

In a 'closed system' where the variables and the relations between them are known, punctuation is a very efficient elementary prerequisite for designing safety policy and rules. However, when the system is an 'open' one, a spatial type of 'accident' may occur—the breakdown of the boundaries of punctuation. It is this type of accident which is conceived as an 'inconceivable event', and the decisions made—when they are made according to the system's safety logic—may cause what is conceived as a 'reasonable choice of disaster'.

The phenomenon of 'inconceivable occurrences' is by no means rare. On the contrary, it seems that they are always present in some cases in a way that does not undermine the assumptions on which we operate, and in other cases, as demonstrated in the two case studies described in this chapter, they foil our attempts to treat them as if they belong to a 'set'.

People have some deep-seated cognitive biases in recognizing 'inconceivable occurrences' as such. We have a consistent tendency toward conceiving the environment as more 'conditional dependent' than it really is. We tend to look for causal connections between things so that we will be able to perceive them as parts of a recognized pattern. We also have a tendency to perceive demarcation lines between things we want to observe or control and between those we do not, even in those cases where such demarcation does not exist except in our minds and our models.

Scientists tend to narrow the 'space of events' in such a way that it will become researchable. Practitioners tend to narrow it so that it will be controllable. Thus, when statisticians, designers and practitioners combine their talents on a common project aimed to control the environment, this tendency may become even more pronounced.

Another bias in the recognition of 'inconceivable occurrences' is that we tend to be satisfied and stop our inquiry at the point where we find a cause that explains the known results. Since every 'inconceivable event' has more causes than needed for a causal explanation of the accident, our inquiries are satisfied before we reach the inconceivable phenomenon.

The tendency to conceive 'inconceivable occurrences' as less probable than they actually are may also be the result of human bias in sampling. Since we remember those cases for which we have an explanation, we tend to treat the inconceivable data as 'noises'. In those cases where their role in causing the results is undeniable, we remember them as surprises. People have difficulties in learning the non-causal 'surprising' lessons from surprises (Lanir, 1987).

The fact that we have developed complex and highly technological systems that enable us to shape our environment means that the 'inconceivable phenomenon' has become a potential for catastrophe. Having also developed better ways of collecting, analyzing and distributing information does not eliminate our being trapped by 'inconceivable occurrences'.

In this context, C3I systems represent our faith in our ability to engineer the ever-changing environment in order to control uncertainty and our belief that more control will eventually bring about more safety. However, the C3I systems we created have themselves become the means of drawing distinctions on what we observe as the environment.

There is at least one basic distinction between human cognition and the 'cognition' we delegate to the C3I systems. It is the human and not the C3I systems that have the unique quality of *punctuating the punctuation* (Keeney, 1983). This cognitive quality may be of the utmost importance when the existing punctuated boundaries break down.

The human realizes his tacit cognitive quality of 'punctuating the punctuation' only by challenging the edges of the existing punctuation, by experience gained when crossing the demarcation lines, the tolerance or the safety limits. It is a non-rational process which, in turn, makes possible the later appearance of rationality (Lanir *et al.*, 1988). In this regard, it is interesting to note that those Israeli safety experts who were surprised to find that 'near-misses' in 'dog fights' were much more common than they had realized before videos took the place of still cameras were even more surprised to find that they did not have a statistical explanation as to why the accident rate was relatively so low. The paradox can be solved if we recognize that the experienced fighters learned by their own experience to challenge the limits of the safety rules and to punctuate their own subjective punctuation.

The human tendency to avoid the recognition of 'inconceivable events' is a 'two-way street.' We estimate negative 'inconceivable occurrences' as being less likely than they are, along with the probability that inconceivable positive occurrences, are also as less likely than they are.

This poses an interesting question. How much encouragement do our C3I systems allow people, who happen to be on the spot, in the use of their talent, expertise and boldness for activating the 'positive' potential of 'inconceivable occurrences'? Thus, for example, in the Russian and the Israeli cases, were not the interceptor pilots the only links in the C3I's DDM chain that could have had the greatest potential for preventing the 'reasonable choice of disaster'?

Finally, we make a 'context of context of context' comment on the meaning of safety and safety management. The punctuation of the environment we call 'safety' is not safety but a word we use to punctuate the stream of human experience in preventing accidents. Therefore it assumes a specific kind of coherence and sense. Safety is only the name of the thing, and as Wittgenstein once said, 'the name is not the thing named'.

If the hypotheses presented in this chapter are sound, and are not just an exercise in a theory on the basis of anecdotal observation, then we must have a paradigm of safety which is more abstract than the categories into which our control tools slice the stream of events. In other words, we must have a better theory of safety that will include the human talent of punctuating reality into new categories by experiencing it through a crisis of the type we have called 'inconceivable occurrence'. Such a theory will include three basic themes:

(1) A shift upward in the level of generality at which safety is defined;
(2) A shift away from the center-periphery type of safety management to a kind of network mode of safety, and
(3) Replacement of our concern for objective standards of safety with one of responsibility.

NOTE ADDED IN PROOF

For a further discussion of the strategic lessons of this study see Lanir (1989), *Journal of Strategic Studies*, **12**, 479–493.

Address for Correspondence:

Professor Zvi Lanir, The Public Policy Programme, Faculty of Social Sciences, Tel Aviv University, Ramat-Aviv, 699878 Tel-Aviv, Israel.

REFERENCES

Athans, M. (1986) *Command and Control (C3) Theory: A Challenge to Control Science*, Laboratory for Information and Decision Sciences, Massachusetts Institute of Technology, LIDS-P 1584.

Bateson, G. (1982) *Steps to an Ecology of Mind.* New York: Ballantine.

Booth, K. (1979) *Strategy and Ethnocentrism.* New York: Holmes & Meier.

Dallin, A. (1985) *Black Box KAL 007 and the Superpowers.* Berkeley: University of California Press.

Hughes, W. J. (1980) Aerial intrusion by civil airlines and the use of force. *Journal of Air Law and Commerce*, **35**, 595–620.

Jervis, R. (1976). *Perception and Misperception in International Politics.* Princeton: Princeton University Press.

Keeney, B. (1983) *Aesthetics of Change*. New York: Guilford Press.
Lanir, Z. (1987) *Fundamental Surprises*. Decision Research, Eugene, Oregon.
Lanir, Z., Fischhoff B., and Johnson, S. (1988) Military risk-taking: C3I and the cognitive functions of boldness in war. *Journal of Strategic Studies*, **11**, 96–113.
Ostberg, G. (1984) Evaluation of a design for inconceivable event occurrence. *Materials and Design*, **5**, April/May.
Rasmussen, J. (1988) On causality—coping safely with complex systems. Paper presented to the American Association for Advancement of Science, annual meeting, Boston, 11–15 February.

Part 3.2

Fallacy of Causal Explanations in Complex Environments

The previous part was focused primarily on problems of decision makers in modelling and predicting behavior of intentional systems. This part is concerned with similar problems of causal analysis and explanation after the fact of chains of events in complex systems. Two important implications of the fundamental problems of causal analysis in complex systems are discussed here.

In his position chapter on responsibility, Rapp discusses the problem of allocation of responsibility. Who is responsible for the direction the development of technology is taking? In this discussion he focuses on the responsibility of the technological development in general, in contrast to Rasmussen, who raises the problem of causal allocation in a particular course of events in the subsequent chapter.

Rapp identifies a number of important aspects of responsibility allocation: only persons can be responsible; the action in question should be within one's power of choice, and he or she should be able to predict the consequences. In addition, there are several sources of references for judgement of the consequences of actions, law, superiors, peers, God, etc. This raises the problem of heuristics and stop-rules in causal backtracking of events, which is discussed in more detail by Rasmussen.

During the discussion following Rapp's presentation, another aspect of responsibility was introduced: responsibility as a 'feeling' by an actor that he or she has to act, i.e. the willingness to be concerned, to feel obliged to act. This distinction appears to be fundamental: responsibility in terms of allocation of blame after the fact depending on a pragmatic stop-rule in causal backtracking, and the *a priori* feeling of a drive to act by the individuals involved. The problem of representing the drive to act, to take on oneself the task of making decisions may be too implicit in the discussion of models of distributed decision making in the subsequent sections.

In Chapter 11 Rasmussen takes up the problem of causal explanations in complex environments. The classical 'causal models' are confronted with the relational models of modern science, and it is concluded that causal models have an important role in analysis of the systems under real-life circumstances. However, causality depends on the definition of objects and events which cannot be established objectively, but which depend on prototypes that are only meaningful within a community-sharing conceptual context. Therefore, the conclusion is similar to Rapp's: stop-rules for causal allocation depend on pragmatic arguments and the determination of causes of accidents is not an objective decision. In addition, it is argued that the dependence of acceptance of causal explanations in a shared context has very important implications for experimental verification of hypothesis and models. This problem is discussed in more detail in Chapter 20.

10. Responsibility Allocation in Modern Technology

Friedrich Rapp
Universität Dortmund, FRG

The systems and processes of modern technology have not arisen spontaneously. They have been created by man. However, the principles on which technological systems are based must conform to natural laws; otherwise the systems in question would not work at all. Hence one could claim paradoxically that technology is natural (as part of the material world) and at the same time it is artificial (since the artifacts of technology do not exist in nature).

The systems and processes of modern technology are brought about in cooperative work by means of a deliberate goal-directed activity. Thus the question arises of precisely who is to be held responsible for both positive and negative results originating from them. One point is clear from the beginning. Taken in its totality, the modern world is the result of a historical process for which no single person can be held responsible. Of course, history is made by man. But it would be preposterous to search for the persons that are, for example, answerable for our modern secularized and pluralist society, for the process of democratization or, for that matter, for bringing about modern science and technology in general. Clearly, some individuals are more important than others. But they are always acting within a network of cooperative activity. Even social groups cannot alone be held responsible for such processes, since directly or indirectly, in one way or the other, all members of society are involved in the collective activity of reshaping the world that has been handed to us by our ancestors.

It is equally clear that with respect to a specific, well-defined action it must be possible to ascertain some sort of responsibility. It is as erroneous to suppose that no-one is responsible for anything as it is to hold everyone responsible for everything. The real problem consists of finding a reasonable middle course between these two extremes. At first, one may be tempted to ascribe the responsibility for a specific piece of technology to all those directly involved

Distributed Decision Making: Cognitive Models for Cooperative Work
Edited by J. Rasmussen, B. Brehmer and J. Leplat

in originating, maintaining and using it. Yet, not all the individuals in question can be held responsible to the same degree. Further distinctions and specifications are needed. Let us start with a conceptual analysis of the notion of responsibility.

DIMENSIONS OF RESPONSIBILITY

In order to arrive at a clear-cut explanation of the many-faceted and usually rather vague connotations of responsibility, perhaps the following dimensions or elements can be distinguished:

(1) In the strict sense, responsibility can only be assumed by *persons*. Also, the inverse holds good; one may define a person as a subject to whom responsible actions can be imputed. That is, that the very concept of a 'person' is inherently linked to the ability of consciously bringing about certain effects, i.e. actual events in the world (cf. the following chapter by Rasmussen). From the close and inseparable connection between responsibility and being a person it follows immediately that responsibility in the strict sense can only be assumed by individuals. Only in a derivative manner can it be assumed by social groups, bodies, institutions, etc. Ascribing agency—and the responsibility derived from it—to juristic persons is only a formal, legal construction in order to deal with the question of guilt in court procedures. It is impossible to solve the problem of responsibility by taking the collective process of decision and action in its undivided totality. One must rather set out to disentangle the complex aggregative process by analyzing it in terms of some internal pattern (for instance, the organizational structure, the hierarchies, and individual competencies). Depending on the questions asked and the strands of decision making followed, one will arrive at different, complementary types of analysis. There is no simple and straightforward way of allocating the authorship and the responsibility to the individuals involved.

Modern technology relies on the division of labour and, by implication, also on the division of responsibility. Yet production of technology, on the one hand, and responsibility for it do not necessarily coincide. Within a hierarchical system, the author of an action may be just a slave or a sort of instrument, since he is only performing orders that are given to him. The result is that it is easier to identify the physical activity, the concrete contribution of a certain individual in generating a certain state of affairs than to specify his or her share of responsibility for the result. At this juncture we can observe a further divergence. It is not only the case that in complex, hierarchical organizations being the author of (that is, causing something to happen in the material world) and being responsible for (that is, giving orders or being in charge of something) may differ. In addition, causing something and being responsible for something have different normative connotations. As a rule, success is taken for granted. But in the case of a failure one is looking for a culprit to be held responsible. Whereas acting and refraining from action do not evoke prima facie either negative or positive moral associations, the idea of responsibility is more often used to punish the guilty than to praise the deserving.

(2) A person can be held responsible only on condition that he or she has *control or power* over the course of events considered. This is implied in the notion of agency. No-one is held responsible for bad weather, hurricanes or earthquakes. Only if I myself or by means of orders that I have given to others have really brought about the state of affairs in question— or if I could have prevented it from coming about—can I be held responsible for what happened. Whereas in (1) the point is about subdividing the *collective actor*, be it a body, a group, a cooperation, an organization, or an institution in a possibly correct way so as to specify the responsibility of the individuals involved, here the stress is on dividing up the *aggregative action-process* as well as the effects arising from it so that the portion of responsibility belonging to a specific individual can be established.

The feature that a person can be held responsible only for things he is in control of is a necessary but not a sufficient condition for his being responsible for the action in question. Obeying, carrying out orders within a hierarchical system reduces the range of control or power, whereas giving orders extends the range of control or power exercised by the person in question. In fact one may distinguish between a connotation of neutrality and one of normativity that are inherently united in the notion of responsibility. The connotation of neutrality refers to being in charge of something and concerns the degree of control or power held by a person within a hierarchical system. The connotation of normativity refers to the moral dimension of actions, i.e. consideration, helpfulness, altruism. The connotation of neutrality refers to occupancy of supervisory functions within a given decision structure. Both connotations are present when the question of responsibility is posed.

(3) Power and control alone are not enough. Responsibility can only be imputed to a person who has sufficient *knowledge* about the results to be expected from the actions he performs. Various degrees of reliability can be observed here. Whereas states of affairs that are contiguous in space and time allow for rather reliable predictions, the precision of our foreknowledge tends to decrease when it comes to more distant events. The most striking feature is that our predictive power is much higher in the field of the natural and the engineering sciences than in the sphere of the social sciences. At this point we can observe a clear-cut epistemological hierarchy of reliability. We can predict a lunar eclipse with high precision; statements about the safety of technological systems are less reliable; and any forecast concerning social

and cultural change can be nothing but a more or less subjective extrapolation of the trends observable at present.

(4) Furthermore, the action to be imputed to an individual must be performed *deliberately* and not just by chance, or in a careless or unintended manner. This re-emphasizes the feature that responsibility can only be imputed to a consciously acting person. In a lawsuit, certain distinctions (carelessness, gross negligence, acting with intent) as well as operational procedures of forensic psychology are applied in order to distinguish various degrees of deliberate and intentional action, and correspondingly various degrees of imputation and responsibility (von Wright, 1971).

(5) The notion of responsibility does not only apply to an accomplished action. To a lesser degree, it also applies to the *preparational stages* that precede the performance of the action in question. With respect to technology, various stages (conception of the idea, research and development, prototype, use of the finished system) can be distinguished here, in each of them a certain kind of responsibility being relevant. This holds good notwithstanding the circumstance that in the view of conceptual analysis there is an inherent logical connection between an action and its result (von Wright, 1971). If the result does not arise, the action has simply not been performed; in other words, the result is an 'essential' part of the action.

(6) The basic notion of being responsible is derived from communicative interaction. In everyday speech to be 'responsible' means to be accountable or answerable for an act to some other person or a group of persons. In a more general way, to be responsible means to be called to account by some *authority*. This authority can be specified in social terms (peer group, superiors, posteriority, mankind), in legal terms (codes of law), in mental terms (consciousness) or in theological terms (God). Regarded from a merely functional aspect, what matters is not the origin of the authority but rather the feature that there is some last, final authority of an absolutely commanding character towards which one has to give account for what one has done. Taking the functional analysis further, one can even consider responsibility as a means of avoiding anarchy. Taken in these terms, responsibility has the function of controlling people who otherwise might act arbitrarily, comparable to the Freudian superego supposedly controlling the unconscious.

(7) Finally, the *standards or commands* maintained by the authority in question must be specific in one way or another. This can be achieved by positive law, and in a less definite manner by moral obligation or by a system of positive values. In modern pluralistic societies provisions must be made to maintain standards that are homogeneous enough to ensure a cooperative and nondestructive social life. On the meta-theoretical level this can be achieved by certain rules of procedure that allow comprehensive solutions to be reached (for example, by legislation).

Responsibility can be imputed only if free will is taken for granted. Yet, the age-long metaphysical dispute about freewill versus determinism need not concern us here. In everyday life as well as in all legal hearings and trials, freewill is actually presupposed, irrespective of the intricate conceptual issue of how the actor's motives can be conceived as falling or not falling under the realm of causal law. The question under discussion concerns intention and motivation and is thus confined to the mental sphere. The choice in question pertains, by definition, exclusively to the mind, and therefore it exists irrespective of whatever external constraints or compulsions may exist outside of the person in the physical world. It is unnecessary to mention that this is only an artificial, conceptual distinction, since in a real situation of choice both aspects, the internal motivation and the external constraints, are always relevant.

ASPECTS OF TECHNOLOGICAL CHANGE

The other element of our topic, namely the dynamics of modern technology, is also a multi-dimensional concept that requires specification. At least three different aspects can be distinguished here:

(1) The state of affairs we are faced with is the result of the technological *development up to the present time.* From the very beginning man has been the tool-making animal (Benjamin Franklin) or the *Homo faber* (Henri Bergson), but only in recent times has this feature been given closer attention. Until the Industrial Revolution, technology was so closely integrated into the social, political and cultural structures that it was not considered a subject that deserves special attention. Within the last 200 years a fundamental change has taken place in this respect, and today our modern world is globally shaped by a science-based technological structure. This structure forms a second nature, a technosphere, which, to a large degree, is replacing the biosphere that evolved in nature untouched by man.

The technology of our time, like that of any other epoch, is the result of an historical process. Thus if we want to find out why things are the way we find them now, we have to turn to the past to learn how they came about. Who, then, is to be held responsible for the type of technology we inherited from our ancestors? Clearly, the technological change that took place in history is the outcome of an highly aggregative, complex process of collective decision making and acting. When turning to the seven dimensions of responsibility listed above, it becomes evident that in the strict sense there are no individuals that can be held responsible for what happened. This for the simple reason that no-one had control or power of the whole development, and furthermore no-one could predict the practical outcome that would result from the technological actions performed. In fact, it can be said only of a small amount of the actions involved that the decision makers and actors were fully aware of what they were doing. Take the example of inventors and high-ranking decison makers: in neither of these groups did the persons involved really know what the far-reaching results of their action would be. Clearly, their decisions and activities were more important than those of the average person. But they, too, were caught in a complex web of constraints, trends, habits of behaviour, and of counteracting and mutually interfering interests and actions which far exceeded their capacity to control and understand them. Thus technology as a whole is the result of human actions but not of human intentions.

(2) The virtually inexhaustible complexity of the historical process can only be made accessible to theoretical understanding by means of *simplifying models* that concentrate on specific aspects, thereby inevitably neglecting other features that are also relevant but are not considered in the specific model in question (Rapp, 1982). In order to arrive at some structure, one can distinguish two mutually exclusive models. These aggregative models are intended to cover the whole field in an exhaustive way by concentrating on important aspects (and in doing so inevitably neglect the other, complementary aspect):

(a) In the structural model of *technological determinism* the historical process is regarded in much the same way as processes in nature. In this case, the historian assumes the pose of a detached observer who merely states what is going on at a highly aggregate level, without considering the individuals involved or their intentions or aims, etc. The 'objective' features that escape the power, control and foreknowledge of the individual are stressed in this approach. Just as no-one is held responsible for natural processes, so technological development is regarded as a phenomenon that just happens.

(b) This, however, is only part of the truth. After all, technology only comes about and is maintained and developed further by purposeful, goal-directed human decisions and actions. The individuals involved in deciding and acting aim at fulfilling some sort of (perhaps unconscious or implicit) goals, interests, priorities, or value patterns. In this conception of purposeful decision making and acting it is presupposed that men are, in principle, free deliberately to change the overall trends of existing technological development. It is only within the conceptual framework of this model of *value determinism* that some sort of responsibility for technological development can be conceptualized in a consistent way. However, any attempt at doing this will be subject to the severe restrictions mentioned; in fact, these restrictions are overemphasized in the model of technological determinism.

One must always keep in mind that any process of technological change takes place in a society which is shaped by particular cultural attitudes, legal institutions, social structures, and political forces. It is within the framework of economic processes that technological systems are produced and applied on the basis of the given technological knowledge and skills, with regard to particular conceptions of values and goals, and by use of material resources. This process then exerts its influence on the areas first mentioned and thereby furthers, in its turn, the course of technological development. This being the case, there is no hope for a simple, monocausal or one-dimensional explanation of technological change. Thus the structural model as well as the model of value determination are only simplified constructions in order to conceptualize in some consistent way the otherwise overwhelming complexity of the actual process.

More than other historical processes, technological development seems to be subject to impersonal, structural determinants. Individual judgements and decisions, the role of great individuals, combinations of special circumstances, and established historical traditions have less significance than the physical reality of technological systems. Technological measures, which are ultimately subject to the laws of nature, are largely tied to a material, functional context—availability of raw materials and infrastructure, interchangeable parts, division of labour and specialization—since only in this way can the goal of higher efficiency be attained. In consequence, the self-regulating progress of technological rationality with its objective of continuing dynamic advance takes, on the whole, the place of unique and 'fortuitous' historical occurrences. The result is that only in a vague, overall sense which does not allow for clear-cut and precise specification is it possible to speak about responsibility for the technological development up to the present.

(3) No-one (perhaps with the exception of journalists and historians) can change what happened in the past. But it is up to us to bring about the future. We are *introducing new technologies*, and hence we should be able to shape the future course of technological development. From a practical point of view, the conceptual and theoretical reconstruction of the processes of decision making and acting *in the past* is of a merely academic character. Even if we knew who was responsible for the results that were achieved, we would not be able to change them. In contrast, it makes sense and is even necessary to realize what is actually going on and to consider what ought to happen *in the future*. Of course, here again the intricate complexity of the process of technological change just mentioned comes into play. After all, we cannot expect that the future will completely differ from the past. Each of us must face the 'dialectics of history', namely the fact that, on the one hand, things will happen, irrespective of what a single person is doing; and that, on the other, we are obliged to consider carefully what we are going to do and consider ourselves responsible for the results arising from our actions (Jonas, 1979). This holds good at least with respect to the short-term consequences we are in command of. But we must also be aware of the further consequences of our decisions and actions to the extent that we can

actually foresee their results. The notion of technology assessment is intended to provide some guidance by identifying, as far as humanly possible, methodological rules and institutional procedures for shaping future technological innovations in a humane way (Rossini, 1979; Rapp, 1983).

MODELS FOR ASCRIBING RESPONSIBILITY

In order to handle the complex problem of responsibility conceptually, perhaps the following models can be distinguished:

(1) As a *voter* and as a *participant in the market*, every citizen and every consumer has a vague co-responsibility for technological change in so far as he or she can and actually does influence the political and economic decision processes. But clearly his share is only a fraction of the responsibility of the whole collective body involved. In terms of a highly simplified model one may take it for granted that the same 'amount' of responsibility can be ascribed to each and every member.

(2) In modern democratic societies the knowledge, understanding and attitudes of individuals are, to a high degree, shaped by the media. As a result, journalists often have the function of *opinion leaders*. Similarly, politicians as well as scientific and technological experts may exert a decisive influence on public opinion and hence indirectly on the decisions finally made. If one assumes that, roughly speaking, the responsibility a person holds with respect to technological development can be weighted according to the influence the person exercises on the final decisions, one arrives at the result that the opinion leaders, no matter what their professions are, will have a greater responsibility than the 'man in the street'.

(3) Corresponding to the dimensions (2) and (3) of responsibility mentioned above, one can assume that power and foreknowledge are important criteria of responsibility. Consider those who, within a firm or a bureaucracy, hold a well-defined *position of authority* within the hierarchy in a decision-making process involving technological development. Clearly, they will have more responsibility for what is going on than those on the lower levels. Usually the hierarchical structure will be of such a type that the decision maker is not necessarily the physical agent. It may well be that the real culprits are well hidden in the hierarchy, while the apparent agent is actually innocent.

(4) There are different ways of dealing with responsibility and technology in the interrelated and complex modern world. With respect to technological change we can distinguish different *systems* (science and engineering, research and development, the media, economics, politics). Following the approach of systems theory, one may regard these systems as self-sustained entities which are defined by their organizational structure and reproduce

and reinforce themselves without being influenced by the environment. The value-neutral objectivizing perspective of systems theory and of technological determinism takes whatever happens for granted. From this viewpoint responsibility, as it were, vanishes. But at the same time, a sort of *meta-theoretical responsibility* arises for designing and/or maintaining the appropriate organizational structures, including the processes of decision making.

The material mode of responsibility is thus replaced by a formal one. The person in question is no longer held responsible for a specific decision or action, but rather for enabling 'responsible' decisions and actions by providing the appropriate framework in terms of an orderly organizational structure. Providing the framework is only a necessary procedural tool, but by no means a sufficient condition that would guarantee 'responsible' ways of action. Even the most sophisticated formal organizational structures cannot replace the material dimension, i.e. the 'responsible' decision of the person in question. These structures are of crucial importance, since it is only by means of such decision structures that in the highly complex and interrelated modern industrial societies any aim, goal or value whatsoever can be realized. The importance of this feature becomes evident from *ex negativo* examples. When the organizational patterns and the structures of decision making are inefficient and counterproductive, reasonable and appropriate decisions will only arise by chance, but never as a rule.

A further important feature is the emotional environment that is present in any given organization. Here again the higher-ranking people are responsible for creating a mental or moral atmosphere, some sort of internal corporate identity, that encourages 'responsible' decisions and actions. In this way, the rational element of a clear-cut structure of decision making must be supplemented by appropriate emotional support for doing the right thing. The prevailing moral climate is so important, because in a decision situation people do not usually start considering rational arguments; they rather tend to follow their entrenched habits and attitudes. Psychology, training and character are at least as important as decision-theory, thinking and the intellect.

(5) Another approach would be to deal with technological innovations in terms of a one-dimensional time-sequence model. One could start with the statement that the stock of scientific findings and technological knowledge hitherto acquired constitutes the basis from which further innovations can arise. As this stock is handed down to us by our ancestors, they are—in whatever form—to be held responsible for it. But it is up to us how we will use these elements. The successive *stages of technological innovations* by means of which the technology of the future is brought about comprise: invention, research and development, and acceptance by the market.

This model of time sequence once again brings to mind the intricate character of technological change. If one was to allocate responsibility, whom should one address? The research scientist, the person in the development department, the managerial decision maker, the banker (who gives the money), the buyer (who puts the product to use), or the maintenance person (who keeps it running)? Evidently, this chain would break down if a single one of the elements involved were missing. When the final result – and not a single intermediate stage – is taken as a point of reference, strictly speaking, the decision makers of all of the stages involved must be held responsible. As a rule, at every stage there is a group of persons who are to decide and hence are to be held responsible. There may be ways of breaking this chain of connections by replacing one or the other of the elements mentioned by a functional substitute. Furthermore, a person may claim that if he would not have done the job, somebody else would have done it. But this argument does not really relieve the decision maker and/or actor from his share of responsibility in the process he was actually engaged in. The lesson is once again that there is no convenient and straightforward way of splitting up corporate responsibility.

At this juncture it may be helpful to distinguish between two models or ideal types of causation and hence also between two types of responsibility. In a well-defined organizational framework with a linear, hierarchical decision structure the series connections model applies; one step follows the other like the links in a chain. The person who is situated on a higher level and thus has more power and more control contributes more to the result and also takes more responsibility. Things are different if causing or bringing about of the state of affairs in question results from the joint combination of various causes which have been instigated by various actors acting on the same level. If all these actors are equally relevant, they would all bear the same share of responsibility. Only if their contribution is different might one try to quantify the share of their respective responsibility. In the linear series as well as in the combined influences model each and every actor is needed to bring about the final result of the cooperative activity. For this reason, none of them can be freed from his or her responsibility for the final state of affairs, though one may feel the need to estimate his or her share.

MORE OPERATIONAL APPROACHES

Even if the problems of authorship and distributing responsibility for collective decisions and actions were solved, the question of the standards or commands, as mentioned in (7) above, would still be open. If we counterfactually assume that it is clear who holds which share of responsibility, the question still remains in terms of which interests, goals, values, standards or commands he should have acted. The formal, organizational aspect of responsibility must be supplemented by the material, ethical aspect. In order to correctly assess the responsibility of a person the criteria, standards or commands he should have obeyed must be known. Assuming the same type of formal responsibility, a change in the commands or standards taken into account will result in a change of the moral responsibility to be ascribed to the person in question.

In all of the cases mentioned, namely the responsibility of the citizen and consumer, the responsibility of the opinion leader, the responsibility of the decision maker, the meta-theoretical responsibility for providing an efficient organizational structure as well as for a favourable emotional atmosphere, and the responsibility of the people involved in the different stages of a technological innovation, one may refer to general normative ideals like progress, the common good of mankind, the ideal of a fulfilled life, or the meaning of history. In order to arrive at more precise statements, the standards to be taken into account or the criteria to be fulfilled must be specified in more detail.

There are different ways of doing this. In the case of professional ethics the generally accepted standards of an occupation, as shared by all members of the peer group, are taken as the decisive point of reference. These standards are, by their very nature, closer to concrete reality and hence much more specific than general notions such as human rights, liberty, or self-determination. But the standards of professional ethics do not by themselves and in every case coincide with the interest of a firm, the organization or the bureaucracy in question. At this point, as everywhere in human life, value conflicts can easily arise. For example, professional ethics may demand a safe, expensive solution, whereas the interest of the firm consists in solving the given problem in a more profitable way (Schelling, 1984). These value conflicts can be interpreted as conflicts of loyalty to different types of responsibility. The loyalty to the goals and interests of the firm or organization can conflict with the standard or moral code a person may hold on weapon production or ecology. In this case two types of responsibility must be reconciled or balanced against each other, namely the responsibility towards the employer and the responsibility towards the moral code of the person in question.

Still more specific are the provisions made by positive law. They prohibit certain actions, but at the same time they leave open a wide range of a conduct which is exempt from jurisdiction but subject to moral assessment. In terms of the rules and principles laid down in a code of law, responsibility is no longer a private affair that concerns only the individual mind and defies public assessment. It is rather turned into a public, as it were, palpable matter which is threatened with negative social sanctions and specific types of public punishment in cases of contravention. It is the merit of the rules of law that they give an operational definition of responsibility by assessing the decisions made, the actions performed and the results brought about. On the social level the punishment laid down by the law can largely be analyzed in operational and behavioristic terms without explicit reference to the morality of the person in question. What happens is a sort of social game that consists in threatening a contravention with a certain punishment as laid down in the law, the punishment consisting in the social sanction of conviction. Guilt and punishment are elements in the social mechanism of maintaining responsibility (Kochen and Deutsch, 1980).

This seems to eliminate responsibility in the moral sense. To be more precise, moral responsibility is turned into a private affair and split off from adherence to the law. However, the legal procedure has the great advantage of giving clear commands and turning the question of responsibility into a public affair that can, in principle, be decided in a definite way. In this case, the complicated task of specifying commands or standards in terms of which a person has to exercise his or her responsibility is solved by the code of law. He is no longer forced to listen to the perhaps vague and weak voice of his conscience. Some people feel that it would be helpful to regulate technological development by means of as much legislation as possible. Yet this would counteract the idea of self-determination, liberty and the free market, and in the last analysis such an approach would result in perfect control by the state. As everywhere in politics, the task in legislation is to find a reasonable compromise between the two extremes of complete *laissez-faire* and perfect control, i.e. between anarchy and dictatorship.

Only in the stylized scheme of rational decision making do individuals aim at a consistent choice in order to maximize their expected utility, or, for that matter, to arrive at the most 'responsible' decision. In a more realistic approach at least two important non-rational counteracting influences must be considered. The first consists of the psychological feature of the entrenched habits and attitudes mentioned above. The second influence consists of the soft or hard constraints imposed upon the decision maker by the social environment. Clearly, there is a broad spectrum of options between the extremes of other direction (being guided by others) and inner direction (being guided by oneself). A self-imposed, reasonable type of social direction can help to enhance social responsibility when it comes to acting 'responsibly' towards nature, i.e. taking care of the environment and of the natural resources. Each and every individual is much more willing to refrain from acting selfishly if he has no other choice, because he is forced to act in a responsible way by moral social pressure and perhaps even by a law for which he himself has voted.

The legal approach to responsibility, i.e. imputing the authorship for certain actions, in view of the punishment laid down by the law also provides some help for dealing with the more vague and more basic moral notion of responsibility. In both cases, the charge of neglecting (legal or moral) responsibility can and must be sustained by establishing the relevant chain of events which triggered the faulty process. This procedure presupposes that the decision and/or action in question has already taken place. At first, it therefore works only with respect to the *ex post* assessment of responsibility. However, it may also be found to be useful when being applied *ex ante*. After all, in everyday life as well as in business, there are often complicated situations in which the competence for making decisions is not at all well defined. In such cases, the process of tracing events and agents back and simultaneously constructing alternative scenarios can serve as a heuristic model for identifying certain chains of responsibility.

The lesson is that the notion of responsibility so frequently referred to in opening addresses and speeches is found to have a very broad meaning and a highly complex structure, ranging from an indefinite feeling of involvement to a very specific commitment in legal terms. Clearly, it would be false to conclude that one should dismiss all aspects of the concept of responsibility that resist a well-defined operational interpretation. If we want to adhere to the traditional notion of man as a rational animal, i.e. as a creature that acts intentionally and consciously with certain value patterns in mind, we must also maintain the idea that he has to account for what he does. This is to say that there is no way of giving up the notion of responsibility.

As we have argued, due to the highly complex and aggregative decisions and actions which produce and maintain technology, there is no unequivocal and straightforward solution for responsibility allocation in modern technology. There is no way of placing responsibility for large-scale technological change. The same is true for any other far-reaching historical process. Nevertheless, it is possible to assign responsibility to individuals in small-scale specific situations on the micro level. When people undertake specific tasks, occupy functions or positions within given decision systems or within a clear-cut organizational structure, it is more feasible to define their responsibility in legal terms, in terms of professional ethics, and even in terms of moral criteria. However, even in this case a host of problems remain (appropriate weighting of the share of responsibility for collective actions, but also the role of carelessness and of lack of vision, etc.).

Notwithstanding these problems, the discussion about responsibility allocation is by no means inconsequential. Conscious activity is guided by the mind, and the state of mind is, among other things, shaped by the notion of being answerable for one's actions and by the ideals referred to. Public discussion about our responsibility for other persons, for our fellow-creatures, and for future generations will increase moral awareness.

Address for Correspondence:

Professor Friedrich Rapp, Universität Dortmund, Abteilung 14, Postfach 50 05 00, D 4600 Dortmund 50, Germany.

REFERENCES

Jonas, H. (1979) *Das Prinzip Verantwortung*. Frankfurt: Insel Verlag, pp. 222–33.

Kochen, F., and Deutsch, K. W. (1980) *Decentralization. Sketches Toward a Rational Theory*. Cambridge, Mass./Königstein: Oelgeschlager/Hain, p. 193.

Rapp, F. (1982) Structural models in historical writing. *History and Theory*, **21**, 327–46.
Rapp, F. (1983) The prospects of technology assessment. In P. T. Durbin and F. Rapp (eds), *Philosophy and Technology*. Dordrecht: Reidel, pp. 141–50.
Rossini, F. (1979) Technology assessment: A new type of science? In P. T. Durbin (ed.), *Research in Philosophy and Technology*, Vol. 2. Greenwich, Conn.: JAI Press, pp. 341–55.
Schelling, T. C. (1984) *Choice and Consequence*. Cambridge, Mass.: Harvard University Press, p. 32.
Wright, G. H. von (1971) *Explanation and Understanding*. London: Routledge & Kegan Paul, pp. 64–8.

BIBLIOGRAPHY

Baumgartner, H. M., and Eser, A. (eds) (1983) *Schuld und Verantwortung*. Tübingen: J. C. B. Mohr.
Ströker, E. (ed.) (1984) *Ethik der Wissenschaften? Philosophische Fragen*. Paderborn: Schöningh.
Ingarden, R. (1970) *Über die Verantwortung*. Stuttgart: Reclam.
Lenk, H., and Ropohl, G. (eds) (1987) *Technik und Ethik*. Stuttgart: Reclam.
Passmore, J. (1974) *Man's Responsibility for Nature*. London: Duckworth.
Sachsse, H. (1972) *Technik und Verantwortung*. Freiburg: Rombach.
Sosa, E. (ed.) (1975) *Causation and Conditionals*. London: Oxford University Press.
Watson, G. (ed.) (1982) *Free Will*. New York: Oxford University Press.

11. Event Analysis and the Problem of Causality

Jens Rasmussen
Risø National Laboratory, Denmark

INTRODUCTION

Science and engineering depend on a representation of the laws of nature in control of the behavior of physical systems. This representation can take different forms. The classical representation from Aristotle and onward was formed in terms of causal connections between events. The breakthrough of modern science was due to Galileo and Newton, who replaced observations of events by measurements of variables and causal laws by mathematical relations among variables.

The quantitative, mathematical representation of the physical sciences and engineering has been so successful that the qualitative concept of causality has been discredited by scientists. In his classical essay on the notion of cause, Russell (1913) finds the concept of causality to be so diffuse that it should be banished from science. Russell's conclusion, that causal explanations should be replaced by relational, mathematical representations, appears, however, to be mistaken. The two methods of representation are complementary approaches and they are both necessary for engineering analysis.

The quantitative, relational representation of physical sciences is not applicable for analysis of the courses of events when the structure of technical systems breaks down, e.g. during accidents. Likewise, this representation is not suited to describe the interaction of human decision makers and technical systems. The consequence is that a representation in terms of causal flow of events has become an important tool for accident analysis and for modelling decision making in the control of technical systems.

Causal explanations describe objects which interact in chains of events. Neither the objects nor the events can, however, be defined objectively. Their identification depends on a frame of reference which is taken for granted, and causal explanations are only suited for communicating among individuals

Distributed Decision Making: Cognitive Models for Cooperative Work
Edited by J. Rasmussen, B. Brehmer and J. Leplat

having similar experience who share more or less intuitively the underlying definitions. In a period of rapidly changing technology and the involvement of laymen in arguments about the impacts of large-scale technical installations, the ambiguity caused by the very nature of causal explanations is an important problem.

RELATIONAL AND CAUSAL REPRESENTATIONS

The causal and the relational representations are supplementary. They are based on fundamentally different methods of generalization and will serve different purposes for scientific and engineering analysis.

A mathematical, relational representation of physical phenomena is based on mathematical equations relating physical, measurable variables. The generalization depends on a selection of relationships which are 'practically isolated' (Russell, 1913). This is possible when they are isolated by nature (e.g. being found in the planetary system) or because a system is designed so as to isolate the relationship of interest (e.g. in a scientific experiment or a machine supporting a physical profession in a controlled way). In this representation, material objects are only implicitly present in the parameter sets of the mathematical equations. The representation is particularly well suited for analysis of the optimal conditions and theoretical limits of physical processes in a technical system which, by its very design, carefully separates physical processes from the complexity of the outside world.

A causal representation is expressed in terms of regular causal connections of events. In his essay, Russell discusses the ambiguity of the terms used to define causality: the necessary connection of events in time sequences. The concept of an 'event', for instance, is elusive: the more you strive to make the definition of an event accurate, the less is the probability that it is ever repeated. In this way, the regularity of causal connections disappears when attempts are made to define the concepts objectively. The weakness of Russell's request to have causal concepts defined objectively is its root in the quantitative, mathematical representation. In order to qualify the argument that a stone thrown against a pane of glass breaks it, you have to specify the weight and velocity of the stone. This argument is basically wrong. Events and causal connections cannot be defined by lists of objective attributes. An attempt to qualify a causal statement objectively by events in conjunction with the conditions which are jointly sufficient and individually necessary for a given effect to occur is, as Russell observed, without end. Completeness removes regularity. The solution is, however, neither to give up causal explanations nor to seek objective definitions. Regularity in terms of causal relations is found between kinds of events, not between particular, individually defined events.

The behavior of the complex, real world is a continuous, dynamic flow which can only be explained in causal terms after decomposition into discrete events.

The concept of a causal interaction of events and objects depends on a categorization of human observations and experiences. Perception of occurrences as events in causal connection does not depend on categories which are defined by lists of objective attributes but on those identified by typical examples, prototypes (Rosch, 1975). This is the case for objects as well as for events. Everybody knows perfectly well what 'a cup' is. To define it objectively by a list of attributes that separates cups from jars and vases and bowls is no trivial problem, and it has been met in many attempts to design computer programs for picture analysis. The problem is, that the property to be 'a cup' is not a feature of an isolated object but depends on the context of human needs and experience. The identification of events in the same way depends on the relationship in which they appear in a causal statement. An objective definition, therefore, will be circular.

A classical example is 'the short-circuit caused the fire in the house' (Mackie, 1965). This statement in fact only interrelates the two prototypes: the kind of short-circuit that can cause a fire in that kind of house. The explanation that the short-circuit caused a fire may be immediately accepted by an audience from a region where open wiring and wooden houses are commonplace, but not in one where brick houses are the more usual kind. If not accepted, a search for more information is necessary. Short-circuits normally blow fuses, therefore further analysis of the conditions present in the electric circuit is necessary, together with more information on the path of the fire from the wiring to the house. A path of unusually inflammable material was probably present. In addition, an explanation of the short-circuit—its cause—may be needed.

The explanation depends on a decomposition and search for unusual conditions and events. The normal and usual conditions will be taken for granted, i.e., implicit in the intuitive frame of reference. Therefore, in causal explanations, the level of decomposition needed to make it understood and accepted depends entirely on the intuitive background of the intended audience. If a causal statement is not accepted, formal logical analysis and deduction will not help: it will be easy to give counter-examples which cannot easily be falsified. Instead, further search and decomposition are necessary until a level is found where the prototypes and relations match intuition.

In the same way as it is impossible to define the meaning of words by linguistic analysis of one separate sentence, it is impossible by analysis to define the elements in a causal statement separated from its verbal context in the total description. In effect, causal explanations are only suited for communication among individuals who share prototypical definitions of objects and events because they have similar experience and, therefore, common 'tacit knowledge' (Polanyi, 1967). The great effort spent to formalize causality and to cope logically with counterfactual statements (Sosa, 1975) is probably misdirected. Instead, efforts should be focused on recent linguistic developments such as relevance theory (Sperber and Wilson, 1986) and situational semantics (Barwise and Perry, 1983) and on psychological theories of conceptualization and categorization (for a review see Murphy and Medin, 1985).

The causal description is an analog representation including physical objects as separate elements. The generalization implies categorization and identification of prototypical objects and events. The great value of causal reasoning is its immediate relationship to the material world, i.e. to physical objects and their configuration. The representation is therefore very easy to update in correspondence with changes in the real world. This is not the case in the relational representation in which a complex set of parameters and variables must be changed in order to incorporate physical changes.

In this way, qualitative, causal reasoning is useful to guide reasoning during design or in a choice of physical systems for some purpose. On the other hand, mathematical reasoning, related to formal analysis of relations between variables, is particularly useful to optimize a design and find its theoretical limits. The complementary nature is similar to that found between the use of intuitive judgement and formal proof by mathematicians (see Hadamar, 1945).

PROBLEMS IN ANALYSIS OF MODERN TECHNOLOGY

In the more traditional use of technology the problems related to the ambiguities of causal representations were rather innocent. Quantitative engineering analysis was applied for the design of machinery. A classical steam locomotive could be considered by the designers to be a well-defined micro-world in which the relationships of the thermodynamic laws were undisturbed by external factors. The description of the interaction of the locomotive with the environment in the course of an accident would be the concern of others, who could then view it as one integrated object with certain characteristics. Its behavior in the environment could be described with no reference to its internal physical functioning.

This separation cannot be maintained for the engineering analysis of large, centralized systems. Large systems present the potential for great losses and damage to people and the environment in cases of internal malfunction. Systems such as large chemical process plants cannot be considered to have 'practically isolated' internal functions, well contained by system boundaries and, therefore, adequately described by classical engineering analysis. Accidents happen when system boundaries break down. In this case, the preconditions for formal, mathematical analyses of system function also break down and the formal methods are replaced by different methods for analysis of accidents based on causal representations.

Such causal representations are important for two purposes. One is the analysis of accidents and incidents in order to gain experience and to collect data for the improvement of the safety of future designs. Another purpose is risk analysis, i.e. predictive analysis of hypothetical courses of events following technical faults and human errors.

PROBLEMS IN CAUSAL ANALYSIS OF ACCIDENTS

Analyses of accidents in, e.g. chemical process plants, are made in terms of accidental chains of events, i.e. causal representations. Since no two accidents will be identical, accident analysis will depend on prototypical categories of causes, events and consequences. A direct reference to elements in the physical world makes causal analysis a very effective technique for identifying and representing accidental conditions. It is, however, important to consider the implicit frame of reference of a causal analysis.

In the analysis of accidents, decomposition of the dynamic flow of changes will normally terminate when a sequence is found with events which match the prototypes familiar to the analyst. The resulting explanation will take for granted his frame of reference and only what he finds unusual will generally be included: the less familiar the context, the more detailed the decomposition. By means of the analysis, a causal path is found upstream from the accidental effect. This path may be set up by abnormal conditions which are latent effects of earlier events or acts. In this case branches in the path are found. To explain the accident, these branches are also traced backward until all conditions are explained by abnormal but familiar events or acts. The point in question in the present context is: how does the degree of decomposition of the causal explanation and the selection of which side-branches to include depend on the circumstances of the analysis? Another question is: What is the stop-rule applied for termination of the search for causes? Ambiguous and implicit stop-rules will make the results of analysis very sensitive to the topics discussed in the professional community at any given time. There is a tendency to see what you expect to see. During one period, technical faults were in focus as causes of accidents, then human errors predominated, while in the future the focus will probably move upstream to designers and managers.

The perception of stop-rules is very effective in the control of causal explanations. Everyone from college knows the relief felt when finding a list of solutions to mathematical problems. Not that it gives the path to solution to any great extent, but it provides a clear stop-rule for the search for possible mistakes, overseen preconditions, and calculation errors. The result: hours saved and peace of mind. A more professional example of the same point is given by Kuhn (1962). He mentions the fact that chemical research was able to come up with whole-number relations between elements of chemical substances only after the acceptance of John Dalton's chemical atom theory. There had been no stop-rule for the efforts in refinement of the experimental technique until the acceptance of this theory.

Stop-rules are not usually formulated explicitly. The search will typically be terminated pragmatically in one of the following ways: (1) an event will be accepted as a cause and the search terminated if the causal path can no longer be followed because information is missing; (2) when a familiar, abnormal event is found to be a reasonable explanation; or (3) if a cure is available. The dependence of the stop-rule upon familiarity and the availability of a cure makes the judgement very dependent upon the role in which a judge finds himself. An operator, a supervisor, a designer, and a legal judge may very likely reach different conclusions.

To summarize: identification of accident causes is controlled by pragmatic, subjective stop-rules which, to a large extent, also depend on the aim of the analysis, i.e. whether the aim is to explain the course of events, to allocate responsibility and blame, or to identify possible system improvements in order to avoid future accidents.

Analysis for explanation

In an analysis to explain an accident, the backtracking will be continued until a cause is found which is familiar to the analysts. If a technical component fails, a component fault will only be accepted as the prime cause if the failure of the particular type of component appears to be 'as usual'. If the consequences of the fault make the designer's choice of component quality unreasonable, or if a reasonable operator could have terminated the effect, had he been more alert or been trained better, a further search would probably be made. In such a case, a design or a manufacturing error can be found.

In most recent reviews of larger industrial accidents it has been found that human errors are playing an important role in the course of events. Frequently, errors are attributed to operators involved in the dynamic flow of events. This can be an effect of the very nature of the causal explanation. Human error is, particularly at present, familiar to analysts: to err is human, and highly skilled people will frequently depart from normative procedures. The problem of defining human error will be discussed in a separate section.

Analysis for allocation of responsibility

In order to allocate responsibility, the stop-rule of the backward tracing of events will be to identify a person who made an error and, at the same time, 'was in power of control' of his or her acts. The very nature of the causal explanation will focus attention on people directly and dynamically involved in the flow of abnormal events. This is unfortunate, because they can very well be in a situation where they do not have the 'power of control'. Traditionally, a person is not considered in power of control if physically forced by another person or when subject to disorders such as e.g. epileptic attacks. In such cases, acts are involuntary (Fitzgerald, 1961; Feinberg, 1965), from a judgement based on physical or physiological factors. It is, however, a question as to whether psychological factors also should be taken into account when judging 'power of control'. Inadequate response of operators to unfamiliar events depends very much on the conditioning taking place during normal work. This problem also raises the question of the nature of human error. The behavior of operators is conditioned by the conscious decisions made by work planners or managers who will be more 'in power of control' than an operator in the dynamic flow of events. These decisions may not be considered during a causal analysis after an accident because they are 'normal events' which are not usually represented in an accident analysis or because they are to be found in a conditioning side branch of the causal tree, not directly involved in the dynamic flow.

In conclusion, present technological developments require a very careful consideration by designers of the effects of 'human errors' which are commonplace in normal daily activities, but unacceptable in large-scale systems. The present concept of 'power of control' should be reconsidered from a psychological point of view, as should the ambiguity of stop-rule in causal analysis.

Analysis for system improvements

Analysis for therapeutic purpose, i.e. in order to identify events or conditions which can be a target for system improvement, will require a different focus with respect to selection of the causal network and of the stop-rule. The stop-rule will now be related to the question of whether an effective cure is known. Frequently, a cure will be associated with events perceived to be root causes. In general, however, the effects of accidental courses of events can be avoided by breaking or blocking any link in the causal tree or its conditioning branches.

Explanatory descriptions of accidents are, as mentioned, focused on the unusual events. However, the path can also be broken by changing normal events and functions involved. The decomposition of the flow of events, therefore, should not focus on unusual events but also include normal activities.

The aim is to find conditions sensitive to improvements. Improvements imply that some person in the system makes decisions differently in the future. How do we systematically identify persons and decisions in a (normal) situation where it would be psychologically feasible to ask for a change in behavior when reports from accidents focus only on the flow of unusual events?

In conclusion, the choice of stop-rules for the analysis of accidents is normally left to the subjective judgement of the analyst, depending heavily on the aim of his analysis. Analyses made for one purpose may, therefore, be misleading for other purposes.

EVALUATION OF THEORIES AND SYSTEMS

The internal consistency of a quantitative, relational model can be tested logically and mathematically, and systems designed from such theories can be validated by means of controlled experiments. Implementation of these models in the real world is considered to be an 'application' and, therefore, irrelevant to science. Such rigid distinctions are not appropriate when considering theories relating to complex environments and based on causal representations obtained from the generalization of observations.

Research into artificial intelligence offers effective tools for simulation of complex systems by object-oriented languages. This has created a new 'cognitive science' in which theories are only acceptable if they can be tested for consistency by computer simulation. Until now, this has only been successful for very well-formed micro-worlds like games, cryptograms and theorem proving. The basic reason for this appears to be that objects, events and causal connections in such restricted worlds can be objectively defined in the classical way by lists of attributes.

This is not possible for simulation of complex systems. Objects, events and causal relations in models then represent classes, not instances. It is, of course, possible in simulations to replace the classes by particular members, but then the entire exercise will be an *ad hoc* demonstration of selected examples. There will be no formal stop-rule to terminate the additions of new relations or objects in order to match simulated performance to observed real-life performance. An empirical testing of the internal consistency of a theory in causal terms by simulation of scenarios is not a satisfactory solution. As Davidson (1967) suggested, causal descriptions and causal laws should be kept apart from each other.

Simulation of causal chains of events in entirely technical systems is eased by their well-structured and relatively stable anatomy. Simulation can be planned from invariant relationships at a higher level of abstraction, typically derived from mass and energy conservation laws. Classes of events related to state changes of physical components can be mapped onto model parameters and the completeness of representation of a set described by a prototype can be judged.

This is not the case for the activity of people with free will, mobility and subjective goals. During actual behavior, members of a causal chain will be selected from prototypical classes and adjusted to match particular conditions. In simulation based directly on explicitly formulated causal relations, e.g. production rules, this is not the case. The set included in the database of a simulation, therefore, has to include all possible variants of a class.

This is unrealistic. Consider, for instance, the variety of actions necessary to represent the class of 'human errors'. Simulation based on 'first principles' corresponding to physical conservation laws is therefore necessary to avoid *ad hoc* selection and model fitting. For human error, this implies that particular errors should be generated from higher-level behavioral laws.

A first approximation is to categorize error according to generating mechanisms: effects of adaptation guided by the law of least effort; interference between cognitive control structures; lack of mental processing resources, etc. When such principles underlying observed scenarios can be formulated, an 'object-oriented' simulation can 'generate' entire families of scenarios from higher-level relationships.

Similarly, representing human knowledge in terms of explicit 'production rules' appears to involve a category mistake, taking the particular for the kind. Taken as models of human expertise, the old GPS system was more valid than the recent expert-system approach. Advice from an expert system will probably only be understood and accepted by a person who has the same frame of reference as the expert supplying the rules, and therefore is able to regenerate the prototypical classes (i.e. in practice; only the expert himself?).

In order to avoid *ad hoc* demonstration in simulation of human decision making, independent representations are necessary of the work domain, the task requirements and of the human cognitive mechanisms. This, in fact, is a request for the revival of the Brunswikian ecological psychology (Brehmer, 1984).

Another example is simulation of organizational behavior. Decision making is typically modelled in terms of a separate sequence of mental acts of one person. Observations are made, an analysis supports a diagnosis and, finally, acts are planned. In reality, however, actual decision making is a continuous process to control the state of affairs in a dynamic work domain in cooperation with other decision makers.

Models of organizations are, however, normally based on normative, effective decision strategies, and the cooperation on the role allocated in formal organizations. Again, simulation based on such representations will be *ad hoc* demonstrations. Instead, simulation should be based on principles that will dynamically generate the decision scenarios. One approach can be from a control-theoretic point of view in terms of a self-organizing, distributed control system in which the actors are allocated control of a defined sub-space of a loosely coupled work domain defined by the available means–ends relations. The actual organization of actors can then evolve from a specification of the conventions and constraints defined for their cooperation and communication.

CONCLUSION

During the past period of slowly evolving technology the ambiguity of the causal representation of commonsense reasoning was a rather innocent academic problem of philosophy and human sciences. In a rapidly developing technology, change inhibits the maintenance of common experience and intuition of groups involved in the development, use and assessment of technology. At the same time, design of large complex systems makes the use of causal analyses mandatory. Basic research and application can no longer be separated.

Address for Correspondence:

Professor Jens Rasmussen, Risø National Laboratory, PO Box 49, DK-4000 Roskilde, Denmark.

REFERENCES

Barwise, J., and Perry, J. (1983) *Situations and Attitudes*. Cambridge, Mass.: MIT Press.

Brehmer, B. (1984) Brunswikian psychology for the 1990s. In K. M. J. Lagerspetz and P. Niemi (eds), *Psychology in the 1990s*. New York: Elsevier Science.

Davidson, D. (1967) Causal relations. *Journal of Philosophy*, **64**, 691–703. Reprinted in E. Sosa (ed.), *Causation and Conditionals*. Oxford: Oxford University Press.

Fitzgerald, P. J. (1961) Voluntary and involuntary acts. In A. C. Guest (ed.), *Oxford Essays in Jurisprudence*. Oxford: Clarendon Press. Reprinted in A. R. White (ed.), *The Philosophy of Action*. Oxford: Oxford University Press.

Feinberg, F. (1965) Action and responsibility. In M. Black (ed.), *Philosophy in America*. London: Allen and Unwin. Reprinted in A. R. White (ed.), *The Philosophy of Action*. Oxford: Oxford University Press.

Hadamar, J. L. (1945) *The Psychology of Invention in the Mathematical Field*. Princeton: Princeton University Press.

Kuhn, T. (1962) *The Structure of Scientific Revolution*. University of Chicago Press.

Mach, E. (1905) *Knowledge and Error*. English edition, 1976, Dordrecht: Reidel.

Mackie, J. L. (1965) Causes and conditions. *American Philosophical Quarterly*, **2.4**, 245–55 and 261–4. Reprinted in E. Sosa (ed.), *Causation and Conditionals*. Oxford: Oxford University Press.

Murphy, G. L., and Medin, D. L. (1985) The role of theories in conceptual coherence. *Psychological Review*, **19**, No. 3, 289-316.

Newell, A., Shaw, J. C., and Simon, H. A. (1960) Report on a general problem-solving program for a computer. *Proceedings of the International Conference on Information Processing*, Paris: UNESCO, pp. 256–64.

Newell, A., and Simon, H. A. (1972) *Human Problem Solving*. Englewood Cliffs, NJ: Prentice Hall.

Polanyi, M. (1967) *The Tacit Dimension*. New York: Doubleday.

Rasmussen, J. (1987) Approaches to the control of the effects of human error on chemical plant safety. *International Symposium on Preventing Major Chemical Accidents*, February, American Institute of Chemical Engineers.

Reason, J. (1986) Cognitive under-specification: its varieties and consequences. In B. Baars (ed.), *The Psychology of Error: a window on the mind*. New York: Plenum.

Reason, J. (1988) *Human Error: Causes and Consequences*. New York: Cambridge University Press.

Rosch, E. (1975) Human categorization. In N. Warren (ed.), *Advances in Cross-Cultural Psychology*. New York: Halsted Press.

Russell, B. (1913) 'On the notion of cause'. *Proc. Aristotelean Society*, **13**, 1–25.

Sosa, E. (ed.) (1975) *Causation and Conditionals*. Oxford: Oxford University Press.

Sperber, D., and Wilson, D. (1986) *Relevance*. Oxford: Basil Blackwell.

Section 4

Field Studies of Cooperative Work

A number of field studies which have been made, particularly in Europe, can shed light on the problem of taxonomies of organizational and work domain characteristics. This section is focused on a discussion of the problems and prospects identified in the previous chapters in the light of specific examples from field work.

Part 4.1

Process Control

The chapters by Van Daele and De Keyser and by Kasbi and de Montmollin illustrate two very different cases of distributed decision making in industrial settings.

Chapter 12, by Van Daele and De Keyser, is concerned with the situation as it exists today. They study the case of a centrally located operator whose task it is to coordinate and synchronize the work of a team in relation to a continuous process. This task is made difficult for the operator by the fact that he lacks the necessary instrumentation in the control room to construct an adequate representation of the state of the process. Therefore, he has to rely on the team members as human sensors to obtain the data he needs. On the basis of the information they provide, he then constructs a representation of the problem and issues orders to the other team members. However, depending on the task facing the team, he cannot always expect these orders to be carried out without question. Consequently he sometimes has to enter into negotiation with the team members to reach an acceptable course of action. Van Daele and De Keyser provide a number of interesting and important suggestions about how different forms of production and working conditions lead to different forms of cooperation and communication in distributed decision making. In addition, the chapter offers interesting insights into the advantages and problems in using the communication among team members as a source of data for the study of cooperative work.

Chapter 13, by Kasbi and de Montmollin, offers more of a view towards the future. They discuss, among other things, the new control concept for French nuclear power plants. According to this concept, each operator works at his or her own workstation with a separate part of the plant. Thus, there is one operator for the primary circuit and another for the secondary circuit in the plant, etc. Similar forms of organization can, of course, also be found elsewhere in industry (e.g., pulp plants), and may be an important trend for the future. It is easy to see how this form of organization will lead to operators who have partial models of the process because they see it through different 'windows'. The future evaluation of the new French control room concept should provide extremely valuable data to guide the development of new forms of work organization that are adequate for the new possibilities now offered by technology.

12. Distributed Decision Making and Time in the Control of Continuous Processes

Agnès Van Daele and Véronique De Keyser
University of Liège, Belgium

INTRODUCTION

Automation has changed the role of the operator. His work is no longer so much a question of direct control of the process as of synchronizing and coordinating a system. Moreover, the operator does not work alone: he works in a team. This chapter is concerned with the relations between a centrally located operator in a control room, on the one hand, and the rest of the team, consisting of workers closer to the actual process, on the other. It is focused on problems faced by the operator in this team work. Specifically, we aim to show the role of the operator in the decision process and the effects of distributed decision making on the problems faced by him. Four industrial case studies are given.

Decision making is seen as a process involving three different steps: diagnosis (detecting a need for intervention from an estimation of the systems' state); planning (based on this estimation and according to a system's target state, to selecting among a set of possible actions one (or, more often, a set of actions) to carry out); and execution (carrying out the actions decided upon in the planning step and evaluating the feedback obtained).

FORMS OF TEAM ACTIONS AND THE PROBLEMS FACED BY THE OPERATOR

We can distinguish among three different forms of team actions:
(1) Actions that intersect, or are linked, without affecting the process directly;
(2) Actions on the process where the operator functions as a relay;
(3) Direct actions on the process.

The operator often decides on these actions by giving orders to the members of the team. However, the team members frequently have the means to regulate

Distributed Decision Making: Cognitive Models for Cooperative Work
Edited by J. Rasmussen, B. Brehmer and J. Leplat

their own activity, although this is not always so, and especially not in the case of incidents. In this event, the operator will have to assume control over the work process in a more direct way.

To fulfil his role as coordinator of the system (De Keyser *et al.*, 1987; Van Daele, 1988) the operator must make sure that the actions of different individuals in the team are compatible, and are directed towards the overall goal of the work process. The operator is thus responsible for the temporal organization of individual actions. This activity, that encompasses his own actions, involves problems for the operator.

The first of these problems is that of achieving a representation of the system as a whole in real time. The operator needs to know 'who makes what, when and for how long'. Because the team is dispersed geographically, the operator often has to achieve this representation on the basis of verbal communication (e.g. via telephone, radio). However, there can be delays in or lack of information transfer that prevent the operator from making an efficient decision, the more so since he has a centralized position and must make decisions within a broader horizon. In the case of incidents, the workers close to the actual installation tend to communicate among themselves and attempt to solve the problem before they communicate with the operator. This may lead to delays, and since the operator will need information to prevent the incident from spreading, this may cause the disturbance to become worse than it should have been.

A second problem relates to the need for the operator to synchronize the actions of the team members, and the actions of the team, with his own actions. This synchronization is based on estimations of the duration of different actions. To be able to give a command at the right time the operator has to consider a number of durations: the time required to carry out an action, the time required for a command to reach the worker who is to carry out the action, the time it will take for the worker to reach the location where he is to undertake the action, etc. Moreover, the operator has to consider the temporal order among his own actions and those of the team members. To decide this order, he must know the momentary state of the system, and this takes us back to the need for the operator to have a representation of the system as a whole.

A third problem for the operator is to make the actions of the team members coincide with the evolution of the process. This is especially important under conditions of disturbance. A disturbance such as a delay in relation to a plan, or an incident, that generally takes place out of the operator's reach, requires from him very rapid actions to modify possibly the evolution of the process and limit the consequences and then to decide on new actions for the team. Finally (but this occurs later in most cases), he must determine the causes of the disturbance. Besides the difficulties linked with the detection of the disturbance, other problems are due to conflicts that can occur between the productivity and security of the installation in the choice of actions to be fulfilled.

These problems are exacerbated by the way today's control rooms are designed. Indeed, it seems that, up to now, informational supports have not been designed to help the operator in his mastery of the evolution of the system. So a unitary logic 'one captor/one measure' still very often applies to the design of displays (Woods, 1985). This logic favours a presentation of instantaneous variable values without any trace of their evolution. Now it is known that what is significant for the operator is generally some kinds of variable evolution in which the evolution speed is an important parameter (Rogalsky, 1987). The operator often relates these variable evolutions functionally to each other in patterns. However, the latter are most often split into several displays, which does not facilitate checking. Moreover, the displays are often not designed for team work but for individual work. Consequently, the operator may have to construct his representation of the evolution of the system on the basis of verbal communication from persons looking at instruments in different locations.

COOPERATION AND DISTRIBUTED DECISION MAKING IN PROCESS CONTROL

When there is a problem, cooperation among the operator and the rest of the team can take at least two different forms. It may occur at the level of the resolution of the problem (i.e. it is a matter of gathering information or coordinating action), or it may be found at the level of the solution of the problem (i.e. it is a matter of reaching consensus on the appropriate course of action among the workers (Savoyant, 1984)). At this level, we may speak of distributed decision making among the workers in the sense suggested by Fischoff (1986), i.e. that those who shape the decision do not share completely the same information.

The operator's role in the decision process may be more or less important. It depends on the form of coordination between the operator and the other team members. Following Mintzberg (1984), we may distinguish three forms of coordination. The most common form may be described as coordination through task distribution. In this case, the total task is broken down into a number of subtasks that can be compared to the different stages of the product's transformation, for instance. Here, coordination among the workers is generally operated by a plan fixed *a priori*. However, given the variability of the situation, an operator is responsible for a part of the process (several stages of transformation) and must control the coordination of the team's actions in real time. The mode of cooperation which affects the decision on new actions is performed basically at the level of solution. The workers close to the process signal possible variations to the operator. The operator transmits the information, gives orders to cope with the disturbance, and maintains a choice of actions to carry out. The other members of the team contribute to the decision in that they supply information during the diagnosis stage and perform the actions required.

Coordination through distribution of objectives represents a second form of coordination. Here, the overall goal for the work is divided into a number of subgoals and each worker is made responsible for reaching one (or more) of these goals. This is the classical form of coordination of different functions in a company which will have a production department, a sales department, a marketing department, etc. With this form of coordination the operator will often have to negotiate with different workers whose objectives are in conflict, in order to reach a consensus on what course of action should be taken, or what should be given priority. The cooperation mode of the operator and the other workers is at the resolution level. In this case, the operator's role is more restricted than in the first case in that he is no longer the only person to choose the actions to be performed by the team.

The third form is called coordination through reciprocal adjustment. In this case, each team member takes on whatever task is not performed by other team members. In the control of continuous processes this mode of coordination seems to be limited to tasks such as maintenance, i.e. they are not subject to the constraints imposed by the evolution of the process itself. In this form of coordination the operator's task is reduced to that of information transfer. The operator signals to workers separated geographically what other team members are doing to achieve coordination in the team. Here, cooperation among team members is more restricted than in the other cases, and the operator's role is that of a relay.

In each form of coordination, distributed decision making based on information supplied by the team members will help the operator to cope with problems. This is especially true when coordination is achieved through distribution of tasks. Here, verbal communication from the team members is an important source of information about the state of the system as a whole, and makes it possible for the operator to be informed of changes in the process as well as of the possible consequences of these changes. This is true both when these changes cannot be detected from the control room and when changes in the process are ignored because the operator fails to detect them due to information overload, because they do not occur as regularly as expected, or because he fails to inspect some parameter that has a very low probability of deviating from the normal. In the first case verbal communication from the team members makes up for the ergonomic deficiencies of the control room. In the second and third cases it makes up for deficiencies in the operator's ability to use the information provided in the control room. Moreover, since the operator is not only a passive receiver of information but can search for it actively by asking the team members, he can update his representation of the state of the system. This updating is a fundamental prerequisite for the synchronization both of the actions of the various team members and of those of the operator and the other members of the team.

As for the planning stage of the decision process, i.e. the choice of actions to be performed at the appropriate time and in the appropriate order, resorting to the team enables the operator to broaden the scope of these actions. In addition, it often helps him to reach a consensus on a solution. Reaching a consensus may not in fact be a problem for the team because the members often share the same values and norms, and this allows them to give priority to a solution, even if it involves a potential conflict among contradictory objectives.

At this level, we could draw a parallel with what happens in sport teams. A series of studies on a high-ranking football team show that effective social cohesion is a prerequisite for effective playing, that is, for operational cohesion (Chapuis and Thomas, 1988). Moreover, this is true even when the players do not share the same representation of the dynamics of a game. When the team is both an instrument of goal achievement and an object of solidarity, action reinforces effective cohesion, and this becomes the important aspect to preserve; failure does not weaken this but may enrich it instead. If, on the other hand, the football team is only an instrument of goal achievement, and if the objectives of the players do not coincide, participation in the collective effort required for success becomes problematical. As noted by different authors, social objectives become important, and even decisive, in the decision making of a work team in the same way as in sport teams (Mariné and Navarro, 1980; De Keyser *et al.*, 1985).

However, the effects of distributed decision making on the operator's ability to overcome his difficulties are not always positive. Distributed decision making may also have negative effects, and it may introduce new problems. For example, there may be problems in the communication network. Additionally, interaction between the operator and the team may reinforce a misjudgement of the situation, or it may lead the team to give priority to the course of action that requires the least effort or the most risky one. Moreover, it may bring about new conflicts as the number of workers involved increases.

CASE STUDIES

Four different situations have been analyzed: one of these involves a transformation process and the other three, dispatching. In each case, the study focused upon the interaction between the operator and the team.

Brief presentations of the four case studies

Situation 1. This study (see De Keyser *et al.*, 1987; Van Daele, 1988, for further details) concerned the main control room of a continuous casting in a steel plant. This control room is located in a large production system with two stations upstream (steel works and ladle metallurgy), one station downstream (storage) and two transfer stations (overhead cranes). From the control room the operator supervises solidification of steel in the casting machine. Since this transformation process is highly automated, the main part of the operator's work consists of coordinating the actions of the team in the different stations. The operator has to meet goals with respect to time, quality and quantity set in the production planning. In cases of disturbance (e.g. when a station is late or ahead of its schedule, when there is a quality defect, or a technical incident) the operator must intervene.

Situation 2. This study (see Gonnay, 1984, for further details) focused upon the planner in the steel works of the same plant as that in Situation 1. The main task of this operator is to create a forward production plan, i.e. to decide on the sequence of castings and to check on how production develops during a shift. In the case of a disturbance, the operator must take action, i.e. modify the production plan, in cooperation with the workers upstream (the blast furnace), those downstream (pouring basins, slabbing, rolling mill) and those in the transfer stations (overhead cranes and internal railway traffic).

Situation 3. This study (see Feyereisen, 1987, for further details) involved an internal railway station in the same firm. The objective of the railway is to supply the various sectors with raw materials. From a control room, an operator controls the movements of a locomotive by transmitting information to the driver, who drives the locomotive by remote control. Signalmen give clearance at strategic points of the network. Movement of locomotives from the outside (external traffic) are controlled by a second operator. There is planning with respect to those operations in the normal production situation that can be foreseen. This involves monthly and daily production as well as the type of material to be carried by the trains. The task of the operator is to ensure that transportation complies with this planning.

Situation 4. This study (see Bahlan, 1987, for further details) involved two railway traffic control stations in a Belgian regional center. In each station there is an operator who controls a certain number of lines. The stations differ with respect to the type of traffic to be regulated (freight versus passenger traffic) and the type of technical equipment (a manual graph instrument, which requires the signalmen to indicate the position of the trains to the operator, who then updates the instrument, versus an automatic graph instrument, where the positions of the trains are detected by means of electrical contacts along the tracks and transmitted automatically to the instrument). Each station has a typical train timetable which is to be complied with. However, trains are sometimes delayed, and this requires regulation. Taking the number of constraints into account, the operator must avoid or minimize any delay by modifying the sequence and the timetable of some trains, take adequate steps to clear the tracks in case of obstruction, and apply protective measures in cases of incidents.

Objective and methods

Our objective here is to discover traces of distributed decision making in the content of verbal communication. Even though we know that the analyses of verbal data present a number of problems, especially when the subjects are required to verbalize their thoughts (Leplat and Hoc, 1981; Ericsson and Simon, 1985), analyses of the verbal communication between the operator and the team in real time may reveal important aspects of the operator's reasoning as well as the difficulties he meets, and it is an elegant way of circumventing certain methodological obstacles.

In each case, spontaneous verbal communications between the operator and the team have been noted or recorded for at least a hundred hours of work. To analyse these data, we have adopted the segmentation principles proposed by Falzon (1988). According to these, a communication consists of one or more messages to the same interlocutor during the same communication event. A message is a unitary whole of information expressed by a single interlocutor and for the purpose of reaching a precise goal. A conversation is a set of communications involving the same interlocutors.

Quantitative and qualitative analysis of the communication have been made. The differences between the communication from and to the operator have been noted in each situation. The communications have been categorized according to the interlocutor of the operator, the point in time in the shift, and whether the context was normal or not.

The communications have also been analysed with respect to their content. In the analysis we looked for the usefulness of the communication. Important questions here were the following. What role does it serve in the coordination of the actions of the team? How is the information conveyed different from that available from other forms of support in the control room?

Discussion

For each situation we note that the operator does not make the decisions alone. Indeed, the verbal communication proves that the decisions are frequently made in cooperation with other workers. Distributed decision making can be seen in all four situations. This is especially clear when the operator works to coordinate the actions of the team. We find all three modes of coordination discussed above.

Distributed decision making and the three modes of coordination

In situations 1 and 2, we observe coordination through task distribution in which elementary tasks can be assimilated in the different stages of steel processing. The coordination of the workers involved in these steps is achieved by the production plan decided *a priori*. However, given the variability of the system, an operator is needed to regulate coordination among the workers close to the installations. In situations 3 and 4, coordination by task distribution is also found among the personnel located close to the network (signalmen, engine men, station masters, track maintenance staff, etc.). A plan coordinates the actions of the team *a priori*. Due to the high variability of the system, we also find an operator who is responsible for part of the system and who must control coordination of the team's actions in real time. In all four situations, the operator's attempts to control coordination sometimes leads to decision processes aiming at modifying the team's activity. The mode of cooperation involved in selecting and performing these new actions works essentially at the level of resolution. The workers close to the installations signal some variation in relation to the plan to the operator, and he issues instructions concerning how to cope with the situation.

Coordination by goal distribution is also found in all four situations analysed. The problems involved in this form of cooperation have often been emphasized: economic problems, linked to quality defects or processes stoppages, maintenance taking too long, etc. The organizational dimension has often been used to explain these difficulties, e.g. it is said that the timetables become desynchronized, that it leads to different forms of hierarchical dependence, etc. However, it seems that the problems with this form of coordination cannot be summed up in terms of interference with respect to isolated points only. For example, in situation 1, quality is an essential aspect of the product. Good maintenance is a guarantee of the stability of the process's parameters and thus for the reliability of its automation. The traditional domination of production personnel decreases, and this is indicated by a number of factors: a relative decrease in the number of the staff, rules of material design specific to other departments, and modification of the work content, to give some examples. As for the last point, it must be noted that the operators try less than before to produce at any cost. They are putting less effort into anticipating incidents than in trying to recover from them as quickly as possible. Whether it will be possible to reduce the time for stoppages by contacting the appropriate maintenance staff at the right moment is now a constant source of worry.

However, it is still often noted that the goals of workers belonging to different departments are in conflict, and this leads to the need to search for compromises. The dominating form of cooperation is seen at the solution level. In situation 1, the problems usually arise from the need to stop the casting machine for maintenance. Before maintenance begins, contacts between the operator and the maintenance staff relate to maintenance time. There are three possibilities, depending on how urgent is the need for maintenance: immediate action, with process stoppage; action postponed to when the process is regularly stopped for changing machine parts (about every eight hours); or to the next 'cold shift' reserved for installation maintenance (every month).

Coordination by reciprocal adjustment is less frequent than the other forms in the four situations discussed here. In situation 3 (the control room for the internal railway traffic, which is the only control room with more than one operator), coordination through reciprocal adjustment was observed, but only during the night shift. During day shifts, coordination through task distribution is the dominating form and a decrease in the amount of verbal communication among the operators is observed.

The usefulness of verbal communication in distributed decision making

Analysis of the content of the verbal communication reveals how the operator uses his contacts with the team. A surprising amount of communication is concerned with temporal positioning. There are two forms of such communication. The first helps the operator to position himself within the usual chronology of action, i.e. to help him decide where he is with respect to the plan, to determine the probable duration of some processing steps, to estimate delays, etc. The second helps him to position himself within an unusual chronology of action (e.g. maintenance, repair and tests), where the problem is to determine when these actions begin and end, their probable duration. If information of the second type is not available from the computer system and if the operator has no knowledge to infer it, this puts him in a more difficult position than if the first kind of information is lacking, and it has different consequences for how he uses the verbal communication with the team.

There are at least two explanations for the difference. The first is related to how the operator overcomes part of the problem caused by the instruments in the control room giving no direct information about the beginning and the end of the activity of the workers assigned to a given production stage. Here, the operator is often led to use information for a purpose different to that for which it was provided. For example, one way to know whether or not a product processing stage has been finished is to check whether analysis of the product in question had already been made. In this case, it is not the contents of the analysis that interests the operator but whether the analysis has been completed or not. This tells the operator whether the processing stage had been completed. However, this information comes at a relatively late stage, so the operator often prefers to ask the workers concerned. A second explanation is pressure of time, which favours exchange of information through verbal communication rather than the computer system.

Beside helping to coordinate action in time, verbal communication also helps the operator to be informed of possible deviations from the normal evolution of the process. When the operator asks for information to help him position the work temporally, he also receives information with respect to disturbances. Both types of exchange allow the operator to update his representation of the system as a whole, which sometimes implies an updating of the computer system. Thus, in situation 3, for example, 60% of the communication came from engine men. For the operator, this information is useful in two ways. First, it informs him of any variation in the network compared to what has been planned. It also allows him to update the computer system. Indeed, in this situation, the engine men may be seen as 'human captors' for a process for which there are no technical sensors. In situation 4, where each operator has a different form of information support (manual graph instrument for station A versus automatic graph instrument for station B) to carry out the same task (regulation of railway traffic), 20 hours of recording during normal operation showed a much higher level of communication for station A (681 messages) than for station B (127 messages). For station A, 50.7% of the communication came from the network (signalmen, station masters, etc.) and allowed the operator to update his graph. For station B, there is practically no communication between the operator and the team that could be used to update the graph, since this is automatic.

In the case of disturbance, other variations in verbal communications have been observed. For both stations in situation 4, a disturbance led to an increase in the amount of communication, +32% for station A and +388%(!) for station B. This increase shows how cooperation between the operator and the team increases in such situations. Analysis shows that the increase in communication is caused by a growth in the number of requests for information from the network, rather than by an increased number of messages from the operator. The operator is in fact overwhelmed by the demands for information from the workers concerned by the failure, asking him to take steps to bring the system back to normal. To minimize the effects of the disturbance, the operator must make a number of decisions: whether or not a train should be allowed to depart, whether a single track should be used, etc. As a rule, communications used for regulation are more frequent, and there is a reduction in the number of messages that support updating of the manual graph instrument in station A from 50.7% to 36.3%.

There are at least two reasons for this reduction. First, the operator asks the train personnel when traffic is very low and not affected by the disturbance not to communicate until the situation is normal again. Second, the network workers will, on their own initiative, gather information about the checking points for the trains, i.e. they will communicate with the operator at longer intervals but the exchange will be richer in information. Both strategies relate to collective regulation of the operator's workload to prevent errors in his decision making.

An increase in regulation activity and a decrease in the updating of the computer in the event of a disturbance has also been observed from analysis of the verbal communication in situation 2. The time when an operator enters data into the computer may thus be regarded as an indication of his workload. If the entry does not take place until the end of the shift, just before the new operator takes over, this is a sign of a high workload during the shift.

Despite the positive effects for the operator with respect to the problems that stem from the temporal evolution of the system, he complains that he does not get enough information about the disturbances. The workers concerned by them first try to correct them before they contact the operator. These delays in information transmission prevent him from making the most efficient decisions. To have certain information early can be important for the operator, who has to make decisions on a wider timescale. It enables him to develop anticipatory strategies preventing the disruption from spreading throughout the whole system. The best examples of such anticipatory strategies that have been observed in situation 1 are linked with an implicit goal, shared by all the workers, of producing more than had been planned. The aim of these strategies is to reduce the time required for processing the product at some stages that leads not only to a reduction in overall production time but also to an increased risk of lower quality and problems with the casting machine. The urgency of these strategies is due to competition between the teams, and is encouraged by the display of production outputs in the firm. To try to attain this implicit goal enables the operator to reach a consensus on what action should be taken. He must not negotiate when he asks the team to intervene. In this situation, only 1.8% of the communication is used to negotiate, and this is restricted to exchanges between the operator and the maintenance staff. To reach a consensus on the action to be taken, the team must not necessarily share the same implicit objective. A good understanding and a certain solidarity among the workers can be enough. Indeed, in situation 2, we have noted that a high proportion of the communication is what we have called 'dispatching' and 'personal service' (more than 50%). The form of communication called 'dispatching' does not require any modification in the plan except, perhaps, indirectly and in the longer perspective. Examples of this form of communication are when the operator facilitates the transfer of information, or when he makes a general call to the maintenance staff. As for 'personal service', it is an extension of 'dispatching' but it concerns personal matters. An example would be when the operator locates another worker who is wanted on the phone. These two forms of communication are not directly useful for production purposes, and they are not formally required by the hierarchy. This illustrates the role played by communication when concern about the relations within the team can be more important than the prescribed work goals. More often, social utility is added to the functional utility of communication and it helps the operator reach a consensus more easily when giving orders to the team. For example, in situation 1, one of the operators observed begins all his requests for action by saying 'We're from the same family so we can do this favour for each other'.

CONCLUSIONS

The evolution of continuous processes has often been neglected up to now. However, it affects decision making in the control room. When new information appears, the nature of the problem to be solved changes. It causes several problems for the operator: to estimate the fluctuation of the process, to achieve a representation of the process in real time, to synchronize his own actions with those of the team and those of the team with the evolution of the process, and to cope with ergonomic deficiencies. However, as shown by verbal communication, the operator does not have to make his decisions alone. There is often cooperation with the team, and the decision making is distributed among many individuals. If we divide the decision process into three main steps (diagnosis, planning, and execution of the action), the relative importance of the operator and the team will depend on the mode of coordination. If coordination is through task distribution, the operator makes the choice of action to be carried out. The role of the team is mainly to supply information to establish the diagnosis and to carry out the action effectively. Cooperation thus takes place at the level of problem resolution. When coordination is through goal distribution and through reciprocal adjustment the operator's role is less well defined. In the first case, the operator must try to reach a consensus on the actions to be taken. Cooperation takes place mainly at the level of problem resolution. In the case of coordination through reciprocal adjustment, the operator works as a relay for information and intervenes very little in the team's decision making. All three modes of coordination are clearly seen in the four case studies.

The second theme of this chapter was that the effects of distributed decision making on difficulties met by the operator are ambivalent. They are sometimes positive, when they make up for some deficiencies, but they may also lead to new problems. In the present analyses of verbal communication, we mainly found the positive effects. Indeed, we have shown that a number of important exchanges with the team allowed the operator to position himself in the evolution of the system and to be informed of possible deviations in this evolution. These two forms of information are particularly important in the diagnosis step. With respect to the planning stage, i.e. the selection of actions, the studies showed that it is fairly easy for the operator to reach a consensus within the work team. This consensus is sometimes supported by an implicit objective shared by all team members, or simply by good understanding and a certain solidarity among team members. The negative effects of distributed decision making appeared less clearly in the four case studies. This may be due to the methods employed. Indeed, the only negative effects observed concern delays in the transfer of information, and have been detected from the complaints made by the operators, not from analysis of the verbal communications. It is possible that other negative effects were also ignored in the analysis. Further analysis will require a more diverse set of methods involving, among other things, attempts to relate the content of the verbal communication to performance criteria, analysis of errors resulting from the distribution of decision making and systematic analysis of the worker's complaints.

Address for Correspondence:

Agnès Van Daele, National Fund for Scientific Research, Université de Liège, Faculté de Psychologie et Sciences de l'Education, Service de Psychologie du Travail, Bd du Rectorat 5, Box 32, B-4000 Liège, Belgium.

REFERENCES

Bahlan, C. (1987) Etude de la pregnance des caractéristiques d'un système technique sur l'activité d'opérateurs polyvalents appréhendée à travers les communications verbales. Mémoire de licence en psychologie du travail. Université de Liège, unpublished.

Chapuis, R., and Thomas, R. (1988) *L'équipe sportive*, Paris: PUF.

De Keyser, V., Decortis, F., and Perée, F. (1985) Collective control in an automatized system apprehended in verbal communication. *2nd IFAC/IFIP/IFOR/IEA Conference on Analysis, Design and Evaluation of Man–Machine Systems*, Varése, 10–12 September.

De Keyser, V., Decortis, F., Housiaux, A., and Van Daele, A. (1987) *Les communications hommes-machines dans les systémes complexes.* Brussels: Services de Programmation de la Politique Scientifique.

Ericsson, K. A., and Simon, H. (1985) *Protocol Analysis. Verbal Reports as Data.* Cambridge, Mass.: MIT Press.

Falzon, P. (1988) *Ergonomie cognitive du dialogue.* Grenoble: Presses Universitaires de Grenoble.

Feyereisen, F. (1987) Communications verbales, images sur écran: match nul. Mémoire de licence en psychologie du travail. Université de Liège, unpublished.

Fischoff, B. (1986) Decision making in complex systems. In E. Hollnagel, G. Mancini and D. D. Woods (eds), *Intelligent Decision Support in Process Environments.* Berlin-Heidelberg: Springer Verlag.

Gonnay, N. (1984) Traitement de l'information et régulation chez le planning-man d'aciérie. Mémoire de licence en psychologie du travail. University of Liège, unpublished.

Leplat, J., and Hoc, J. M. (1981) Subsequent verbalisation in the study of cognitive processes. *Ergonomics.* **24**, 743–55.

Mariné, C., and Navarro, C. (1980) Rôle de l'organisation informelle du travail en équipe lors d'un dysfonctionnement technique. *Bulletin de Psychologie*, **XXXIII**, 344, 226–9.

Mintzberg, H. (1984) *Structure et dynamique des organisations.* Paris: Editions de l'organisation.

Rogalsky, J. (1987) Analyse cognitive d'une méthode de raisonnement tactique et de son enseignement à des professionnels. *Le Travail Humain*, **50**, 4, 305–18.

Savoyant, A. (1984) Définition et voies d'analyse de l'activité collective des équipes de travail. *Cahiers de Psychologie Cognitive*, **4**, 3, 273–84.

Van Daele, A. (1988) L'écran de visualisation ou la communication verbale? *Le Travail Humain*, **51**, 1, 65–80.

Woods, D. D. (1985) *Integral Display for Dynamic Worlds.* Pittsburg, PA: Westinghouse Research and Development Center.

13. Activity Without Decision and Responsibility: The Case of Nuclear Power Plants

Catherine Kasbi
Electricité de France, Etudes et Recherches
and
Maurice de Montmollin
Université Paris-Nord and MAST Group

INTRODUCTION

The work summarized in this chapter is still under way. Theoretical and methodological discussions are in progress, but the data collected are numerous enough to assess the plausibility of the following assumptions, which are, at present, restricted to local working conditions (we are conducting an ergonomic research, not a psychological one):

(1) The—mainly cognitive—interactive activities of the crew members in control rooms in nuclear power plants (NPPs) cannot easily be described in terms of distributed *decision* making. The concept of decision has, to say the least, to be diversified. It is more appropriate to speak of 'distributed reasoning' and of 'distributed competence'.
(2) Nevertheless, some people are *responsible* for controlling the process. This responsibility should be traced to the different persons (the whole hierarchy, in industrial settings) who contributed, at their respective level, to the actual situation which resulted in the success or failure of the process. Success means the normal (i.e. prescribed) production of electricity; failure means some incident or accident. In this perspective, there is no such thing as the responsibility of the sole operator who, at the very end of the operating sequence, took the so-called 'erroneous decision'.

Distributed Decision Making: Cognitive Models for Cooperative Work
Edited by J. Rasmussen, B. Brehmer and J. Leplat

In this chapter, point (1), which is typically related to an ergonomical analysis, is examined at length whereas the second point is only briefly covered in the conclusion, as it is more general and less directly related to situations met in NPPs.

OPERATORS' 'DISTRIBUTED ACTIVITIES'

The main characteristics of the operators' activities in NPPs, as inferred from the analysis of data (see below), are the following. Continuous process control implies a *continuous working process*. In contrast with some other descriptions (long periods of boredom, short periods of stress, etc.), operators are seen to be often active: they observe, infer, verify, check, discuss, act. As time is a vital agent for them, and often the bitter enemy, they continuously try to follow and, if possible, prevent the evolution of the process. Of course, during an incident their activity is more intensive. However, the distinction between 'normal' and 'incident' conditions is often artificial, and is derived more from an *a posteriori* consideration of the final results of the activities than from a detailed sequential analysis of these activities.

Consequently it is *not easy* to split the continuum of the operators' activities by identifying their 'decisions', even if we merely apply this term to 'decisions under uncertain circumstances'. This apparently trivial and evident concept becomes irrelevant after careful ergonomic work analysis. More precisely, everything could be called a 'decision'. Any of a thousand glances at VDU displays can be regarded as a 'decision' to request information. The 'decision' to start a pump may seem to be a 'real' decision, whereas this action probably stems from and is conditioned by the preceding cognitive sequence, and therefore cannot be explained outside this context of numerous micro-decisions. Similarly, the 'decision' to follow one of the prescribed procedures is predetermined by the preliminary cognitive, sometimes unconscious, orientation imported by the diagnosis which resulted in the choice of this procedure. When the operators are discussing a problem, who is making the 'decision': the person who says the final words of a sequence, 'OK, let's try to shut this valve!' or one whose arguments demonstrated the necessity of the action?

As a consequence, we have focused our analysis on the following types of operators' *activities*: (1) cognitive processes (including actions) and (2) cognitive structures. The way these activities are distributed (the so-called collective aspects of work) will be analysed in the working environments of the two control rooms (see the next section). *Cognitive processes* (or 'information processing') in continuous process control are, to a high degree, conditioned by the temporal aspects of work (see Chapter 12, this volume). It means that the operators' activities are strictly sequential, without any possibility of going backwards (as is the case in administrative matters, for instance). *Cognitive structures* here mean hypothetical models of relatively stable, organized mental structures built by the observer to *explain* behavioral patterns and cognitive processes. Ergonomists call *competence* the structures explaining (at the basis of) the professional activities corresponding to precise tasks or families of tasks. Examples of constituents of competence are the different types of knowledge, knowhow, representation (too polysemic a concept), skills (or routines), etc. The more experienced the operators in the team, the more difficult the modelling of their competence, as a large part of their cognitive processes is more heuristic than algorithmic, and thus cannot be easily verbalized. *Interactions* between operators (undoubtedly an essential aspect in any research on work distribution) are directly related to their competence (one could speak of 'interactions between competence').

After a brief description of the study performed at Electricité de France we will return to the main concepts above and consider a specific case: the control room redesign.

STUDY BACKGROUND

The advanced control rooms of the new French power plants

On the whole, the future French 1500 MW PWR power plants (N4 PWR series, whose first unit will be commissioned in 1991) are similar to the present 1300 MW ones as far as the process and automation levels are concerned. However, their advanced control rooms, with fully computerized workstations, will be provided with very different means of data acquisition and control, as explained above, thus requiring the performance of a new task: the so-called workstation management.

The technological leap forward from conventional control rooms to computerized ones was considered so great that it was decided to build a prototype control room connected to a 1300 MW PWR process simulator (called S3C), for technical ergonomic design validation. Therefore an ergonomical study program was designed.

Ergonomical evaluation: overall method

This evaluation is based on tests on the S3C simulator and observation of operators' activity. This activity is compared with that in a conventional control room.

Tests are performed with a multidisciplinary (ergonomists, engineers) evaluation team and with experienced operators requested to work on the simulator in different operating conditions. These tests are performed after one week of training in workstation management.

Ergonomic evaluation deals with many aspects:

(1) The control room's physical environment (especially visual aspects), including the design of the man–machine interface: display structure, man–machine dialogue and workstation management;
(2) The cognitive aspects: operators' reasoning strategies;
(3) The collective (or 'organizational') aspects.

Figure 1 summarizes the overall method.

Many *tests* have thus been performed with plant operators who were placed in a wide range of normal operating situations and accident conditions. Information is available from an *automatic acquisition system*, recording data on the actions of the operators at their workstation and from a real-time acquisition system recording precoded events corresponding to the *direct observation* of other aspects of the operators' activity (all these data and their precise time of occurrence are sent to a database, and various statistical treatments are performed on them). *Interviews* are organized at the end of the tests.

Focusing on collective aspects

We are studying the collective aspects of plant operation that this new man–machine interface is likely to affect. Indeed, it is important to assess the considerably modified operating conditions in a nuclear unit from a collective point of view and not only at the level of the individual operator. These collective aspects have to be studied inside the control room and for the complete operators' crew (including field operators).

It was decided to devote the first phase of this work to the preparation of simulator tests. In this perspective, the organization of the operating crews has been studied in existing power plants (observations, individual and collective interviews). Analysis resulted in assumptions on the impact computerization may have on the collective aspects of plant operation. The control room is of central importance for those collective aspects.

On the S3C simulator the collective work of the two control room operators was particularly analyzed (the rest of the crew did not take part in the simulator tests). On the basis of the data obtained by the method presented above, the aim was to describe the different types of task allocation between operators and the organization of their collective activities.

To this end, attention has been focused on the following data:

(1) Type of images viewed (primary or secondary systems) and of orders sent (primary or secondary systems) by the operators during a scenario;
(2) Type of alarm allocation chosen (no specialization at the workstation level, total or partial differentiation);

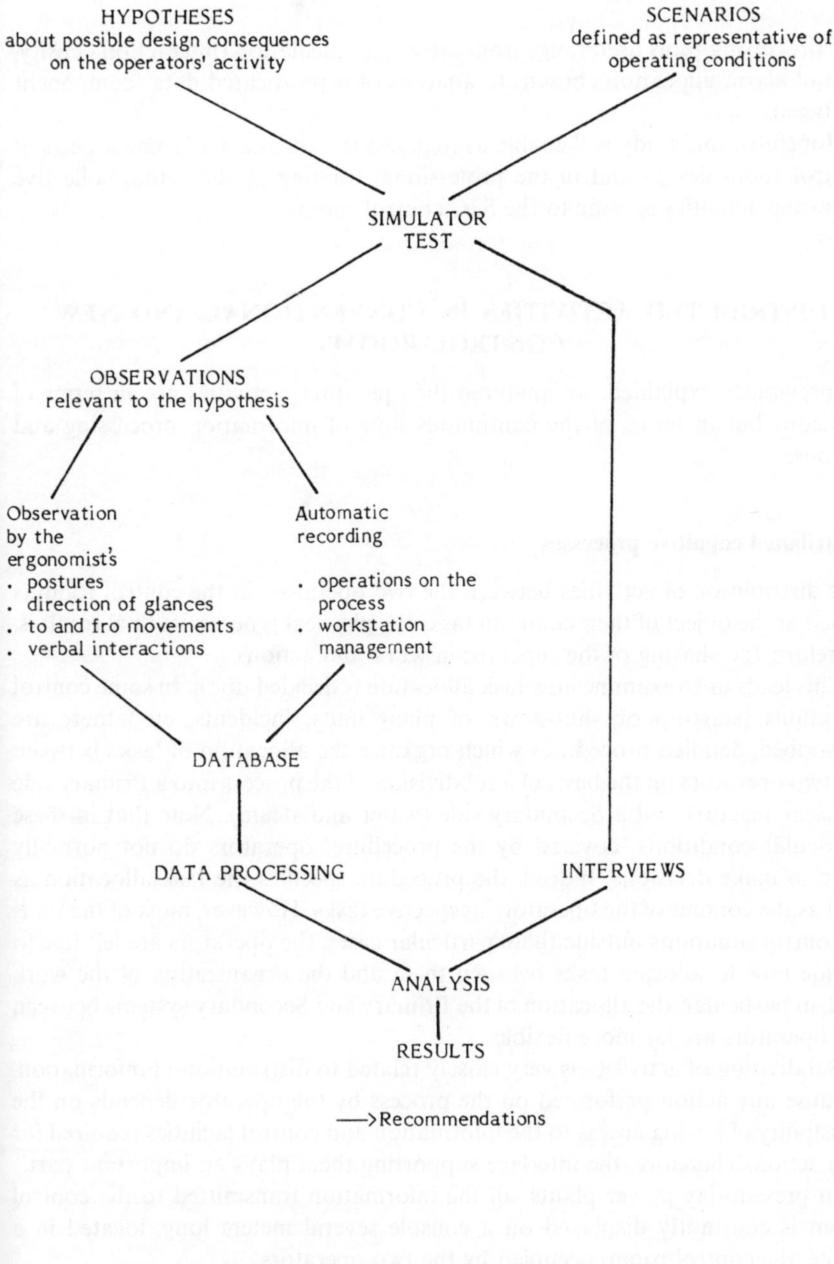

Figure 1. Overall method of S3C ergonomic evaluation

(3) Amount and type of verbal exchanges (from a verbal exchanges grid);
(4) Number of to and fro movements between the stations.

The processing tools used range from mere rate calculation (interaction density, type of alarm allocation chosen) to analysis of sophisticated data (component analyses).

Hopefully, this study will enable us to assess the adequacy of some aspects of control room design and of the professional training in the actual collective operating activities specific to the S3C control rooms.

DISTRIBUTED ACTIVITIES IN CONVENTIONAL AND NEW CONTROL ROOMS

As previously explained, we analyzed the operators' activities not in terms of decisions but in terms of the continuous flow of information processing and actions.

Distributed cognitive processes

The distribution of activities between the two operators in the control room is aimed at the object of their common task: the physical *process*. Its final result is, therefore, the sharing of the supervision work and actions.

This leads us to examine how task allocation is decided upon. In some control situations (start-up or shut-down of plant units, incidents, etc.) there are prescribed, detailed procedures which organize the allocation of tasks between the two operators on the basis of a subdivision of the process into a Primary side (nuclear reactor) and a Secondary side (water and steam). Note that in these particular conditions 'covered by the procedure' operators do not normally have to make decisions. Indeed, the procedure specifies the task allocation as well as the content of the operators' respective tasks. However, most of the time, in control situations outside these particular cases, the operators are left free to decide how to allocate tasks between them and the organization of the work and, in particular, the allocation of the Primary and Secondary systems between the operators are far more flexible.

Subdivision of activities is very closely related to distribution of information, because any action performed on the process by the operator depends on the possibility of having access to the information and control facilities required for this action. Therefore, the interface supporting them plays an important part.

In present-day power plants, all the information transmitted to the control room is constantly displayed on a console several meters long, located in a space, the control room, occupied by the two operators.

The S3C control room is the product of a totally novel design, because each operator sits at one of the two workstations. However, the design principles do not impose a rigid distribution of data between the two stations, as might have been expected. Indeed, from each station it is possible to have access to all the process images and all the controls. This configuration, however, requires the distribution of the information. First, each operator can only display a limited amount of data at the same time (three graphic display units are available). Second, two operators are really needed to control the process so that their activities must not be redundant but coordinated.

The results of the actions performed by the two operators in order to maintain the plant in a safe state or to bring it back to safe conditions is indicative of how efficient their *collective* work is. In fact, the complementarity of the two operators is essential. As already mentioned, their complementarity cannot be easily explained by a clear-cut division of the decisions between them. It would be more appropriate to speak of the overall distributed cognitive processes which will contribute to the best interaction of information and complementary competence so that the proper actions may be arrived at collectively through the contribution of each. This collective work concerns the physical process itself and the process of task allocation.

In an S3C-type control room the coordination of activities demands a more formal distribution of tasks. This does not necessarily mean that it is more rigid. Most of the time, at the beginning of the session, the operators agree on the allocation of the Primary and Secondary systems. However, during their work, they often have to handle tasks concerning the system initially assigned to the other operator because of the workload, of the specific skills and the display units overloading. This intertwinement of activities also occurs in a conventional control room, but it is more informal because it does not need any action to be carried out on the information media. On the S3C this leads to more precise verbalization and to workstation management actions.

Task allocation, which is more formal in the S3C control room, is not simply dictated by a third party. During tests it has been observed that the task allocation negotiated between the two operators resulted in a better coordination. If the monitoring operations and the information processing are distributed, data must, nevertheless, be exchanged so that the operators may share a common knowledge of the general state of the unit. In the S3C control room it is more difficult to have access to all the information and to follow what the other operator is doing.

Indeed, in a conventional control room an operator is informed on the part of the process being monitored by the position of the other operator, and he has only to take a few steps to have a clearer idea of what is happening without disturbing the activities underway. He thus can find out not only what the other operator is doing but also whether he is coping in order to help him when necessary (see Distributed Cognitive Competence). In the S3C control room it is not easy for two men to be facing the same display unit at the same time, and the calling up of new pictures on the station requires workstation management which may disrupt the activity underway.

Interactions between operators (oral exchanges, glances, movements to and fro), on the one hand, and the information sources available in the control room (alarms, pictures, mimic panel) are the means the operators working in pairs use to monitor the overall process and/or the other's activity. Note that operators gradually learn to use these means provided to support the collective work. Thus the crews' behavior can be seen to evolve towards more interaction in the course of the tests—a greater number of to and fro movements, of oral exchanges (spontaneous transmission of information, statement of task allocation rules)—and towards greater organizational flexibility associated with the diversification of the task-allocation modes adapted to the situations. The conventional primary/secondary system allocation becomes more varied and less rigid as operators divide the control operations between them, depending on the interaction level between the tasks related to the Primary and those related to the Secondary system, on the task concentration and hence on the workload, on the availability of the displays, etc.

Distributed cognitive competence

The respective activities should not be totally separated. The different circuits of a plant are functionally linked, and control is a complex task. Each operator involved must be able to utilize not only the other's information but also his competence. In some situations the operators not only want to work in coordination but really need to identify a process status or a diagnosis together. This is a typical situation in which the competence of both operators interact. In this case, in conventional control rooms they are accustomed to standing in front of a common information medium. Such a situation allows them to share—and perhaps also to build up—their competence. The configuration of the new control room does not facilitate these types of collective activities.

The division of the control room into two control areas could have resulted in the specialization of the stations and of the operators. On the contrary, the chosen design, under normal operating conditions, preserves the organizational flexibility between the operators. This flexibility is better adapted to the continuous sequence of cognitive activities involved when the operators collectively control the process. Depending upon its own characteristics, and on the control situation, each crew can adopt the task-allocation pattern and the method of exchange they find the most suitable.

CONCLUSION

Responsibility is not directly linked with activity. If an incident has severe consequences (economic loss or human injury), there are two ways of ascribing responsibilities. One is to investigate the so-called (here 'erroneous') decisions. We believe this procedure to be pointless and time consuming (see above). The other is to attribute the responsibilities in the light of the end product of the different systems and subsystems, regardless of the many complex and intricate factors which produced this result, that is, to consider the 'situations' and not the 'decisions'. This *social* distribution of responsibilities is one of the justifications of hierarchy, which in turn has to obtain the technical and human resources necessary to achieve the required results.

Of course, it is always necessary and interesting—but different—to explore the complex processes which resulted in the final failure (we are drawing a distinction between failure and error). Many conclusions can be derived from such an ergonomic approach, resulting in modifications of the workplace, of the interface, and, of course, of the operators' competence (e.g. by training). However, for NPPs at least, there must be no confusing merging of the ergonomic analysis of the multiple and complex processes involved in the system control with the managerial and legal approach, consisting of tracing the responsibilities after an incident by investigating the so-called erroneous decisions. Legal analysis affects the efficiency of the ergonomic analysis. For similar reasons, we are not very fond of the concept of 'human error', but that is another story.

Address for Correspondence:

Catherine Kasbi, Electricité de France, Direction des Etudes et Recherches, Département Etudes de Sûreté et de Fiabilité, 'Groupe Facteurs Humains', 1 Avenue Général de Gaulle, F92140 Clamart, France.

Part 4.2

Emergency Management

The contributions of Van Daele and De Keyser and of Kasbi and de Montmollin have, as their source of data, process plants, that is, systems which are well structured, with behavior generally controlled by laws of nature. The operators have the opportunity to be thoroughly familiar with the plant and its components, although faults and stoppages can bring surprises. Decision making during emergency management, which is the source of data in Rogalski's study, is of a substantially different nature. The work domain is changing for each task occasion. It will be badly structured and, consequently, will only in very general features be known to the actors. Finally, the team involved will change from time to time. The chapter by Rogalski illustrates the application for distributed decision making, of a model Method for Tactical Reasoning (MTR), described in detail in the chapter by Samurçay and Rogalski.

The chapters are methodologically interesting in that they give an example of an analysis in which the cognitive decision task and the allocation of roles to individuals are kept separate. This has several important implications. First, it makes it possible to evaluate the transfer of models of decision tasks between different domains. In the present case, a model of a single operator's decision making in process control appears to be useful to represent the overall task in cooperative decision making. The approach is based on an analysis of the decision task as if it was taken care of by one, virtually omnipotent, operator. Then the requirements for parallel and sequential efforts in the decision process are analyzed. For this, the logical as well as the temporal organization of the global task is considered, and in addition to the temporal constraints, parallelisms can be required due to properties of the emergency situation itself, of the organization, of the command structure, and of the pre-existing organization of command and resources. In other words, the approach supports the conclusion from Section 2 that a separate representation of the work domain, the cognitive decision task, and the allocation and organization of the roles of the individual decision makers will be a useful way to generalize and transfer results and data among application areas.

14. A Method for Tactical Reasoning (MTR) in Emergency Management: Analysis of Individual Acquisition and Collective Implementation

Renan Samurçay
and
Janine Rogalski
CNRS, Université de Paris 8, France

INTRODUCTION

In the domain of emergency management operators have to deal with risky and evolving situations such as industrial fires, traffic accidents, pollution, forest fires, earthquakes and floods. Their goal is to organize a set of coordinated actions (a safety device) in order to reach a stable state, reducing as far as possible the consequences on human, material and economic environment.

These situations can be analysed from various points of view. First, they can be seen as particular cases of dynamic environments, and the tasks can be analysed in the general theoretical framework of dynamic environment control. Second, controlling such situations requires the coordination of numerous agents. Although the final decision is the responsibility of only one person, the global task involves various specific tasks (design, implementation and control of the safety device) which have to be shared between various operators. In this sense, emergency management has to be considered as distributed decision making.

This last issue is developed in the next section. Thereafter we will focus on cognitive task analysis in emergency management, presented in a framework given by the Method for Tactical Reasoning (MTR). This method expresses invariants in the cognitive decision task for the class of emergency situations. It describes a decomposition of the overall task into specific tasks (involved in

Distributed Decision Making: Cognitive Models for Cooperative Work
Edited by J. Rasmussen, B. Brehmer and J. Leplat

analysis and in planning), as prescribed tasks in the sense developed by Leplat (1988).

CHARACTERIZATION OF EMERGENCY MANAGEMENT

Emergency situations as dynamic environments

In emergency management, as in process control, operators have to intervene in situations evolving with their own dynamic, interacting with operators' actions. The main consequence is that emergency management requires operators to construct and use two models:

(1) A system in 'free' evolution;
(2) A model of the effects of their own actions.

Hence, the two types of knowledge defined by Bainbridge (1988) for process control—goal-action knowledge and system-operating knowledge—also have to be integrated into emergency management.

Emergency management situations differ mainly from process control by the fact that they concern open systems. There is no model of normal functioning in which it would be necessary to replace a process after appropriate diagnosis of dysfunctioning. The central purpose of emergency management is to intervene on the consequences of the release of a process which is essentially irreversible, and the source of which cannot always be known. Here the mental models related to risks and their evolution are crucial for controlling situations. Means of information purchase and resources for control are not integrated into the process on which operators are intervening. However, process accessibility and directness of control are important parameters in process control, as are response delays (for information as well as for action) (Hoc, 1989). Because of the indirect control, diagnosis and planning demands are very strong. Moreover, the indirectness of access to information on which the decisions are based increases the demand for identification of relevant descriptors or indicators for system evolution.

Typology of emergency management situations

An emergency situation can be described as a multidimensional space of states, each state being a function of time. Three dimensions can be used in order to categorize emergency management situations. The speed of evolution ('tempo' of the dynamic event) determines the rapidity with which elaboration has to be processed when dealing with a particular situation. When the situation evolves quickly (such as in case of a forest fire), the representation of the intervention time and of the related constraints are more important than in situations which evolve slowly (floods, consequences of earthquakes, etc.). As in process control, some of the 'state parameters' are time derivatives: gradients of quantitative evolution (speed of a forest fire or of a poisonous cloud), or 'gradients' of qualitative evolution (aggravation of the state of wounded people, explosion risk). For each dimension, parameters may evolve in a computable way (in general, for an order of magnitude only), or in an hypothetical one, requiring 'reasoning under hypotheses.'

MTR AS A MODEL FOR TASK ANALYSIS

A method for tactical reasoning (MTR) was elaborated by expert fire officers with the aim of rationalizing situation analysis and optimization in decision making. It was a transposition of the military method for tactical reasoning. This method expresses common processes for elaborating and choosing strategies for the class of emergency problems. It does not describe effective procedures for problem solving but defines two types of conceptual invariants. The first expresses common points between the problems; the second, common points between the treatment processes.

The difficulties encountered by operators in diagnosis and decision making (selection of relevant information, confirmation biases, uncertainty processing, etc.) have been emphasized by many authors (Fischoff, 1986; Jacob *et al.*, 1986). With respect to these difficulties the MTR satisfies three main functions.

(1) *Information processing*: the method defines the field of necessary and sufficient data to be processed. It gives an orientation basis for information purchase and data processing;
(2) *Option generation*: the method constrains operators to define exhaustively the possible goals and subgoals leading to the target state and prescribes the construction of various means of effective realization;
(3) *Optimization*: the method requests the definition of a set of choice criteria, and the evaluation of their values for the proposed solutions.

MTR is included in an officer's training curriculum. There exists a textbook presenting the method, its content and functions, the general aim of the method and its place in the overall framework of emergency management. It then describes successively the phases corresponding to different activities in safety device elaboration. For each phase, the textbook presents the function, the organization of the data which have to be collected in this phase and the conclusions which have to be drawn at the end of the processing. It defines the possible interactions with other phases, and the specific difficulties encountered in implementation of the phase.

For each phase, keywords were defined in order to facilitate operative communication. Figure 1 expresses the MTR phases by using Rasmussen's symbolic representation of operations and states of knowledge (Rasmussen, 1986). Using this representation shows that MTR as a framework for task analysis in emergency management is quasi-isomorphic to the model elaborated by Rasmussen for cognitive task analysis for process control. The functions of information processing, option generation and optimization are distributed along the various MTR phases.

Diagnosis concerns, on the one hand, the static environment and, on the other, the dynamic event. Prognosis is needed to anticipate possible further states. The main goal has to be decomposed into possible sets of subgoals. Resources to reach each subgoal have to be defined in qualitative, quantitative and temporal terms (delay) and compared with the resources available. The operations corresponding to these tasks produce definite states of knowledge. They concern the dynamic environment, the alternative or coordinated possible subgoals of the overall goal, the 'balance' between adapted means needed and resources available.

The subsequent phases (1) define strategies (manoeuvres), specifying the possible ways and means to reach the global goal, chosen subgoals, possible space and time, means and actors; and (2) present the values taken by the criteria chosen for each manoeuvre, depending on the possible further states of the dynamic environment. The final result is the choice of a strategy, after a multidimensional optimization.

Although isomorphism is stressed above, comparison between Figure 1 and Rasmussen's original framework shows that differences appear between tasks of process control and emergency management: three differences must be noted. First, diagnosis and prognosis distinguish between static environment and dynamic event; they are mainly oriented by analysis of consequences rather than by causal analysis. Second, goal analysis is one of the most important prescribed tasks: this point is related to the existence of hierarchical levels in the public safety device (see Chapter 15). Third, determination of resources is split into definition of adapted resources, evaluation of available resources and comparison between the two sets (balance). This partly reflects the fact that resources are not integrated into the dynamic environment to be controlled.

SOME ISSUES ABOUT COGNITIVE ACTIVITIES IN INDIVIDUAL ACQUISITION AND COLLECTIVE IMPLEMENTATION OF MTR

Evaluating the efficiency of MTR as an aid for decision making appears as a quite difficult question. On the one hand, it is necessary to identify to what extent it has been acquired by operators. On the other hand, studies in other fields (as, for instance, in programming) indicate that using methods is independent neither of problems nor of the operators' knowledge of the content

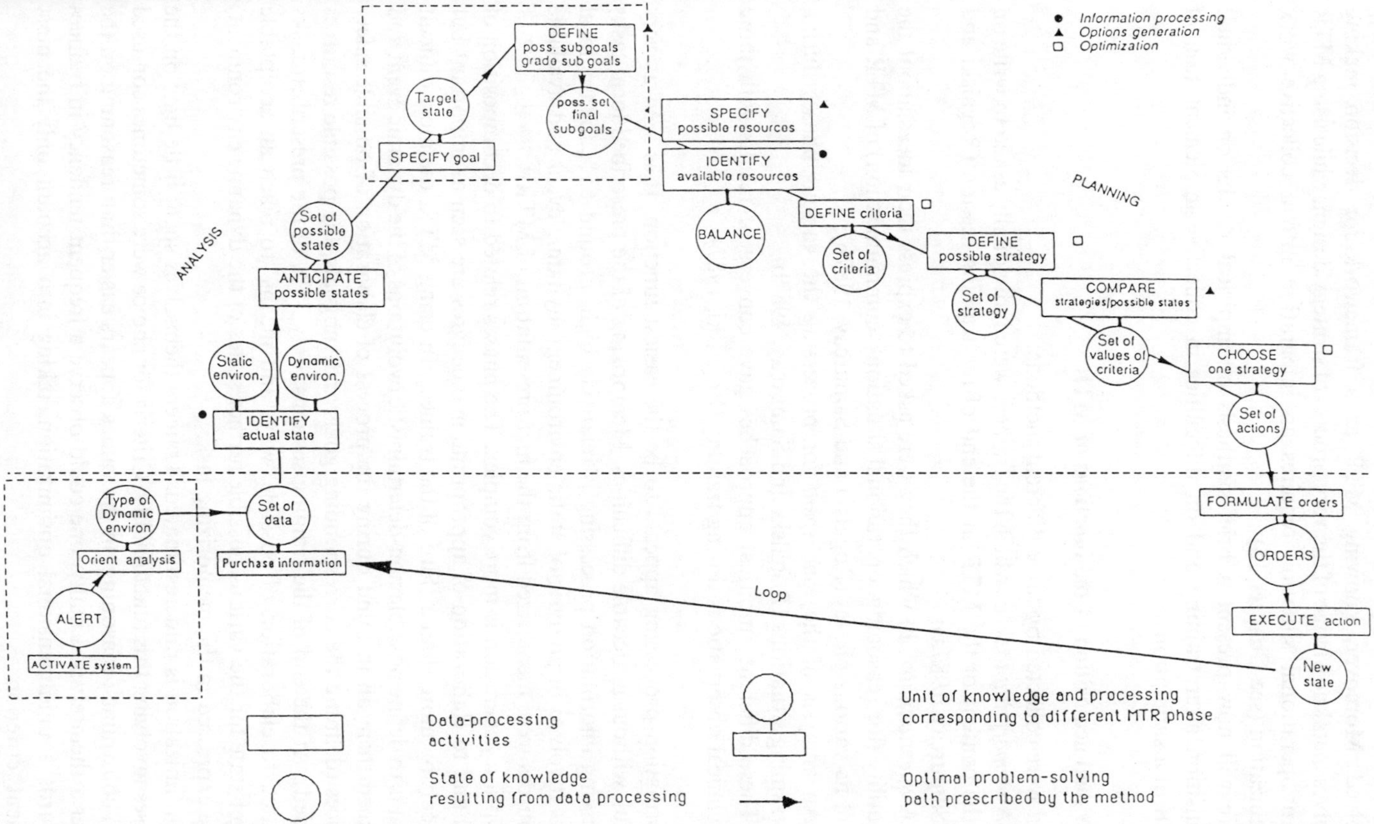

Figure 1. The MTR phases using Rasmussen's (1986) symbolic representation of operations and states of knowledge

involved. Moreover, knowing MTR as a framework for decision making involves metaknowledge of the very process of strategy design, while using MTR in an operational situation requires an integration into a collective work organization (see Chapter 15).

We will now present a brief synthesis of empirical results on individual acquisition after training and on difficulties in collective implementation of MTR in a simulation.

Individual acquisition of the functions of MTR

Data were collected by three different methods:

(1) A *memorizing task*, in which the trainees were individually asked to write on the content of the MTR at the end of the training session (Rogalski and Samurçay, 1987a);

(2) A *questionnaire*, in which they were asked to express their ideas about the utility (for reasoning, operational situations, communication) of MTR and of its various phases (Rogalski and Samurçay, 1987b);

(3) An analysis of the *time spent* for processing the various phases during training situations (Rogalski and Samurçay, 1987b).

These different empirical approaches gave convergent results with more clinical observations during training (Rogalski, 1987).

Information processing appears to be the easiest function. It is seen as very useful, without noticeable difficulties. Memorizing of the prescribed local tasks involving information processing is relatively high: around 65% for the local tasks involved in analysis of static environment, dynamic event and available resources were memorized from the first presentation of MTR.

Option generation is more complex. The phases related to decomposition of goal and to elaboration of appropriate manoeuvres are seen as important but difficult by more than a third of the trainees. In using MTR, the most difficult point is to define possible non-deterministic evolutions of the dynamic event and to keep them all in mind during the process of elaboration of possible safety devices (defining the corresponding goals and subgoals, the possible resources needed). At the end of the training sessions, only 35% of the prescribed tasks (related to elaboration of possible 'ways and means' to reach an acceptable target state for the various possible further states of the dynamic environment) were expressed in the memorizing task.

Optimization is underestimated. Trainers themselves spent little time on the phases involving this functionality. Criteria for choice were sometimes confused with constraints; reasoning on the values appears easier than reasoning on the criteria themselves. Finally, one could observe a frequent tendency in trainees towards a unidimensional optimization, taking into account only the most 'salient' criterion.

At the end of the training sessions (around 28 full hours) the trainees did not appear really convinced about the utility of MTR as an aid in decision making for operational situations with a fast 'tempo'. For many of them MTR was considered useful as a guideline for reasoning and communicating, as a tool in foreseeing or in long and complex operations (with a slow 'tempo') (Samurçay and Rogalski, 1988a).

Collaborative implementation of MTR

During training, trainees were working in small groups without any specific distribution of tasks. It was therefore possible to observe collaborative work which can be seen as one dimension in collective working (see Chapter 4, this volume). Studies on problem solving generally lead to the conclusion that collaborative working allows people to engage in more difficult problems and to present generally more efficient strategies.

Teams of operators were observed in problem-solving situations (during training) with the aim of characterizing their strategies. One of these situations concerns the search of people lost in a mountain during winter, and has two main characteristics:

(1) The initial state of the situation is hypothetical: the available information is insufficient to ensure precise knowledge on the present state of the situation, several hypotheses are possible and must be processed;
(2) The evolution of the situation can be characterized only in a qualitative way: it is impossible to compute the evolution as a function of time by unidimensional, quantitative methods.

Data were collected during training, and concern two 'critical' phases of MTR implementation: identification of possible situations and definition of possible solutions (Rogalski and Samurçay, 1987b). Depending on previous observations, it was hypothesized that these two phases were sufficient to know the main characteristics of the strategies followed by groups in elaborating a safety device.

The strategies used by operators can be characterized by two main properties. First, the operators establish an indirect relationship between the probability of occurrence of an event and the risk associated with the consequences of this event. When this probability is weak, they do not really take into account all the consequences when elaborating a safety device. For instance, the probability is weak that people were walking very fast, and hence went relatively far into a very dangerous area. Most of the teams defined a safety device inappropriate for such a case. They organized a search, starting with the most near areas, whatever would be the danger for people. Second, operators excluded some hypotheses about the possible situation or its evolution, even when there was not enough information for such an assumption. They were reducing uncertainty, instead of managing it.

Representations, strategies and work organization in collective MTR implementation

In a comparative study, strategies used by two command posts in a simulated situation were analysed in order to identify the relationships between efficiency of strategies, representations and working procedures. In this situation operators had to conceive a global safety device and to plan its 'implementation' in order to face possible further incidents or disasters produced or increased by an abnormal snow fall on a suburban and a rural area. Operators had to deal concurrently with a set of local situations that were usual incidents, for which the interventions were well known, but the conditions of execution of which were modified because of the global situation. Therefore operators had to manage the interaction between global and local situations in terms of resource allocation and work priorities. The efficiency of their respective strategies was analysed (1) from their evaluation by expert trainers and (2) from the time and operations required in order to deal with a specific accident caused by the snowfall (Samurçay and Rogalski, 1988b).

Designing the safety device for the global situation required dealing with:

(1) A large number of various 'static' spatial information as topography, roads and railways, population distribution;
(2) Numerous hypotheses about potential risks related to the snowfall in terms of probability about extent, quality, location and moment;
(3) Possible strategies in terms of decomposing the main goal into related possible subgoals and in terms of adapted and available resources for achieving these subgoals;
(4) A combination of subgoals and resources in global safety devices which have to be evaluated in order to prepare the choice.

In terms of representations (about what content are operators operating?), operators devoted more attention to the analysis of area than to that of the evolving situation itself. In the group with the most efficient strategy, the verbalization concerning the descriptors of area, goals and resources were more frequent than in the less efficient group (71% versus 48%). The less efficient group devoted more attention to current events and actions than to the elaboration of the global safety device (38% versus 16% for the most efficient group).

In terms of processing (what activities are operators developing about a given representation?), the most efficient strategy was characterized by more cognitive activities on available data (computations, predictions, hypotheses), while the less efficient strategy was characterized by more frequent data inquiry activities. Even if the potential risks anticipation existed in both strategies, the most efficient group better operationalized these risks in order to define related goals and subgoals. Globally, planning activities were more important in the most efficient strategy.

The data collected on the previous situation were also analysed in order to identify the effects of work distribution on elaboration strategies and on the efficiency of the safety device (Samurçay and Rogalski, 1988b). MTR was used as a framework for analysing the verbal protocols produced by the teams observed. In terms of work organization the most efficient strategy was characterized by:

(1) An appropriate work distribution, with separate responsibilities, on the one hand, on local 'current' situations, and, on the other, on the global 'abnormal' situation, defining separate problem-solving fields;
(2) A strongly directed interaction between team members inside a given problem-solving field: any locutor was speaking to a specified interlocutor;
(3) A strongly directed information flow: the data were dispatched depending on the problem-solving field;
(4) The existence of more frequent verbal exchanges concerning general work orientation, distribution, control and evaluation of tasks.

Elsewhere, the most efficient group was implementing the MTR in the prescribed order of the various phases, so that there existed few redundancies and little lack of data or computation in their activities.

The main global conclusion of this analysis is that there exists a strong relationship between quality of work organization and efficiency of cooperative MTR implementation. Observations on other teams in simulation situations lead to the hypothesis that the quality of work organization can be more relevant than individual acquisition for MTR implementation.

CONCLUSION

The cognitive task analysis of the Method for Tactical Reasoning as an aid for emergency management allows us to consider MTR from another point of view as a model of the cognitive tasks involved in such situations. The comparison with Rasmussen's model for control process shows a quasi-isomorphism between these two models devoted to two poles in the control of dynamic environments.

Using MTR as a framework for analysing cognitive activities in the elaboration of a safety device allows us to identify some deep cognitive difficulties in emergency management, from the point of view of individual cognitive activities, as well as from that of collaborative working. Reasoning under hypotheses and managing uncertainty appear as particularly difficult points, while option generation and optimization seem to be underestimated.

The beliefs that MTR is useful for operations with a slow 'tempo' are reinforced by the fact that cooperative working requires specific metacognitive tasks such as work distribution, 'current' task identification, control and evaluation and information flow control (for outside and inside team communication) that add their specific difficulties to the cognitive difficulties of emergency management.

Training operators in collaborative and cooperative working appears to be a condition for efficient implementation of MTR in emergency management situations. However, work distribution is not an evident task, even without time pressure. Present research on parallel programming, as well as in artificial intelligence on multi-expert, multi-agent expert systems, indicates that some theoretical work has to be done for modelling tasks distribution between operators, along time.

Chapter 15 is devoted to research using MTR as a framework for this kind of metacognitive task analysis in order to propose a model of distributed decision making in emergency management, taking into account the various constraints acting on operators (tactical constraints related to an organization into levels, material constraints for effectiveness of solutions, temporal constraints, organizational constraints, etc.).

Address for Correspondence:

Renan Samurçay, Centre National de la Recherche Scientifique, Université de Paris 8, URA 218: Psychologie Cognitive Ergonomique, 2 rue de la Liberté, F-93526 Saint Denis Cedex 02, Paris, France.

REFERENCES

Bainbridge, L. (1988) Types of representations. In L. P. Goodstein, H. B. Andersen and S. E. Olsen (eds), *Tasks, Errors and Mental Models*. London: Taylor & Francis, pp. 70–91.

Fischoff, B. (1986) Decision making in complex systems. In E. Hollnagel, G. Mancini and D. D. Woods (eds), *Intelligent Decision Support in Process Environments*. Berlin/Heidelberg: Springer-Verlag, pp. 61–85.

Hoc, J.-M. (1989) La conduite d'un processus continu à long délai de réponses: une activité de diagnostic. *Le Travail Humain*, **52** (4), 289–316.

Jacob, S. V., Gaultney, L. D., and Salvendy, G. (1986) Strategies and biases in human decision making and their implications for expert-systems. *Behaviour and Information Technology*, **5**, 2, 119–40.

Leplat, J. (1988) Methodologie von Aufgabenanalyse und Aufgabengestaltung. *Zeitschrift fur Arbeits- und Organisationpsychologie*, **1**, 2–12.

Rasmussen, J. (1986) A framework for cognitive task analysis in system design. In E. Hollnagel, G. Mancini and D. D. Woods (eds), *Intelligent Decision Support in Process Environments*. Berlin/Heidelberg: Springer-Verlag, pp. 175–96.

Rogalski, J. (1987) Analyse cognitive d'une méthode de raisonnement tactique et de son enseignement à des professionels. *Le Travail Humain*, **50**, 4, 305–17.

Rogalski, J., and Samurçay, R. (1987a) Teaching and learning a method for decision making in public safety: conclusions to design support systems. *First European Meeting on Cognitive Science Approaches to Process Control*, Marcoussis, France.

Rogalski, J., and Samurçay, R. (1987b) *Enseignement et appropriation d'une méthode de raisonement tactique (MTR) dans le domaine professionel de la Sécurité Civile*, Rapport PIRTTEM, CNRS, Paris.

Samurçay, R., and Rogalski, J. (1988a) Analysis of operators' cognitive activities in learning and using a method for decision making in public safety. In J. Patrick and K. Duncan (eds), *Training, Human Decision Making and Control*. New York: Elsevier Science/North-Holland, pp. 133–52.

Samurçay, R., and Rogalski, J. (1988b) Control of dynamic environment with distributed decision making: methodology for analysing collaborative work. *Fourth European Conference on Cognitive Ergonomics ECCE4*, Cambridge, September.

15. Distributed Decision Making in Emergency Management: Using a Method as a Framework for Analysing Cooperative Work and as a Decision Aid

Janine Rogalski
CNRS, Université de Paris 8, France

INTRODUCTION

As seen in Chapter 14, situations of emergency management can be considered as specific cases of dynamic environments. They may change over time, and possibly in space, independently of operators' actions, while causing damage. The operators' goal is to organize a set of coordinated actions in order to reach a stable state, reducing as far as possible the consequences on human, material and economical environment. This state will be referred to as the 'target state'.

The global task for decision makers in such situations can be schematized as a loop:

```
define actual state
while ⟨target-state not reached⟩ do
   define intervention
   order execution
   define actual state
endwhile.
```

Controlling dynamic environments implies coordinating many operators, organized in an operational link, going from the responsible (the *emergency director*) to executives in charge of material execution. Although the emergency director is the only one who has to decide about intervention, one can speak of distributed decision making in emergency management. Indeed, managing an emergency situation implies numerous and complex tasks (decision elaboration, implementation, execution control, communication and support for the inter-

Distributed Decision Making: Cognitive Models for Cooperative Work
Edited by J. Rasmussen, B. Brehmer and J. Leplat

vention) which cannot be ensured by the emergency director himself and have to be distributed among several operators, at various levels.

Modelling distributed decision making in emergency management appeared to us as a prerequisite task in a general project of public safety in which we are involved as researchers: designing a framework for *operational training* of high-level public safety officers and defining the characteristics of *support systems* for training and decision making. These two objectives imply a precise definition of *problem space* for emergency management from the very beginning (alert) to the end (target state reached, means freed).

Training also requires identification of *invariants* in task, analysis, command organization and in information flow organization, in order to train operators for the various situations they may encounter, depending on the type of disaster they may face, on the organization (institution) to which they belong, on the communication structure during the disaster, and on their position in the *operational device*. Such a model is necessary to define how to transpose crisis situations into didactical ones, allowing appropriate learning for the management of decision making in new situations.

A *Method for Tactical Reasoning* (MTR) was elaborated by experts in the field of public safety (high-level fire officers) as an aid for training and decision making. It describes and prescribes a logical task structuring in the process of defining the 'most appropriate' manoeuvres to reach a given target state. It was also designed in such a way as to constitute a basis for *operative communication* (Falzon, 1984, 1986) in the group of operators involved in operational situations.

This method, first developed for training in emergency management, also affords a model for task analysis quite convergent with the well-known model developed by Rasmussen (1984, 1986) for process control. We will take this as a starting point and the core for modelling distributed decision making in emergency management. This model of the overall task of one *virtual operator* will be kept separate from analysis of the allocation and organization of roles to individual *effective operators*. It will provide a basis for analysing the requirements for parallel and sequential efforts in the decision process. These approaches will be coordinated with an organizational approach based on the network of intra- and interorganization for communication (information, demands, orders) and resources.

DECISION MAKING IN EMERGENCY MANAGEMENT: OUTLINES FOR MODELLING THE 'PROBLEM SPACE'

Decision making in the operational flow

The overall task of elaboration and choice, schematized as a time-dependent loop, implies information processing, option generation for 'ways and means'

(Poirier, 1987) to reach the goal (target state) and optimization before choice. Now (distributed) decision making in emergency management has to be seen as a more complex process. It begins with information purchase and implies execution control. Moreover, it may be managed at different hierarchical or semi-hierarchical command levels (Brehmer, 1988).

Therefore the overall task described by MTR (considered as a model) as well as the global cognitive activity supported by MTR (seen as an aid for decision making) have to be embedded in a general operational flow. They must also be related to the tasks and activities of the safety operational device considered as a whole. Indeed, we are referring to the analysis given by Leplat of decision making as a process of control of activity (Chapter 3, this volume).

We wish to stress the importance of the notion of *operational flow* in any model of distributed decision making in dynamic environments. Environment states, cognitive tasks as well as, on the one hand, material tasks to be performed and on the other, networks of organization for communication and resources, have all to be seen as functions of time. Moreover, the global structure of the operational device is also time dependent. This last point will be developed later.

The operational flow is the temporal organization of tasks (required by the dynamic environment control) or of activities (conducted by effective operators) during the intervention. The first perspective on the operational flow is task oriented, the second is activity oriented (Patrick, 1980).

Figure 1 shows the position of elaboration and choice in the operational flow from the point of view of tasks required. This schema concerns a very general level. The model of the operational flow appears as a loop, whereas the embedded processes, involved as a succession of more specified tasks, may act in a parallel or sequential way.

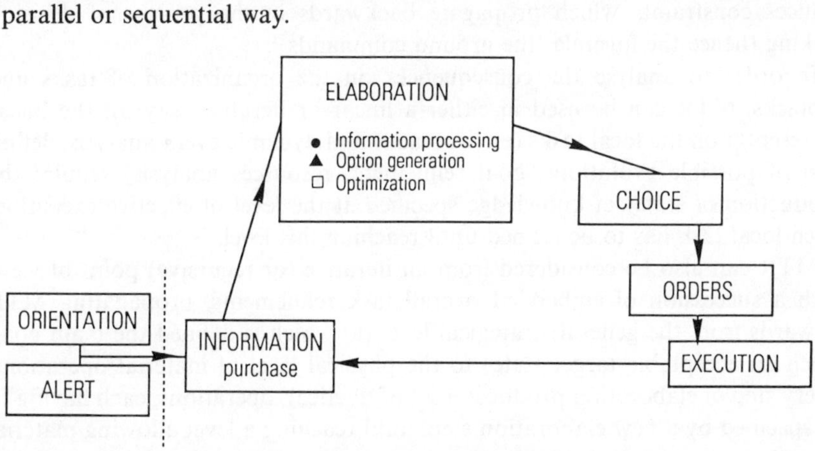

Figure 1. In controlling dynamic environments, such as emergency situations, the phase of elaboration of possible solutions, preparing the choice, is embedded in a loop: information purchase/elaboration/choice/orders/execution, executed while the target state is not reached

The MTR as a model for task analysis

The MTR expresses invariants in the cognitive decision tasks for the class of the emergency situations as prescribed tasks in the sense defined by Leplat (1988). The elaboration and evaluation phases, as organized by MTR in a structure of local tasks embedded in the overall task, must be integrated into the operational flow shown in Figure 1. Moreover, communication and support tasks for the material actions have to be integrated into the operational global task analysed above. In fact, an adapted MTR can be applied to each of them, giving rise to a first instance of 'embedded' Methods for Tactical Reasoning.

Elements will be given below for a decomposition of the orientation phase, the information purchase and the executive phase. Such decompositions are part of modelling emergency management, and will be oriented by the task analysis defined by MTR.

In emergency management the work domain is changing for each task occasion. Most often, it is badly structured, and only very general features are invariant for a given type of situation. Teams, resources nor organization can be considered as uniformly predefined from time to time. This is the most salient difference with control processes (Hoc, 1989). In order to construct a model for distributed decision making it is necessary to develop a deeper analysis of the overall task in the general framework of MTR.

The expected 'production' of the global decision process is a set of coordinated actions (*what*), responding to subgoals (*why*), defined in space (*where*), time (*when*), and resources (*with whom and what*), so that they can be performed, in the field, in real time, by effective actors. This condition of material effectiveness induces constraints which propagate backwards in the process of decision making (hence the formula 'the ground commands').

In order to analyse the consequences on the organization of tasks and subtasks, MTR can be used in either a linear or iterative way. In the linear representation the local tasks (environment and dynamic event analysis, definition of possible evolutions, goal refinement, resources analysis) require the production of states of knowledge specified at the level of effective execution. Each local task has to be refined until reaching this level.

MTR can also be considered from an iterative (or recursive) point of view, with a succession of embedded overall task refinements, propagating MTR forwards from the general strategical level (at which is defined the main goal: reach an acceptable target state) to the physical level of material operations. Every step of elaboration produces a set of 'tactical' operations, each having to be specified by a new elaboration step, until reaching a level allowing material execution.

We will choose this recursive representation of 'embedded' MTR as the most general model for decision making in emergency management. Goal analysis is the core of this recursive model. On the one hand, decomposition of the global goal into possible subgoals is a key point for the change of processing levels. On the other, it propagates backwards conditions on the level at which states of knowledge have to be produced by situation analysis.

Moreover, modelling decision making by embedded MTR takes into account the organizational dimension underlying distributed decision making in complex situations. The 'logical' organization of goals and subgoals is related to the fact that decision making at a given level of responsibility is embedded in a hierarchical frame. This frame results from an adaptation of the operational device to the constraints of tasks sharing and role allocation for complex situations.

Hierarchical levels for decision making and the dimension elaboration/ specification

Brehmer (1988) has shown how an hierarchical organization may reduce complexity for a complex system when it was impossible to really share decision making. He has compared the hierarchized military system to a semi-hierarchized system adapted to emergency situations. In fact, two main reasons are leading to this adaptation of organizational structures to task requirements. One is related to the logic of elaboration, the other to the properties of execution.

First, as in programming tasks (or in other conception tasks: see, for instance, Hoc, 1986), elaborating strategies for emergency management can be top-down defined. General functional outlines can be defined before describing the various parts in more detail, until the material executive level is reached. Second, controlling effective execution of tasks by other operators requires a limit on the parallel controls which have to be managed (from the point of view of workload, as well as the memory load of the operator who is in charge of this control).

Figure 2 shows the fundamental embedding of levels in decision making in emergency management. General and particular situations have to be seen as dynamic. Each involves the sets of (possible) initial situations and of (possible) related further states.

This embedding can be seen as an application of task analysis to organizational structure, conserving a fundamental relation of specification. In fact, specification is involved in the decomposition of goals into related subgoals as well in the hierarchy between general and particular situations, or in the relationship between the mission and the task to be performed. The result of elaboration at a given level becomes the mission given as a starting point for the following level. The new task at this level becomes the specification of the mission. This application is compatible with the theoretical framework defined by von Cranach *et al.* (1986). Hierarchical levels as illustrated in Figure 2 then appear as well adapted tó the important task requirement related to the organization of goals.

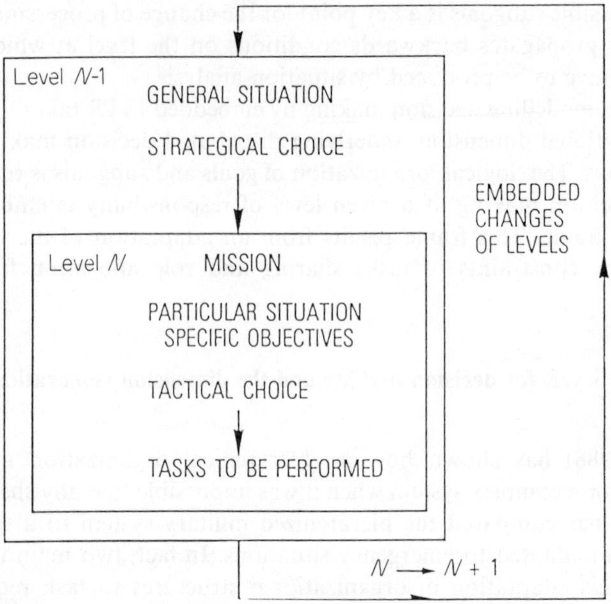

Figure 2. Embedded changes of levels. PARTICULAR SITUATION (for level *N*) becomes GENERAL SITUATION (with respect to level $N + 1$). TASKS TO BE PERFORMED (defined by level *N*) become MISSIONS (for level $N + 1$). TACTICAL CHOICE (of level *N*) becomes STRATEGICAL CHOICE (with respect to level $N + 1$)

It is possible to go further in the model. The process of elaboration/specification, which is related to embedded levels, can be considered as a general dimension for analysing cognitive requirements of a given task. This can describe the change in hierarchical levels defined by Rasmussen of knowledge-, rule- and skill-oriented tasks, as well the hierarchical relationships between methods, procedures and routines related to embedded problem classes (Rogalski, 1987).

MTR can be considered as a method for managing (1) the specification of situations and goals and (2) the elaboration of subsequent missions. Hierarchization of levels is a way of implementing the passage from elaboration to specification in an effective organization. The level of complexity and/or novelty of the situations a given system may face may be increased by an appropriate link between MTR (as decomposing and structuring the overall task) and organization in embedded levels (as organizing local task refinement).

In fact, this framework is a task model for a 'virtual' omnipotent operator. Depending on the situation, the tasks must be shared between several effective operators. Requirements for sequential or parallel efforts are related to task sharing between effective operators (including, eventually, computer-based systems). These will be analysed in Chapter 16.

DISTRIBUTED DECISION MAKING AND ROLE ALLOCATION: FROM VIRTUAL OPERATOR TO EFFECTIVE OPERATORS

Reducing complexity in emergency management

By distributed decision making we mean the whole process, from information purchase to control of execution, involving several functions and various levels for decision/execution. Until now, cognitive tasks involved in decision making (in this broad sense) were presented from the point of view of a virtual, omnipotent operator. The logical as well as the temporal organization of the global task were analysed using the MTR as a framework. Figure 1 and 2 indicate its deep complexity as a continuous process, with a hierarchical, 'recursive', structure.

In fact, cognitive activities in emergency management are complex along several dimensions: complexity in managing embedded levels in task definition (implying coordinating functions of elaboration, communication, physical resource management, support for the decision task itself, command and control), difficulties in achieving and coordinating the numerous local tasks involved in the elaboration phase and complexity of managing communication in real time in order to implement the logical relationships between the various functions at the material level of effective execution.

In order to achieve the decision process in a delay compatible with the 'tempo' of the dynamic environment, complexity must be reduced by deducing from previous task analysis an appropriate role allocation to effective operators. Three dimensions for reducing complexity will be taken into account: organization of processing levels with a functional distribution of global tasks, role allocation to effective operators with sequential or parallel work sharing, and predefinition of organizational settings and elaboration of tools for decision aid. First, we will present a model of organizational structure derived from preceding analyses.

Functional organization for distributed decision making

The embedding of levels shown in Figure 2 will now be modelled as a functional structure, which must be considered as one unit. Figure 3 represents the relationships between the embedded levels, the organization of distributed decision making, the functional roles and the organizational structure. In fact, a complete model of the operational structure would require us to take into account the fact that functional 'global' roles can be devoted to various institutions or administrative organizations, and that the various operational roles have to be allocated to effective operators, with specific organizational places as well as specific individual competences.

For analysing this model we will choose the point of view of the Emergency

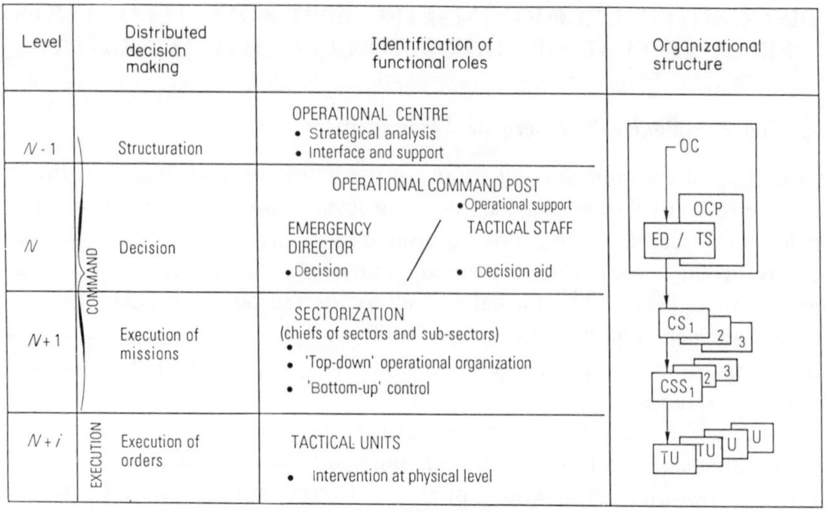

Level
Distributed decision making
Identification of functional roles
Organizational structure
N - 1
Structuration
OPERATIONAL CENTRE
• Strategical analysis
• Interface and support
N
Decision
OPERATIONAL COMMAND POST
• Operational support
EMERGENCY DIRECTOR
• Decision
TACTICAL STAFF
• Decision aid
COMMAND
N + 1
Execution of missions
SECTORIZATION
(chiefs of sectors and sub-sectors)
• 'Top-down' operational organization
• 'Bottom-up' control
N + i
EXECUTION
Execution of orders
TACTICAL UNITS
• Intervention at physical level
OC
OCP
ED / TS
CS1
2
3
CSS1
2
3
TU
TU
U
U

Figure 3. Organization of distributed decision making into hierarchical levels. From the level of general structuring to that of execution of orders, the functional roles are distributed between strategical analysis and intervention at a physical level. The related organizational structure has to be seen as modelling various implementations, with various effective services and operators

Director (ED), responsible for decision making in the situation being considered, managed at level *N*. The functions of the various operators will be defined with respect to his main function of decision making. The ED is supported by the tactical staff (TS) in the overall task of elaborating appropriate 'ways and means' (manoeuvres) to reach the target state. This means that this functional cell has to apply the MTR in order to propose to the ED a choice between several possible 'manoeuvres'. This analysis is convergent with Maleval and Oziard's (1988) functional definition of TS in the military context. Performing this main *elaboration task* requires specific *support tasks*.

First, the subsystem ED/TS needs a wide range of information. Some of this is related to the 'states of knowledge' specified in the representation of MTR (state of the dynamic environment, available resources). Some may also concern the decomposition of the main goal into subgoals, when this decomposition is dependent on the technical specificities of the situation. Therefore the subsystem ED/TS must be supported for information purchase and representation. This is the function of a specific cell in the operational command post (OCP).

Second, the decision must be turned into orders and executed. It is necessary to implement the tactical choice of manoeuvres at a physical level and to control the execution. This implies specifying the physical resources, to ensure that they will take the appropriate position on the operational ground, to guarantee communication with the operators involved.

Organizing hierarchical levels from the ED (level N) to the ground (level $N + i$) is the first means of ensuring transmission of orders and implementation of decisions. Moreover, such a structure allows the definition of manoeuvres by ED/TS at a general tactical level, while refining subgoals and actions is devoted to the sector's chiefs. (These sectors may be defined for a spatial or a functional distribution of responsibilities and tasks.) The organizational tasks are shared by the subsystem ED/TS and by the Operational Center at level $N - 1$.

Another task for implementing the decision is resource management, from the point of view of the relationship between tactical, spatial and communication positions. It is necessary to ensure the link between means (*who* and *what*), space (*where*) and time (*when*) during the whole operation. This task is a function depending on the OCP, in a relationship with the allocation of resources. Computer-based support systems could be shared by OCP and OC in performing this task.

Two other support tasks must be performed in order to ensure efficiency of the operational device: logistic support and communication support. In lengthy situations involving numerous means and operators, performing each of these tasks may require a specific application of an adapted MTR. This function is also dependent on the OCP. It must be emphasized that distributing decision making and task sharing produce internal specific support needs for communication and logistics that have to be taken into account.

The OC at level $N - 1$ intervenes through four decisive support functions:

(1) Interface with organizations which are external to the operational device but are nevertheless concerned with emergency management (for instance, by yielding means or energy, by ensuring transportation or accommodation);
(2) Interface with higher hierarchical levels;
(3) Allocation of resources for information, communication and operation;
(4) Anticipation on the general situation in order to ensure an appropriate safety device at this level (this last function may imply an application of MTR, as seen in Figure 2).

All the OC functions are related to the fact that, on the one hand, the particular situation (managed through the operational device considered as a unit from levels N to $N + i$) is embedded as a general situation, and, on the other, that this unit may have to interact with other organizations (not centered on the goal 'reach the target state') and may depend on higher 'hierarchical' levels ($N - 2$, $N - 3, \ldots$) which can eventually modify the main goal (definition of the target state).

Some cognitive questions are related to this distribution for decision making. A general hypothesis may be that the mental representation an operator obtains about his proper function and position in respect to those of 'connected' operators is an important variable in analysing cooperative work. By 'connected' operators we mean those who share some spatial field and/or who are directly related in at least one of the networks: communication, function, command organization (this could be extended to computers as connected operators for the effective human operators interacting with it).

Some informal observations have been made on this. One could have an SC (Sector Chief) of a higher level in the informal hierarchy than the ED, making his proper choices instead of implementing the mission which was given to him by the ED, with negative operative results (it must be emphasized that the functional role attributed to the ED is prevailing on a formal hierarchy, in terms of ranks); a chief of OCP, taking as his role the decision role of the ED and unable to adapt (using the work done by the TS) to a specific demand of the ED about possible manoeuvres in case of failure of his present decision (in a training simulation); an ED (at level N) trying to specify actions at a very low level without defining missions to be taken in charge by levels $N + 1$, and consequently unable to master the situation (during an exercise).

Sequentiality or parallelism in MTR implementation?

Analysis of the relationship organized by the MTR between the overall task and the local tasks has stressed two main dimensions for work coordination: logical organization and temporal organization of local cognitive activities. For an efficient use of the MTR it appears necessary to share activities between operators in such a way that the time required to carry out these activities should also be shared, and consequently global time reduced. Therefore MTR must not be applied by the subsystem ED/TS in a purely sequential way but with parallel distributed tasks.

Several dimensions affect the requirements of such a parallel planning:

(1) The properties of the emergency situation itself;
(2) The properties of the emergency organization;
(3) Pre-emergency organization by means of a forecast (pre-organization of means and resources, existence of plans for various types of event, etc).

MTR can be used as a framework for analysing the effects of these dimensions on parallel planning. As seen in Chapter 14, the prescribed local tasks produce defined states of knowledge (circles in the schema of MTR). Each task prescribed in MTR requires some of the elements composing the states of knowledge produced by the preceding tasks. Nevertheless, subtasks may involve only parts of the preceding states of knowledge, so that it is possible to organize parallel processing inside the global sequential organization of tasks prescribed in MTR.

For instance, if the evolution is hypothetical, it is possible to develop the study of specific tasks to be performed and adapt necessary means in a parallel way for each main hypothesis before organizing a synthesis. Similarly, when very specific subgoals can be defined for reaching the target state, it is possible to develop their analysis (elaboration of possible 'ways and means') in a parallel way. It is also possible to organize functional sectors to achieve these specific subgoals.

Task sharing and information flow

One core issue for the effectiveness of collective work is the management of the information flow: i.e. information purchase, processing and transfer between operators. The question must be solved for communication between the various operational levels, for communication inside a functional team (OC, OCP or TS), and for communication between organizations (through interfaces).

Let us develop briefly the point about information needs inside a team. Different operators, performing different on-line tasks, may need information on the same content or at the same time on different contents. Does the functional cell devoted to information purchase respond independently to these needs (operators and cell exchanging messages on the relevant data) or is it playing the role of a 'central memory', allowing access for each operator to all the information? The dimension centralized/distributed is an element in modelling information flow inside the overall model for distributed decision making.

Pre-emergency organization

Pre-emergency organization concerns first, preventive analysis for possible emergency situations, either in a specific location (a chemical or power plant) or for a type of risk (a forest fire, chemical pollution, a nuclear transport accident). The only noticeable difference is that the static environment is predefined in the first case and the dynamic event in the last. MTR can be used as a methodological aid for evaluating risks and their possible evolutions, for defining acceptable target states, and ways and means to reach these target states; for designing *a priori* structures for possible interventions, command and resources structuring, pre-planning for interfaces between the various organizations involved in intervention on the given plant.

Preventive analysis has important consequences on MTR implementation in emergency situations. One of the important subgoals in the MTR is the determination and implementation of an appropriate operational structure (for which resources and staff have to be defined). If the command organization and the executive support have been anticipated, this subgoal disappears as a task to be performed, decreasing the complexity of the overall task and the time required for implementation of the operational device. (Nevertheless, knowledge of this organization is required from operators, so that they can take into account the conditions of execution allowed or required by such an organization.)

Globally, a forecast allows us to turn elaboration tasks into specification tasks (applying general procedures), or even into mere application of fully specified procedures (applying routines). It allows implementation of drills involving possible future operators. Moreover, when means are pre-structured in organized tactical units (with their own support organization), it allows us, on the one hand, to define the 'manoeuvres' at a higher tactical level (MTR may be implemented in an easier and shorter way), and, on the other, to reduce the support tasks in execution. Delays involved in the operational flow may be significantly changed, from the level of decision making to those of execution on the ground.

In fact, the importance of pre-emergency was one of the key elements in efficiency reported by Sorensen *et al.* (1985) and it is closely related to stability of functions and roles inside a given organization in pre-emergency and emergency situations.

TIME AS A KEY VARIABLE IN DISTRIBUTED DECISION MAKING

Time can be considered from several points of view and analysed at several different levels. It is a key variable in dynamic environments. Time is also intervening at the level of the 'tempo' of the event with respect to the speed of implementing an operational device. It has also to be analysed as a parameter in the networks for command, resources and communication. Finally, organizations involved in emergency situations are affected by long-term adaptive processes, partly depending on past emergency situation management.

Time as a variable in dynamic environments

Van Daele and De Keyser (Chapter 12, this volume) analyse the cognitive difficulties underlying mastery of time as a variable in control processes. We wish to add one point. In emergency management, uncertainty about information increases the difficulty. During the elaboration phase, operators may have to 'reappreciate' time derivatives such as the mean speed of a forest fire or of a toxic cloud. They must use approximative information about space and time, and they have to appreciate the forward propagation on other variables (risks, necessary and available means, etc.) Brehmer and Allard (Chapter 16, this volume) emphasize the effect of delays in information processes. Appropriate anticipation of the time required for implementing decisions and adequate confidence in other operators appear as conditions for using MTR efficiently from the point of view of coordination of moments and delays in the operational flow loop.

Time as a constraint on cognitive activities

Time running during the operation itself is another crucial point, directly affecting the operational flow. The loop: information purchase/elaboration/execution/control may be seen as a continuous and time-dependent process, related to the dynamic environment itself. This process is discretized by the activities of the various operators involved in the operational device. Discretization may differ depending on the operators involved and the required tasks, and on the 'tempo' of the event.

For instance, it is necessary to choose appropriate moments for integrating new values of parameters or new states for the general or particular situation (including availability of resources), in order to adapt hypotheses about evolution, tasks to be performed and possible actions. It can also be necessary to define specific moments for communication if the supporting network is overloaded.

Therefore it appears necessary to coordinate the 'tempo' of the event with the internal 'tempo' of the overall task in such a way that anticipation can be carried out until reaching the terms of the decision, and that adaptation remains possible, without 'running after the event'. For slowly evolving events, this parameter has no crucial effects. Discretization may be done by the technique of *rendezvous* used in informatical processes as well as in military staffs through the 'reports'. For events such as forest fires the 'tempo' of the event strongly affects all the operators' activities. Collaborative work implies internal information processing as a critical subtask to make different individual discretizations fit together. Designing computer-based supports will take into account these specific temporal requirements.

The operational device as a function of time

Time is not only involved in the dynamic parameters defining the dynamic environment, it is also a key parameter of the operational device itself. The structure of the operational device in Figure 3 must be seen as a function of time. In fact, current activities and goals of the organizations involved in emergency management do not require such a permanent and stable structuring of levels (as is the case for military organizations). Moreover, this structuring for an emergency situation may involve several organizations, with distinct permanent structures. The possibility of change from current to target structuring as well as the temporal modalities of such a change are important parameters for efficiency. The operational device must in fact be described as a complex function of time in its structure, as well as in the functions it can fulfil. This function may be 'top-down' driven, the level $N-1$ taking the organizational decision with the responsibility of the emergency situation. It may be 'bottom-up' driven: the operators on the ground (level $N + i$) may ask for a change in operational level (it is the so-called *montée en puissance*, for resources as well as for command).

Time as a long-term variable in command, resources and communication networks

Finally, time intervenes as a long-term variable in the evolution of permanent networks for resources and communication, in a relationship with preventive decision making and training. Moreover, adaptive processes may affect the various organizations involved in emergency management, as well as their formal and informal relationships. This may give insights into the regulation processes involved in responsibility and distributed decision making.

CONCLUSION

A model—Method for Tactical Reasoning (MTR)—was used as the core of an attempt to model distributed decision making in emergency situations. This method, described in detail in Chapter 14, was taken as a framework for analysing the overall cognitive decision task, independently of the specific problem of task allocation to organizations and/or individuals. It allows us to have a common model for situations in which the work domain is changing for each task, in which the teams involved will change, and for a wide range of initial structures of the safety organization as a whole.

MTR appears as a model for the decision task (including orientation, information purchase, elaboration of manoeuvres, orders for execution and control) of a 'virtual', omnipotent operator. Specifying the position of MTR in the operational flow leads to a deeper analysis of logical as well as temporal constraints on the organization of the global task into subtasks. The notion of 'embedded' MTR implementations, defined at different levels, leads to a structuring of the decision task into levels from knowledge-based decision making to rule-based activities.

From this development of the MTR model, requirements for parallel and sequential efforts in the decision process are analysed and different factors leading to reducing complexity in cooperative decision making are presented. The task analysis provided by MTR, the structuring into levels by embedded MTR, are used in order to define a structure model of a virtual operational device into levels, specifying functions to be fulfilled and functional relationships between the elements in the structure.

This general model for distributed decision making may be used for two purposes. The first aim is to analyse the role allocation to effective operators in distributed decision making, the effective organization of command and resources, and their possible temporal evolution from the initial alert to the end of the emergency situation. The second goal is to elaborate a 'doctrine' on distributed decision making, in order to train those responsible for public safety in operational management in an adaptive way, allowing them to cope with complex and new emergency situations.

The model MTR, as well as the levels at which it can be considered, was the result of a reflexive, metacognitive process of experts in emergency situations, making explicit their operational knowledge in order to teach it. It appeared strongly isomorphic to the well-known model, with its attached levels, defined by Rasmussen for task analysis in process control. This convergence of models (which were designed quite independently, and for different purposes) provides a strong presumption of validity.

With the same 'cross-validation', the present approach for modelling distributed decision making in emergency management supports the conclusion from Section 3 that a separate representation of the work domain, the cognitive decision task, and the allocation and structuring of roles of the individual decision makers allows us to make more explicit the invariants in distributed decision making for various environments. This gives support to the possibility of generalizing and transferring results and data among application areas, allowing us to know more in each domain on questions for which specific experimentation or even observation may be difficult or impossible.

Several perspectives can be taken for further research using this model. Some are related to task analysis, others to cognitive activities analysis. We can use the model in order to define training situations, and particularly situations of simulation. What are the main elements in constructing such situations, taking into account the whole task definition? Which functional roles must be allocated to trainees and which may be simulated? This was the first motivation for this study on distributed decision making in emergency management. It could be extended to other dynamic environments.

Another point of view is the study of real organizations with respect to the functions that must be performed in distributed decision making. Such a study requires us to go further in modelling by defining some (time-dependent) 'mapping' of real organizations onto the preceding organizational framework, and by specifying how the functional allocation of roles can be implemented (depending on the organizations involved and on the emergency situations).

Elsewhere, such a framework may be used for analysing the cognitive activities related to the various tasks involved in distributed decision making, and for analysing training processes. Tasks defined at a meta-level, such as local task distribution and execution control (cooperation between levels, cooperation inside the ED/TS subsystem for sequential or parallel implementation of MTR), or information flow control (between levels, and inside a team sharing elaboration or support tasks) are of particular interest for a better knowledge of the cognitive processes involved in distributed decision making.

ACKNOWLEDGEMENTS

This work was supported by a PIRTTEM-CNRS grant from the French ministry responsible for public safety. It was undertaken in collaboration with Renan Samurçay (CNRS, University of Paris 8) and Monique Baron (University of Paris 6). We wish to extend our thanks to the Directors, the trainers and trainees of the national superior school for fire officers (ENSOSP) and of the interregional school of Valabre, and to the Director of the German federal school for emergency management (KSB), who welcomed us as guest trainees. Commandant F. Robert, responsible for training at the DDSIS83, lent effective help to our study on implementation of MTR at the operational level.

Address for Correspondence:

Dr Janine Rogalski, Centre National de la Recherche Scientifique, Université de Paris 8, URA 1297: Psychologie Cognitive, 2 rue de la Liberté, F-93526 Saint Denis Cedex 02, Paris, France.

REFERENCES

Brehmer, B. (1988) Organization for decision making in complex systems. In L. P. Goldstein, H. B. Andersen and S. E. Olsen (eds), *Tasks, Errors and Mental Models.* London: Taylor & Francis, pp. 116–27.

von Cranach, M., Ochsenbein, G., and Valach L. (1986) The group as a self-active system: outline of a theory of group action. *European Journal of Social Psychology*, **16**, 193–229.

Falzon, P. (1984) The analysis and understanding of an operative language. *First IFIP Conference on Human–Computer Interaction, INTERACT '84*, pp. 237–41.

Falzon, P. (1986) *Langages opératifs et compréhension opérative.* Thèse de Psychologie, Université Paris V. Paris.

Hoc, J.-M. (1986) Aides logicielles à la résolution de problème et assistance aux activités de planification. In René Paterson (ed.), *L'homme et l'écran, aspects de l'ergonomie en informatique*, pp. 53–69, Ed. de l'Université de Bruxelles.

Hoc, J.-M. (1989) Cognitive approaches to process control. In G. Tiberghien (ed.), *Advances in Cognitive Science. Volume 2, Theory and Applications.* Chichester: Ellis Horwood, pp. 178–203.

Leplat, J. (1988) Methodologie von Aufgabenanalyse und Aufgabengestaltung. *Zeitschrift für Arbeits- und Organisationpsychologie*, **1**, 2–12.

Leplat, J., and Hoc, J.-M. (1983) Tâche et activité dans l'analyse psychologique des situations. *Cahiers de Psychologie Cognitive*, **3**, 1, 49–64.

Maleval, M., and Oziard, P. (1988) Impact des techniques de l'intelligence artificielle sur les systèmes informatiques d'aides à la décision. *Actes des Sèmes rencontres internationales d' Avignon sur Les Systèmes Experts et leurs Applications. Conférences Spécialisées*, pp. 281–308.

Patrick, J. (1980) Job analysis, training and transferability: some theoretical and practical issues. In K. Duncan and D. Walis (eds) *Changes in Working Life*. Chichester: John Wiley, pp. 55–69.

Poirier, L. (1987) *Stratégie théorique 2.* Paris: Economica.

Rasmussen, J. (1984) Strategies for state identification and diagnosis in supervisory control tasks, and design of computer-based support systems. *Advances in Man–Machine Systems Research*, **1**, 139–95.

Rasmussen, J. (1985) The role of hierarchical knowledge representation in decision making and system management. *IEEE Transactions on Systems, Man and Cybernetics*, **15**, 234–43.

Rasmussen, J. (1986) A framework for cognitive task analysis in system design. In E. Hollnagel, G. Mancini and D. D. Woods (eds), *Intelligent Decision Support in Process Environments*. Berlin/Heidelberg: Springer Verlag, pp. 175–96.

Rogalski, J. (1987) Analyse cognitive d'une méthode de raisonnement tactique et de son enseignement à des professionnels. *Le Travail Humain*, **50**, 4, 305–17.

Rogalski, J. (1988) Formation à une méthode de raisonnement tactique comme aide à la prise de décision partagée. *7éme European Annual Conference on Decision Making and Manual Control*, Clamart, France, pp. 262–8.

Samurçay, R., and Rogalski, J. (1987) Designing systems for training and decision aids: cognitive task analysis as a prerequisite. In H. J. Bullinger and B. Shackel (eds), *Human–Computer Interaction INTERACT '87*. New York: Elsevier Science/North-Holland, pp. 663–8.

Savoyant, A. (1984) Définition et voies d'analyse de l'activité collective des équipes de travail. *Cahiers de Psychologie Cognitive*, **4**, 3, 273–84.

Savoyant, A., and Leplat, J. (1983) Statut et fonction des activités de communication dans l'activité des équipes de travail. *Psychologie Française*, **28**, 3, 247–73.

Sorensen, J. H., Mileti, D. S., and Copenhaver, E. (1985) Inter- and intraorganizational cohesion in emergencies. *International Journal of Mass Emergencies and Disasters*, 29–52.

Section 5

Experimental Studies in Simulated Task Environments

This section introduces the use of simulation in research on distributed decision making. Simulation is an important tool which can support the modelling of distributed decision making in several different ways.

Simulation of a complex task domain makes it possible to repeat the same decision scenario with several different subjects, recording of interaction data is easy and, consequently, it will be possible to make detailed studies of structural relationships which are not possible in field studies. This is the approach taken by Brehmer and Allard in Chapter 16. In a simulated task environment, representing the basic structural features of a forest fire fighting scenario, they are able in a controlled way to change basic features of the task, such as time delays in the response to decisions, the complexity of the scenarios, etc. In a series of experiments they are able to collect data well suited to study the influence on performance from changes in structural properties. In Chapter 17, on organization for decision making, Brehmer gives the background for these structural experiments.

Dörner and his group have taken a completely different approach in Chapter 18. Their program includes a series of simulations of very different complex work domains. They analyze in detail the mental strategies of the subjects and, in particular, the decision errors made during the sessions. From the data collected from several different work domains they generalize in order to formulate basic cognitive mechanisms in control of human navigation in complex work environments. In particular, effort is spent to account for affective factors and related individual differences.

Dörner introduces another very important application of computer simulation in cognitive sciences, that is, the use of simulation to test hypotheses and models of cognitive systems. Simulation of models formulated in terms of objects and courses of events present some very basic problems, as pointed out by Rasmussen in Section 3, and a number of methodological problems have to be considered in order to avoid experiments which are demonstrations of models, rather than evaluations. This topic was dealt with in a separate discussion session, and a joint chapter by the editors reflecting and expanding on the topics raised is presented in Chapter 20.

These two experimental programs are both considering only a single decision maker at present. The results gained will, however, be very important for simulation of distributed decision making. As the approaches suggested by Rogalski and by Rasmussen show, the decision tasks and role allocation should be considered as separate dimensions.

The state of the art of simulating individual decision makers is illustrated by the chapters in this section in order to show what any modelling of collective and cooperative processes will have to take into account. The experimental approaches by Brehmer and by Dörner can be extended with additional workstations for multi-agent experiments which both teams indicate for future programs.

16. Dynamic Decision Making: The Effects of Task Complexity and Feedback Delay[1]

Berndt Brehmer and Robert Allard
Uppsala University, Sweden

Consider the decision problems facing a fire chief charged with the task of extinguishing a forest fire. He receives information about the location of fires from a spotter plane and, on the basis of this information, he can send out firefighting units (FFUs). These units will then report back to him about their position and activities, and on the basis of this information, he may then issue new commands, sending the FFUs to new locations, until the fire has been extinguished.

This situation has all the characteristics of a *dynamic decision problem* as described by Edwards (1962), i.e.:

(1) A series of decisions are necessary;
(2) These decisions are interdependent, i.e. the decision made at $ti + 1$ depends on that made at ti; and
(3) The environment changes both autonomously and as a function of the decision maker's actions.

However, these three characteristics do not quite capture the essence of the problem. They define a sequential decision task, but they omit one critical aspect of the firefighting problem: the time element. Thus, in the above problem it is not only necessary to make the correct decisions, and in the correct order, the decisions also have to be made at the correct point in time.

The time element sets dynamic problems apart from the kinds of problems usually considered in research on decision making. Moreover, consideration of the time element has an extremely important consequence: it leaves us without a normative theory for the task.

Real-time, dynamic decision tasks of the kind facing the fire chief are quite common. Examples can be found in operator work in modern process plants

---

Distributed Decision Making: Cognitive Models for Cooperative Work
Edited by J. Rasmussen, B. Brehmer and J. Leplat

(Brehmer, 1989), in intensive care in hospitals (A. Brehmer, 1989), and in military contexts (Brehmer, 1988). Despite this, such tasks have not received very much research attention from psychologists. There are at least two reasons for this: the commonly accepted normative decision theory does not apply to these tasks (leaving researchers without a good reference with which to compare the performance of their subjects), and the lack of a suitable experimental paradigm for the study of this form of decision making. Both these matters are discussed in turn. Then an experimental paradigm for the study of real-time, dynamic decision making is outlined. Finally, some first results obtained with this paradigm are presented.

CHOOSING A MODEL FOR A DYNAMIC TASK

Traditional normative decision theory requires us to consider decision making in terms of discrete episodes. A decision problem is defined in terms of a set of possible actions, connected to a set of possible consequences of these actions by means of probabilities. The decision maker's task is to select the action that leads to the best outcome, usually defined as the alternative with the highest expected value. Thus, decision making is seen as a matter of resolving a choice dilemma. Such a conception ignores both the fact that dynamic decision making involves a series of such dilemmas and that these occur in real time.

It is, of course, possible to construct a decision tree to take into account the fact that dynamic decision making involves a series of decisions. To capture the real-time aspect, such a decision tree would have to be constructed with some time base. For example, one could construct new nodes for every minute or every half minute. It is not difficult to realize that this is impossible. Such trees would be quite complex, even for rather simple dynamic problems, and there would simply not be time to construct the trees when decisions are needed. Thus, traditional decision theory does not give a good guide in these kinds of tasks.

However, we need some guide, and when decision theory fails us, we have to look elsewhere. We have followed a suggestion by Broadbent *et al.* (1986), who noted that dynamic decision problems are similar to those considered to be facing control engineers, and we have chosen to view our problem from the general perspective of control theory. In doing so, we have not made use of formal control theory. Instead, we use the theory in a loose, metaphorical way. At some future date, when we know more about dynamic decision making, formal theory may also prove useful, but, as noted by Bainbridge (1981), current forms of control theory are not really congruent with what we know about human behaviour.

Our general point of departure, then, is that decision making in real-time dynamic decision tasks should be seen as an attempt to achieve control over some important aspect of the task. As noted by Conant and Ashby (1970), this is possible to the extent that the decision maker has a good model of the task

('Every good regulator of a system must be a model of that system'). This model should enable the decision maker to predict what the task system will do under different circumstances, so that he or she can choose the appropriate action.

As noted above, the models offered by traditional research on decision making are not particularly useful for this purpose. Control theory does not offer any alternative task model. Task models are not part of control theory but must be supplied to make the control theory work. For the problem considered in this chapter we have not been able to construct a model on the level required for the application of control theory formalisms. We suspect that this will be the case for many real-life dynamic problems. This is an important reason why we have not tried to apply more formal versions of control theory in our work.

In the absence of a good model for the task, traditional normative analyses become impossible. This has two important consequences: it is not possible to know whether a given strategy is optimal, and it is difficult to learn to develop optimal strategies on the basis of experience. This is because it is impossible to decide whether a given strategy needs to be modified except by comparing it to one known to be better, and without a normative theory, there is no ground for ascertaining which strategy is better. This is not to say that experience will not lead to improvement, at least for some people. Indeed, for many dynamic problems there are recognized experts, and one way to learn to perform a dynamic task is to study what experts do (as is done, for example, by officer candidates who study famous battles in great detail). However, if we have no normative model, we have no way of evaluating the experts, and we cannot know how general their knowledge is.

However, the need for a well-formulated model of a dynamic task may not be as great as one would first think. First, as pointed out by Hogarth (1981), many dynamic tasks allow the decision maker to correct earlier mistakes in his later decisions. This is not a feature of all dynamic tasks, however. Correction of earlier mistakes is possible only if the tasks allow the decision maker to rely upon feedback, and this is possible only if the feedback delays are insignificant in relation to the time taken for actions to have an effect upon the system.

Second, some level of control over a dynamic system can sometimes be achieved by means of simple heuristic rules. Military strategy and tactics provide particularly well-worked out examples of such heuristics. However, they are no more than heuristics; had they been algorithms, wars would presumably have come to an end.

If there is no normative model, it will, however, be impossible to evaluate these heuristics, and decide whether an optimal level of control has been achieved. For example, a given method for fighting a fire may be effective in that it leads to extinction of the fire. However, there will always be alternative methods which also lead to extinction of the fire, and in the absence of a normative theory for the task, it will be impossible to choose the best one. After a fire has been put out it is, of course, often possible to form hypotheses about better methods for fighting that particular fire. However, in the absence of a normative theory, it is hard to decide how general the experience with this fire could be, and modification of one's strategy on the basis of such particular information may therefore be quite risky.

In dynamic tasks, then, decision makers have basically three alternatives open to them: (1) to develop a mental model of the task, (2) to develop heuristic rules, and (3) to rely upon feedback, and modify their behaviour gradually. The question for psychological research is which of these alternatives the subjects will choose under different circumstances.

RESEARCH PARADIGMS FOR THE STUDY OF DYNAMIC DECISION MAKING

To study how subjects cope with dynamic tasks we need a research paradigm that allows us to vary the relevant characteristics of the task and to assess the effects of these variations. Earlier attempts to study dynamic decision making by Dörner (Dörner *et al.*, 1983) and Mackinnon and Wearing (1984) have followed contrasting strategies. (We are ignoring the work of Rapoport, 1975, who was concerned with sequential, rather than dynamic, tasks; there is no consideration of the time element in Rapoport's models.) Dörner and his associates have selected a very complex task, that of running a town as a mayor, a task which requires the subjects to cope with a number of different problems by means of different kinds of control variables. Mackinnon and Wearing, on the other hand, have gone in the opposite direction, and have constructed a simple task where a single target variable has to be controlled by means of a single control variable.

Neither of these approaches provides a general experimental paradigm for the study of dynamic decision making as defined in this chapter. Dörner's approach has an appropriate level of complexity, but it is developed from an analysis of a concrete case, and it is not founded upon any general analysis of the characteristics of dynamic decision problems. It does not allow for any variation of the characteristics of dynamic problems. Thus, it is best suited to analysis of individual differences in how people cope with dynamic problems, which is exactly the problem Dörner and his associates have been studying. The approach of Mackinnon and Wearing, on the other hand, uses systems theory as a general framework, but the analysis is limited to problems that involve the control of a single variable.

We have therefore developed DESSY (Dynamic Environmental Simulation System) to serve as an alternative research paradigm. DESSY is an interactive computer program constructed on the basis of a general analysis of the nature of dynamic systems, and it allows us to vary a number of important characteristics of dynamic decision tasks. Our approach has considerable affinity with that of Toda (1962), in his well-known paper on the fungus eater. However, while Toda saw the problems facing fungus eaters as those of search and choice, we have adopted a general systems and control theory approach. Therefore, the concepts we propose for analyzing dynamic tasks differ from those proposed by Toda. Moreover, DESSY is explicitly developed to study dynamic decision making in real time.

This is not the place for a general discussion of the nature of dynamic systems, but a brief statement of the characteristics of such systems is nevertheless needed to put the present work into perspective.

THE CHARACTERISTICS OF DYNAMIC SYSTEMS

The number and nature of the characteristics needed to describe a dynamic system is, of course, dependent upon the level of abstraction and the uses to which the description will be put. In the present context, we need a description that can be used for the purposes of psychological research. We admit that the list given below is somewhat arbitrary, and is subject to revision as we learn more about dynamic decision making. For the time being, however, we have found the following six variables useful for characterizing a dynamic decision task.

Complexity

Complexity is a difficult concept because it has no clear operationalization. Here, we have followed Ashby's suggestion, and define the complexity of a system relative to the capacity of the mechanism that seeks to control that system (Ashby, 1956). In the present case, the control mechanisms are human beings, and we know that humans have a limited capacity for processing information. Consequently, a preliminary definition of complexity could be made in terms of the number of elements in the system to be controlled. However, in so doing, we need to distinguish between different kinds of elements, of which there are at least four: goals, actions, side effects and processes that need to be controlled. Thus, complexity would be related to the number of processes to be controlled, the number of goals, the number of action alternatives, and the number of side effects. In the case of the firefighting example above, complexity would thus vary with the number of fires: whether the subjects' goal is simply to put out the fires as quickly as possible or whether there are other considerations as well (e.g. fires in some areas may be more dangerous than other fires) and the number of action alternatives (i.e. the number of firefighting units and their characteristics), as well as whether the agents used for putting out the fires had other effects as well (e.g. they may have negative effects on the flora and fauna of the forest).

Rate of change

This refers to how quickly the process(es) to be controlled changes. Rates of change may vary within very wide limits, with very fast tasks at one end (e.g. performing a low-level attack with a jet fighter) and extremely slow ones at the other (e.g. controlling a country's economy), with tasks such as firefighting in between. An important question for research is, of course, whether systems with different rates of change are perceived and controlled in the same way.

Relation between the characteristics of the process to be controlled and those of the control processes

This feature is unique to dynamic problems. It stems from the time-dependent nature of such tasks. The object of dynamic decision making is to control a time-dependent process. However, the means used for control will also have process characteristics, i.e. it will take some time for them to have any effect at all, and the magnitude of their effect will vary over time. If the change in effectiveness does not match the change in the process, the decision maker faces a tactical problem. The case of firefighting illustrates this very clearly.

If there is no wind, a fire will spread as a quadratic process, i.e. it will ignite all neighbouring areas, and as the fire grows, it will ignite a larger area. If there is wind, it will spread in the direction of the wind, and its front will increase linearly. The FFUs work in a linear way over time, because each unit can put water only on a limited area at a time. The problem in fighting a fire, therefore, can be characterized as that of trying to control one linear process with another linear process. The extent to which the fire chief will succeed in this depends on the extent to which he manages to match the characteristics of the firefighting process to the fire process. If the fire spreads faster than a single FFU can extinguish it, it will be necessary to use and coordinate a number of FFUs. For example an important consideration in firefighting is that the fire will spread as the FFUs move towards the fire, and when they are in place, the fire will always be larger than it was when they were first sent out. Therefore, the fire chief must remember to send out more FFUs than seem to be initially required.

This particular combination of processes is, of course, only one of many possibilities. Each dynamic problem will have its own combination, and this characteristic will determine what the efficient strategy for the task is. For example, when the process is a cancerous growth, and the means surgery, we are using a step function to control an exponential process.

Delays

The concept of delay refers to a slowing down, or lagging behind, in the transmission of energy, or information, in the system. This variable is, of course, often quite complex in real dynamic systems, for delays may occur in many different places in the system. In the firefighting example, commands may be slow in reaching the FFUs, the FFUs may delay in responding to the commands, it will take time to execute the command, and the FFUs may be slow in reporting their actions to the fire chief. All these different kinds of delay will show up in the same way to the decision maker: as a delay between the moment when a command has been given and the moment when information about the results of this command is obtained.

From the fact that there is such a difference, it is not possible to infer the location of the delay. For that, additional information about the system is needed.

Quality of feedback information

Information about the state of the system may vary in quality. Thus, it may be more or less complete because of the way in which the information system has been designed, or it may even be distorted, perhaps because the lower levels send incorrect reports about their activities.

Distribution of decision-making capacity

In a complex dynamic system, such as the firefighting example, all decision-making power may be centralized in the fire chief, or it may be distributed, so that the local FFU commanders are able to make some of the decisions. The possibility of delegating decision-making power is of extreme importance when there are delays in the system. In that case, it is not possible to control the system centrally (unless one has a model that incorporates the delays), and delegation of decision-making power to local units becomes mandatory.

DESSY

A simulation system which enables us to manipulate the six factors described above can be created only in the form of a computer program. DESSY is such a program.

It is a modular program, where modules can be added or subtracted without reprogramming other modules. The temporal progress is controlled by the computer's internal clocks. The program is currently implemented in a PDP 11/40 computer equipped with a GT40 monochromatic display, a LA 36 DECWRITER keyboard/printer, and two RK11-01 disc drives with 1.2 MB discs (see Allard, 1986, for a description of the actual program).

The remainder of this chapter reports the first experiment performed with DESSY. The experiment is exploratory in character, and the main purpose was to investigate whether subjects could learn to control a complex dynamic system, and whether this was affected by feedback delay and complexity.

METHOD

The decision task in the experiment was a simulation of the firefighting task discussed above. Figure 1 shows how the task appears to the subject. The subject is seated in front of the GT40 display with a keyboard to issue commands. On the screen, there is a map in the form of a grid with 16 × 16 squares, each of which is coded in terms of a letter and a number. Active fire is represented as pluses, minuses denote a fire that has been extinguished. Information about fires is received from a spotter plane, and the subject cannot influence these reports. Thus, he cannot, for example, ask the plane to go to a certain location to investigate whether there is a fire there. Each FFU is represented by its identification number (between 1 and 8 in the present experiment, where the subject had eight FFUs at his disposal). In the centre of the map, four squares are outlined with heavy lines. These represent the base where the fire chief (= the subject) is located. Directly below the map a weather report is provided with information about the general weather conditions, the direction of the wind, and the time when this report was issued.

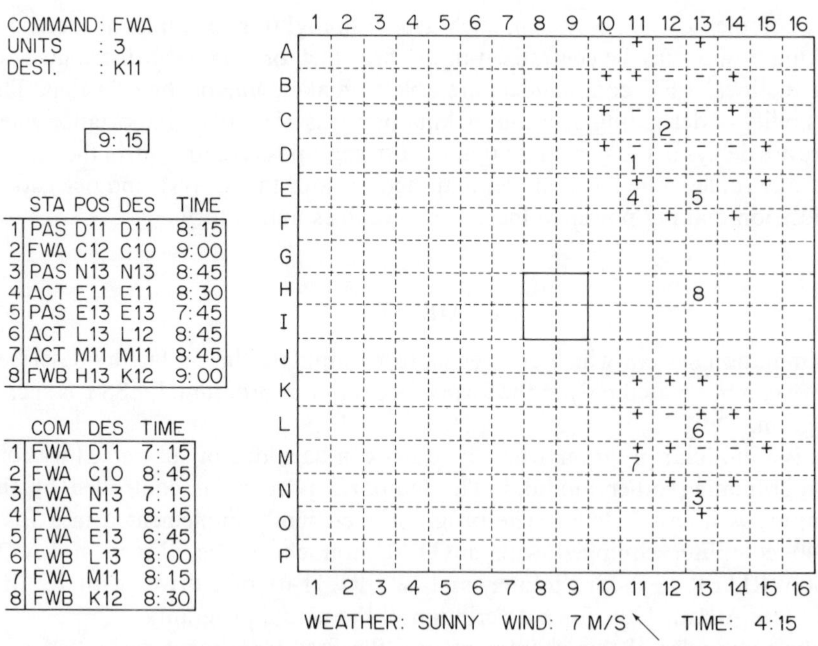

Figure 1. The experimental task as seen by the subject (for explanation, see text)

To the left of the map there are four displays. The top display shows the last command, the next shows the current time, and the third display the status reports from the FFUs. The first column in this display shows the reported status, which may be ACT (active in fighting fire), PAS (passive, i.e. the FFU is doing nothing, perhaps because it has put out the fire in its area), FWA (the FFU is on its way under central control, i.e. it is not allowed to fight fires that it encounters *en route* to its destination) or FWB (the FFU is on its way under decentralized control, i.e. it is allowed to fight fires that it encounters *en route* to its destination). The second column shows the reported position of the FFU, and the third the destination to which the FFU has been ordered to go. The fourth column, finally, shows the time when the FFU reported. The bottom display is a list of the last command given to each unit, with information about when these commands were issued.

The subject sends FFUs to different locations by means of either the FWA or FWB command described above. A command must include information about the mode of control, i.e. FWA or FWB, the name of the unit (a number between 1 and 8), and a map reference, e.g. 'K11', indicating the destination. The information on the screen is updated once every 20 seconds.

The subject has two goals: to protect the base and to put out the fire(s) as soon as possible. A trial ends when the fire(s) have been put out or when the fire has reached the base.

A fire starts in one of the high-risk areas C3, C14, N3 or N14 and spreads in the direction of the prevailing wind. The first fire starts at $t = 5$ time units (each time unit is 20 seconds). Ten time units later, a second fire starts in one of the nearby high-risk areas, and at the same time, the direction of the wind changes, so that it now blows in the direction from the second fire towards the base. If the subject does nothing, the second fire will reach the base at $t = 60$ time units. Thus, the second fire is always the most dangerous one in this experiment.

The FFUs move at the rate of one square per time unit. The subject has eight FFUs at his or her disposal. The effectiveness of these units was varied in the experiment as described below.

Independent variables and design

Two factors were varied in the experiment: feedback delay and complexity. In the no-delay conditions, the FFUs reported on their status and activity without delay. In the delay conditions, half of the FFUs reported back on their location and activity with a delay of 1 time unit (20 seconds), while the other half reported back with a delay of 2 time units (40 seconds). However the 'spotter plane' still reported the fire and its location without delay.

Complexity was varied by a manipulation of the effectiveness of the FFUs. In the low-complexity condition, all FFUs were equally effective, and a FFU required 5 time units (100 seconds) to put out the fire in one square. In the high-complexity condition, four of the FFUs were approximately twice as effective as the other four, but the total effectiveness of the eight FFUs as a whole was kept constant. Thus, the effective FFUs could put out the fire in 3 time units (60 seconds), while the less effective FFUs put out a fire in 7 time units (140 seconds).

In the four conditions resulting from a factorial combination of complexity and delay, the subjects received eight trials. Thus, the design of the experiment was a 2 (levels of delay) by 2 (levels of complexity) by 8 (trials) factorial design with repeated measures on the third factor.

Subjects

Sixteen undergraduate students (nine male and seven female) were paid 60 SEK (about $8.50) to serve as subjects. They were randomly assigned to the four experimental conditions.

Procedure

The subjects were informed about the general nature of the task. They were instructed that they had two goals: to protect their base and to put out the fires as quickly as possible. Protection of the base was the most important of these goals for the obvious reason that if the base was destroyed, they could not continue their task. They were then allowed to familiarize themselves with the display and the commands, and to practise the commands on the keyboard for 20 minutes. The subjects came to the experiment on four days, and performed two trials on each day.

RESULTS

DESSY registers everything that happens on every trial. From this information it is possible to construct a number of dependent variables. Five of these will be analyzed here. The first two show the extent to which the subjects were able to fulfil the two goals, and the next three how the subjects used their resources.

Subjects' ability to meet the goals

Base Losses

For each subject, the number of trials that ended in the base being lost to fire was recorded. χ^2 analyses showed that significantly more trials ended in base loss in the delay condition than in the no-delay condition (42% versus 8%, $\chi^2 = 27.56$, d$f = 1$, $p < 0.001$), but that there was no significant effect on complexity (30% versus 23% in the high- and low-complexity conditions, respectively, $p > 0.05$).

Relative Area Lost

This measure shows the number of squares destroyed by fire at the end of the trial, relative to the maximum possible loss at $t = 60$ time units. The results are shown in Figure 2. As can be seen from the figure, the subjects improve in the no-delay conditions but not in the delay conditions. The main effect of delay, as well as the delay by trials interaction, are significant (F 1/12 = 10.2, $p < 0.01$, and F 7/84 = 4.4, $p < 0.01$, respectively). There was no significant effect of complexity and no complexity by trials interaction, but, as can be seen from Figure 2, subjects in the no-delay condition tend to perform somewhat better in the low-complexity condition than in the high-complexity one towards the end of the experiment, resulting in a significant complexity × delay × trials interaction (F 7/84 = 3.97, $p < 0.001$).

Utilization of resources

Allocation to fires

This measure expresses the proportion of FFUs which have received a command to go to a fire five time units (i.e. 100 seconds) after the start of this fire.

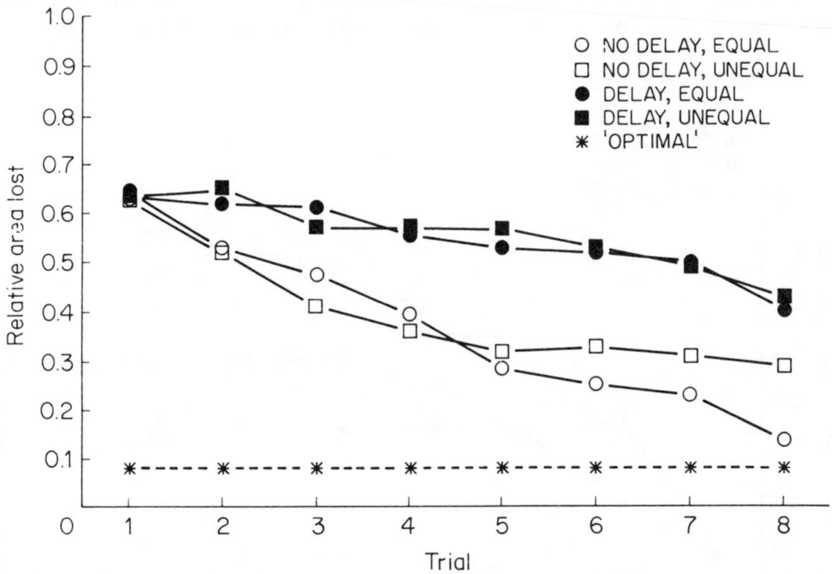

Figure 2. Relative area lost to fire as a function of trials in the four experimental conditions. The 'optimal level' in the figure is not the result of computations; there is no optimal model which allows us to compute such an optimal level. Instead, it is the best performance that the present authors have been able to reach after analysis and considerable practice

The statistical analysis yielded no main effect of task complexity, and no interactions involving this factor. There were, however, strong effects of delay. Figure 3 shows that, over trials, subjects in both conditions learned to respond more quickly and massively. In all conditions, the proportion of FFUs that are engaged increases over the first few trials. The main effect of trials is significant ($F\ 7/84 = 36.6$, $p < 0.001$). However, the effect is strongest in the no-delay condition, as indicated by a significant main effect of delay ($F\ 1/12 = 7.22$, $p < 0.05$), and the difference between the two delay conditions increases over trials, as indicated by a significant delay by trials interaction ($F\ 7/84 = 5.54$, $p < 0.001$).

There is a general tendency to allocate more resources to Fire 1 than to the more dangerous Fire 2 ($F\ 1/12 = 9.37$, $p < 0.01$). In the no-delay conditions, subjects tend to allocate their resources more evenly to the two fires than in the delay conditions. The delay by fire interaction is significant ($F\ 1/12 = 7.27$, $p < 0.01$).

Waiting times

This measure shows the time a FFU is left inactive after it has carried out the command it has received. Waiting times decreased over trials ($F\ 7/84 = 3.85$, $p < 0.01$), indicating that the subjects learned to respond more quickly. Waiting times were longer in the delay condition than in the no-delay condition

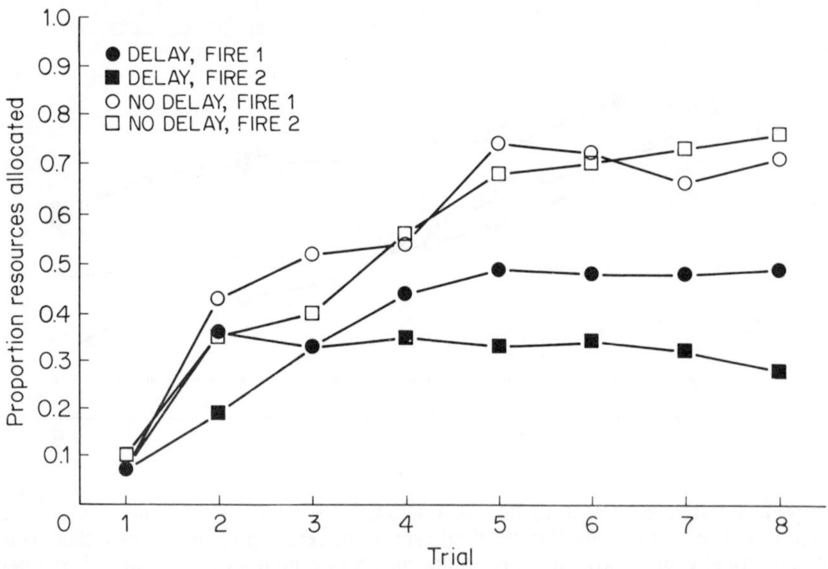

Figure 3. Proportion of FFUs allocated to the two fires as a function of trials in the four experimental conditions

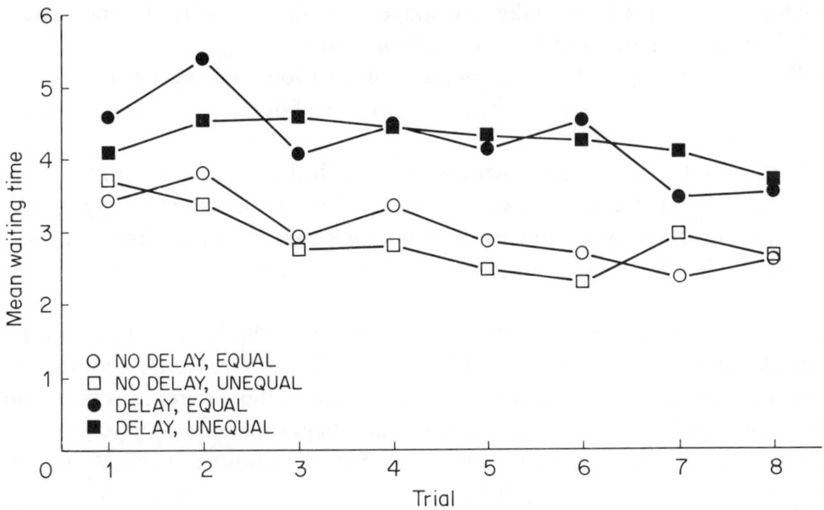

Figure 4. The time FFUs are left inactive after having carried out their orders

(F 1/12 = 28.66, $p < 0.001$). Mean waiting time in the delay condition was 4.26 time units, while in the no-delay condition, it was 2.93. The difference corresponds closely to the mean magnitude of the delay, which was 1.5 time units.

There were no differences in waiting times for the more and the less efficient FFUs in the high-complexity condition, indicating that the subjects did not increase their effectiveness by using the more effective FFUs to a greater extent.

Delegation of decision making

The proportion of FWB commands decreased from 30.9% in the first trial to 15.2% in the last (F 7/84 = 61.1, $p < 0.001$), but there were no main effects of complexity and delay, and no interactions involving these factors. Thus the subjects did not avail themselves of the opportunity to increase their efficiency by delegating decision making to the FFUs, nor did they learn to use the FWB command to combat the effects of information lag in the delay conditions.

DISCUSSION

The results of this experiment are:

(1) That subjects' control over the firefighting task improves with experience; but
(2) Even a minimal delay in feedback has adverse effects on learning to control the task;

(3) That the subjects do not take advantage of the difference in efficiency among FFUs in the high-complexity condition; and
(4) The subjects do not use delegation of decision making as a means to improve effectiveness and combat the effects of delay.

All these results have subsequently been replicated (Brehmer and Allard, 1990a-c), and may thus be seen as stable characteristics of behaviour in this task.

The first result is important because it shows that the task was not in itself unmanageable. This makes the striking effect of feedback delay all the more important.

The results on waiting time give some insight into the nature of the effect of feedback delay. These show that FFUs in the delay condition are kept inactive longer than those in the no-delay condition, and that the difference corresponds to the magnitude of the feedback delay. This suggests that the subjects simply reacted to the information as it arrived on the map, without consideration of the delay.

There are at least three possible explanations for these results. First, it may be that the subjects simply did not detect that there was a feedback delay. Second, it may be that the subjects saw the delay, but that they were unable to develop a predictive model that took these delays into consideration. Third, it may be that the subjects detected the delays, but that they did not interpret them as feedback delays.

It is important to note that although the subjects in this experiment were not informed about the possibility of a feedback delay, this delay was in no way hidden from them. There were three sources of information that they could have used. First, the report time shown in the report display always lagged behind current time with a lag equal to the delay time. Second, there was a lag equal to the delay time between the moment when a command was given and the moment the unit's response to that command was displayed. Third, there was a clear conflict between the report from the spotter plane and that from the FFU. That is, the FFU would report fighting fire in an area where the spotter plane reported that the fire had been put out. Thus, the fact that there was a delay could readily be inferred by someone who inspected the evidence to look for delays. Subsequent experiments (Brehmer and Allard, 1990a) have shown that subjects report that they have detected the delays in conditions with delays, and that they report no delays when the FFUs report the results of their actions without delay. Thus, it seems that the explanation for the strong effect of feedback delay is not that the subjects fail to detect these delays. Instead, the effect seems to be due to subjects' inability to construct an adequate strategy for compensating for these delays.

The complexity manipulation had little effect. The subjects in the high-complexity condition did not avail themselves of the opportunity to increase the efficiency of their firefighting by utilizing the more effective FFUs to a greater extent. There are at least two possible explanations for this. One possibility is that the subjects simply did not detect that there were differences in efficiency, despite the fact that they had all the information they needed in the displays, perhaps because they did not have the relevant hypothesis. However, subsequent experiments (Brehmer and Allard, 1990c) have shown that subjects claim that they detect differences in efficiency among FFUs when such differences exist. Thus, it seems that the explanation here is the same as for the effect of feedback delays, i.e. that the subjects did not understand how to use the differences in effectiveness to their advantage.

The results with respect to delegation show a dysfunctional development. Rather than increasing the use of the FWB command, the subjects decreased it over trials, and they did not use delegation to a greater extent in the delay conditions, where it could have led to a marked improvement in performance. One possible explanation for this is that offered by the results of Dörner (1980), who found that his subjects tended to assume more control as their problems in controlling the task increased. Increased centralization would thus be an indicator of a more primitive mode of thinking due to stress.

In the present experiment there was, however, no indication that the subjects used fewer FWB commands in the conditions where their control was worse, i.e. the delay conditions. This suggests the alternative possibility that subjects simply did not understand the task well enough to realize that they could increase their own efficiency by letting the FFUs make the decisions. These problems clearly merit further study.

Due to computer limitations, we could not analyze the subjects' behaviour in fine detail in this experiment. Therefore, we can only report some impressions here, to serve as a basis for future experiments. First, we noted in running the experiment that the subjects did not seem to understand that when issuing a command they should send the FFU to the location where the fire would be when the FFU was in position, rather than to the position where the fire was when the command was issued. That is, the subjects' decisions did not seem to be guided by any predictive model of the task. Instead, as indicated by the results on resource allocation and waiting times, they seemed to learn a rather simple heuristic: to respond quickly and massively, i.e. to send as many FFUs as quickly as possible in the direction of the fire. This is not necessarily bad strategy, but is not efficient. It agrees with the observations of Dörner and his associates for quite different systems (Dörner *et al.*, 1983).

In conclusion, the present experiment provides one important result: that subjects do not take feedback delay into account when trying to control a dynamic task. This is surprising, because feedback delay is a common characteristic of systems, and there should be plenty of opportunity to learn about delays in everyday life. To understand this phenomenon in more detail and to develop means that help people cope with delays are important tasks for future studies on dynamic decision making.

NOTE

[1] This study was supported by a grant from the Swedish Council for Research in the Humanities and Social Sciences.

Address for Correspondence:

Professor Berndt Brehmer, Uppsala Universitet, Dept of Psychology, Box 1854, S-751 48 Uppsala, Sweden.

REFERENCES

Allard, R. (1986) DESSY: A general interactive computer program for studies of dynamic decision making. Uppsala: Uppsala University, Department of Psychology, manuscript.

Ashby, R. (1956) *Introduction to Cybernetics.* London: Hutchinson.

Bainbridge, L. (1981) Mathematical equations or processing routines. In J. Rasmussen and W. B. Rouse (eds), *Human Detection of and Diagnosis of System Failures.* New York: Plenum.

Brehmer, A. (1989) Intensivvård som ett hierarkiskt kontrollsystem. Uppsala University: Center for Human Computer Interaction Report.

Brehmer, B. (1988) Organization of decision making in complex systems. In L. P. Goodstein, H. Andersen and S. E. Olesen (eds), *Tasks, Errors, and Mental Models.* London: Taylor & Francis.

Brehmer, B. (1989) The cognitive side of process control. Uppsala University: Center for Human Computer Interaction Report.

Brehmer, B., and Allard, R. (1990a) *Feedback Delays in Real Time, Dynamic Decision Making*, Uppsala University, Department of Psychology: Uppsala Psychological Reports.

Brehmer, B., and Allard, R. (1990b) *Effects of Complexity in Real Time, Dynamic Decision Making. I. The effect of a variation in the effectiveness of control processes.* Uppsala University, Department of Psychology: Uppsala Psychological Reports.

Brehmer, B., and Allard, R. (1990c) *Feedback Delays and Strategies in Real Time, Dynamic Decision Making.* Uppsala University, Department of Psychology: Uppsala Psychological Reports.

Broadbent, D. E., Fitzgerald, P., and Broadbent, M. P. H. (1986) Implicit and explicit knowledge in the control of complex systems. *British Journal of Psychology*, **77**, 33–50.

Conant, R. C., and Ashby, W. R. (1970) Every good regulator of a system must be a model of that system. *International Journal of System Science*, **1**, 89–97.

Dörner, D. (1980). On the difficulties people have in dealing with complexity. *Simulation and Games*, **11**, 87–106.

Dörner, D., Kreuzig, H., Reither, F., and Stäudel, T. (1983) *Lohhausen: Vom Umgang Unbestimmtheit und Komplexität.* Bern: Huber.

Edwards, W. (1962) Dynamic decision theory and probabilistic information processing. *Human Factors*, **4**, 59–74.

Hogarth, R. M. (1981) Beyond discrete biases: functional and dysfunctional aspects of judgmental heuristics. *Psychological Bulletin*, **90**, 197–217.

Mackinnon, A. J., and Wearing, A. J. (1984) Systems analysis and dynamic decision making. *Acta Psychologica*, **58**, 159–72.

Rapoport, A. (1975) Research paradigms for studying dynamic decision making. In D. Wendt and C. Vlek (eds), *Utility, Probability, and Human Decision Making.* Dordrecht: Reidel.

Toda, M. (1962) The design of a fungus-eater: A model of human behaviour in an unsophisticated environment. *Behavioral Science*, **7**, 164–83.

17. Organization for Decision Making in Complex Systems[1]

Berndt Brehmer[2]
Uppsala University, Sweden

Conant and Ashby's (1970) principle that every good regulator of a system must be a model of that system as well as Ashby's (1956) law of requisite variety lead to the inescapable consequence that a complex system requires a complex control structure. However, while such a structure will render the once complex problem simple in relation to that structure, the structure will still be complex in relation to those who use it, not to mention those who have to design it.

There are two ways in which a decision problem can be simplified: it can be divided into parts or a hierarchical organization may be imposed upon it. However, neither of these possibilities is a general solution to the problem of complexity. So far, it has not been possible to spell out the conditions for one or other control structure to be effective.

This chapter is concerned with the hierarchical organization, and it will discuss some of the problems and possibilities of that kind of organization. Specifically, it deals with the hierarchical organization of social systems for decision making in dynamic contexts, a problem that does not seem to have received much attention in earlier writings on organizational theory. The discussion will focus upon two systems: the *military system*, which will serve as an example of a supposedly hierarchical system, and *emergency management systems*, which illustrate some of the shortcomings of hierarchical organizations. The purpose of the discussion of the military system is not so much to convey any new insights into that system as to illustrate some of the properties of a hierarchical system.

HIERARCHICAL SYSTEMS

The term 'hierarchical system' may refer to three different phenomena:

(1) It may be a way of *understanding* a system, i.e. a hierarchical conceptual structure is imposed upon a problem to reduce its complexity and make it understandable.

Distributed Decision Making: Cognitive Models for Cooperative Work
Edited by J. Rasmussen, B. Brehmer and J. Leplat

(2) It may refer to a particular organization of a system.
(3) It may refer to a particular principle for the control of a system.

There are no necessary relations among these three phenomena. A system may be analyzed as a hierarchy without having any 'real' hierarchical organization (as in the case of the Linean system), or it may have a hierarchical structure without having any real hierarchical control structure (as in a royal court, where the different levels of nobility form a hierarchical system, but there is no control flowing from the higher levels of the system to the lower ones).

How a hierarchical system reduces complexity

To impose a hierarchical system is to introduce a series of descriptions of the system which differ with respect to their level of abstraction. This makes it possible to control the level of complexity in the sense that only a limited number of units have to be considered at each level of the hierarchy.

Thus, in a military system, for example, the imposition of a hierarchical structure means that a company commander has to consider only three platoons, rather than, say, a hundred individual soldiers, and that a battalion commander has to consider only three companies, rather than, say nine platoons, and so on.

A hierarchical analysis is always possible, for there is no necessary relation between the levels in the hierarchy. The levels are the result of a creative act on the part of the person who creates the system. Consequently, a wide variety of conceptual hierarchical systems can be created for any one system.

However, not every hierarchical organization is equally useful for achieving the objective of the system. For the purpose of control, it is necessary to bring the hierarchical structure in some relation to the variable to be controlled by the system. Specifically, it must be possible to describe the control variable in terms of a hierarchical structure as well, where the levels of the control variable must be congruent with the description of the controlling hierarchical system. If this is not possible, the hierarchical structure will not serve any control purpose (as in the above case of the organization of the nobility).

For the purpose of control it is, of course, the number of levels of the control variable that determines what the number of levels in the hierarchical system should be. If all levels in the control variable are not covered in the control structure, the system will be subject to *surprises*, i.e. to unforeseen consequences of long-term trends that have not been monitored by the system.

However, an organization that only takes control into account when deciding upon the number of levels may not serve to control the complexity of the tasks of the decision makers at different levels in the system. The need to control the complexity of these tasks may lead to the introduction of new levels in the hierarchy, or to the assignment of tasks on different conceptual levels to the same organizational level. As a consequence, the organization of the system will not match the conceptual analysis of the task or the analysis in terms of control needs. This emphasizes the importance of distinguishing between the three different meanings of the term 'hierarchical system'.

THE MILITARY SYSTEM

The modern military system is, of course, an extremely complex organization with a variety of purposes. It is beyond the scope of this chapter to describe this organization in its entirety. We will limit the discussion to certain aspects of one particular task of that system—that of fighting a battle—in which the hierarchical organization of the system and its problems are especially apparent. It also illustrates some important conditions for a successful hierarchical system, as well as the problems and opportunities created by the introduction of modern information technology into a hierarchically organized system.

The control variable for the military system is that of *area*, area gained in the case of attack and area retained for defense. The control variable can be described in terms of different levels. These levels simply represent areas which differ in size. Thus, we are discussing the military system as a control structure for dominating geographical area, a system that achieves that purpose by allocating the appropriate resources to an appropriate size area.

The general principle for creating the hierarchical control structure thus also relates to size, and in this case it is the size of the unit. Thus, there is the hierarchical organization of platoons, companies, battalions, divisions, etc., each of which will be charged with an area of a given size. This is clearly not the whole truth. The size of the unit committed to a given area is also dependent upon the size of the unit that the enemy commits to that area. Thus, an area might at one time be given to a company, and at another to a battalion. However, although the size of the area may vary, the principle of a congruence between the relative size of the unit and the relative size of the area to which it will be assigned still holds.

The military system, then, employs a hierarchical organization because the primary conditions for this kind of organization are met. There is a control variable that can be described at different levels, and it is possible to find a hierarchical structure for the control system that matches the levels of the control variable. As noted above, this system serves to regulate the complexity of each commander's decision task by keeping down the number of units that he has to consider in his decisions.

However, even though the military system meets the conditions for a successful hierarchical organization, this may not be sufficient for the system to actually achieve control over the area with which it is charged. There are at least three problems here. The first is the enemy, and the difficulties of getting information about what the enemy is up to; the second, that of keeping track of one's own forces, and the third, the delays that are an inescapable feature of hierarchical systems.

The flow of control and information

The levels of the military hierarchy differ not only in the size of the units involved but also in the level of abstraction. Whereas a platoon sergeant is responsible for some twenty individuals in practical terms, a brigadier-general deals with the abstract entity of a division.

The actual control of the system thus involves moving through a series of abstract descriptions down to the level of actual soldiers. In the military system, moving from one level of abstraction also means moving from one person to another, for the military system is distinguished by the fact that the organization of the system follows the same principles as the control structure and the conceptual structure.

Ideally, the level at which a commander finds himself should determine how he thinks about the system. Not only should there be a separate set of concepts for describing the system at each level in the hierarchy, there should also be a set of commands appropriate to that level. Moreover, the information needed at each level will be specific to that level. That is, the division commander needs to have a different conception of the system than that of the company commander, and he needs to have the information for his decisions structured in a way different from that of the company commander. Thus, information going up the system needs to be transformed and reinterpreted.

This is true also for commands going down the hierarchy. The commander on each level is to interpret the commands received in terms of the actions appropriate to the level at which he finds himself.

However, while control flows from the top of the hierarchy, much of the information about the state of the system necessarily comes from below. With respect to information flow, hierarchical systems of this kind have built-in problems. One of these is delays in information.

Delays

Only individual soldiers move; battalions and divisions do not. That is, even though an order may be issued to a division commander, nothing will actually happen until these orders have passed down the various levels in the command hierarchy to the individual soldiers. This takes time: the hierarchical organization introduces delays that cannot be avoided.

There will, of course, be corresponding delays in the information that emanates from the bottom level of the hierarchy. In short, the higher levels will always be early in their commands (relative to the actual action in the system) and late in their information about the state of the system.

Delays of this kind introduce important restrictions upon the kinds of orders that can be issued by a higher level to a lower one. Even if the higher level could have exactly the same *kind* and *amount* of information as a lower level, it would nevertheless have this information at a later time, and when it may no longer be relevant. Therefore a higher level could never issue commands that requires information of the kind and detail required at a level below, for then its commands would generally come too late. This illustrates what was said above. Each level in the hierarchy needs information that is appropriate to the decisions made at that level. Conversely, the commander at a given level should only make the decisions appropriate given the information that is available at that level.

This problem has been recognized by the military system, and it is handled by never issuing detailed orders about what should be *done* on a given level. Instead, all commands from a higher to a lower level involves transmission of *goals* for the lower level. The decision concerning how these goals should be achieved is left to the commander at the lower level, who has superior knowledge about current conditions at that level.

It should be noted that this is, at best, a partial solution to the problem of delays. It may very well be that in the interval between the moment when information about conditions was transmitted and the moment when commands were received, conditions have changed so drastically that the goals just cannot be achieved any longer. This is not an uncommon situation, as every student of military history knows.

This means that there are important limits to the level of control that can be achieved in an active dynamic environment. The environment introduces a number of constraints that change over time, and the actual constraints will generally be known only imperfectly by the higher levels. Hence the stress, in military thinking, upon surprise attacks, which allow the attacker to fight the battle on the basis of feedforward control.

Planning time

In a hierarchical system there will not only be delays in the upward flow of information, there will also be delays in the execution of commands, as has been indicated above. The longer response times for the larger units create delays, as we have already noted. This is not always bad, for it creates opportunities for planning provided that the system is not changing too rapidly. Because the larger units are so slow to respond, commands cannot be given very often. That is, there will be time to think between commands, and the planning time will increase as one moves up the hierarchy. Thus, a platoon sergeant may be issuing several orders every minute with very little time for planning, while division headquarters may issue only one order every day, and have considerable time.

This is why staffs, which are planning devices, are found only at the higher levels in the military systems, but not at the lower levels.

Time for planning is also created by the more abstract character of the activity at the higher levels. While the lower levels in the hierarchy will be subjected to a rapidly changing physical environment which requires new decisions at a fast rate, the rate of change in the information available at the higher levels will be much slower, provided that a means for transforming the information from the lower levels into a form appropriate for the higher levels has been found. We will return to this problem.

Trade-offs in the hierarchy

There are a number of restrictions and possible trade-offs in a hierarchy. Thus, the more complex the hierarchy, the longer orders will take, and the more planning time there will be at the higher levels in the hierarchy. However, a more complex hierarchy also creates a greater *need* for planning. Since the complex system is slower to react as a whole, there is a greater need to look ahead and plan to be able to respond appropriately and in time. The balance between the need for planning and the opportunity for planning is a delicate one, and there are as yet no general rules on how to strike this balance. However, one important restriction in this connection is that, to function as a *useful* model of the environment, the control structure must run at a rate faster than that of the environment it seeks to control. That is, the system must have the ability to respond before the consequence that the system seeks to avoid has occurred. If not, the system will lose control. While true, this conclusion may nevertheless not be very useful in the design of systems, for it requires information about all problems that the system will be asked to handle. This is clearly impossible. All we can do is to design a system that will be able to cope with most problems, but not one that can handle all. This means that a system should be designed to have the ability to reconfigure itself. We will return to this problem.

The appropriate number of levels in a hierarchy

One of the basic functions of a hierarchical system is to regulate the complexity of the decision tasks in the system. In an ideal system, the complexity of the tasks at each level in the system should not exceed the capacity of the decision makers to control the system on that level. As the tasks facing a system become more complex at a given level of the hierarchy, this will create a need for new units at that level. However, as new units are created on a given level, this will result in a need for new levels above that level, so as not to increase the complexity of the decision tasks at the original higher level of the system. These new levels will be introduced for managerial reasons, and they have nothing to do with the original control structure. This is how the control structure and the organizational structure become separated in a hierarchical system. Consequently, we cannot assume that an analysis of the organization of a system will reveal the control structure of that system.

In a stable environment we would expect a hierarchical system to have a number of levels that would regulate the complexity in an appropriate way. Moreover, we would expect that as the systems faced increasingly complex problems, the complexity of the command and control systems would also increase. This is, of course, exactly what has happened in the evolution of military systems. No longer do we see the supreme commander of an army lead his troops into battle, sword in hand, as was the case during the Middle Ages. Instead, we will find him well behind the actual front, communicating with his troops via a complex hierarchy of intermediate levels of command.

In an unstable environment, on the other hand, we should not expect to find stable systems that would regulate the complexity of the decision tasks in the systems as well as the military system supposedly does. Instead, we would expect systems with considerable overload at one or more levels. We would also expect that these systems would be in a process of reorganization.

Presumably, the problems in an increasingly complex environment would be most noticeable at the higher levels of the hierarchy, which have to monitor the performance of the system as a whole, and there would therefore be a tendency for these higher levels to introduce new units into lower levels, with an attendant need for new managerial levels in the hierarchy. There would thus be a tendency for the hierarchy to expand upwards.

An alternative way would be to issue more global commands from the top. There are costs associated with both these strategies. Expanding the hierarchy leads to longer delays in the system, while more global commands may result in longer implementation times because the translation of these global commands into appropriate actions will be more difficult and will demand more time. Moreover, this strategy would presumably lead to horizontal expansion at the lower levels to handle the greater number of tasks implied by the more global commands. This would, in turn, create new managerial levels in the hierarchy. In short, it is not possible to escape from the conclusions from Ashby's law of requisite variety that more complex problems will require more complex control structures. That is, there is no hope for less bureaucracy, unless we ask the bureaucracy to do less.

At least in civilian systems, both tendencies described above are observed at different times, with a dialectical interplay between increasing centralization and decentralization. However, there never seems to be a substantial reduction in bureaucracy. Nor should we expect such a reduction, unless the tasks with which the bureaucracy is charged are made less complex.

Only a historical study of such systems would reveal whether there has ever been any kind of stable equilibrium with a well-functioning hierarchical system. In a changing environment, no such equilibrium is likely to be found. One of the factors currently destabilizing hierarchical systems is modern information technology. We now turn to this problem.

New technology and hierarchical systems

Because the decision makers at the higher levels in a hierarchical system are removed from the actual events they are seeking to control, and because they are likely to have very little information about what actually takes place at the lower levels, they are likely to experience undue delays in the execution of their commands by the lower levels and in the information they receive from these levels.

Because the higher levels are likely to feel that they are never getting enough information or are not getting it fast enough, they are likely to see modern information technology as an answer to problems that are important to them. But although modern information technology offers a number of new possibilities here, it is not self-evident that it will have only beneficial effects. Indeed, the new information technology constitutes a threat to the very hierarchical structure. Specifically, it creates problems of mismatches in the response times at the different levels in the hierarchy, and of information overload. We will discuss each in turn.

Response times

Information technology in the form of modern computers makes it possible to collect and transmit great amounts of data at a rapid rate. It thus becomes possible for the higher levels in a hierarchy to obtain a very detailed picture of the state of the lower levels, and to use this information for issuing very detailed orders to these levels. In the extreme case, this would seem to make it possible to abolish the hierarchy altogether, and to control each unit at the lowest level centrally. This should have significant effects upon response times of the system, for there would be no delays in information transmission or in the transmission of orders. This is highly desirable in the military system because other forms of technology in that system (e.g. new methods of weapons delivery and of transporting troops) have cut down the execution times for orders, and have created a need for faster information processing at the higher levels.

Assuming that such a system would be technically feasible, we face the interesting problem of what the program in this computer would be like. Such a program would, of course, reflect our understanding of the task facing the system. That is, it would reflect our hierarchical conceptual understanding; there is simply no alternative to this concept at present. This means that the program would have to perform the translation from one conceptual level to another in this hierarchy to process the information it collects, and to execute the commands it would issue.

However, as we have already noted, the number and nature of the levels in a hierarchy is somewhat arbitrary, and the relation between levels is not one of derivation. That is, there are no algorithms for translating information from one level to another, or for deriving orders at a given level from the goals that are being transmitted from above. Consequently, the primary problem here is not one of programming but of finding out how the information in the system is interpreted. This requires that the program models the understanding of the people in the system being computerized. The system would thus have to be a so-called expert system that simulates the cognitive activities of the commanders at different levels. Whether such an expert system could be constructed is an open question at present.

If such a system could be constructed there would be a price to pay. Planning times at the top of the hierarchy would be reduced as the processing at the lower levels became faster and the number of levels in the hierarchy decreased. Consequently, something would have to be done at the higher levels also.

Of course, the problem of processing information fast enough is not new to the military system. It exists also with more traditional forms of information technology. Historically, the military system has tried to solve this problem by trying to introduce feedforward control, rather than feedback control. That is, command decisions at the top level involve developing a plan and then this plan is carried out, no matter what the consequences are. We do not have to imagine what such consequences would be; military history is replete with examples. That the procedure has not been abandoned, despite spectacular failures, illustrates that there is no alternative, given the nature of the information and control system. Modern information technology would only accentuate the problem. Considering the characteristics of modern weapons technology, the prospects seem rather bleak, to say the least, and it is doubtful whether the kind of control structure represented by the traditional hierarchical system is functional in the present circumstances.

Using information technology to speed up processing at the lower levels of a hierarchical system is thus no solution to the problems of information and control. To use such technology at the higher levels is equally problematic, for it might lead to commands being issued at a higher rate than could possibly be executed by the lower levels. This might easily bring the system to a standstill.

The introduction of information technology at one level which leads to faster processing at that level will therefore create a need for redesigning the system as a whole. It is an important task for the art of systems design to find methods for evaluating the effects of information technology and to redesign the systems as new technology is introduced.

Information overload

As noted, different levels in the hierarchy differ with respect to abstraction, higher levels being more abstract. The information needed for decisions at the higher levels in the hierarchy therefore needs to be different from that at the lower levels, and the representation of a system at a given level must be appropriate to that level.

This leads to the important question of what the relation between a more abstract level and a more practical level could be. As noted above, the relation between levels in a hierarchy is arbitrary, and so is that between a more abstract level of representation and a less abstract one. What is considered more abstract is the result of a more or less conscious decision to consider one aspect of the information available, rather than some other aspect. This means that although it may be possible to derive the more concrete representation from the more abstract representation, the converse does not hold.

This is an important obstacle to the creation of a useful information system that would collect information from lower levels in a hierarchical system for use at a higher level. Moreover, it is a problem that is often not solved in management information systems. Instead of transforming the information collected in useful ways for decision making at higher levels, the system often simply presents more information, and information that is appropriate to lower levels in the hierarchy rather than to the higher levels. Such systems create problems of information overload, without actually helping the decision makers at the higher levels of the hierarchy.

These information systems, therefore, need to be expert systems that perform some of the creative acts of abstraction in producing the information needed for the higher levels of the hierarchy.

The problem of incomplete modelling

As noted above, the conclusion from the argument by Conant and Ashby (1970) is that a control system must be a model of the system it seeks to control. A hierarchical control structure is, however, only a limited model of the system with which it is charged. It has a bottom level. This is the level where the environment of the system makes some significant impact on the system. That is, at this level, the behaviour of the units is not only a function of the commands arriving from above, it is also affected by the environment. At this level part of the control is transferred to the units.

In the case of a military system, the bottom level consists of individual soldiers. In battle, the soldiers will not only respond to commands, they will also be reacting to a changing environment. In so far as what happens in this environment has not been foreseen by the higher levels, control is transferred to the soldiers, and the system takes on a self-organizing character. This is why commanders at the higher levels in the hierarchy await news from the lower levels with such anxiety, for in the actual battle, control has often slipped from their hands.

Every command and control system will have such a lower level which is imperfectly modelled in the system. However, the designers of the system may have misjudged where the bottom level is, and they may have created a hierarchical system which seeks to control levels that are so imperfectly modelled that the system will not function. Systems for emergency management seem to have this property.

EMERGENCY MANAGEMENT: A QUASI-HIERARCHICAL SYSTEM

The military and civilian bureaucracies exist in stable forms to cope with a set of more or less well-defined problems. Systems for emergency management, on the other hand, are created *ad hoc* to cope with problems as they occur, and involve the creation of a temporary system of information and control, using the resources society can provide. Such systems offer a number of unique problems, and there is no guarantee that it will be possible to create a system where the conceptual analysis of the system, its organization and the flows of information and control will be in harmony as they are in the more stable military systems. Moreover, it is not clear that it will be possible to find a control variable which can be analyzed at different levels, comparable to that of area in the military system, or an organization of the actual system of information and control that is congruent with the levels of the control variable. That is, as we move up the hierarchy in the emergency management system, it is not only the case that we become concerned with increasingly greater catastrophes; we also become involved with qualitatively different decisions.

Emergencies will differ with respect to the extent to which they can be modelled and controlled by a hierarchical system. If there were a major earthquake in Uppsala tomorrow, something that has never occurred before, the existing emergency system would presumably not be very effective in dealing with that problem, but would need to reorganize from the top. If, on the other hand, a house was on fire, the emergency system would work quite well, and no reorganization would be needed. While both these emergencies involve unforeseen events, the unforeseen events in the earthquake example concern the highest levels of the system, while the unforeseen events in the example of the house on fire will be found in the lowest level in the emergency system for fires, and thus no reorganization is needed.

It is interesting to note that exercises involving hierarchically organized systems generally relate only to those aspects of the system that can be modelled hierarchically. This is true both for military systems and for emergency management systems. Thus, there are more staff exercises and war games than full-scale manoeuvres, and there are many exercises involving the higher levels in the emergency management systems than those involving the general public. For example, in the Swedish system for managing nuclear emergencies there are regular exercises for the County Emergency Centres, but none involving the public. This is likely to create an exaggerated faith in the capabilities of the existing hierarchical control system.

The capacity to reorganize as the need arises must be an important aspect of emergency systems, and we cannot expect that this reorganization can take place top-down, for the entire existing system may be inappropriate and there may be no top level capable of carrying out the reorganization. Moreover, there may simply not be time to carry out the reorganization required for a functioning hierarchical system. To further complicate matters, the design of functioning hierarchical system involves a number of delicate problems, as noted above, and there is no guarantee that a good system will be found under circumstances that change rapidly, as they are likely to do in an emergency.

The discussion above may lead to despair, but this would be misplaced. The results from studies of actual emergencies suggest that there may not be a need for a hierarchical system (e.g. Dynes, 1983). The basic assumption behind the felt need for a hierarchical command and control system is, of course, that the emergency creates total disruption, so that a command and control system is needed to create some order, and to get the social system going again. In fact, the results from studies of emergencies suggest that there is no general disruption, and that major parts of the social system go on functioning in very much the same way as they did before the emergency (Dynes, 1983). That is, there is no need to create a new system, but there may be a need to coordinate existing resources in the system, one that will have strong self-organizing properties. This is a problem very much different from that for which the military kind of command and control system was designed. The military system is one which imposes structure, but the social system presumably already has a structure, and will resist the attempts of the hierarchical command and control system to impose another.

The problem for emergency management, then, is to design a system that could aid the processes of coordination and self-organization, rather than one for creating a new structure. This is a problem that has received very little attention from researchers so far, and it is not clear how such a system should be designed, what sort of information it would need, or what decision aids will prove useful. To investigate these problems is an urgent task for future research in the area of emergency management.

NOTES

[1] This chapter originally appeared in *Tasks, Errors and Mental Models*, edited by L. P. Goodstein, H. B. Anderson, and S. E. Olsen, 1988, Taylor & Francis, London, and is reprinted by permission of the original publishers.

[2] This is one of a series of a papers from ongoing research on the application of modern information technology to emergency management (NKA/INF 620) in which the present author and Jens Rasmussen cooperate. Although this chapter has no direct references to Rasmussen's work, discussions between the author and Jens Rasmussen have been important in shaping the ideas expressed here.

Work on this chapter was supported by a grant from the Nordic Council of Ministers for Project NKA/INF 620.

Address for Correspondence:

Professor Berndt Brehmer, Uppsala Universitet, Dept of Psychology, Box 1854, S-751 48 Uppsala, Sweden.

REFERENCES

Ashby, W. R. (1956) *Introduction to Cybernetics.* London: Hutchinson.

Conant, R. C., and Ashby, W. R. (1970) Every good regulator of a system must be a model of that system. *International Journal of Systems Science*, **1**, 89–97.

Dynes, R. R. (1983) Problems in emergency planning. *Energy*, **8**, 653–60.

18. The Investigation of Action Regulation in Uncertain and Complex Situations

Dietrich Dörner
Max Planck-Projekt Gruppe, FRG

In this chapter we investigate how individuals behave while dealing with uncertainty and complexity. This means researching how humans behave in dynamic situations about which they are not fully knowledgeable, which exert time pressure since they are constantly developing, which are too complex to be grasped completely and, finally, for which the goals for action are frequently unclear and not very extensively specified. In order to examine the manner in which humans cope with such situations we use various computer-simulated scenarios. We use, for example, simulated models of industrial companies, of political situations in Third World countries, models for the local government politics of a small town, ecological situations, etc. We try to work with a variety of simulated models so that as many different requirement profiles of such situations as possible can be investigated with regard to their effects on human actors.

The challenges presented by situations of this kind can be detailed as follows:

(1) The subjects have both to specify goal criteria which are, for the most part, unclear and poorly defined and to recognize and balance out contradictions among partial goals.
(2) The subjects have to complete their incomplete knowledge of the system in question by constructing a model of the reality segment in question, trying at the same time to visualize the situation by asking questions and collecting information. Most of the time this will not be possible in any complete sense, and for this reason the subjects must try to expand and refine the given stock of information by means of inferences. The same holds for the future state of the system in question. In making their plans and decisions, the subjects must, of course, take into account the future state of the system. To this end, they must try to predict and, in planning and making their decisions, to bear

Distributed Decision Making: Cognitive Models for Cooperative Work
Edited by J. Rasmussen, B. Brehmer and J. Leplat

in mind the course of developments, doing so on the basis both of the situation and of the established model of the system.

(3) In order to attain their goals, the subjects must put together paths of action, to analyze these with regard to long-term and side effects, to change courses of action and to translate their plans into action. Here the problem often arises that not all problems can be solved simultaneously, and that instead, areas of concentration, or focal points, must be formed.

(4) After making the decision for a particular course of action, the subjects must monitor the effects of their action, checking at the same time whether the prognoses they have made turn out to be true. If these checks show negative results, that is, if the effects of action are not those expected, or if events other than had been predicted occur, then the subjects must examine their own behavior critically. They must analyze the extent to which they made errors in forming goals, in collecting information or in planning action, as the case may be. In doing this, they must not only investigate whether, possibly on the basis of incorrect information, they have planned wrongly or have gathered the incorrect information, but, over and above this, they must subject even their own strategies of goal formation, of gathering information and of planning to critical analysis. On the basis of a self-reflexive analysis of this kind, the subjects may be obliged to reprogram their own self-organization.

We are not only interested in how subjects manage the requirements mentioned above. We are also concerned with how they coordinate the various activities which arise in the context of dealing with the demands of uncertain and complex situations. Typically, the course of finding decisions in a complex situation is not at all characterized by an 'orderly' sequence of the form 'goal formation–attaining information–prognosis–planning action–checking effects–self-organization'. Their behavior appears to be rather more chaotic.

The main purpose of our investigations is to draw up a general theory of human action regulation. Figure 1 shows the outline of one such model. Our ideas about a theory for explaining human action regulation at the moment comprise a system which consists of four information-processing units (GENINT, SELECTINT, RUNINT, HYPERCEPT in Figure 1).

GENINT generates intentions, and in doing so creates a data structure (Memint in Figure 1). Generally, intentions are goals plus plans. The goal state of an intention is related to the repair of a discrepancy between the momentarily given value of a variable and the set point of that variable.

SELECTINT selects one of the intentions to be run by RUNINT.

RUNINT runs an intention either by starting an automatic sequence of behavioral steps, if such a sequence exists in the memory of 'reality models' of the system or by constructing such a sequence if it does not exist, i.e. by problem-solving processes.

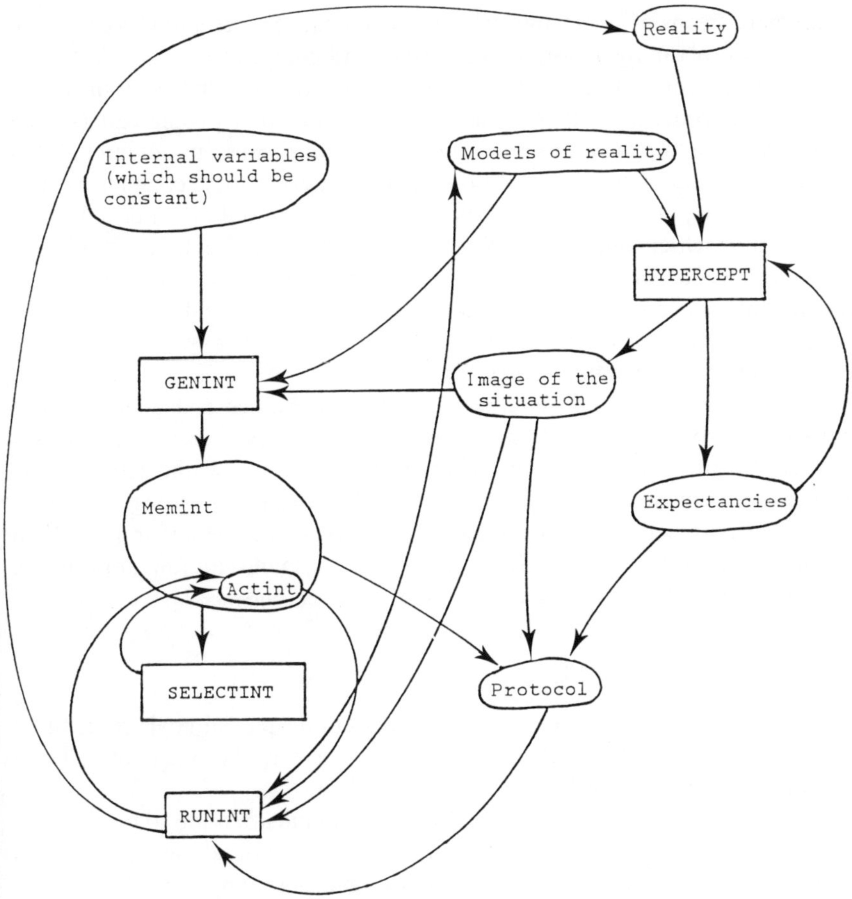

Figure 1

HYPERCEPT provides an 'image of the environment' for the system and produces a 'horizon of expectancies' for the planning and decision-making activities of RUNINT.

This is a sketchy outline of a model of the human 'action-regulating system'. At present we are implementing the system as a computer model and are conducting experiments to test the predictive power of the model for human behavior.

Our research efforts are primarily aimed at further developing theoretical psychology. Apart from this, we are striving for a practical application of our results in two respects. First, we are of the opinion that training methods for dealing with uncertainty and complexity can be developed on the basis of our results. Second, we believe that the simulated games we use may prove useful as a diagnostic means of ascertaining the particular capabilities and weaknesses of persons when planning action in uncertainty and complexity.

Our present conception of effective behavioral training in uncertainty and complexity appears such that it leads us to believe that people can best be trained by subjecting them to a multitude of situations and scenarios, and that in this way one can diagnose their action errors, analyzing these errors as well as the backgrounds and possible remedies. The subjects should then be subjected once again to self-encounter (in simulation experiments). We do not think that conveying *general* strategies of acting in complex and uncertain situations is very helpful. It is a question of proceeding in small steps and of analyzing in detail which action errors this or that person makes and what the psychological backgrounds of these action errors are.

We do not so much base diagnosis of the capabilities and deficiencies of individual persons in dealing with uncertainty and complexity on the successes or failures of behavior in a complex situation, but rather on the action errors which a subject makes in a particular situation. For this reason, we endeavour to draw up as complete a list as possible of the action and behavioral errors in complicated situations, using these as the background for an appropriate diagnosis. A list of such action errors might look as follows.

ERRORS IN GOAL FORMATION

(1) The deficient decomposition of a global goal into partial goals results in a 'repair service mode of behavior', or in *ad-hoc*ism, as the case may be, i.e. in reacting to immediate deficiencies.

(2) Deficient goal balancing (that is, not giving enough attention to the fact that partial goals may contradict one another) results in not taking the long-term and side effects of one's own actions into consideration.

(3) Deficient explication of 'implicit' goals (that is, not enough consideration is given to the fact that, in a complex situation, it is a question of keeping the 'good' states good). This usually leads to deficient goal balancing, to an insufficient consideration of the contradictory relation obtaining between various partial goals.

(4) Formation of areas of concentration and goal selection according to their obviousness and to competence. This arises as a consequence of the deficient decomposition of a complex goal. One does not solve the problems which *are supposed* to be solved but those which one *can* solve or those which are especially conspicuous.

ERRORS IN GATHERING, INTEGRATING AND ELABORATING INFORMATION

(1) No explication of the reality model is used; the implicit model is thus 'absolutely set'. This often results immediately in a 'dogmatic entrench-

ment'. Due to fear and insecurity, contradictions appearing between the implicit model and what is actually happening in reality are denied, not recognized, interpreted into insignificance or repressed. A dogmatic entrenchment can also result in no further information being looked for, since the subject thinks it already possesses the data in question.

(2) 'Incomplete' conclusions in elaborating data. Among these errors are included a great number of cognitive errors; subjects do not use the available stock of information completely, thereby arriving at erroneous conclusions. This leads to linear extrapolations for growth processes which actually run exponentially and also results in errors of the kind named 'availability heuristics' and 'representativity heuristics' by Kahneman and Tversky (1982) as well as in 'base rate fallacies'.

(3) Hypothesis formation by means of 'central reduction'. All phenomena of a particular segment of reality are reduced to *one* cause: over-generalization of single findings and single correlations.

(4) Formation of hypotheses on 'magical' forces. (This form of hypothesis formation is a special kind of central reduction.)

ERRORS IN PLANNING STEPS FOR ACTION

(1) Not considering long-term and side effects.

(2) Not including frictions in calculations (that is, not including the many minor frictions and incidents).

(3) Replacing steps for action by naming goals ('The production should rise by 50%!').

(4) 'Vertical' or 'horizontal' escape ('project making', planning with 'unreal' steps of action, encapsulation).

(5) Methodism (that is, unreflected replication of courses of action which have at one time or another proved successful).

(6) Assuming a linear correlation between the step of an action and the effect ('a lot helps a lot').

ERRORS IN DECIDING AND IN CHECKING EFFECTS

(1) 'Ballistic' steps of action (the effects of steps of action are no longer checked: by merely taking a step, the problem is regarded as solved).

(2) Actionism ('doing' without planning).

(3) 'Total planning' (the subject no longer relies on the planning stage; when asked, they justify this by indicating that everything has first to be precisely analyzed and checked before one might be in a position to make any decisions).

(4) Acting without checking the background (it is no longer taken into consideration that even the variables which may at first be in a good state might possibly change into a poor one).

(5) Progressive conditionalizing (this is an error concerning the management of hypotheses). Instead of discarding a hypothesis once it has been proved to be erroneous, very specific reasons are given for the hypothesis not having worked *in this case*, although generally it remains valid. This method ensures that hypotheses can maintain their validity for an indefinite period of time.
(6) No self-check or self-reflection; one's own strategies and ways of acting are not regarded self-critically.

All the various cognitive errors enumerated here can be traced back to a few causes. One cause is the limited capacity of conscious human information processing resulting in humans' having, when in complex situations, a strong tendency to utilize strategies which strain their cognitive capacity to the least extent possible. This is, for instance, how 'incomplete' conclusion procedures, abandoning checks and, generally excluding cognitive steps which are really necessary arise.

A second source of errors is the high tendency of humans, in every case, to retain something like a feeling of competence in acting in a situation of uncertainty and complexity. For the purpose of ensuring one's own self-esteem, for the purpose of ensuring one's own image of competence in acting, obtaining negative signals and, generally, also everything which could endanger one's own self-image is eliminated.

Another source of errors could be the human tendency to think abstractly. The low incidence of converting abstract, extremely general schemata into ideas of concrete situations results in 'overinclusive' thinking, which does not include the frictions of the respective situation and the specifics in its generality. (The poor ability of humans to render abstract concepts into images—their weak 'powers of imagination'—could be of great significance here.)

Address for Correspondence:

Professor Dietrich Dörner, Max Planck-Projekt Gruppe, Kognitive Anthropologie, Frauenstrasse 6, D-1000 Berlin 45, FRG.

Section 6

Simulation of Decision Processes

This section presents an approach to formalization of decision-making models in the frame of artificial intelligence tools such as knowledge-based systems and object-oriented languages. Lind attempts to formalize a decision-making model into a rational, normative framework that can be made consistent, and therefore is well suited to serve as a basis for simulation experiments. When the model has been tested for internal completeness and consistency, it will be possible to introduce perturbations in the model structure representing 'error mechanisms' and, in this way, to adapt the model's performance to match actual, real-life performance. This approach requires first a normative model of decision making, as described by Lind.

19. Decision Models and the Design of Knowledge-based Systems

Morten Lind
Technical University of Denmark, Denmark

BACKGROUND

The work reported in this chapter is part of an effort to apply systematic approaches to the design of a knowledge-based system (KBS) for realistic (i.e. usually complex) domains. In most cases, KBSs are developed with a strong orientation towards analysing the domain in terms of the mechanisms supported by existing programming paradigms. The dangers of this tool-oriented approach is that the system designer is not encouraged to analyse and specify the task to be solved in a way independent of the actual implementation. As a result, the process of acquiring knowledge from the expert becomes very difficult and may even be inadequate. Another result may be lack of transparency of the final KBS architecture.

Top-down methods has gained a certain popularity for the development of traditional software, and the question is whether a similar approach is possible for KBS design. By adopting a top-down approach to the KBS design problem we need concepts which are suitable for the specification of KBS functions. We have considered the use of decision or task models of the type described by Rasmussen (1986), Breuker and Wielinga (1985) and Kepner and Tregoe (1960) as possible candidates for guiding the development of KBSs. We will select the decision model developed by Rasmussen as the basis for our discussion. The model is shown in Figure 1, and it is assumed that the reader is acquainted with it.

Decision models are interesting because they are very general and informative and apply on many task levels. Generality is a desirable feature but it creates problems when the models are applied in KBS design because the task context should be precisely defined. Most people would intuitively understand the meaning of a decision model like that presented in Figure 1 because it has so

Distributed Decision Making: Cognitive Models for Cooperative Work
Edited by J. Rasmussen, B. Brehmer and J. Leplat

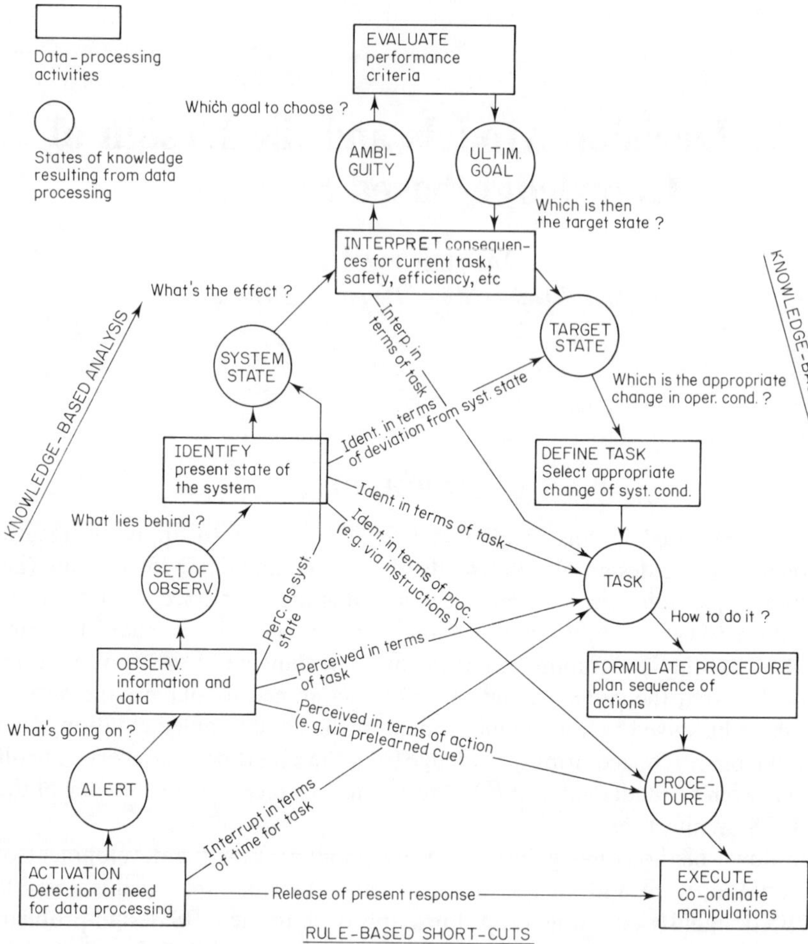

Figure 1. The decision model (Rasmussen, 1986; reproduced by permission)

many possible interpretations. However, this makes it difficult to distinguish what is actually represented in the model and what is inferred or implied by a person looking at it.

We have attempted to use Rasmussen's decision model as a design tool in the development of a KBS for diagnosis of a process plant. In this study, we considered the decision model as representing control knowledge which could be used by the KBS if properly identified and formalized. The diagnosis system is based on the use of multilevel flow models (Lind, 1990b) of the process plant to be diagnosed (Lind, 1982; 1988) and requires a fairly elaborate control structure to guide the problem-solving processes. Concepts which could aid in the specification of control structures would be very useful for this design task.

As part of this work, we have identified some inherent ambiguities in the decision model shown in Figure 1. An analysis of the problems encountered has led to the identification of some fundamental problems with the decision model. These problems should be solved if the model were to be used as a formal tool for specification of control structure and KBS functions. It is one of the aims of this chapter to describe these problems for later clarification.

THE DECISION MODEL

The decision model defines a framework for the planning of different problem-solving activities in a KBS for dealing with systems diagnosis and control. Initially, the model was developed for describing problem solving of operators in process plant control rooms. However, as shown in this chapter, it can also be used as a useful conceptual tool in the design of advanced KBS architectures. In such an application it is utilized as a normative model, i.e. for prescribing the functional structure of the system. The decision tasks included in the model are included in the taxonomy of expert tasks presented by Stefik (1982). The model in Figure 1 shows how these tasks can be considered as subtasks in systems control and how they relate to each other.

A unique feature of Rasmussen's model is the distinction between so-called knowledge-based problem solving corresponding to the use of deep knowledge of the system in diagnosis or planning and the use of rule-based problem solving based on shallow knowledge. In this way, it makes a distinction between the way a novice would solve a problem (by reasoning through a rational sequence using deep knowledge) and how an expert would short-cut the rational sequence. By integrating these different types of problem solving into one framework the decision model may be used for planning the use of different types of knowledge in problem solving.

We will use the model mainly for discussing decision making in diagnosis and control of a system. The decision tasks relate accordingly to the environment of the decision agent (human operator or KBS). However, another interpretation of the decision model is possible which relates to the description of the decision processes going on internally in the computer. That is, it describes how the KBS inference machine manipulates symbol structures representing domain knowledge in the knowledge base. The two interpretations are related by the way domain knowledge is represented in terms of knowledge representation formalisms. These relations will not be considered here.

HOW CAN THE DECISION MODEL BE USED IN KBS DESIGN?

The decision model can be used in two ways for the design of KBSs. It can be employed normatively as a conceptual framework for specifying the tasks to be done by the KBS or it can be used descriptively for the interpretation of human problem-solving performance.

When using the decision model as a normative one it is employed to specify the tasks involved and the relations between tasks via states of knowledge. This can be considered as a high-level informal specification which can guide the further development of the system. However, if the model is formalized (which is the core topic of this chapter) it can be used as knowledge represented explicitly in the KBS and for controlling the problem solving.

The use of decision models or similar models representing task networks for interpretation of human problem-solving performance has been described by, for example, Breuker and Wielinga (1985). They consider the use of so-called interpretation models similar to the decision model for the analysis of verbal data as part of the process of knowledge acquisition.

DECISION TASKS AND INFORMATION PROCESSES

In the following we will mainly deal with the decision tasks on an abstract level and will consider the decision model as describing a network of tasks related by knowledge states. However, although we consider each task as an abstract entity, we will mention briefly how a task relates to the actual information processes which are required to solve the task. The basis for solving a task is knowledge about the system controlled (be it a physical system such as a process plant or a symbol manipulation system). Each decision task can, in general, be performed by using many different categories of knowledge and they may be implemented as KBSs. A KBS for solving a specific task in the model can, accordingly, be considered as a resource which is available for achieving the task in question and the choice between information processes as a resource-allocation problem. Rasmussen (1986) discusses different strategies for diagnosing system faults based on different types of knowledge of the system diagnosed. These strategies define different information processes with different requirements to information about the plant and processor resources (e.g. memory size and complexity of inferences).

WHAT DOES THE DECISION MODEL REPRESENT?

Although the decision model is very helpful and would provide a useful tool for the design of knowledge-based systems it is not directly suitable for this purpose in its present form. The problem is that many important aspects are left unspecified or implicit. In the following we will analyze the decision model with the aim of uncovering this implicit information. The analysis is a step towards the formalization of the model. Only when the model is formalized can it serve as a tool for KBS design.

There are two main aspects of the decision model which we will discuss. First, the model does not describe fully the information flow in decision making but only the flow of control from one task to the other. As an example, we could mention that the 'DEFINE TASK' subtask requires both the system state and the target state as input information (see Figure 2). This fact does not appear explicitly in the figure, although it is implicitly assumed. It is not made explicit that each decision task in the general case can be based on all plant data for both measured or computed values of the plant parameters available or models of plant structure and function. This fact does not appear in Figure 1, and the

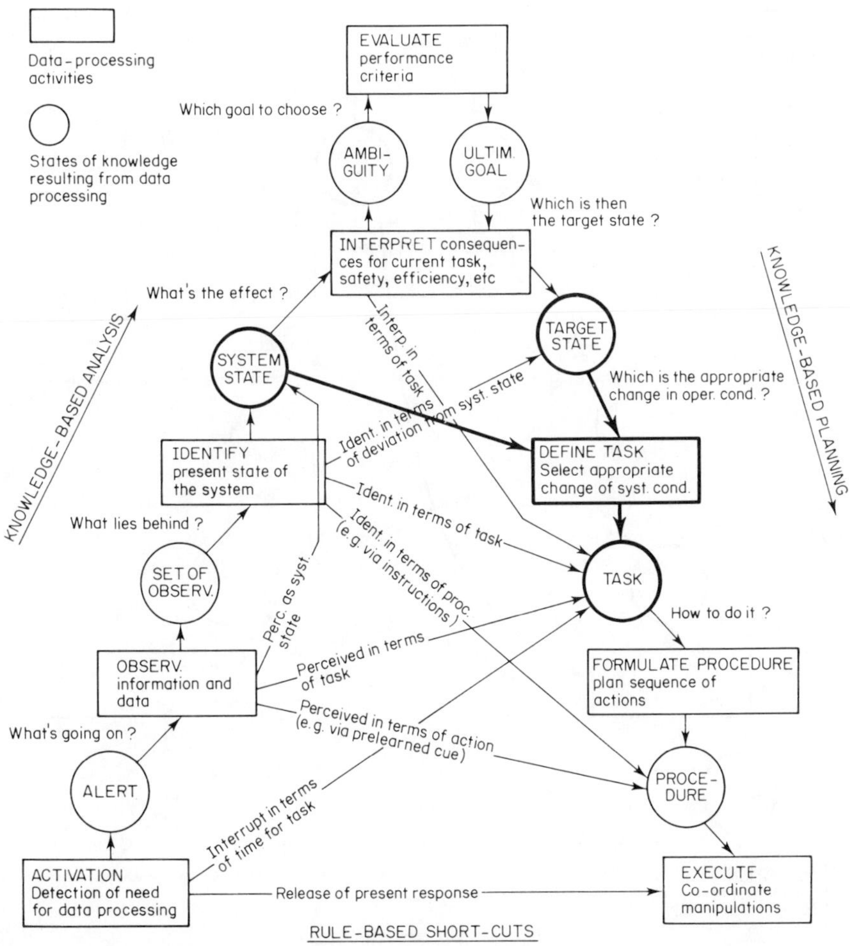

Figure 2. The definition of task is dependent on system state. The dependence is shown as an additional link

knowledge states in the model correspond therefore to different stages of elaboration of the plant information. Each knowledge state represents new information created by performing the previous decision task. Another example illustrating the same problem is due to the inherent circularity of the diagnostic process (Lind, 1984). The circularity occurs because it is necessary to know the goal (protect system, protect operation or locate fault) before a proper level of state identification can be performed. On the other hand, the goal can be chosen only when the system state is known. This means that the goal (which is one of the knowledge states on the top of the decision model) may provide information

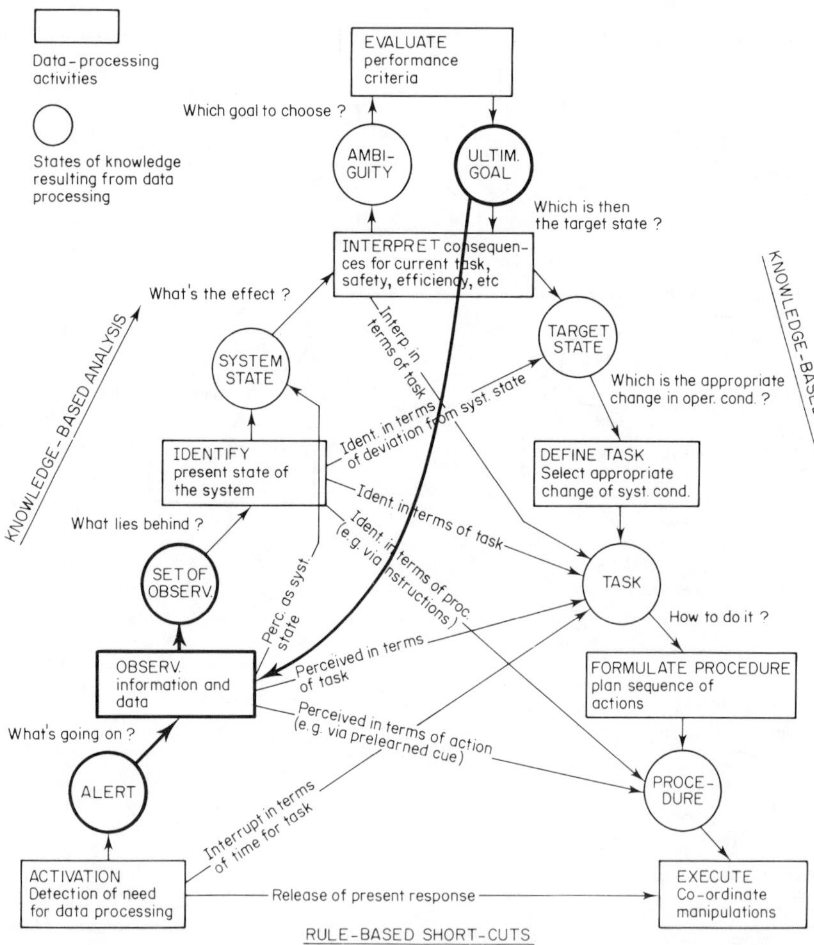

Figure 3. The observation task depends on the goal chosen. The dependence is shown as an additional link

for the observation or identification tasks (see Figure 3). These dependencies are not made explicit in the present form of the model.

Second, it should be noted that the knowledge which provides the basis for the decisions made in a given task changes with time. This is obviously the case when the state of the plant controls this change. However, it is more important to realize that the result of a decision task may also depend on the state of the decision-making processes themselves. Thus, if the same type of decision task is performed several times within a longer task sequence (e.g. in a diagnosis–planning–execution–diagnosis cycle) the information processes involved may be different at the various steps. Another way to state this fact is that a decision maker may choose the information-processing strategies on the basis of the current knowledge acquired. A method of coping with this aspect in a formalized way is to consider each decision task in the model as a task category or class that has different instantiations (corresponding to different information processes) which applies for different kinds of knowledge available.

The distinction between rule- and knowledge-based decision making deals with a part of the problem mentioned above, but it does not take into account that there may be different 'shallow and deep' decision processes which can be applied under different conditions of knowledge available. The problem can be described in general terms as a lack of means to represent the flow of data or information during problem solving. This deficiency makes it impossible to describe the dynamic aspects of decision making described above.

However, we need to consider another dynamic aspect of the decision processes. This deals with the problems occurring when a decision task cannot be completed due to lack of sufficient information or decision criteria. This is illustrated below by a small scenario describing a simple diagnostic process:

> *Example scenario*:
> We assume that the initial situation in the diagnosis is that the decision maker is waiting to be alerted by plant signals indicating that the plant is disturbed and a diagnosis of plant state is required. When alerted, the decision maker begins to observe plant parameters. After the collection of a set of observations has been completed plant data are interpreted in order to identify the system state. Up to this stage the sequence of tasks performed fits well into the sequence prescribed by the decision model on the left branch. However, as the interpretation of plant state is ambiguous (as would be the case when multiple competing fault hypotheses has been generated), the decision maker collects more plant data in order to be able to discard one or several hypotheses.

It is realized that in this case the control flow reverses, and it is determined by the actual problem-solving state inside the interpretation box. The fact that it was impossible to distinguish between two hypotheses makes the decision maker collect more observations (i.e. to initiate a task which is not in the direct sequence described by the decision model). We can therefore conclude from this example that a problem occurring inside one of the boxes will invalidate the sequence prescribed by the decision model in Figure 1. The sequence described by the decision model presumes that the tasks are solved, so there is no need to change the control flow.

THE DECISION MODEL REPRESENTS A PROBLEM SPACE FOR DECISION PLANNING

The first step in solving the problems with control flow in the decision model is to declare that the model does not prescribe a unique sequence of tasks but represents the problem space for planning of task sequences. This means that the model does not imply in itself any specific ordering in time but describes only the logical dependencies of the individual tasks involved. However, removing the sequence information does not solve our problem directly: it only makes it possible to reformulate the task-sequencing problem as a planning one. Before we examine this decision-planning problem we will explore the consequences of considering the model as a problem space for decision planning. We will study the left branch of the decision model in Figure 1, i.e. the tasks involved in diagnosis.

There may be several alternative ways of carrying out state identification using deep knowledge of the system structure and function or shallow knowledge such as fault symptom–cause pairs. This means that we can expand the decision model (the part we consider for the present purpose) by decomposing the individual tasks, as shown below. The tasks may be distributed among separate problem solvers (KBSs). In Figure 4 we have decomposed the identification task into three subtasks. Each subtask produces one or several state hypotheses and the SELECT task deduces the system state from these hypotheses using knowledge about the relations between the IDENTIFY subtasks. The observation task may also be decomposed into several tasks if the individual identification tasks are based on different sets of observations. In this case we obtain the structure depicted in Figure 5.

DECISION PLANNING

The task network can be used to plan the execution of the individual tasks, as it describes how the different states of knowledge are connected via decision tasks. Assume, for example, that observed (measured) plant data are given. Then we can plan a sequence of tasks which may lead to a goal state where the state of the system diagnosed is known (the top nodes in Figures 4 and 5). The plan (sequence of tasks) is generated by finding the path(s) which lead from the initial node to the goal node (forward reasoning in the task network). However, more elaborate structures may be used which apply a combination of forward and backward driven reasoning in the task network. The top node may be taken as the goal node and the possible plans may be generated by backward reasoning.

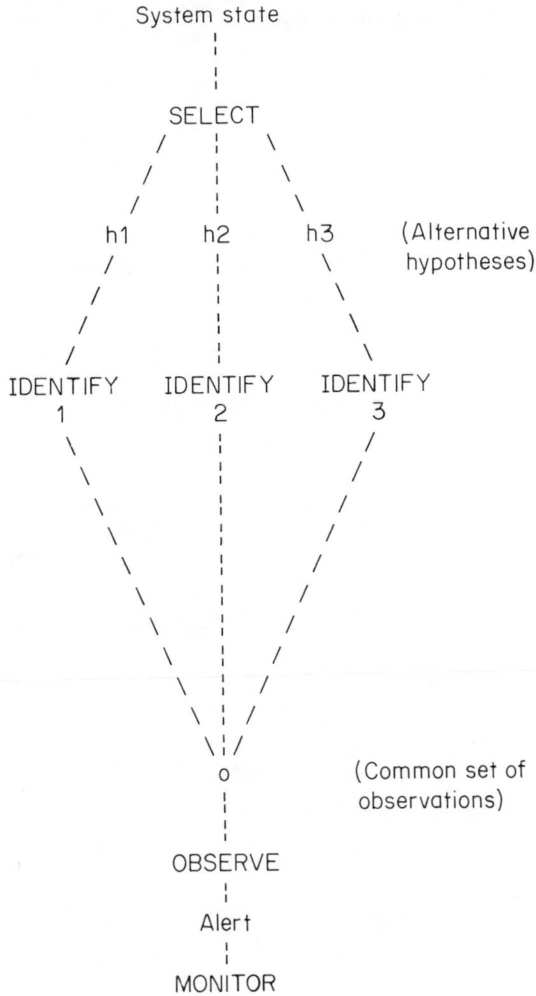

Figure 4. A decision network with three identification tasks

The two cases correspond to two different ways of controlling the decision processes. In the first case it is data driven and in the second it is goal driven, leading to two possible architectures for implementation of the expert system.

There may be tasks which relate states with observations such as a verification task which, from a hypothesis about the system state, can produce the observations necessary for hypothesizing the given system state.

We can consider the planning of the execution of decision tasks as a meta-level decision problem. This means that we can apply the decision model again, but we need to define a new context in which the decision planning can be

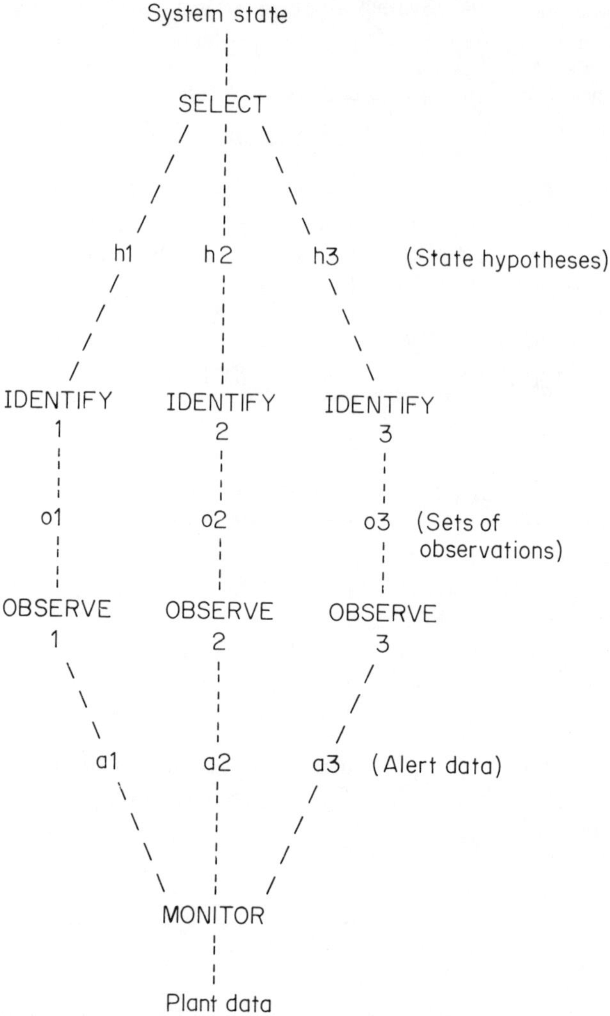

Figure 5. A task network with three identification and observation tasks

formulated. This context is defined by the decision model being considered as a task network. In this context, 'system state' will represent the states of knowledge reached on the base level (i.e. how far the base level decisions have reached) and plans and actions will relate to base-level decision task sequences which have been selected by the (meta-level) decision maker in order to change the state of the base-level decision process. Accordingly, the meta-level decision processes may include both diagnostics and planning functions. When a problem occurs in one of the information processes on the base level, a shift may be made to the planning (meta) level to evaluate the possible actions to be taken.

We can summarize the description of meta-level decision making in terms of three questions which can be made about problem solving on this level:

(1) Where am I (what is known at the base level)?
(2) What are the goals (what is the current knowledge state to be achieved on base level)?
(3) What are the options (what base-level information processes are available)?

THE DECISION MODEL AND THE CONTROL CYCLE OF AI PROGRAMS

In the analysis of the decision model we have up to now been concentrating on decision planning as seen from the point of view of the external task. We have indirectly assumed that the task was related to the diagnosis and control of a system in the environment of the KBS or the decision maker. However, we can also apply the decision model for describing the internal operations of the computer. Adopting this view, we consider the decision tasks as related to the manipulation of the symbol structures in the computer's memory.

This interpretation of the decision model is interesting, because the control cycle of production systems (and basically of all AI programs, according to Nilsson, 1979), can be mapped directly into the decision model as a specific choice of sequence of tasks and intermediate knowledge states (see Figures 6 and

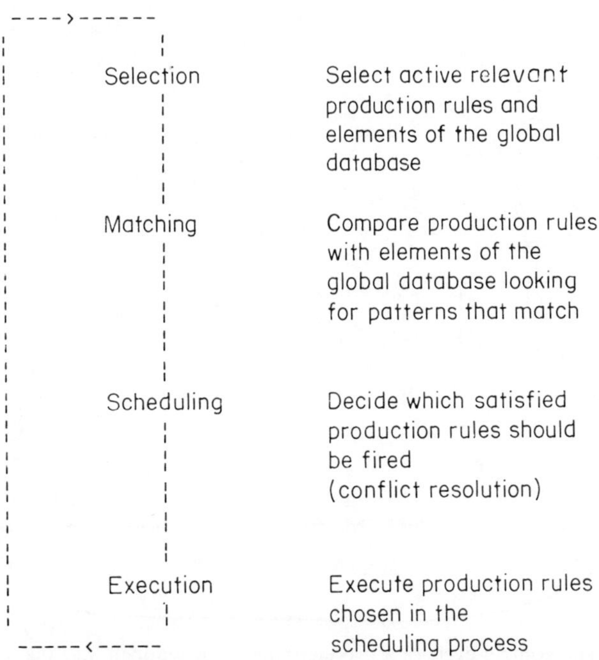

Figure 6. The control cycle of a production system

7). This is presumably not a coincidence, and raises some interesting questions related to the conceptual basis of the production system cycle or to the origin of the decision model.

CONCLUSIONS

In this chapter we have analyzed a specific decision model from the point of view of KBS design. We have identified some problems of what the decision model actually represents, as it only implicitly deals with control and information flow.

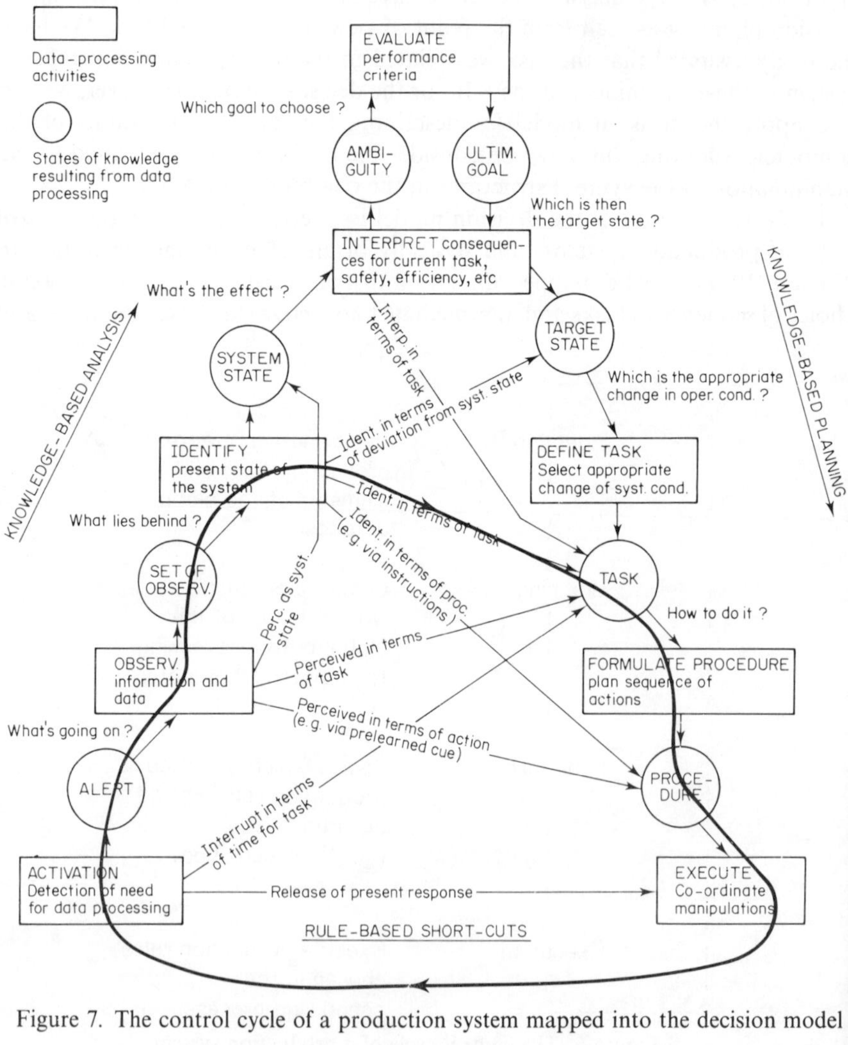

Figure 7. The control cycle of a production system mapped into the decision model

Two major findings have been obtained. The decision processes have been separated into three distinct categories or contexts, one (base level) related to decisions in terms of the external tasks and a meta-level decision process related to planning the sequence of decision tasks on the base level. The third context is an interpretation of the decision model in terms of the control cycle of a production system. As this production system may implement one of the decision tasks, we have demonstrated that the decision model applies on at least three functional levels of a KBS.

Furthermore, the identification of the close similarity of the decision model and the basic control cycle of AI programs raises some basic epistemological issues in systems theory, because there is a one-to-one mapping between production systems and Turing machines. It indicates a possibility of using the decision model to extend the control cycle of AI programs to include the top levels in the decision model. The significance of this extension is a topic for further research. AI architectures (e.g. blackboard-based systems) which can support the dynamic control and information flow structures identified in the decision model are under investigation (see Lind, 1990a, c).

Address for Correspondence:

Professor Morten Lind, Danmarks Tekniske Hojskole, Institute of Automatic Control Systems, 2800 Lyngby, Denmark.

REFERENCES

Breuker, J., and Wielinga, B. (1985) KADS: structured knowledge acquisition for expert systems. *Proc. of the Fifth Internl. Workshop On Expert Systems and their Applications*, Avignon, France, 13–15 May.

Kepner, C. H., and Tregoe, B. B. (1960) *The Rational Manager: A systematic approach to problem solving and decision making*. New York: McGraw-Hill.

Lind, M. (1982) Multilevel flow modelling for process plant diagnosis and control. *Riso-M-2357*, Riso National Labs, Denmark.

Lind, M. (1984) Information interfaces for process plant diagnosis. *Riso-M-2417*, Riso National Labs, Denmark.

Lind, M. (1988) *Diagnosis using Multilevel Flow Models.* Report from ESPRIT project P96.

Lind, M. (1990a) *Abstractions, Description of classes and their use.* IACS report 90-D-380.

Lind, M. (1990b) *Representing Goals and Functions of Complex Systems.* IACS report 90-D-381.

Lind, M. (1990c) *Modelling Control Tasks in Complex Systems.* Paper presented at the NATO ASI on Automation and System Issues in Air Traffic Control, June 1990, Maraten, Italy.

Nilsson, N. J. (1979) A framework for artificial intelligence. *AD AO68188*, March.

Rasmussen, J. (1986) Human–machine interaction: An approach to cognitive engineering. North Holland.

Stefik, M. *et. al.* (1982) The organization of expert systems: a prescriptive tutorial. Xerox rept *VLSI-82-1*, January.

Section 7

Methodological Conclusion

In this section an overview is given of the use of computer simulation for research in complex dynamic decision making. Modern computers are very effective tools for simulation of complex work settings as well as cognitive processes of decision makers. Simulation is therefore useful for bringing the complexity of real-life work into the laboratory for experiments with human problem-solving and decision-making strategies, and it offers new possibilities for evaluation of models and hypothesis regarding cognitive processes. There are, however, several basic problems in such simulations, and the chapter focuses on some of the problems which were subject to formal and informal discussions throughout the workshop.

One problem stems from the nature of causal models which are dealing with prototypes of objects and events while simulation runs present particular tokens. In consequence, the chapter focuses attention on the difference between illustrating demonstrations of mechanisms and actual validation of hypothesis, and it is argued that we need some rules for establishing prototypal significance of experiments in analogy to the way we require statistical significance in classical experimental settings. Another problem discussed is the relationship between the internal structure of simulation models and the structure of the 'cover story' which is used to introduce subjects to experiments and which will determine the context in which the subject perceives the simulation. It is concluded that more work, both of a theoretical and an experimental kind, is needed to make simulation of problem spaces and of cognitive processes into reliable research tools.

20. Use of Simulation in the Study of Complex Decision Making

Berndt Brehmer, Jacques Leplat and Jens Rasmussen

INTRODUCTION

Modern computer systems offer increasingly effective means for simulation of complex systems. As a consequence of this development, simulation has now become a widely used tool for research on human interaction with complex work environments. In particular, object-oriented programming systems provide very flexible tools in such research. Indeed, without the tool of simulation, much research of the kind described in this book simply could not be undertaken.

Experimental studies in which subjects interact with a simulation of complex environments offer a combination of the advantages of analysis of performance in the complexity of real-life scenarios and in well-controlled laboratory experiments. There is a close connection between this new form of experimentation and the simulators used for training. Simulators of complex systems are expensive to develop, and when they have been introduced for training purposes as, for instance, in aviation and the nuclear power field, it has been a natural extension of the application to use sessions with expert operators also for scientific analysis of behaviour. Therefore, in addition to training, complex 'high-fidelity' simulators are now used to study human behaviour under conditions more complex than those in typical laboratory experiments.

This has also led to a new approach to analysis of behaviour in complex situations, as illustrated by the contributions to this volume by Brehmer and Allard and Dörner. Most important, the new 'experimental simulators' make it possible to study behaviour in dynamic tasks, i.e. tasks where the state of the tasks is dependent not only upon the actions taken by the subject but also upon some autonomous process driving the task.

Such dynamic environments have, of course, been studied before in social psychological research, e.g. in the form of experiments with groups. In these

Distributed Decision Making: Cognitive Models for Cooperative Work
Edited by J. Rasmussen, B. Brehmer and J. Leplat

kinds of situations the dynamic aspects are introduced by the interaction between two or more subjects. However, as noted in Section 5, the dynamic aspects in ordinary social psychological experiments, e.g. experiments on group decision making, are limited to the social aspects. The tasks used in this research are static, and are usually quite simple ones. This makes these experiments poor simulations of modern forms of work, which are characterized by both social and task dynamics. For example, in process control in a modern plant one typically finds a group of operators working together to control a dynamic task, and an important field of research is their response to unforeseen disturbances. In such situations it is important to be able to study their dynamic process and the reallocation of roles in the cooperative decision making which will influence performance at the same time. This can only be done by means of simulated scenarios due to the scarcity of occasions in real life. The advantage of complex simulation, however, has its price, which is the topic of this chapter.

MODELS AND SIMULATION

Simulation depends on the implementation of a model in some kind of computer. Basically, two kinds of models are used today for analysis of the behaviour of complex systems and, consequently, also for simulation: the relational, mathematical model of natural science and the causal model in terms of interaction among objects (Chapter 11, this volume).

The classical model of natural science is based on mathematical relations (deterministic or stochastic) among quantitative variables. This kind of model is well suited to the study of practically isolated relationships. Simulation based on such models has been used extensively in engineering for study of the dynamic behaviour of complex systems. This kind of model has advantages because its internal consistency can either be tested logically or mathematically or be verified by controlled experiments with a simulated model as long as we are concerned with 'practically isolated relationships'. Validation of an implementation of the relationships in the real world is a separate issue.

In the causal model, quantitative relations among variables are replaced by objects interacting in chains of events. Causal models are advantageous for representation of complex real scenarios because there is a close relation between objects in the real world and elements of the model. For this approach, the advent of the object-oriented simulation languages has opened up new possibilities for experimental work in complex settings. This work raises special problems with respect to verification of model consistency and validation of real-life relevance.

TWO USES OF SIMULATION

In the study of complex behaviour two different kinds of simulation are used for different purposes:

(1) *Simulation is used to create task environments* in which experiments can be made with human subjects for study of their individual as well as cooperative cognitive behaviour. This application can be conceived as an extension of the classical experimental psychology to also include complex tasks for which the subjects frequently have themselves to define the task and the goal. In terms of work context, this can involve simulation of some well-structured technical system, e.g. an industrial process or a more loosely coupled environment (the activities of inhabitants of a town). The ability to make simulations of this kind is a prerequisite for experimentation, and provides relevant task environments for the studies both on individual operators (e.g. in investigations of mental models and how they depend on task characteristics, or of individual differenccs in performance) and for studies on groups in investigations of different forms of organizations on distributed decision making. We now have quite a number of such simulations that have proved useful in experiments on individual decision making, e.g. Lohhausen (Dörner *et al.*, 1983), DESSY (Chapter 16, this volume) or PLANT (Morris, 1985), to give but a few examples.

(2) *Simulation of cognitive processes is used to describe the cognitive systems* of the subjects' interacting with dynamic tasks. There are quite a number of such simulation programs in cognitive psychology, going back to the General Problem Solver of Newell *et al.* (1965). However, these simulations tend to be concerned with performance on static tasks, such as cryptarithmetic, rather than on dynamic tasks, such as process control. Moreover, there seem to be no simulation programs concerned with the functioning of groups facing dynamic tasks.

Simulations of cognitive processes have been used for mainly two purposes:

(1) Verification of hypotheses about human cognitive processes and mechanisms. In AI-based cognitive science it has been widely accepted that the consistency and completeness of a model has been proved when it has been demonstrated that a model is 'computational', i.e. that it can run on a computer and produce behavioural traces similar to those of a human subject in the tasks under study. In essence, such simulation can be used to verify hypothesis about cognitive processes that *can be used* by human actors.

(2) Validation of models of human behaviour in actual complex work environments. This includes tests of hypotheses about human intention formation and subjective criteria of choice, emotional and resource-related process criteria in order to determine what cognitive mechanisms and process *will be used* in a complex setting. This is clearly an extension of the previous verification simulation and it presupposes that such a simulation has been successful. Furthermore, this validation of behavioural models requires a

simultaneous simulation of the cognitive system and a complex work environment, if not for other reasons, then only to be able to interface the cognitive simulator with its problem environment. Such joint simulations of operators and processes could be used not only to test theories of dynamic decision making but for deciding the best allocation of functions between operators and the automatic system, the effects of different forms of organization, and so on. So far, only very few examples of such simulations have been reported in the literature (see Dörner *et al.*, 1989).

Each of these uses has its own problems. We discuss each in turn, but first we need to consider some more general problems with simulation as a method that are common to all tasks.

GENERAL PROBLEMS WITH SIMULATION

Simulation is basically an empirical method, and many of the problems associated with simulation are common to all empirical methods. One of these stems from the fact that a simulation, just as any experiment, must be limited. It cannot include all potentially relevant variables. A second problem is that each variable in a simulation must be given a real value to make the simulation run.

It is not possible to include all potentially relevant variables in a simulation. This is also a well-known problem in experiments, and for experiments, a special method has been developed to handle it: to hold all the variable constants that are not being evaluated in the experiment. In some treatments of this problem it would appear that the variables that are held constant somehow mysteriously disappear. This is not true, of course. What actually happens is that the effects of the variables that are evaluated in the experiment will also reflect the effects of constant values of the variables that have not been evaluated, but are held constant at some value. This feature of experimental design is similar to the problem of causal models which only include what the analyst finds abnormal and, therefore, interesting while the usual and familiar is taken for granted. (See the discussion by Rasmussen in Chapter 11, this volume.) This means that there is a potential confounding of the main effects of the experimental variables with an interaction that is not being evaluated, since only one of the rows in the potential interaction table is being included, i.e. the row representing the constant value. In fact, it is, of course, not only one single row, it is one row from many interaction tables. Sooner or later, someone will run a new experiment including more rows from these implicit interaction tables, and as a consequence, the results of the original experiment may not replicate, i.e. if the interaction is indeed important.

What variables are held constant in experiments? As is the case for the elements included in a causal model by an accident analyst, these variables are, of course, those about which the designer of the experiment has explicit or implicit beliefs that they are unimportant for the problem at hand. Thus, what is included in an experiment tends to express the cumulative wisdom of the scientists in a given field, the intuition of the profession, and if an experiment will contribute nothing else to science, it will show that a certain variable can be safely ignored in future studies. Thus, experimental findings are always made against a background of explicit (or implicit) beliefs about what is and what is not important (see Brehmer, 1986, for further discussion), and therefore, isolated experiments are normally of little general interest.

These considerations are even more important when we are dealing with object-oriented causal models because, as discussed in Chapter 11 by Rasmussen, objects and events in such models are prototypes of classes which cannot be objectively defined, i.e. it is impossible to list and control all defining attributes. What will be included will depend on shared beliefs of what is and what is not relevant to explain the behaviour of interest, as in the case of experiments. We will deal more explicitly with these difficulties when discussing the different applications of simulation.

The basic problem is very pronounced for simulation of causal models because of their prototypical nature. In causal models, the context and the normal conditions along the causal path will be taken for granted, because, as mentioned above, we cannot include everything in models of complex systems. There is, unfortunately, no clear-cut rule telling us what to include and what to leave unspecified. As mentioned below, this creates serious problems when simulation is used to test models and hypotheses against empirical evidence.

In contrast to experiments in the actual, complex work setting, simulation gives us the real possibility to ignore those variables that we think are unimportant, and simply leave them out of the program. Consequently, simulation makes radical simplification possible, but this also means that the results of a simulation can never precisely match those of an experiment in a complex setting.

The variables in a simulation must have values

A simulation cannot remain in the abstract, it needs actual concrete values for each of the variables in the simulation program. This means that the types and categories and the acceptable ranges of variables of the conceptual model have to be replaced by particular members and values. Types are replaced by tokens, ordinal values by numbers. Again, we recognize this problem from experiments, where we have to give values to all variables in the experiment. This is, of course, not unimportant when the variables are true variables with many levels, or when objects and events with real attributes are studied.

In experiments, this problem is solved by so-called functional designs, i.e. the experiment is designed to evaluate the form of the functional relationships between dependent and independent variables in the experiment. This leads to two problems: that of selecting the correct number of levels for the variables in question to make it possible to evaluate the actual function (the degrees of freedom problem), and that of deciding a range of levels so that the function can be evaluated. This requires considerable pre-experimental information to make the correct choice. The functional design is an attempt to get away from the inherent limitations of fixed-effects designs, i.e. that all generalization is limited to the exact values included in the experiment. The argument here is, of course, that it is only for those levels in the experiment that we can argue that our design allows the potential interactions between variables in the experiment to cancel.

The same arguments are relevant in simulation, and a simulation will be valid only for those values that were included in the original simulation. For other combinations, there may well be unforeseen interaction effects that make the simulation invalid.

Discrete simulations—continuous models

The behaviour of objects and people in a real-life environment presents to a human actor a continuous flow of changes. For a complex environment which cannot be represented by a set of continuous, albeit non-linear differential equations, simulation models must be based on a causal representation of events which implies a decomposition of the environment into discrete objects which interact in discrete events. However, discrete simulations have different properties from the continuous environment, and a discrete simulation of a continuous world will not necessarily behave in the same way as the continuous world because the level of decomposition and, therefore, the definition of objects and events by agents in the world may not be stable. If simulation is to be the preferred method of testing systems for consistency and stability, perhaps it will be necessary to acknowledge this fact and limit the use of causal models to scenarios with a stable level of discretization.

SPECIFIC PROBLEMS

Simulation used to create task environments

The tasks used in studies of complex decision making must be interactive, i.e. what happens next must be dependent upon what the decision maker has already done. Such tasks, except when they are very simple, are hard to realize in any form other than as simulations of 'complex fields of reality', to use Dörner's phrase. This is indeed how research on complex decision making is made, and a number of different programs have been developed for these purposes (see Chapters 16 and 18, this volume). Experiments with such dynamic simulations introduce a series of new problems in evaluating the results, for what actually happens in the experiment will be dependent upon what the subjects choose to do in pursuit of their goals. Thus, the traditional psychological idea of a strict causation from stimuli to responses must be abandoned, for in these experiments, stimuli are produced by the subjects. This requires a circular, or cybernetic, view, rather than the traditional linear one. Indeed, the independent variables in these experiments cannot be defined as stimuli at all, but have to be defined in terms of system characteristics, such as feedback delays (see Chapter 16, this volume, for a list of potentially relevant system characteristics), rather than in terms of specific stimulus values or decision problems. As a consequence, experiments with such systems provide information of a kind different to that obtained by conventional psychological experiments. This problem is further discussed below.

The problem is particularly important in object-oriented simulations, because the underlying causal model is based on prototypes, representing classes of events and objects involved in typical chains of events, i.e. dealing with 'types' whereas the experimental trajectory is a 'token'. Testing the membership of a token in a type is no simple matter; two different judges may come to disagree depending on what they take for granted in the context. One possible test would be to ask subject experts from the actual task environment whether they 'understand' the behaviour shown in the simulation and find it 'reasonable'. This would constitute a loose form of a Turing test of the validity of the simulation.

Simulation programs for experiments can be designed from two different points of departure. First, a task simulation may be designed with the intention to model some specific domain of reality, e.g. a specific control room. It would then be a simulator of that particular control room. This approach is the German 'complex problem solving' approach to the problem (see e.g. Eyfert *et al.*, 1986), and shares many of the problems involved in observational studies, e.g. in control rooms, such as problems of generalization of results and of determining what are the causally effective variables. In most cases such studies are performed in 'high-fidelity' training simulators, in which not only the simulation of the underlying physical process but also the physical appearance of the experimental system have face validity.

The second approach is to design a simulation that focuses on functional validity, so that it will be possible to evaluate the effects of various system characteristics, e.g. feedback delays. In this case, the approach is more akin to the classical study of 'practically isolated relationships', and the problem is one of judging the validity of the 'isolation'. These are two very different kinds of approach. If, for example, one is interested in the effects of feedback delays as such, one cannot follow the first approach, for if a simulation is designed to picture an actual domain of reality, one is not free to vary feedback delays in such a way as to be able to evaluate the effects of the feedback delays. One can only evaluate the effects of such variables by a comparison between tasks that vary naturally with respect to feedback delays. However, such a comparison offers problems, in that the simulations are also likely to differ in many other respects and the effects of the feedback delays will then be confounded with those of other factors. Consequently, one will be hard put to argue that the effects are due to the feedback delays and nothing else.

In the second approach, other problems arise. The task will have to be given some content or 'cover story' (and even if the task is abstract and without explicit content, some cover story must nevertheless be used to explain to the subjects what they are supposed to do in the experiment). This leads to the problem of the extent to which the underlying dynamic structure, which determines the subjects' performance, matches their understanding of the task and the intuition which they bring into the task. As shown in various experiments (e.g. Warg and Brehmer, 1983), a cover story is a very powerful means of directing the subjects' thinking about the formal nature of a task, and if there is a discrepancy here, the results may be hard to interpret.

When a limited-fidelity simulation is used, the influence of the context which the subjects will add to a scenario should be carefully considered. Physical systems with known and invariant internal structure are responding to changes and to human acts according to basic laws of nature, which therefore can be used to predict their behaviour. In a simulation involving such a system it is important that the simulation does not contradict any expectation based on such laws, i.e. the experimenter is not free to change the laws of nature just to suit his or her experimental needs. In intentional social systems, behaviour is controlled by attributing motives or intentions, and it is harder to determine what expectations subjects may have. The distinction between physical causal systems and intentional systems is nevertheless basic, and must be considered when subjects' behaviour in simulations is used to explain performance in real-life systems.

Many formal systems such as games are only defined as one single level of abstraction (e.g. geometrical theorem proving and construction, cryptarithmetic problems, puzzles and purely logical problems). It should, however, be realized that problem-solving behaviour may be very different in one-level formal systems compared to a problem context of an abstraction hierarchy, in which means–end relations connect values and intentions, functions and physical processes.

An illustrative example of the role of means–ends levels can be found when comparing a decision task which has to be performed in a one-level description with performance when the context is also available. Good empirical evidence is the experiment by D'Andrade (discussed by Rumelhart and Norman, 1981), which repeats the experiment by Wason and Johnson-Laird (1972). This was based upon a set of cards representing a concept (e.g. if one side shows a vowel, the revese displays an odd number). A subject was given a sample of four cards and was asked which to turn in order to test the hypothesis. The experiment was repeated with the same concept disguised in a bill-signing context. If the amount of a bill exceeded $50, the supervisor had to sign the reverse side. The ratio of correct solutions in the two conditions was 13% to 70%.

In the first condition, the problem solving is based on formal logical arguments at only one level of abstraction. Specifically, it must be based on syllogistic logic which requires manipulation of abstract symbols and storage of intermediate results in short-term memory. In the second experiment, the context defines an intentional system, in which the effects of the different decisions can very easily be inferred at the higher goal levels.

This distinction between problem solving performed by formal logic within a problem space with only one level of abstraction and problem solving based on transformation through levels of an abstraction hierarchy has important implications for laboratory experiments on decision making. Frequently, more or less context-free problem representations are used for experiments on problem-solving strategies and decision making. These experiments are very effective when the aim is to model logical reasoning in closed formal systems or in 'isolated relationships', but the implications for real-life tasks may be difficult to establish, because the context subjects add to the scenario may not be in correspondence with the structure of the simulation.

Simulation of cognitive processes

Verification of hypotheses about human cognitive processes and mechanisms

Experiments with complex dynamic systems yield great masses of data, and these need to be reduced in some way. One possibility here is to assume a number of possible strategies for handling the task, writing programs that simulate these strategies and then comparing the results for these simulated strategies with subjects' behaviour to find out which strategy fits best. This creates problems in defining and evaluating criteria of approximation in a simulation.

Feigenbaum (1961) has discussed three possible approaches to the testing of information-processing models of the kind involved in simulations:

(1) The first approach involves simulation of a model of an 'average subject', i.e. the simulation is limited to the generation of mean outcomes of different conditions of an experiment. Thus, one might simulate times for a task, or the number of correct answers. In this case, the testing of the validity of the simulation model seems unproblematic. It should be easy enough to see whether the results obtained (on the chosen criteria) with the simulation under different experimental conditions are similar to those obtained with subjects (see Feigenbaum and Simon, 1961, for example).
(2) Simulation programs, however, are generally designed to produce more than just a final outcome. They also give a trace of the cognitive process

leading to this outcome and validation involves a comparison with some analogous trace obtained from a subject, e.g. in the form of a verbal protocol or eye movements. A problem in comparing such traces is that an error at a single node, with the program going in one direction and the subject in another, may give too high a count of deviations between model and data. Had the program and the subject not parted company at this particular node, the degree of correspondence might have been high. To handle this problem, Feigenbaum (1961) suggested the method of conditional prediction, i.e. the program would be reset at each node where there was a deviation. The number of resets would then provide a measure of lack of fit. The problem with this method is obvious. Some nodes may be more important than others, and if there is a deviation at one of the important nodes, agreement in the rest of the traces may be unimportant. Moreover, for some simulation systems it may also be very difficult to make the reset. Reitman (1965) notes that for a simulation system like Argus the reset would involve going back and changing all previous steps, not just the last state. In this case, then, even a small reset would involve massive changes in the model, and just counting resets would not give a good measure of fit.

(3) The third approach proposed by Feigenbaum is the Turing test. This is problematic in at least two respects. First, since we do not know how people make the judgment required by the Turing test, it is difficult to interpret the results of such a test, especially if the outcome is negative. Second, the test could presumably not be used on protocols of individuals about whom the judges could never know enough, but would have to be used on some 'average' or 'typical' protocols and would involve a judgment concerning 'people in general'. Protocols that give a good representation of people in general may be hard to find.

As noted by Reitman (1965), interest in simulation as a method is often accompanied by a de-emphasis upon the usual distinction between prediction and reproduction of data. Traditionally, successful prediction has always been seen as a stronger test than successful reproduction. However, the goal in much simulation work is to produce a model for an individual subject, and the impossibility of repeating an experiment with the same subject often puts the person designing a simulation program in the position of having to go back and forth between a protocol from a subject and the simulation program. What is prediction and what is reproduction thus becomes unclear, and the strength of the evidence for the program as a simulation of the subject becomes correspondingly unclear.

Validation of models of human behaviour in actual complex work environments

Newell and Simon (1961) describe three levels of testing applied to GPS:

(1) The crudest level would involve ascertaining whether the program in fact is able to solve the kinds of problems that humans solve. For the domains in which it has been applied, GPS passes this test. This is the model consistency test, discussed above.
(2) At an intermediate level, one could look for the kinds of methods used by the program in subjects' protocols. For example, one could look for evidence of means–ends analysis of the kind assumed by GPS in verbal protocols from experiments. This is also a test that GPS passes; there is evidence of the principal methods used by the program in actual protocols. This is the verification of the model's ability to generate strategies which *can* be used by subjects.
(3) The highest level of validation discussed by Newell and Simon would involve a detailed line-by-line comparison of the output from the program and the protocol from the subject. The protocols presented in Newell and Simon (1972) give some rather impressive evidence of similarity also on this level. This represents the ultimate validation that the model can predict the trajectory the subjects *will* use. However, traces from the program and verbal protocols are seldom identical, so in the end, the investigator's Turing test becomes the final criterion of validity.

Reitman (1965) proposes that one could use the similarity between different programs used to predict the same subject on the same kind of task as a measure of validity. Thus, one would first develop a simulation program for one sample of behaviour, then use the program to simulate another sample, and if the program does not simulate this second sample as well as one would wish, the program should be modified until it does and the number of modifications used as a measure of fit. This seems to raise many of the same problems as the conditional prediction method proposed by Feigenbaum.

Reitman also proposed that testing of a simulation model should be made not at the level of the actual protocol but at the level of psychological constructs employed in designing the simulation. Thus, one might collect a verbal protocol, use part of that protocol to look for, e.g. certain learning strategies. Then a program incorporating these learning strategies would be used to predict the rest of the protocol data. Reitman (1965) offers some concrete suggestions as to how this could be done. This seems to be a promising approach in that it would uphold the distinction between prediction and reproduction of data, and put the resulting theory at a level more useful than that of the total protocol.

The nature of causal models, as discussed above, creates basic problems when simulation is used to test models or hypotheses about human behaviour in complex environments about cognitive processes that *will* be used. In 'cognitive science', theories are only acceptable if they can be tested for consistency by computer simulation. Until now, this has been successful except for very well-formed micro-worlds such as games, cryptarithmetic and theorem proving. The basic reason for this appears to be that objects, events and causal connections in such restricted worlds can be objectively defined in the classical way by lists of attributes. This is not possible for simulation of complex systems. Objects, events, operations and causal relations in models then represent classes, not instances. In simulations, we have to replace classes by particular members, but then the entire exercise will be an *ad hoc* demonstration of selected examples unless we can demonstrate 'prototypical significance' (which in some way replaces statistical significance). This means that we have to be able to relate the particular scenario to the prototype. This is no easy matter. There will be no formal stop-rule to terminate the additions of new relations or objects in order to match simulated performance to observed real-life performance. Such stop-rules will only come from a deeper theoretical understanding. Consider the following example given by Kuhn (1962). He mentions the fact that chemical research was able to produce whole-number relations between elements of chemical substances only after the acceptance of John Dalton's chemical atom theory. There was no stop-rule for the efforts in refinement of the experimental technique until the acceptance of this theory.

Simulation of causal chains of events in purely technical systems is eased by their well-structured and relatively stable anatomy. Simulation can be planned from invariant relationships at a higher level of abstraction, typically derived from mass and energy-conservation laws. Classes of events related to state changes of physical components can be mapped onto model parameters and the completeness of representation of a set described by a prototype can be judged.

This is not the case for the activity of people whose behaviour is determined by their goals, intentions and interpretations of the information available to them. During actual behaviour, members of a causal chain will be selected from prototypical classes and adjusted to match particular conditions. Therefore, the correspondence of the 'cover story' and the internal structure of the simulation is crucial. In the case of simulations to study 'practically isolated causal relationships' the secret is to find a simple yet reasonably complete scenario (very likely found in a different real-life context) grasping the intended relationship, rather than a simplified simulation of the complex source of the problem. That is, even though the simulation is necessarily simplified, and will be recognized as such by the subjects, it should embody the same kinds of relations among events as those among the corresponding events in the 'real' system being simulated. Moreover, it must include those events that are essential to the solution of the problems presented to the subjects in the simulated scenario, so that they can use reasonable methods for solving these problems. For example, in simulations of firefighting, the simulated fires must spread in the way real fires spread, and the means available for fighting fires must share the essential characteristics of actual firefighting units with respect to how they move from one place to another, and with respect to the time taken to extinguish a fire, and to the area over which they can be effective. This is especially important when the scenario simulates problems that are reasonably well known to the subjects, such as fires. If the underlying laws in the simulation do not agree with the corresponding laws in the system being simulated, the experiment is transformed from an experiment on decision making into one on the learning of arbitrary and counter-intuitive relationships.

CONCLUSION

Computer simulation is a very important tool for the study of human behaviour in complex work domains. Simulated work domains can be used efficiently and reliably as a source of data for modelling human behaviour. It is, however, important to consider carefully the cover stories used to instruct subjects in experiments based on simplified simulation models. When experiments are planned to study relationships identified in a complex work setting such as, for instance, communication delays, it may be better to find an actual, simple task environment to serve as a cover story for which the relationship in question is a dominant feature than to design experiments with a simplified version of the original environment but maintaining this as the 'cover story'. Unless this is done, the intuition and context brought to the experiment by subjects will be difficult to predict.

In addition, simulation of cognitive processes and mechanisms is an important tool for verification of the internal consistency of models with reference to hypotheses about mechanisms that can be used by human agents as well as for validation of hypotheses of the processes that will be used by agents in an actual work context. In this respect, the basic nature of causal models expressed in terms of objects, actions, and events brings with it problems of prototypical significance of the experimental trajectories obtained being particulars, whereas the hypothesis interrelates types and classes. In all, more work, both of a theoretical and an experimental kind, is needed to make it possible to distinguish demonstrations from reliable validations.

Finally, it should be mentioned that simulation is an important tool in the analysis and modelling of complex work domains in combination with actual field studies. There is a reciprocal and continuous relationship between field studies and studies by means of simulation. At every step, one casts light on the other. Therefore, a coordinated development of methods for field analysis and simulation is important, particularly of cooperative work and distributed decision making, because study in this area until now has not been focused on the cognitive aspects.

Address for Correspondence:

Professor Berndt Brehmer, Uppsala Universitet, Dept of Psychology, Box 1854, S-751 48 Uppsala, Sweden.

REFERENCES

Brehmer, B. (1986) Politike rollen och forskarrollen: inga gräns-overskridandan men ömsesidigt stöd. Om kvalitet och relevans i samhällsvetenskaplig forskning. In B. Sollbe (ed.), *Vishets frukter*. Gavle: Statens institut for byggnadsforskning.

Dörner, D., Kreuzig, H. W., Reither, F., and Straudel, T. (1983) *Lohhausen. Vom umgang mit Unbestrimmtheit und Komplexität*. Bern: Huber.

Dörner, D., Schaub, H., Staudel, T., and Strohschneider, S. (1989) Ein System zur Handlungsregulation oder-Die Interaktion von Emotionen, Kognition und Motivation. *Sprache & Kognition*, **4**, 217–32.

Eyfert, K., Schomann, M., and Widowski, D. (1986) Der Umgang von Psychologen mit Komplexität. *Sprache & Kognition*, **1**, 11–26.

Feigenbaum, E. A. (1961) The simulation of verbal learning behavior. *Proceedings of the Western Joint Computer Conference*, **19**, 121–32.

Feigenbaum, E. A., and Simon, H. A. (1961) Comment: The distinctiveness of stimuli. *Psychological Review*, **68**, 265–88.

Kuhn, T. (1962) *The Structure of Scientific Revolution*. University of Chicago Press.

Morris, N. (1985) PLANT: an experimental task for the study of human problem solving in process control. *IEEE Transactions on Man, Systems and Cybernetics*. **SMC-15**, 792–8.

Newell, A., and Simon, H. A. (1961) Computer simulation of human thinking. *Science*, **134**, 2011–17.

Newell, A., Shaw, J. C., and Simon, H. A. (1965) Elements of a theory of human problem solving. *Psychological Review*, **65**, 151–66.

Newell, A., and Simon, H. A. (1972) *Human Problem Solving*. Englewood Cliffs, NJ: Prentice Hall.

Reitman, W. R. (1965) *Cognition and Thought*. New York: John Wiley.

Rummelhart, D. E., and Norman, D. A. (1981) Analogical processes in learning. In J. R. Anderson (ed.), Cognitive Skills and their Acquisition. Hillsdale, NJ: Erlbaum.

Warg, L., and Brehmer, B. (1983) *Both congruent and ingruent task contents facilitate learning of probabilistic inference tasks*. Uppsala University: Uppsala Psychological Reports No. 321.

Wason, P. C., and Johnson-Laird, P. N. (1972) *Psychology of reasoning: Structure and Content*. London: Batsford.

Author Index

Subject Index